FAT ALBERT

Shropshire Blue, Volume 3

Ron Powell

Copyright © 2022 Ron Powell

All rights reserved

No part of this book may be reproduced, or stored in a retrieval system, or transmitted in any form or by any means, electronic, mechanical, photocopying, recording, or otherwise, without express written permission of the publisher.

ISBN-13: 9780957669284
ISBN-10: 0957669284

Cover design by: Martin Butler

This book is dedicated to the Lockheed C-130 Hercules (Fat Albert) and all the crews that have flown the aircraft over its many years in RAF service

CONTENTS

Title Page
Copyright
Dedication
Introduction — 1
Nearing the Front Line — 7
Meeting Fat Albert — 11
Operational Conversion and Bonding — 17
Groundschool — 26
More Bonding — 33
Flying Fat Albert — 50
Intro to Route Flying — 59
The Argentineans Intervene — 80
Gibraltar and Dakar — 90
Ascension Island — 106
Welcome to 24 Squadron — 134
The Pace Continues — 145
Cyprus — 156
Ascension Again – And Again — 169
Op Banner and Berlin — 180
New Zealand — 192
Bread and Butter — 229

Cape Canaveral	239
Volcanoes, Medevacs and Cracker Boxes	259
Beirut and the Red Arrows	277
Combat Survival and Rescue	297
Taceval and Flight Safety	331
New Year, New Challenges	340
Las Vegas	368
Ascension and The Falklands	376
Bits and Bobs – Oh, and Ethiopia	405
Farewell to Albert	431
Author's Note	435
Acknowledgements	436
About The Author	437
Ron's Other Books	439
Glossary and Abbreviations	443

INTRODUCTION

Our C-130 Hercules is 20,000 feet above the white-capped waves of a stormy South Atlantic Ocean between Africa and South America. After nearly six hours, we're 1,800 miles southwest of our departure point, Wideawake Airfield on Ascension Island. But that still leaves us 2,000 miles short of our destination, Port Stanley in the Falklands. And although we might have just enough fuel to make it that far, if bad weather or anything else prevents us landing, we won't have enough to reach our diversion airfield in Uruguay.

There's only one option – refuel in the air.

That's why another Hercules is spearing in and out of the cloud tops about fifty yards to our front left. It's one of six that have been modified as tankers, and it's just trailed an eighty foot long black rubber hose into the airflow from a lozenge-shaped port in the bottom skin of its sloping rear cargo door.

Sitting to my left on the other side of the throttle quadrant, our captain, a tall wiry man in his early forties, reduces power, eases us back a smidge and slides behind the tanker. He waits a couple of seconds, then takes a deep breath and advances the throttles, edging us forward until the other aircraft's wide tailplane and towering tailfin fill our field of view.

Impressive as this is, my eyes are locked on a much smaller object bobbing in the airflow about ten feet ahead.

Known as a basket, it resembles a large shuttlecock, its silver metal spokes spreading out from the end of the hose to form a funnel with a circular opening about two feet in diameter. I take a few moments to check that the spokes and fabric rim of the funnel are undamaged, then look up at our refuelling probe, a four-inch diameter pipe thrusting forward a couple of yards from a rough fairing bolted to the outer skin above my head.

The captain is making ready to prod this probe's shiny metal tip - like a small artillery shell with a rounded nose – into the four inch diameter hose valve at the centre of the basket. If his approach is a little off-centre, the metal spokes of the basket will guide the tip in, although he'd prefer to manage without their help.

My job is to give him directions.

It would be hard enough in good weather. But we plunge into the flank of another dark storm cloud, bucking and bouncing in its violent up and down draughts. The tanker becomes little more than a shadowy presence in thick fog, as does most of the hose. All we can see clearly is the basket, flailing about like the head of a demented cobra.

During groundschool at RAF Marham, an air-to-air refuelling instructor had emphasised the difficulty of getting the probe into the basket in such conditions.

Like taking a running fuck at a rolling doughnut!

Sitting in a warm classroom on terra firma it had seemed little more than a funny turn of phrase. Now, staring wide-eyed at the dancing basket, we understand only too well what he meant.

We steel ourselves for a difficult thirty minutes.

The Hercules tanker is heavy with fuel, its four turboprop engines working hard to maintain airspeed. We, on the other hand, fairly skip along at relatively light weight. But as we take his fuel and become heavier, we'll find it harder to keep up, let alone make the delicate changes in speed required to maintain our connection.

The solution is a technique specially devised for such occasions: *tobogganing*. Basically, we'll chase the tanker downhill, using gravity to help us maintain speed and stay in contact as we take on the fuel we need.

Before all that though, the captain has to drive the tip of the probe into the hose at just the right speed. Approach too slowly and he won't push the tip in firmly enough to gain a leak-free connection. Even more annoying, he might nudge the hose just enough for it to wind all the way back into the tanker's belly, in which case we'll have to wait for it to re-stream before he can have another go.

Approach too fast, though, and he risks a hard contact that could damage the tanker's refuelling mechanism and snap the tip off our probe. Alternatively, he could drive the probe through the metal spokes of the basket, rendering the hose unusable, even locking our two aircraft together.

Unsurprisingly then, some captains find *plugging in* incredibly stressful. Not ours, though. He's brilliant at it. Operating the controls in response to a combination of visual cues on the tanker and my voice - *up a bit, left a bit, steady*, etc – he invariably plugs in at the first attempt, rarely needing the spokes to guide the tip into the bullseye. Even in today's turbulence, he manages to edge us forward at just the right moment, nail the hose and push it in far enough to make all the right connections. A few seconds later, green lights appear to either side of the port on the tanker's cargo door and we begin taking on fuel.

So far so good. But as the moments tick by, the tension on the flight deck mounts.

There's another wrinkle to air-to-air refuelling.

We're so close to the tanker that its slipstream and spiralling prop-wash swirl around our airframe and onto the high tailfin. We become a huge weather vane, eager to swing in response to every air current. Countering this would be difficult enough if the forces were constant. But the turbulent air and every twitch of each aircraft's throttles and flying controls combine to make the swing totally unpredictable. Despite this, most captains manage to hold reasonably steady for the duration of the refuelling bracket, while the best can so manipulate throttle, stick and rudder that it's impossible to spot any movement, no matter how trying the conditions.

Our captain is not one of these. Before long, we're swaying from side to side like a pendulum, the delicate tip of our probe dragging the heavy hose further and further to the side with every oscillation.

We're allowed to swing a certain amount – within a cone of safety – but if we pull the probe too far in any direction, we could snap the tip off, meaning we'll have to cope with the fuel we have, either returning to Ascension or making for our en-route diversion, usually Rio de Janeiro. How serious matters are beyond that depends on where tip of the probe ends up.

If it stays trapped in the hose, the tanker can't give fuel to anyone else, not really a problem out here; we're his only customer. But if the weighty hunk of metal flies out of the basket into the slipstream, it could clatter along the airframe and into a propeller or engine, causing untold damage. It could even start a chain of events ending in the dark waters below.

So there are sound reasons for the underlying tension.

And of course, the more the captain tries to correct the swing, the worse it becomes. We should be used to it. He always explores the cone of safety. But every occasion is different, and this time we seem to be gearing up for a full rolling circle around the tanker's tail. I suggest he pulls out, while we still can, and before the tanker crew put the red lights on.

The captain eases the throttles aft a smidge and we drop back until the probe pulls out and the basket bounces away, spraying fuel for a few moments as the hose valve shuts. Once clear, he takes no more than a few moments to control the swing, although the hose continues to flail wildly. Then the cloud thickens, the tanker disappears and the basket becomes little more than a dancing smudge, hard to see, let alone capture.

Over the next twenty five minutes, we have to pull out several times. And while the captain gets us back in first time every time, the hiatus slows down the transfer of fuel and edges us ever closer to the angry southern ocean and the end of the refuelling bracket. If we haven't taken on enough fuel by that point, we'll probably have enough to make it back to Ascension, but we certainly won't be going to Stanley.

Passing 5,000 feet, we begin another series of wild swings and I glance down at the waves. I really don't want to suggest pulling out again, but...

'Tanks full,' the navigator announces, as if the news is of no more than passing interest.

I exhale like a deflating balloon.

After an exchange of light signals, the tanker crew reel in the hose, turn away and climb into cloud. It'll be six hours before they reach Ascension.

We also climb, contemplating our own 1,800 mile flight into the notoriously unreliable weather around the Falklands, and an approach to Port Stanley's makeshift runway.

This is one of many adventures I enjoyed on the RAF Hercules fleet. In the company of an amazing cast of characters, I flew the sturdy freighter, affectionately known to its crews as Fat Albert, to places as far apart as the western USA, New Zealand,

Iceland and The Falkland Islands, and as unlikely as Cape Canaveral, East Berlin and the highlands of eastern Turkey near the Soviet border.

Highlights included touch and go medical evacuations, buddy/buddy starts, flying a damaged aircraft out of Ethiopia during the famine relief operation, and many other experiences I could never have imagined when growing up in Shropshire. While revealing these, I hope to give a flavour of what it was like to be an RAF Hercules pilot in the early 1980s. As I do so, I make no apology for passing on the same health warning as in the previous two volumes of Shropshire Blue.

Even with the aid of log books, diaries, scrap books and photo albums, memory can be slippery and unreliable, as well as partial and self-serving. As no less an authority than Her Majesty Queen Elizabeth II put it, *recollections may vary*. So what follows are my recollections, my story.

NEARING THE FRONT LINE

After the award of my wings in July 1981, Geraldine and I finally left RAF Finningley in the second week of August, heading for RAF Lyneham and our third married quarter in fifteen months of marriage.

RAF – now Ministry of Defence - Lyneham sits about twenty miles northeast of Bath and ten southwest of Swindon in the southern English county of Wiltshire. Work on its airfield began in 1939 and for most of its life it had been home to elements of the RAF transport force, most recently, the C-130 Hercules fleet.

As we settled in, the warm glow of gaining my wings was already beginning to fade. A new question was rearing its ugly head. Exactly how would I cope with flying the Hercules?

But as usual in the RAF, there was to be a short delay before the question could be answered.

My course on the Hercules Operational Conversion Unit didn't start until late November, so a junior officer at RAF Support Command with the snappy job title of P2 Air had to find something to do with me for a couple of months. I hoped it involved flying, and that it was as close to Lyneham as possible.

In the end, I was posted to RAF Abingdon, an airfield about five miles southwest of central Oxford and close enough to Lyneham for me to commute daily.

In 1981, Abingdon was a maintenance unit responsible for the servicing of the RAF's Buccaneer, Jaguar and Hawk fleets. The airfield also hosted three flying units: two University Air Squadrons (UASs), London and Oxford, and No 6 Air

Experience Flight (AEF), one of thirteen similar units dotted around the British Isles. Something for future volumes, but later in my career, I was to command 6 AEF and two University Air Squadrons, Wales and London, while my final appointment made me responsible for, among other things, all the UASs and AEFs.

On this occasion though, at the age of twenty six, Flying Officer Powell was to become a holding officer on 6 AEF.

The task of the AEFs was – and still is - to provide air experience flights to teenage cadets in youth organisations affiliated to the RAF, primarily the Air Training Corps and Combined Cadet Force, the former located within the community, the latter usually within fee-paying schools.

As a teenager, I'd been a cadet on 333 Ludlow Squadron of the Air Training Corps, and during my five years of membership I'd enjoyed tens of air experience flights. As it turned out, that was more than I was to enjoy during my three months at Abingdon.

The squadron leaders in charge of each AEF were like one-armed wallpaper hangers, single-handedly responsible for tens of volunteer pilots, the groundcrew who serviced the aircraft and the myriad of secondary duties and admin tasks required on a flying unit. Invariably, they were flying instructors of vast experience and, in military terms, vast age. Some were in their sixties.

The Officer Commanding 6 AEF was one such.

On the few occasions we sat in the crewroom to chew the fat, he delighted in relating stories from just after the end of the Second World War, when he joined one of several night-fighter squadrons flying the RAF's first operational jet aircraft, the Meteor.

At the time, his station was losing about one aircraft a week to accidents, many of them fatal. Some occurred in sight of the airfield, horrified spectators watching Meteors roll and arrow into the ground in what became known as a phantom dive. Ejection seats were yet to be fitted and without them the pilots and navigators were invariably killed.

He'd heard the stories, but when he walked into his new squadron's crew room on his first day, he was confronted with grim reminders of the reality, blackened collar studs hanging from the ceiling on pieces of string. Later, he was given the names of the dead owners, and brief details of how and when they'd met their demise.

'Just the way things were,' he'd say with a resigned shrug and a faraway look in his eyes.

I sat there wondering how I'd feel if I was about to join my first squadron in similar circumstances.

Eventually it was discovered that the phantom dive was caused by the disruption of airflow over a Meteor's elevators and rudder when the aircraft yawed with the airbrakes out at speeds below 170 knots. The yaw could be initiated by something as simple as the undercarriage coming down or an engine failure, real or practice. If the swing wasn't caught immediately, the result was always the same: a phantom dive that often left pilots with insufficient time or height in which to recover.

Sadly, when I was on the staff of the Central Flying School at RAF Scampton in 1988, one of my fellow instructors, Pete Stacey, was killed by a phantom dive when performing a display in a Meteor at Coventry Airport.

I didn't know Pete well, but he was quite a character, renowned for his clever heckling at dining-in nights. Shortly before his death, we were both at a dinner where the Station Commander was being dined out at the end of his tour. As often happens, to add spice to the farewell speech, someone had managed to get hold of reports from early in the Group Captain's flying career.

One of the examples read out on this occasion was from the Station Commander's first posting to a squadron. *If Pilot Officer Scroggins continues to apply himself, he may yet make an average pilot.*

The Group Captain squirmed in embarrassment, but the muted laughter turned to roars when Pete shouted, 'Still got a week to go then, sir!'

Perhaps this explained why Pete was a career flight lieutenant. I was at his funeral a few weeks later.

The AEF boss had obviously survived his time on the Meteor, and he went on to become a highly respected flying instructor.

The volunteer pilots that turned up for a day or half a day to fly the cadets were a mix of RAF veterans flying with the airlines, and serving pilots, often senior officers in ground appointments. Because of Abingdon's proximity to southern England's airports and military headquarters', 6 AEF was blessed with more volunteers than any other such unit. This was good for the cadets, but gave Don an unenviable workload, training his pilots, keeping them up to date with all manner of currency requirements, testing them regularly to ensure they were competent and dealing with the paperwork all these tasks generated.

The upshot was that apart from the odd day when someone took pity on me and gave me a flight, I rarely flew. Most of my days were spent briefing and supervising the visiting cadets and relieving the boss of some of his admin burden.

MEETING FAT ALBERT

I was very aware that I knew little about the Lockheed C-130 Hercules beyond the fact that in the RAF at large its name was shortened to Herc, while its crews also called it Fat Albert. I knew even less about the way it was operated, so I organised myself a couple of short flights. Both proved to be something out of the ordinary.

About half the Hercs at Lyneham had recently been lengthened by fifteen feet so they could carry more passengers and freight. The original Herc became the Mk1, while the stretched version was designated the Mk3, and I was to fly in one of these.

I joined the crew in the Operations Block, where they were preparing to fly sixty four soldiers of the Parachute Regiment around the UK for a couple of hours before kicking them out over Salisbury Plain. Most of the flight would be at 250 feet with a climb to 800 feet for what I discovered was to be the crew's first experience of dropping paratroops from the Mk3.

Some elements of the flight planning process were familiar, like reviewing the weather and taking note of the various aviation warnings. But much was unfamiliar, or so different in scale from flight planning on the Jetstream as to be unrecognisable. I tried to keep on top of things without getting in the crew's way.

Planning complete, we were driven across a pan brimming with C-130s, long and short. When we reached our Mk3, the co-pilot ushered me toward a door in the port side just behind the crew compartment. I climbed a couple of steps into the aircraft, then a further set to emerge on the spacious flight deck. To my right against its rear wall – bulkhead - was a bunk bed. As directed, I sat to one side of the lower tier and sorted out a set of lap straps.

A few minutes later the captain gestured me forward to one of the left side windows behind his seat. He pointed at a line of soldiers walking out to the aircraft. They were a curious sight. The tallest and most heavily built seemed to be carrying little more than a parachute and a rifle; while the shortest were weighed down with all manner of heavy equipment, from machine guns and bandoliers of ammunition, to mortar barrels and base plates. They could barely walk.

I pictured them jumping from the aircraft and plummeting straight down like cartoon characters stepping into a lift shaft, parachutes flapping uselessly behind them. But of course the distribution of equipment was to make each man roughly the same weight, so they'd descend at a similar rate and land in a predictable pattern based on the order they left the aircraft, thirty two from each rear side door of the cargo bay.

I'd always enjoyed low flying, and it seemed especially spectacular in the Herc. The terrain streamed past its panoramic flight deck windows with a cinematic quality, never more dramatic than when we weaved along the steep-sided valleys of mid-Wales. The co-pilot did much of the map-reading, deftly manipulating and interpreting a series of maps as the route unfolded.

I was impressed with the teamwork throughout the flight, instructions and information being passed between crew members in clipped, confident, tones. But during moments when the workload relaxed, they also found time for exchanges of playful humour that cut across the normal conventions of rank, crew position, age and experience.

It gave me an early insight into crew cooperation – a form of group dynamics - and the place of leadership within it, something which became a lifelong fascination.

Periodically, I looked into the freight bay where the young Paras sat on red canvas seats. At first, they sat upright, interested and alert. But as we manoeuvred among the hills, some looked pensive, while others bowed their heads, retching into little blue and white sick bags. The two loadmasters were busy handing out more bags.

It crystallized something the co-pilot had said. After a relatively short time flying in a wildly bucking metal tube with few windows, most Paras were so desperate to be on the ground that they'd jump - with or without a parachute.

Approaching the drop zone, the tension throughout the aircraft mounted and communication became evermore terse and clipped. When the navigator put on a green light to initiate the drop, I stuck my head into the freight bay again. On each side, a line of men edged purposefully toward the rear side doors. All had one arm raised holding onto a cord clipped to a line above their heads that ran the length of the freight bay. Each slid the cord and its clip along the wire as they edged forward, glancing up every now and then to check that it was still connected and running freely. The other end of the cord was connected to their parachute opening mechanism.

As each Para reached the open door on his side and received a pat on the back from the dispatcher, he jumped out into the airflow. Immediately, he shot back as if hit by a bus. Somewhere behind the aircraft, the trailing cord would pull open his parachute, although this vital part of the operation was lost to me.

Earlier trials had explored the possibility that the modified slipstream of the Mk3 might cause parachutists exiting each side to crash together behind the aircraft and fall to their deaths in a jumbled mass of flailing bodies and flapping silk. I couldn't believe we'd have been doing it if that was even a remote possibility. But as we sped away from the drop zone, I couldn't help wondering what we were leaving in our wake, both in the air and on the ground. I never did find out, the co-pilot explaining that even the crew were unlikely to hear unless there were problems beyond the odd broken leg, which happened all the time.

Thinking about it, broken legs seemed inevitable when you kicked someone out of an aircraft holding the equivalent of a blacksmith's anvil!

My second flight involved the dropping of something other than parachutists.

The Mk1 Herc could drop two large metal pallets loaded with all manner of freight. It was hoped that the Mk3 would be able to drop three. I was to join one of the trial flights looking into this.

In flight planning I heard that the ramp and door would be lowered to the horizontal and a large extractor parachute or chutes would deploy to pull the pallets along rollers and out of the aircraft, slowing them a little before they thudded into the ground. Cameras would film how the three pallets travelled along and out of the freight bay, and the captain would note how the extraction of the extra pallet affected the handling of the aircraft.

When we arrived at the aircraft, I had a quick look into the freight bay where, as advertised, three pallets loaded high with boxes sat. Unlike the Para drop sortie, the flight to the drop zone was relatively short. At a nod from the captain, I rose from the bunk and looked down the back just as the ramp and door opened.

A short time later, a large parachute sprang from the rear pallet and snaked into the airflow behind the aircraft. As the silk inflated, the pallets began to move, slowly at first but then faster and faster until, amid a cacophony of scrapes, clatters and bangs they flew out of the rear door. The ensuing silence was accompanied by an unvoiced, *Wow!*

Having not experienced anything like it before, I'd found the sound and fury - the violence – of the extraction quite something. But had it been normal, I wondered?

It seemed to me that the third pallet had been just about airborne as it neared the rear of the aircraft and shot into the airflow. Thankfully it hadn't hit anything, but it had looked a bit close for my liking. It turned out that the loadmasters felt the same way. So, although the pilot said there was nothing unexpected in the handling characteristics, the extraction certainly seemed worthy of review.

I never found out what the cameras revealed, but if it had been a major problem, it was solved on later trial flights because the Mk3 went on to be capable of dropping three pallets.

The two flights had clarified one thing. If I survived my operational conversion course, I wanted to join one of the two squadrons at Lyneham that operated Fat Albert in the tactical role, flying at low level, delivering paratroopers and air dropping freight.

Back at Abingdon, I was sometimes loaned to the Station to host visits, usually by local schools. Among the thank you letters in my scrap book is one from primary school pupil, Warren Cartwright. He informs me that he had to sit on the floor of the minibus on the way to 6 AEF, but was allowed to sit in the front between the driver and his teacher for the return journey. Health and safety!

I had at least one other period of respite from 6 AEF. Each

September, RAF Abingdon hosted an air show. Much of the organisation fell to the Unit Test Pilot, the man responsible for testing the Buccaneers, Jaguars and Hawks when they came out of the hangars after maintenance. Most of the year, his air show duties weren't too onerous. But as the date approached, he needed help, and I was one of the people drafted in.

So I spent the week before the show troubleshooting, and much of the day before meeting display crews and making sure they were content. On the day itself, I ran the odd errand, but spent most of the time watching the displays, including a Vulcan, the delta-wing bomber I'd worked on as a corporal two and a half years earlier.

The highlight, though, was the Red Arrows. I watched in awe, unaware that my career path would involve several periods in close proximity to the team and culminate in a flight with them.

As the day unfolded with aircraft whizzing around overhead, I felt immensely proud to be walking around with a set of pilot wings on my chest. But I also felt a bit of a fraud. After all, I had yet to prove that I deserved them.

OPERATIONAL CONVERSION AND BONDING

My most vivid memories of my time on the Hercules Operational Conversion Unit, 242 OCU, are not of the flying, memorable as some of that was, but of the fun I and my fellow course members had during our four and a half months of training.

As we assembled in one of the OCU classrooms on 30th November 1981, there were about thirty of us, roughly equal numbers for each of the five crew positions: captain, co-pilot, navigator, air engineer and loadmaster. Although a couple of female loadmasters had appeared on the Herc fleet by then, our course was all male. We were replacements for aircrew leaving Lyneham for reasons such as retirement, promotion or posting to other aircraft types or ground appointments.

Four of the six prospective co-pilots had been on my course at Finningley. The other had taken a more circuitous route via the Nimrod OCU, having discovered that the aircraft's underlying Dutch roll motion made him violently ill, not only during flight, but for several hours afterwards. So here he was trying a different aircraft, a ploy that I'm pleased to say worked, because he had no trouble with airsickness on the Herc.

All the captains were men with wider experience returning to Lyneham after periods on the ground or on other aircraft types. But the vast majority of the rear crew were, like the co-pilots, relative youngsters straight out of flying training.

So, on that first morning, we graduates of the various Finningley courses were catching up after a few months in holding posts, while many of the older hands were also seeing one another again after a break of several years. The room seemed full of re-unions. It was also full of laughter.

The tone was set.

Situation comedies, jokes and sketches before the era of political correctness were often based on racial or gender stereotyping. We soon discovered that crew positions on the Herc were the same. No matter what personality traits we as individuals displayed, there was no escaping the stereotype. To rail against it, or worse still, display irritation, would only lead to more jokes, and greater enjoyment for those delivering them.

All co-pilots, regardless of age or experience, were type-cast as callow youths prone to stupid mistakes. Of course, there was some truth in this. After all, many of us were young, straight out of training and, therefore, bound to make mistakes. But when I reached my squadron, I discovered that some of my fellow co-pilots were in their fifties with many more flying hours than most of their captains. It didn't matter, the stereotype still held.

And no matter how slim and health conscious they might be, co-pilots were also portrayed as eating machines, constantly hungry. One oft-repeated joke had the loadmaster treading on the co-pilot's foot every time he delivered food to the flight deck.

Asked why, the loadie replied, 'Sorry, Co, I thought you were a pedal bin!'

Navigators sat sideways at a metal desk to the rear right of the flight deck behind the co-pilot. They faced a wall of dials and switches for monitoring and controlling nav kit, some of which dated back to the Second World War. But in addition to their navigation duties, they were responsible for reading out checks and procedures, and for keeping a beady eye on the pilots, monitoring their actions and encouraging them to fly as directed.

As was only right and proper, they took these duties seriously, but it meant they could be stereotyped as earnest and geeky, wedded to check lists, charts, slide rules and sextants. This image wasn't helped by the fact that most of their expertise was hidden from and little understood by the rest of the crew, like some arcane form of magic.

A fair number of navigators tried to play on this element, seeking to appear eccentric, even wizard-like. One used to exit the crew bus and walk straight to the bulbous black nose of the aircraft and greet it in French.

'Bonjour, Albert,' he would say, 'comment allez-vous?'

Then he'd cock his head as if considering the reply, before patting the nose and saying, 'Bon, bon,' nodding his head in contentment as he joined the rest of the crew to board the aircraft.

Any passengers witnessing the performance would wonder if they should board an aircraft crewed by such an oddball. If they'd seen the fluffy tartan bedroom slippers he donned when he settled himself down on the flight deck, they might have been even more concerned.

Finally, it's a simple statement of fact that many navigators only occupied that crew position because they lacked the aptitude to be selected as pilots, or had fallen out of pilot training at some stage. This could leave some with a chip on their shoulder, making them defensive and confrontational if they sensed their advice being given too little weight by the rest of the crew, and especially the pilots.

As a result, some captains thought it great sport to wind up their navigators, calling them mere *directional consultants*, and taking every opportunity to over-ride or modify their advice – just enough to rile them.

Some people went to extremes to put the knife in.

The cocker spaniel of a friend of mine had been taught to

respond to the question, '*Would you rather be a navigator - or be dead?*' by letting out a pathetic whine and rolling onto its back with its paws in the air.

Air engineers sat in the middle of the flight deck, immediately behind and between the pilots, beneath their own panel in the flight deck roof. Its bank of dials, switches, circuit breakers and fuses allowed them to monitor and manage most of the aircraft systems, from fuel and electrics to air conditioning and pressurisation.

On long overseas trips to destinations where engineering support was likely to be limited, the crew was often augmented by one or two ground engineers, senior NCO tradesmen trained to diagnose and fix most problems. Otherwise, the air engineer was expected to deal with anything that went wrong, or at least have a damn good go at doing so before calling in the cavalry.

As a result, they could fit into one of two stereotypes; grease monkeys, eager for any opportunity to show their prowess with a spanner; or shirkers, eager to declare their aircraft unserviceable, preferably in a pleasant location with nice hotels and good allowances.

In my experience, there were few that merited the label shirker. In three and a half years and more than fifteen hundred hours of Herc flying, I spent additional nights on the ground with an unserviceable aircraft only a couple of times, once because we were flying an aircraft that had sustained major damage during the Ethiopian famine relief effort. A story for later in this volume.

The stereotypes of captains and loadmasters can perhaps best be explained by an exchange in the Officers' Mess bar at RAF North Luffenham, where we spent a few days at the school of aviation medicine, my third visit.

Captains were the pilots who sat in the front left hand seat, kings of all they surveyed. As a result, they were less used to being the target of banter than other crew members. But early in the proceedings that night in the bar, an experienced commissioned loadmaster told the story of a tremendously popular gun-dog named Co-pilot that worked on a shooting estate in Scotland. The dog was so efficient at retrieving birds brought down by shooting parties that he commanded a high price. One party returned every year, happy to meet the ever-increasing cost of hiring Co-pilot for a few days. And then, one year, they were surprised to be given the dog at a much reduced rate.

'Why,' they asked,' has Co-pilot gone down so much in value?'

With a twinkle in his eye, the loadmaster looked across the bar at the senior captain on the course, a squadron leader, soon to be wing commander. As their eyes locked, he delivered his punch-line.

'Och,' the gamekeeper replied, 'a few weeks ago some idiot called him Captain. Now all he does is sit on his arse and bark!'

Cue uproarious laughter, and the captain wagging his finger at the loadmaster as if to say, *just you wait*.

Which leaves the loadmasters?

As the name implies, they were responsible for the safe loading and unloading of freight and passengers. But they were also in charge of the aircraft galley, a small *kitchen* at the rear left of the flight deck used to prepare meals and drinks for the crew. Sadly, no matter how hard-working and effective loadmasters were in their primary role, they were likely to be judged mainly on their provision of food and drink. Any shortfall in quantity or quality of the crew's rations would see them labelled lazy, or worse, incompetent.

They could also be stereotyped as shifty wheeler-dealers, again slightly unfair, because very often they had to be entrepreneurial. No matter how remote or primitive the location, they were expected to provide for the crew. Somehow, they all managed, but the best went the extra mile, securing a candle-bedecked cake for a crew member's birthday, or a gourmet meal way beyond expectations. And of course, once again, on such things they were judged.

Anyway, back to that night in the bar, where you could sense the senior captain mulling over a response to the gun-dog joke.

During a lull in proceedings, he began the story of a Herc crashing in the jungle and its crew setting off to walk to safety. After hours of toil, they came to a clearing, in the middle of which was a temple, fronted by a stone figure. As they approached, it was revealed to be a tall, naked, female idol with an enormous blue gemstone in her navel.

When they stepped onto the base holding the statue, a voice boomed out. 'To attain the jewel, you must make love to the idol.'

Sure enough, a few feet below the jewel in the navel was a strategically placed hole. The captain was the tallest and they lifted him up. But he was a few inches short of both the hole and the jewel, and the stone was too smooth to climb. One by one, the others attempted to scramble up the smooth stone and make love to the idol. And one by one, they failed.

The fifth, the loadmaster, was the shortest. Before he could make his attempt, the captain said, 'This is a waste of time. Come on, let's go.'

They turned to leave, but the commanding voice boomed out again.

'Let the loadmaster try.'

The captain paused and looked across the bar at the purveyor of the gun-dog joke.

'After all, everyone knows that loadmasters are idol fuckers.'

The riposte had been worth waiting for, and while the rest of the room laughed, the flight lieutenant loadmaster and the squadron leader captain raised a glass and nodded in mutual respect, honours even.

After forty years, I still remember the highlights of that lively night at North Luffenham. It was one of many events that helped meld us into a band of brothers.

I've said in both previous volumes that forging bonds strong enough for individuals to risk their lives for one another is vital to military success. I know from experience that many civilians express doubt that such bonding can happen in a matter of days, hours even.

I can only assure such sceptics that it can.

Of course, not all the OCU course was in the bar that night. All the air engineers and all bar the flight lieutenant loadmaster were NCOs and therefore enjoying their own bonding session in the Sergeants' Mess.

When he joined his squadron, the flight lieutenant would lead a section of twenty or so NCO loadmasters, mostly young sergeant aircrew, with a smattering of flight sergeants and a few master aircrew, the aircrew equivalent of warrant officer. The air engineer sections were the same, one officer and about twenty NCOs.

Such segregation might seem strange when officer and NCO aircrew flew the same aircraft and shared the same risks. But it was a well-established norm on most multi-engine aircraft. I covered the general principles of rank etiquette between officers and airmen in a previous volume, but that between officer and NCO aircrew was even more nuanced.

Irrespective of rank, from the moment a Herc crew entered flight planning until they reached the accommodation at the destination, they addressed one another using crew positions, in the form, captain, co, nav, loadie or eng (pronounced as in penge).

Otherwise, on the ground at service bases, normal rank etiquette usually applied. But on long overseas routes – *down route* as it was called – things could become more complicated. Senior officers were still invariably addressed as sir – unless they were specialist aircrew squadron leaders, but let's not go there – while junior officers and NCOs could *sometimes* be on first name terms.

The relaxation was dependent on a complex cocktail of factors, including age, experience, familiarity, mutual respect and individual preference. But basically, if an officer and NCO on a crew respected one another enough, they could slip into the use of first names.

In the 1980s, most Army and some RAF officers still thought such intimacy outrageous. They were convinced it would lead to a breakdown in discipline that would reduce military effectiveness. In my experience, the opposite was true, the relaxation, when done for the right reasons, tightened the bond between officer and NCO, enhancing both morale and effectiveness. Indeed, not to have slipped into first name terms when all the stars aligned would have seemed strange – on the Herc at least.

So, if I was to work as effectively as possible with everyone around me regardless of rank, I had to learn to navigate the nuances.

I can't remember exactly how quickly I cracked the code, but once I did, away from the cockpit, where an NCO and I shared a bond of mutual respect, we would use first names; although the personalities of the rest of the crew would dictate whether we did so openly or only when on our own. And the more experienced I became, the more NCOs I knew and respected, and the more likely it was to happen.

Of course, for a multitude of reasons, there were still those who preferred convention.

I once spent several weeks flying with a very experienced master aircrew loadie nearing retirement at the age of fifty five. You'll have to take my word for it that we shared a high level of mutual respect. And yet, although he was perfectly happy and expected me to call him by his first name, he refused to do the same. His training and experience meant he just couldn't address an officer as anything other than sir.

He was a product of the *old* air force, when bases had stretched across the Middle East and Asia as far as Hong Kong and Singapore. Some *old school* officers were the same, and this was accepted. But there was another breed of officer that expected always to be called sir. I struggle to describe them as anything other than arrogant assholes.

I run the danger of damning myself by association now, but it seemed that these were often the most likely to be promoted. They tended to be averse to risk and experimentation. For them, sticking to convention in every area of life was safer, reducing the scope for misunderstanding and error. As a result, the promotion system often saw them as a safe pair of hands, when, in some cases, they really were just assholes.

Mercifully, in my assessment, they were few in number.

To anyone without a military background, this whole discussion may seem trivial, pointless even. But you'll have to take my word for it that the nuances of crew interaction were very important to squadron life, allowing those in the know to figure out in quick time everyone's position in the hierarchy, and their worth, regardless of rank or crew position.

And recently, I was surprised to find similar issues alive toward the end of the second decade of the 21st Century. A Chinook helicopter pilot told me that they went further than we did, using first names in the air.

GROUNDSCHOOL

Our simulator and flying exercises weren't due to start until February. Before then, we had to learn as much as possible about the Herc and how to operate it.

The process kicked off with an introductory visit to see a Mk1 and a Mk3 in one of the engineering hangars. There was only one Mk2, a weather research aircraft based at Farnborough and affectionately known as Snoopy because of its long, lance-like, nose.

There sat two high wing monoplanes, each with a wingspan of 132 feet 7¼ inches (40.41m) and a high tailfin reaching up 38 feet 2½ inches (11.66m) from the ground. The Mk1 was 99 feet 6 inches (29.79m) in length and the Mk3 fifteen feet (4.9m) longer, with two tubular fuselage plugs inserted, one just in front of the wings, another just behind.

Each fuselage sat horizontal and quite low to the ground, supported on a squat nosewheel assembly beneath the flight deck and four mainwheels with chunky, relatively low pressure, tyres, two in tandem each side of the fuselage beneath the wings. The upper surfaces of the aircraft and most of the fuselage were painted in a grey/green camouflage pattern, the lower surfaces a sort of duck egg blue.

On each high wing were two Alison T56-A-15 turboprop engines, each powering four, paddle-like, Hamilton Standard Hydromatic propeller blades. With the engines running, these rotated to form hazy circles of whirling metal, and a distinctive sound, a combination of high-pitched whine and low, rhythmic, thrum. They could also produce enough power to carry 45,000 pounds (twenty tons) of freight nearly 2,500 miles, or half that weight more than 4,500 miles

Like all early Hercs, the cargo compartment of the Mk1 was based on the dimensions of an American railroad boxcar, forty one feet long, ten feet wide and nine feet high. This allowed it to carry anything from two Gazelle helicopters or Ferret armoured cars, to two Land Rovers and forty troops, or countless other combinations of passengers and freight.

One frustration with the Mk 1 was that the cargo compartment tended to fill to capacity before it reached the maximum weight limit. Hence the decision to lengthen thirty one of the sixty six-strong Herc fleet and designate them Mk3s.

Most freight was loaded and unloaded through the opening made when a large portion of the back end hinged down from beneath the tail. The resulting slab of metal, known as the ramp, could be lowered to the horizontal so that loads could be pushed in or out along rollers built into the freight bay floor. It could also be dipped to the ground, forming a sloping ramp up and down which vehicles could be driven. The ramp could also be dropped to the horizontal in flight for the air-dropping of freight, as I'd seen during one of my two Herc flights to date.

Passengers could enter up the ramp or via the crew door to the front left of the fuselage. A full load would be ninety two troops or seventy four stretcher cases, or sixty four paratroopers, thirty two jumping from each rear side door. Paratroopers could also jump from the rear ramp and door, but this reduced the maximum number to forty.

To my eyes, the Herc is not without aesthetic qualities, but the emphasis is on utility rather than beauty. Basically, Fat Albert is a winged truck, reinforced to withstand the rigours of carrying a vast range of gnarly freight over long distances. As a result of this analogy, the RAF crews that flew it were known as Truckies.

We were proud to bear the name, but to the Army, Navy and most of the RAF, it was a term of abuse, based on the perception that we had two things in common with earthbound truckers: an over-fondness for food, and unfathomable rules limiting the length of our working day. Our detractors would quote instances where some seemingly trivial problem, like a lack of food for the crew, had delayed their departure to the point where the flight had been cancelled, preventing them and their kit getting from A to B.

Dealing with the time issue first, a trucker's driving hours could indeed be compared to what we Truckies called a crew duty day. For us it was normally a maximum of sixteen hours, starting two hours before take-off and ending when the chocks were put round the wheels at the final destination. Unless there were exceptional circumstances, we couldn't take off on even a relatively short flight if it meant exceeding this sixteen-hour limit. After all, we couldn't just pull off the road into a convenient lay-by or truck-stop for a nap.

The argument regarding food was similar. If we were going to be working for anything up to sixteen hours, our bodies and, perhaps more importantly, our minds, had to be fed. So if there was no food available for a long flight, we couldn't go because we couldn't just pull over at a truck-stop or roadside eatery.

So the rules were nothing more than sensible flight safety measures to ensure we were reasonably alert and well fed.

In my three and a half years on the Herc, I never experienced a delay due to lack of food, or a galley failure, although I know it happened on occasion. And the only time I had to stay somewhere because of a problem with crew duty hours was when the Royal Navy were several hours late arriving to collect a load.

That said, it was in Barbados!

During groundschool on the OCU, we rarely met as a complete course. Mostly, the pilots, navigators, air engineers and loadmasters received their own, tailored, lessons in separate classrooms.

I found the names of most of the subjects familiar from Linton and Finningley - Aerodynamics, Aircraft Tech, Systems, Avionics and Flight Instruments, Performance and Flight Planning, Operations and Loading, Meteorology and Combat Survival. But the scope of each had broadened immeasurably.

Nowhere was this more apparent than when studying the technical aspects of the Herc. It wasn't just that it was bigger than the Jetstream, it was also more complex.

Learning about the additional hydraulic, electrical and pneumatic systems was bad enough. But coming to grips with such things as how the network of sensors measuring fuel flow, turbine inlet and outlet temperatures, rpm, torque and a plethora of other things interacted to finesse the operation of the engines, propellers and fuel system proved a real challenge.

From an early stage, I started pencilling notes in a little blue book that slotted into the flying suit pocket at the bottom of my left leg. Constantly added to and updated throughout my time on the Herc, it provided, in my own words, facts or snippets of wisdom that wouldn't otherwise be easy to access in flight. It proved worth its weight in gold on numerous occasions, not only when faced with questions during ground and airborne tests, but more importantly, when faced with real dilemmas and emergencies down route.

I have the book open on the desk in front of me now. It

contains a mix of theory and practice, not all of which I fully understand after the passage of thirty years. So, while I don't want to bamboozle any of us with too much technical detail, I do want to give a flavour of the broad range of things I thought worthy of note.

Within the pages devoted to the letter A, the subjects covered include situations when the handling pilot might have to *abort* a take-off, the calls to be made on the flight deck and the checks to be made afterwards; the briefing to be given before flying an *asymmetric* approach on two or three engines rather than four; the limits and constraints on the use of the *auto-pilot*; the phone number of *AOS San Francisco*, an aircraft handling agent; the actions in the event of a brake *anti-skid* failure; the effects of a failure of the *altimeters* and *air speed indicators*; information about *Andros* airfield in the Bahamas, including arrival and departure procedures; notes on the *air conditioning* system and how to deal with various problems with it and the *air turbine motor*, a turbine that rotated at 43,000 revs per minute; and the contact details for the RAF staff at *Addis Ababa* during Op Bushel, the Ethiopian famine relief effort.

There are similar notes for every letter of the alphabet. For instance, four pages of tightly written pencil script are given over to the letter P, with notes on propellers, including details on the blades and their normal operation; the synchrophase system that, among other things, could be tweaked to keep the thrum of the engines in some sort of harmony; the various propeller protection measures, such as pitch stops, safety couplings, negative torque systems, fuel topping; and a page of detail on the ramifications of propeller pitch locks at different phases of flight.

As a co-pilot, I was expected to be particularly knowledgeable about the aircraft hydraulic systems. The panel for monitoring and controlling them sat in front of me.

The Herc had three hydraulic systems – utility, booster and

auxiliary. These used a combination of engine, electrical and, as a last resort, hand pump power to pressurise hydraulic fluid and force it through a network of pipes, sensors and valves to operate the flying controls, landing gear, wing flaps, nosewheel steering, wheel brakes, anti-skid system and rear ramp. The three systems were designed to offer redundancy, ensuring that vital services would continue to operate if one or more failed.

My little blue book gives detail, not only on the operation of the systems, but also the sort of trivia I could expect to be asked by an examiner seeking to ascertain the depth of my knowledge.

For instance, it tells me that there were separate tanks for the utility, booster and auxiliary systems, with capacities of 3.2, 2 and 3.4 US gallons respectively. The engine driven pumps were nine-piston variable angle swash plate pumps with run-around circuits. During engine start, a light on the hydraulic panel would come on when the hydraulic pressure reached 900 to 1,100 pounds per square inch and go out at 1,300psi.

The hydraulic pipes were tested to two and a half times system pressure and a relief valve would begin opening at 3,400psi and be fully open at 3,800psi, at which point, if the pressure kept rising, it might be necessary to shut down the appropriate engine. If temperature was a problem, a thermal cut-out would operate at 121° Celsius, necessitating a cooling off period of between four and twenty minutes, which could be shortened by operating the flying controls.

The hydraulic suction pumps were powered by alternating current from the essential busbar to produce pressures of between 70 and 100psi, with a warning light coming on at 20psi and going out at 30psi. There's a warning not to switch pumps off when a high flow rate exists, for instance when operating the flaps or landing gear, as this could lead to the venting of hydraulic fluid.

The neat pencil script goes on to cover various problems

that might occur with the hydraulic system on engine start, as well as how to deal with them.

For instance, if both engine driven pump lights remain unlit when one engine starts, you have to stop the start sequence. The diagnosis is that No 4 non-return valve is unserviceable, not No 4 engine driven pump. But the problem now is that if that pump were to fail in flight, there would be no indication of the failure. A solution is to swop No 4 NRV for No 3 and remove the drive from No 3 pump, although this will leave you with only half the booster system.

I could go on with another dozen hydraulic problems over a couple of pages, but you'll be relieved to know that I won't.

MORE BONDING

If the scope of the groundschool subjects had changed out of all recognition, so had their relevance.

At Finningley, learning about monsoons and trade winds, jungle survival and how to plan a flight into Hong Kong had seemed little more than academic exercises. But now, if all went well, I really would be flying into areas of the world where such knowledge would be vital. The survival elements were driven home in January, during a short spell of combat survival training at RAF Mountbatten.

Much like our earlier detachment to North Luffenham, this one provided lasting memories, starting with the domestic arrangements.

Mountbatten occupied a peninsula to the south of Plymouth, a maritime city on the south-west coast of England. It had been a flying boat base but was now the RAF School of Combat Survival and Rescue. While it had some accommodation, there was too little to house all the officers on a Herc operational conversion course. So we were put up in the naval equivalent of an officers' mess, the Wardroom at HMS Drake, a Royal Navy shore establishment a few miles across Plymouth.

As well as using several pejorative terms for the RAF, like penguins – all flap and no fly - the Navy love to focus on the relative youth of our Service, measured in decades rather than the centuries they'd been around. They like to assert that while they have traditions, the RAF merely has bad habits. It also allows them to treat us with disdain bordering on contempt. As a result, we set out to be, if not contemptible, as irritating as possible. This may sound childish, but it was all part of inter-

Service rivalry. It was expected.

Our first opportunity came with an assault on the Navy's idiosyncratic language and naming of things. For instance, whereas the RAF live in barrack blocks or messes with rooms on various floors, even when on dry land, the Navy live in mess decks or wardrooms with cabins and decks. And they're very picky about what they call their vessels. The bigger ones tend to be ships, while most small ones and submarines are boats.

Whenever we were in the presence of sailors, we made sure to get everything wrong, calling our cabins rooms and their ships boats, or vice versa. So schooled are they in using the correct terms that we never failed to elicit an irritable correction. And the more often we made our little mistakes, the more exasperated they became.

Such fun!

One of the highlights of being accommodated at HMS Drake was eating in one of the most impressive dining rooms of any Service base in the world – all oak panelling and maritime art. At first we were a bit nonplussed by tens of cords dangling from the ceiling. But it was explained that on the occasion of the annual dinner celebrating Admiral Nelson's victory at the Battle of Trafalgar in 1805, large models of Royal Navy, French and Spanish ships were attached to the cords to float above the heads of the diners, in positions they'd occupied at a pivotal point in the Battle.

I attended several dinners in Royal Navy wardrooms, but never a Trafalgar night. So I could only imagine the ships hanging above tables laden with silver and crystal, all glittering in the light of candles. The room must be quite a sight on such occasions.

Sadly, we tended to enter it only for breakfast. But when we did, we'd be in line astern, the leader sporting a raffish false moustache and a white silk scarf, held out by a piece of wire as if fluttering in the wind. As we walked, we'd lurch from side to side as if on the deck of a ship in a storm.

The Navy officers merely rolled their eyes and carried on with their cornflakes.

After our morning commute from Drake to Mountbatten, the fun continued in the classroom. We were there to learn about the survival equipment on the Herc and how to use it in a range of scenarios, from ditching in the sea to crash landing in differing terrains and climates. It was a serious business, especially when you added the possibility of ending up in enemy territory. But our tutors were adept at introducing humour to drive their messages home, an element we embraced with great enthusiasm.

Many lessons were shared with a handful of would-be Harrier pilots nearing the end of groundschool on their own operational conversion course. All bar one were fresh from fast jet flying training at RAF Valley. And much like us Herc newbies, they were learning what was expected of them from the more experienced man in their group who was returning to the Harrier after a ground tour.

It was the first of several occasions when I was to come into contact with Harrier pilots, not least when I commanded a detachment at a base in Italy from which the versatile jet flew on operations over the Balkans – something for a future volume. That detachment drove home something I first encountered at Mountbatten. Harrier pilots were incredibly intense, driven to the point of obsession to perfect every minute detail of their trade.

It all stemmed from the fact that they had only one aim in life: to hit the target; or, as it was described in large letters above the entrance to one of their squadron buildings, '*Our mission is to kill people and bust their stuff*'.

The Harrier force had no way of knowing that within three months they'd be acting out this mission statement in the white heat of battle over the Falkland Islands. Their preparation had always been for a very different war, one against the Soviet Union. Wherever the red hordes attacked

– the East German border, the frozen wastes of northern Norway or the mountains of eastern Turkey – they'd be ready to kill as many as possible and bust their stuff. It was the war we all expected to fight, and even at this early stage of training, the Harrier OCU students brought the intensity and professionalism required to fight it into the classroom at Mountbatten.

Now, Herc aircrew also prided themselves on being professional. But we'd learned from the other experienced Herc aircrew that our professionalism should be worn casually. In stark contrast with the Harrier pilots, to be seen to take things too seriously, to be too intense, would be to invite ridicule.

This gulf in outlook set up a clash of cultures that was both illuminating and, to us at least, alive with comic opportunity. The more laid back and un-military we appeared, the more intense and irritated the Harrier pilots became. The chasm was perhaps most apparent in lessons in which we discussed what we might do after being shot down over enemy territory.

Asked what their priorities would be, the steely-eyed Harrier pilots said, 'Escape and evade, get home, jump into another jet and have another go at the enemy.'

The Herc aircrew offered several alternatives, from, 'Book into the nearest hotel,' to 'Escape and evade, get home, claim your allowances and take any outstanding leave.'

The Harrier pilots joined in the laughter, but you could tell that they weren't entirely sure we were joking.

Later in the same lesson, asked who they'd aim to capture if they came across a section of enemy troops, the Harrier pilots had no hesitation in going for the officer, 'Because he'll have the map, which will help us to escape and evade, get back to base, jump into another jet, etc, etc.'

But while we correctly identified the officer as the one to nab, the reasons offered were somewhat different.

'Because he'll have the map, which will help us find the nearest hotel.'

I know I'm over-using the word, but it was great fun. Although, you may be pleased to hear that we had our comeuppance on the final afternoon of the course.

We and the Harrier pilots boarded an RAF Air Sea Rescue launch and set out across Plymouth Sound to complete dinghy drills in the harsh environment of the open sea. It would be a new experience for those of us who'd only done drills in a pool. Spirits were high. I even remember a sing song, including a profane rendition of a staple of the Last Night of the Proms in the Royal Albert Hall: *Rule Britannia, marmalade and jam, five Chinese crackers up your arsehole, bang, bang, bang, bang, bang!*

Spirits dipped somewhat when we moved out of the shelter of land into an Atlantic swell several feet high. A few faces took on a pasty hue, and we began to suspect that the spaghetti Bolognese served up for lunch had been someone's idea of a joke. But no-one had actually been ill by the time the launch slowed to sit, pitching and rolling in the choppy seas. Almost immediately, there was a loud whoosh and a rectangular bag that had been pushed off the back of the boat burst open, its contents inflating rapidly until we were looking at a large, circular, black and orange dinghy.

We were about to replicate the aftermath of an emergency that had forced us to land our Herc on the sea. In such a situation, pulling handles inside the aircraft or on top of the wings would make two of these twenty six-man dinghies burst from panels on top of each wing. To prevent them floating off into the distance, they'd be connected to the aircraft by a seventy foot line.

That afternoon, we were treating the drill with more than our usual dose of scepticism. This was because no RAF Herc had ever been ditched successfully. On the mercifully infrequent occasions it had been attempted, the aircraft had broken up and sunk, drowning those few souls that hadn't been killed in the impact. But, academic as it seemed, on this occasion, we had to pretend we'd all survived the ditching and were in a fit state to exit the aircraft and swim to the dinghy.

The crew of the launch invited us to inflate our Mae Wests and, one by one, jump into the rough sea.

The Harrier pilots had been looking forward to this.

While they were cocooned from neck to toe in neoprene rubber immersion suits that would keep them dry and, for a short time at least, warm, we wore only flying suits over woolly long johns and vests. And it was January!

As each successive Herc mate hit the freezing water, they gave a loud gasp. And when they bobbed to the surface, they shouted endless variations of the sentiment, *Fuck me*!

The performance added to the trepidation of those of us still waiting to jump. But it reduced the Harrier pilots to tears of laughter.

In due course, I jumped in, gasped as the icy water closed around me and added my own expletives when I surfaced. The sharp intake of breath had been entirely involuntary, my body's natural reaction to the sudden immersion in cold water. In similar circumstances, those without buoyancy aids can breathe in enough water to drown in a few seconds, while the expansion of the chest can be enough to crack the ribs of those who fasten their Mae Wests too tightly.

Anyway, once I'd bobbed up and regained my composure, I joined the stream of people swimming toward the dinghy.

Among the many things I learnt that afternoon was that there's a world of difference between swimming in a pool or close to a beach, and swimming in the open sea.

Out there, waves arrived unexpectedly, sometimes from two or three directions at once, making it difficult to maintain any sense of control or direction; and as each wave hit, it was as if a bucket of seawater was being thrown in my face, filling my nose and mouth, usually just as I was in the process of breathing.

And it really was bloody freezing. I hadn't been in the water many minutes before I could feel my fingers and toes going numb. I sensed that it wouldn't be too long before the residual warmth drained from the muscles in my arms and legs too, leaving me paralysed.

Swim the Channel! I'd be lucky to swim the length of an average pool in such conditions, even with a Mae West keeping me afloat.

Additionally, as I sank into the frequent troughs, the dinghy disappeared. And when I crawled back up to a crest, it was no longer where it should be, but to the side, or worse, nowhere to be seen. If it really had been at the very end of a seventy-foot tether, I might have struggled to find, let alone reach it. And on my own I might well have given in to panic.

But on this occasion, of course, all I had to do was follow the stream of swimmers. Soon I was bobbing alongside the dinghy awaiting my turn to grasp hands waiting to pull me up onto one of two protruding rubber *doormats* and through the large flap above it.

It afforded me the chance to see the launch pulling away and the first Harrier pilot jump from the back on the end of parachute lines. Although immediately lost behind the waves, I knew he'd be struggling to release his parachute harness to stop himself being dragged. Then he'd have to inflate his single-man dinghy and perform drills similar to those I'd practised in the pool.

When I was eventually pulled into my own rubber sanctuary, I found myself in a circular space with a two foot high wall comprising two inflatable tubes on top of one another. A roof canopy sloped up from the top tube to a central point five feet above the floor atop an inflated pillar, like a tent pole. Despite the door flaps being open, the interior had a murky, orange, tinge. And when the final person was pulled in and the flaps were closed, leaving only a couple of small plastic *windows*, it became dark and claustrophobic.

The waterlogged floor heaved, taking on the contours of the waves coursing beneath us and making it impossible to maintain balance, even when sliding along on our bottoms. Not that there was much room to move, with twenty six occupying the space. Dark shapes huddled around the circumference, coughing and swearing as they brushed against one another in a quest for personal space. There was just enough room round the outside for twenty six pairs of shoulders, but too little in the centre for twenty six pairs of legs and feet. In the end we took it in turns to stretch out or huddle up. Had we been spending a night in there, I doubt any of us would have slept until genuine exhaustion took hold.

I looked around at my drenched compatriots. Any lingering high spirits had evaporated. Some, like me, were shivering, and I suspected from the pale faces and white lips that many were, also like me, feeling queasy.

In a real ditching, we were pretty certain the dinghies would have been at the bottom of the sea with our Herc. But, under the senior captain's direction, we acted as if everything had turned out well and someone pretended to cut the line tethering us to the aircraft – before it sank.

Some were detailed to inflate the floor and canopy, others to bail out the inches of water we were sitting in, or to set off the emergency locator beacon or to rummage in the various bags. These contained survival aids and goodies, including a small amount of food and water, which would have to be rationed.

The brief flurry of activity had banished my seasickness, but soon there was nothing to do but sit back and ponder our predicament. At first, there was lots of banter, but as the odd person made for the door flaps, forced them open, leaned out and began retching, the bonhomie became more difficult to maintain.

Faced with a real survival situation, what would we do next?

Should we stay where we were, or, if we could work out where the nearest land or shipping lane was, try and paddle toward it?

The perceived wisdom was to stay put for about seventy two hours in the hope that rescue forces would converge on a last known position. Already uncomfortable and bored, I knew that would be a very unattractive proposition.

As it turned out, I don't think we spent more than fifteen minutes in the twenty six-man dinghy before we were unceremoniously turfed out and made to swim to a larger one bobbing in the swell about twenty yards away.

When the Mk3 Herc had been introduced, its stretched fuselage could accommodate more passengers than the Mk1. So larger, thirty-three man, dinghies had to be crammed into the wing panels. We were about to board one.

The twenty six-man's door flaps had been replaced with soft tubular entrance chutes, two large ones opposite one another, and two smaller at ninety degrees. One at a time, the people in front of me placed their heads in one of the large chutes and wriggled forward until their feet disappeared. When I'd wriggled my way in, I found myself in what seemed a cavernous space compared to the twenty six-man dinghy. It could actually hold forty one people.

Strangely though, this increase in space didn't seem to mean an increase in comfort. The chutes were sealed with draw strings that, although waterproof, seemed to seal off the air, making the interior darker and more claustrophobic. And so wide was the floor that it tended to span more than one wave. As you bobbed up and down, the person opposite would rise into the air then disappear as he dipped into a trough. It was quite disconcerting, and so disorientating that I wasn't the only one to suffer a rapid onset of queasiness.

It wasn't long before people were frantically undoing the drawstrings on all four chutes, forcing their heads and shoulders into the fresh air and retching loudly. The sounds were the final straw for many of us. Soon, I was in one of four queues of pasty-looking people awaiting their turn. When each man eventually pulled back and vacated a tube, there'd be a muttered, *thank you*, as the next disappeared and added to the chorus of retching. We'd laugh about it later. But it was very unpleasant at the time.

There was something about the 33-man dinghy that made even the hardiest sailors among us violently seasick. And when I popped into the fresh air, I found the sea awash with spaghetti. Somehow, as the waves swept past, the strings of pasta just bobbed up and down, remaining in formation with the dinghy.

A cruel joke indeed.

Although I didn't want to delay the person tapping me on the backside for too long, I couldn't resist taking a few moments to watch a Harrier pilot being winched from the sea by a yellow Sea King search and rescue helicopter. I was envious. When we were finally allowed to vacate the thirty three-man vomit comet, it would be to re-board the launch.

I didn't know it then, but I'd have my chance to be winched into a Sea King about eighteen months later.

As we sat on the deck of the launch wrapped in blankets for the journey back to Mountbatten, we were much more subdued than on the outward journey. The major lesson I took from the afternoon, beyond avoiding the sea, was that if I was fortunate enough to survive a ditching, I hoped to be in a Mk1 with twenty six-man dinghies, rather than a Mk3 with its thirty three-man alternatives.

Luckily, during my time flying both types, I never came close to a ditching situation. Within a year, though, one of the air enges involved that afternoon had come very close indeed, a story covered later in this volume.

Before the first flying exercise on the course, I had five sorties in one of Lyneham's simulators. They were old school, lacking the complex movement and visual systems that were appearing elsewhere. But they were exact replicas of the Herc flight deck and allowed us an early chance to come to grips with the mundane tasks of setting seat positions, storing nav bags and documents, strapping in, donning headsets and positioning and connecting emergency oxygen masks.

More importantly, at much less cost than flying, they allowed us to practise the full range of normal flight procedures and emergencies, including those you couldn't, or wouldn't want to practise in a real aircraft. We could also screw things up, even crash, with no danger of injuring anything other than our professional pride. And although they were earthbound, it was surprising how much tension and fear the sims could generate when things began to go wrong.

Mostly, there was total blackness beyond the sim's flight deck windows, but runway lights could be projected for take-offs and landings, while those lucky enough to practise low level flying could see live images from a video camera running over a model of a rural scene, complete with tiny fields, livestock, trees and villages.

Apparently, there were occasions when a spider minding its own business among the model houses would rise up in front of a crew like a B-movie monster, a heart-stopping experience not covered in the Flight Reference Cards.

When we began flying multi-leg routes on our squadrons, captains and co-pilots would swop responsibilities for successive legs. So, on every other leg, one would fly the take-off and landing and control the bits in between, while the other would operate the radios maintain contact with operating agencies and air traffic control, and update the en-route, diversion and destination weathers.

Of course, the captain was always the captain, so even if I was operating pilot, he might over-ride my decisions, or take control at any point. Sim sorties were more likely to see the captain doing the flying, but there was generally time for me to have at least some time in control,

Our first three sim sorties concentrated on start procedures and faults, then graduated to take-off and climb, instrument approaches and landings. Each sortie lasted three hours and they became increasingly complex; the second included search and rescue and ditching techniques, while the third found us dealing with an assortment of more or less dire propeller problems.

Sims four and five were an hour shorter, but packed with emergencies. These could include failures of the engines, propellers or any other aircraft systems from electrics to fuel and hydraulics, flight instruments, air conditioning or pressurisation, and sometimes all of them. Some emergencies would necessitate fitting oxygen masks to our headsets, adding another layer of complication and discomfort.

The most severe and sinister emergencies were practice fires, sometimes in the engines or fuel tanks, and sometimes among the freight, in the galley or behind one of the many instrument panels on the flight deck. For an engine fire, we'd pull T-handles on one of the overhead panels to operate fire extinguishers in the affected engine or engines. For cabin fires, there were hand-held extinguishers.

Of course, even if we failed to overcome a fire in the sim, we could un-strap and walk away unharmed. But the ramifications of a fire raging out of control in flight didn't bear thinking about. We didn't carry parachutes.

The combination of weeks in groundschool and the first five sims had given me some idea of what was expected of a Herc co-pilot during flight. But over the same period, I'd also gained an insight into my wider role within the crew.

The day before any route flight, I'd be expected to visit the Ops Block to check the contents of a large canvas *route bag* or bags containing the documents the captain, nav and I would need for the entire itinerary, be that a day shuttling between airfields in the UK, or a longer period taking in several countries or continents. The documents would include maps, books containing the air traffic control procedures for the countries we were to over-fly or visit, plus folders of arrival and departure procedures for, not only the destination airfields, but all the airfields we might divert to in the event of bad weather or an emergency. I'd then be responsible for picking the bags up on the day of the flight and depositing them on the flight deck. They invariably weighed a ton, but luckily, once they were stowed, they tended to stay on board for the duration of a route, tucked down next to our seats, ready for us to dive in and find the documents we needed when we needed them.

I also started to become familiar with radio logs, separate sheets for each leg of a route bearing a wide range of information, such as major geographical way points or navigation beacons and their frequencies, the tracks and distances between them and the air traffic control frequencies we were likely to be allocated as we progressed.

In flight, both pilots would have a radio log. Both could fill them in, but the non-operating pilot, captain or co-pilot, was responsible for annotating their sheet with air traffic control clearances, changes of frequency and updated weather for the destination and diversion airfields. He'd also keep a note of height and actual times of arrival at way points or beacons, plus the estimated time of arrival at the next point. In areas of the world without radar coverage, these details were passed to air traffic control, and in areas without air traffic control, they were broadcast on a flight information frequency monitored by other aircraft in the area.

I'd also be responsible for picking up the *imprest*, that is, the money and supporting paperwork we'd need for the duration of our itinerary.

By the time I left Lyneham in 1985, co-pilots were being issued with credit cards. But for most of the three years I flew down route, I carried cash or cash and travellers' cheques in a mix of currencies to the value of several thousand pounds, £13,000 on one occasion.

Whatever the amount, it was invariably more than I could ever have imagined seeing, never mind holding, when growing up on a council estate in Shropshire.

Luckily, down route we tended to stay in large international chain hotels where the cost of the rooms was covered by local contracts. I merely had to check and sign the hotel bill, which found its way back to Lyneham via a handling agent or the British Embassy. But I had to have enough cash for incidental expenses at each location, items such as taxis and baggage handling, known as porterage. And most importantly, I had to issue each crew member their *allowances*, cash for meals – but not drinks.

It could be a complicated process. What qualified as an incidental expense or allowance varied from place to place, as did the rates to be paid. And inevitably, safeguarding the money was a big issue.

During flight and when moving to and from hotels, I tended to put it in a money belt. But when carrying large amounts, a belt could be too bulky, so on occasion some or all of the money had to go in my nav bag – a big, blue-grey, service issue canvas bag that sat next to me on the flight deck. I always guarded this jealously, but especially when it contained the crew's money.

Even the larger hotels didn't have safes in rooms, but most had safety deposit boxes behind reception. As soon as possible after checking in, I'd put as much of my imprest as possible in one of these, hoping to remember it before check-out.

Inevitably there were stories of co-pilots forgetting their imprest and having to rush back to the hotel to retrieve it – if they remembered before take-off. If they didn't, they'd have to try and secure funds at the next location, and find a way of sorting out the mess at the last one. Either way, they'd be very unpopular with the crew and everyone else involved in the process.

Smaller hotels rarely had any provision for protecting valuables, so it was back to the money belt. No matter how well it was hidden, it was impossible not to feel vulnerable when carrying thousands of pounds, especially in cities where your appearance marked you out as a potential target.

Experience showed that my fears were far from groundless. Two of my fellow co-pilots were robbed, the first walking back to a hotel in Nairobi, Kenya. He was jumped, beaten with a baseball bat and relieved of his wallet. Luckily it contained only his personal money. The imprest was in the hotel safe. The second was walking with his crew through a crowded street-market in Dakar, Senegal. He actually felt his wallet being lifted, but in the few moments it took him to alert the others, it had sailed over the heads of the crowd and disappeared. It contained the crew imprest.

Such dangers were the reason I tried to distribute the money for the entire route as soon as possible, ideally not long after we'd left Lyneham. This could be relatively straightforward if only one currency was involved. But if there were multiple currencies, or the captain didn't want the imprest dished out in this way, I was forced to retain the cash and dole it out in penny packets in each new country. A real pain.

After receiving advice from more experienced co-pilots, among the many things stuffed into my flying suit pockets was a little blue book. I still have three of them. They contain details of each route I flew, its crew and the allowances issued, alongside which they had to initial. Of course, it carried no legal weight whatsoever, but it kept me on top of things until I had the opportunity to fill out the paperwork.

Managing the imprest was one of a co-pilot's most onerous duties. Not only was it complicated, time-consuming and stressful, but the legal ramifications of mistakes when dealing with large amounts of taxpayers' money – or The Queen's money as we put it – could be very severe. Every last dime or penny had to be accounted for.

On return to Lyneham, I'd hand the paperwork and any remaining funds to the accounts section in Station Headquarters. Even then, it was a few days before you could relax, just in case they found a mistake and called you in for interrogation.

A final couple of titbits on imprests.

Only pounds and dollars were afforded their proper titles.

Other currencies, even such staples as francs and marks, were known as blats, and they were always given to us by The Queen, as if in person.

I ran out of currency only once, when a blizzard and ice storm trapped us in Gander, Newfoundland, when returning from the USA. The solution was to visit the nearby Royal Canadian Air Force base and uplift currency there.

The hotel was surrounded by six feet of snow, while icicles several feet long hung from buildings and trees, and overhead wires sagged under the weight of several inches of ice. A RCAF police corporal turned up at reception to collect me. We slipped and slid to his station wagon.

Beyond the hotel, the streets had been cleared, or more accurately, the snow had been swept off a solid coating of ice that crunched under the chains on the station wagon's tyres. The roads were quiet, but not deserted. Used to stories of how seamlessly other countries coped with such conditions, I was surprised to see a few cars driving without chains. Moving in a straight line they looked fine, but I couldn't help wondering how they'd fare if they had to manoeuvre or brake suddenly.

It didn't take long to find out.

As we slowed for a set of traffic lights, they turned to green and the corporal put his foot down. A moment later, he swore and braked to an abrupt halt. After rocking back and forward, I sat there wondering what the problem was. Then two cars appeared, one from the left, one from the right. Without chains, they skidded past their respective red lights, then spun round one another in the centre of the junction like dance partners. They missed by inches before, somehow, ending up facing the way they wanted to go and carrying on as if nothing had happened.

It was a surreal scene that lacked only The Blue Danube as background music.

Still a few years short of political correctness, this prompted my driver to tell me that the natives of Newfoundland were known as Newfies and were the butt of many a joke in Canada, a bit like the Irish back in the UK at the time.

Shortly after, he pointed at someone clearing his front path with a small snow blower. As the man pushed the machine along, it ejected a continuous plume of white powder onto the tops of tall snow banks lining the footpath leading to his front door.

My driver looked at me and said, 'See what I mean, six feet of snow and the Newfies are out mowing their lawns!'

It's another thing that has stayed with me ever since.

FLYING FAT ALBERT

So this was it, Friday 10th February 1982 and my first flight on the Herc OCU. As our crew bus drove along the line of aircraft parked on Lyneham's enormous pan looking for XV203, groundcrew beetled away at their various tasks. My mind was awash with conflicting thoughts and emotions.

Less than three years before, I'd been a tradesman toiling away beneath the giant delta wings of 617 Squadron's Vulcans as the crews arrived on their buses. We used to joke that if we became aircrew we'd never have to walk again. It may have been a throwaway remark, but being driven around really was one of the things that seemed to mark aircrew apart.

So as I stepped down from the bus that morning I felt quite an emotional jolt. I don't think any of those around me would have understood, or been interested, and the feeling was gone in an instant, but it was no less real for that.

The day had begun much earlier with flight planning. But unlike my training to date, where meteorological and other information had been given in formal mass briefings, on the Herc force, we collected the information on paper – there were few screens - and briefed ourselves.

On most occasions, it was just the captain, nav and co-pilot that met for flight planning. The eng and loadie would head straight for the aircraft to prepare it and its load for flight. At some point, the loadie would send a message to confirm the aircraft's all up weight and any other information about the load that might be relevant to our planning. We were unlikely to hear from the eng unless there was a problem, but we might contact him if we needed the fuel contents topped up or reduced for some reason.

Where we did our prep down route could vary enormously, from swish American planning suites, to less swanky rooms in air traffic control and operations complexes, sheds on the edges of airfields, the bonnet of a truck or the ground under the aircraft wing. But wherever we did it, the process invariably started with a study of meteorological charts and the forecast and actual weather conditions for both the airspace in which we were about to fly and the key airfields within it. We'd also check for warnings of unusual activity along our route, taking careful note of any that might pose a hazard and/or necessitate a change of plan.

For routes across the Atlantic, we were seeing the beginning of computerisation with a printout called a Jetplan that gave the route and heights to be flown and the fuel load required. The advance was not universally welcomed, especially by the navs, who sensed technology nibbling away at their role. They tended to pick fault with the computers' calculations and suggest changes, usually extra fuel above and beyond that the Jetplan recommended.

And of course, history shows that the navs were right to worry. The J Model Herc introduced at the turn of the Millennium had no seat for a nav.

When routes, heights and timings had been finalised, I'd be responsible for submitting a flight plan telling the air traffic control agencies along our route who we were, how many we had on board, where we were departing from, when and where we expected to enter and exit their airspace, and at what height, and finally, where we were going and where we'd divert in the event of a problem at our destination.

With that done, we'd work through performance tables to check whether the runways at our departure and destination airfields were long enough for us to take off and land at our weight. The factors to be considered included temperature, wind speed and direction, height above sea level and runway slope. Conditions such as the presence of standing water, snow or ice could also be factored in.

Finally, we'd use the weather, runway and weight details to calculate a set of speeds for our take off. These included Rotate, the speed at which the handling pilot would raise the nose of the aircraft from the runway; V1, the speed above which we'd have to continue the take-off even if an engine failed - because we'd be unable to brake to a halt in the length of runway remaining; V2, the speed below which we'd be unable to climb in the event of an engine failure; and VMCA1 and 2, the minimum speeds at which the aircraft could be controlled if one or two engines on one side failed.

As explained in more detail in On The Buffet, you didn't want to suffer an engine failure between V1 and V2, and you wanted to accelerate above VMCAs 1 and 2 as quickly as possible. Modern passenger aircraft rarely if ever operate within these zones, but it was, and probably still is a feature of military flying at high weights. That said, it was something we noted rather than worried about. There was no point.

Armed with all this information, the captain, nav and I would climb on the bus and join the eng and loadie at the aircraft. That makes it sound as if there were only ever five of us. But, in reality, for all sorts of reasons, there were often more, especially on a long route, when there could be extra crew and/or examiners testing one or other crew members.

On the OCU, there were invariably extra people. For a start, there were usually two students for each crew position, plus their instructors. The trainee captains, co-pilots, navs and air engineers would take it in turns to occupy their respective crew seats, while more than one loadmaster trainee could be down the back tending the load.

In the case of trainee co-pilots, one would occupy the right hand seat while the other stood behind watching and waiting his turn. I tended to be paired up with the guy who'd transferred from Nimrods because of airsickness. In the left hand, captain's seat, was our instructor, a moustachioed Specialist Aircrew squadron leader in his early 40s. He'd flown the Herc for much of its time in service.

I was to enjoy remarkable continuity with him, flying fifteen of my nineteen OCU sorties under his tutelage. He was one of the gentlest and most patient men I ever met; not without the odd acid barb to drive a point home, but entirely free of the hostility and contempt for students I'd witnessed in some instructors at Linton and Finningley - although thankfully not mine.

On many of his flights with me, he needed plenty of patience.

Ever since my first visit to Lyneham in a Jet Provost fifteen months earlier, I'd set my heart on flying Fat Albert. Now, my wish was about to come true, and although it hardly seemed possible, I think I was even more excited and nervous than when approaching my first Chipmunk or JP. A large part of the excitement was down to the layout of my new office.

When you squeezed onto the flight deck of RAF multi-engine aircraft of British design, they were so cramped you had to wonder if any thought had been given to ergonomics or crew comfort. So, although the preponderance of bare metal and sharp corners marked the Herc out as undeniably military, it was a surprise to find that its designers had provided a flight deck that was both spacious and comfortable.

About ten feet wide and fifteen feet long, it stretched forward from the bunk running along the flight deck rear bulkhead to the pilots' instrument panel, leaving ample room for the crew, all the necessary hardware and numerous hangers-on.

Perhaps the most striking features beyond the space and confusion of gauges, switches and circuit breakers, were the seats. To either side of a raised *throttle quadrant,* captain and co-pilot sat on large, padded, fully adjustable seats with armrests. Think Captain Kirk on the Starship Enterprise, or at least the captain of a warship. Behind the throttle quadrant, roughly in the middle of the flight deck, the air engineer sat on a similar seat within easy reach of the controls for most aircraft systems, either directly in front of him on the rear of the throttle quadrant, or on a large panel above his head.

To the rear right of the flight deck, the navigator sat sideways at a small desk jutting from the fuselage side wall, facing his nav kit controls and instruments. His seat could be swivelled to face front for take-off and landing, or when he wanted a chat.

To the rear left of the air eng was the galley, from where the loadie dispensed hot food and drinks for the crew, when not busy in the freight bay.

The flight deck was also well lit, with fifteen rectangular windows wrapping round from in front of the pilots to a few feet behind their shoulders. These gave an excellent view of any potential threats to the front, sides and rear through the hazy propeller discs. There were even windows low down to the side adjacent to the pilots' feet.

I had two hundred and seventeen flying hours under my belt and many of the rituals and sensations of RAF flying were familiar. But the principle outlined by Tom Scott on my first Chipmunk flight still held firm. With every action from climbing onto the Herc before take-off, to re-boarding the bus after landing, I felt my IQ reduce by half.

I was also introduced to sensations and sounds that would become all-too-familiar over the following three years: the gentle rocking of the airframe when the engines started; the rhythmic thrum of the propellers at different power settings; the banter on the intercom; the calm unfolding of checks by challenge and response, the nav detailing actions to be completed, the relevant crew member responding as they flicked a switch or confirmed a setting; the noting of clearances from air traffic control; more gentle rocking as we trundled along the taxyway; the increase in noise and the violent shaking as the throttles were opened against the brakes; the lurch as the brakes were released and we accelerated down the runway for take-off; the call of *Rotate* from the non-operating pilot; the sudden smoothness as the wheels left the ground; and finally, the joy of being airborne and in control of such a large machine.

The excitement of flying into foreign airspace and landing overseas was still to come, but the first few trips in the local area were stimulating enough to be going on with.

One statement my dad made at some point every time we met over the next three years was, '*It must be hard work heaving that great big aircraft around?*'

And every time, I'd try and explain that apart from a little heave to raise the nosewheel on take-off, I didn't have to exert much muscle power at all. The control surfaces on the wings and tail assembly were moved by high pressure hydraulic fluid in reaction to and in proportion to my inputs. I merely received feedback that gave me a feel for what I was asking the aircraft to do.

Simplistically, if I was trying to manoeuvre at high speed, I'd have to pull relatively hard on the control column to overcome the airflow. In contrast, if I was manoeuvring gently at slow speed, I'd have to apply relatively little pressure. But in either instance it was the hydraulic fluid doing the work.

Dad would nod sagely, and ask the same question next time we met.

Just to finish on the topic of flying controls, those on the Herc were so well harmonised that it was a delight to fly and any residual control forces were easily removed by trimming, another process explained in On The Buffet. And anyway, much of the time from shortly after take-off until the start of the final approach, the aircraft was generally being flown by the autopilot.

As a result, once I mastered the take off, the mechanics of flying from A to B proved relatively easy. Just as in training though, instrument flying and approaches remained a major challenge, not least because there were now so many instruments to monitor and interpret, and so many new approach patterns and procedures to learn. As an added complication, on most training flights, we invariably pretended one or more engine had failed.

And yet in contrast with flying training, I never failed or had to repeat an OCU exercise. So perhaps I had made some progress.

Landing was the other major challenge.

I knew what I had to do – fly down to the runway, close the throttles and raise the nose to the landing attitude with the mainwheels just above the runway, let the aircraft settle onto the tarmac, gently lower the nosewheel and brake to a halt. But much like instrument flying, knowing what to do it and doing it were two totally different things. Approaching the ground, conflicting sensations and my own excitement tended to overwhelm me, causing my higher brain functions to falter and my actions to be impulsive rather than considered.

And although there are larger aircraft, the Herc is *big*, so big that sitting just above the runway is a relative term. In the landing attitude, with the mainwheels about to touch down, the flight deck is at least fifteen or twenty feet up, the instrument panel obscuring all but the far end of the tarmac.

I found it hard to judge how high above the runway to begin closing the throttles and raising the nose for touchdown. Sometimes I'd round out too early and therefore too high, floating along until we ran out of flying speed and crunched onto the tarmac. Other times I'd hardly round out at all, flying the aircraft into the ground for an equally firm arrival.

Once on my squadron, I don't remember an occasion when the captain felt the need to take control from me, but I never produced landings that would have elicited a round of applause from the passengers – not that that was a regular occurrence on the Herc. The passengers were usually a hard-nosed bunch, little given to displays of appreciation!

In my defence, it was said that landing a Herc was like trying to land a small hotel from an upstairs bathroom window. It certainly felt like it in those early days. And it may be a statement of the bleedin' obvious, but there's much more to watch and do when trying to land a Herc than a smaller or more automated aircraft: four throttles and four sets of engine instruments for a start.

We also used to visit airfields with characteristics that made landing more difficult, such as exceptionally wide, narrow, long or short runways, runways with strange surroundings or surfaces, unusual up or down slopes, humps, or even a series of humps like a rollercoaster. All these could combine to create visual illusions, especially at night, when lighting or the lack of it added another dimension. Cloud, fog, snow and ice could further complicate matters, and create their own illusions.

And then there was a new method of crosswind landing to learn. If you attempted to fly the Herc down to the runway using the conventional method of angling the nose into wind, gusts could get under the high, into-wind wing, and lift it – forcing the other wing down - not a good idea close to the ground. So you had to fly toward the runway with the into-wind wing low.

In the early stages, I found nearing the ground in this attitude very strange. I had to steel myself to do it, especially in the latter stages of an approach. And of course, you couldn't land like it. Just before touchdown, you had to level the wings and stop the aircraft drifting sideways so that both sets of mainwheels touched down at the same time, pointing straight ahead down the runway.

Given the inconsistency of my landings at the best of times, this proved far from easy.

An experienced captain once told me he'd spent his career compiling a list of excuses for poor landings – crosswinds, unexpected gusts, downdraughts, wide, narrow, sloping, wet or frozen runways – any number of things. If he crunched the aircraft in, he'd pick an excuse from his list, whether it was valid or not and dare anyone to challenge him. He advised that I adopt the same ploy. It was a great idea, but I never had the gall to blame anything other than myself for my frequent *firm arrivals*.

On the OCU, my instructor did his best to iron out my faults, remaining patient as I tried to shake the aircraft to bits with one bone-crunching touchdown after another. It's a testament to Fat Albert that this punishment was accepted without complaint, and the instructor also tried to keep me upbeat. But I was often desperately disappointed with my performance, especially in comparison with my peer, who was much more adept.

Just like flying training, I think, *tries hard, could do better* would be a fair summation of my performance on the Herc OCU, certainly in terms of flying skill. Luckily, my performance in other areas – such as pre-flight prep, flight planning, running an imprest and being a good crew member – seemed more promising. At the time though, I'd have swopped any of these attributes for skill in the air.

INTRO TO ROUTE FLYING

Growing up in a working class family in Shropshire, I assumed that I'd rarely leave my home town. I still joke that I was only the second local to have left Ludlow in the 1970s, and I was only let out to track down the other chap and drag him back. Until I went to the Grammar School, I'd met no-one who'd taken foreign holidays or been overseas, except, that is, for men like my dad, who'd travelled during their military service in the Second World War. Foreign adventures seemed an impossible dream.

Since then, the RAF had widened my horizons beyond Shropshire. But my appetite had been no more than teased by two visits to Germany, the first as a teenager with the Air Training Corps, the second during my multi-engine training.

Now though, just five weeks after my first flight on the Herc OCU, I found myself flying a transatlantic route that would take in Canada and the United States.

Some people like to appear blasé about overseas travel, feigning indifference in an attempt to appear worldly and cool. Plenty of RAF aircrew are the same, expressing boredom at the hours spent in the air between destinations.

I never felt this way.

Throughout my life, I've retained an almost childish excitement about flying to different countries. And while I'm no great fan of sitting down the back of an airliner for long periods, as a pilot on the Herc, I enjoyed my time in the air. When not actively engaged in some activity, I'd enjoy the banter between crew members and the constantly changing view through the flight deck windows.

And it all began on that first transatlantic route.

Another co-pilot flew the first leg, while I spent much of the time standing behind him. Our destination was the Royal Canadian Air Force base at Goose Bay, in the province of Newfoundland and Labrador, north-eastern Canada. We tracked across the North Atlantic to the south of Iceland and Greenland. The weather was good and we were at little more than 20,000 feet. There was little to see bar ocean and the odd ship until we were several hundred miles from the Canadian coast. Then I had my first sight of icebergs calved from the glaciers of western Greenland.

Numbering in tens at first, they were all shapes and sizes, some large and relatively flat, others smaller in surface area but thrusting up like jagged alpine peaks. I'm not sure how tall these were, probably nowhere near the record, a monster towering five hundred and fifty feet above the water, but tall enough. A glimpse of turquoise just beneath the surface hinted at the seven-eighths of their bulk hidden beneath the waves.

It was sobering to think that they were drifting south into the transatlantic shipping lanes, where several hundred more lay in wait for unwary seafarers. During 1984, the busiest year ever, two thousand two hundred were counted. I'd probably seen a few hundred, and I had no doubt a collision with even the smallest would be catastrophic for any of the ships we'd seen.

You had to wonder why there weren't more Titanic-like incidents. I guess it's testament to the way the ice is tracked and reported, and to equipment that alerts ships to the danger, especially in poor visibility and at night.

Closer to the coast of Newfoundland, the bergs gave way to an enormous sheet of sea ice. Cracked into a crazy jigsaw, it stretched away to the north. Each jagged block was tens of square miles in area and surrounded by narrow channels of dark seawater far too tortuous for any ship to navigate.

The expanse of white continued when we crossed the Labrador coast, broken only by large forests of fir trees and a few rocky outcrops. Lakes of various sizes stood out because of their unblemished surfaces, while rivers were smooth ribbons of meandering white, the odd dark section marking faster stretches and rapids.

The airfield at Goose Bay sits close to the base of Hamilton Inlet, the longest of the narrow fjords cutting into the coast of Labrador. It was built jointly by the Canadians and Americans in 1941, becoming a vital link in the supply route between North America and the UK in the build up to D-Day and beyond. During the Cold War, Goose hosted aircraft from the USAF Strategic Air Command and many NATO air forces, including the RAF.

With a population of less than 30,000 occupying 115,000 square miles of terrain similar to much of the Soviet Union, Labrador was ideal for NATO low flying training. During my time at Scampton, it had been a regular destination for the Vulcan force, affording crews the opportunity to practise their war role over realistic distances and topography.

By the time of my first visit in 1982, the Vulcan fleet was disbanding and Goose was hosting squadrons of Tornados, Jaguars and Buccaneers for low level training and large scale exercises with other NATO air forces. It was also a staging post for British military deployments to other parts of Canada and the USA.

I forget exactly what freight we were carrying, but we were fielding a genuine supply task that meant offloading and/or taking on kit at each location we visited.

One of the things that suddenly came into sharp focus as I stepped onto the tarmac at Goose was how quickly our fourteen hours on the ground could be eaten up. The countdown began the moment chocks were placed round the wheels on arrival and ended two hours before they were removed again for departure.

On this occasion we were staying on base. So after putting the aircraft to bed, there was little time lost in travelling to our accommodation. But this wasn't the norm. After arrival at most overseas airfields, we travelled to hotels off-base, usually by taxi, which ate up about an hour of our fourteen hours on the ground, often more.

Dissecting the remaining thirteen hours before departure, we usually allowed about an hour and a half for flight planning, and a similar period for the process of waking up, dressing, having breakfast if the dining room was open, checking out of the hotel and travelling back to the airfield, usually by taxi again. This left about ten hours, eight of which were meant to be for complete rest, and ideally sleep.

So we were often left with no more than two hours for debriefing the previous leg over a wind-down beer, getting a meal – again if the hotel dining room or local restaurants were open, and – in my case - swapping over documents, completing paperwork and planning for the next day.

Sometimes a little time could be saved, especially if the hotel was near the airfield, but more often, delays in traffic and journeys to more distant hotels could add 30 minutes at each end, leaving little more than an hour of *free* time.

It's no wonder I rarely managed eight hours' sleep or left the various hotels to see the sights. It was one of the reasons I spent as much time as possible looking out of the flight deck windows, trying to take in as much as possible from the air.

On the sixth day of longer routes, or if we'd flown for forty hours in three days, we were allowed thirty three hours off, an incredible luxury you hoped to enjoy in an interesting location. That said, the thirty three hours usually flashed by as you caught up on sleep and performed admin duties neglected in the shorter stopovers.

The timings on our itineraries were always given in Greenwich Mean Time (GMT), which we knew as Zulu, written Z. But the difference between Z and local changed with every time zone you crossed, local time becoming earlier as you flew west or later as you travelled east. For example, 1000Z would be 4.00am (Z-6) in Washington, and 6.00pm (Z+8) in Hong

Kong.

As a result, when flying multi-leg routes across several time zones, the concept of day and night soon evaporated. We adopted a pattern of work and sleep dictated by the itinerary rather than our body clocks. If forced to sleep in daylight, I prayed for a room with double glazing and black-out curtains.

Jet lag is a subject often discussed in the media, with all sorts of theories on how to alleviate its worst effects. The general practice on the Herc force was to accept the local time wherever you were and never relate it to the time *at home*. To help in this, we set our watches for the next destination as soon as we departed the last.

It worked for me, and Geraldine and I still adhere to the same routine now, shunning conversations that begin, *do you know what the time is at home?*

In terms of aids to sleep, the vast majority self-medicated with a wind-down beer or two in someone's room before we adjourned to get our heads down. The chosen room was always known as the party room, although I don't remember any parties.

Nowadays, the use of alcohol as a relaxant would be discouraged by both the medical and Service authorities, but that's how it was in my day.

I know these problems with shifting time and sleep patterns are nothing compared to those faced by sailors with their fragmented watch systems, or soldiers forced to live in tents or foxholes. I merely wish to point out that life wasn't necessarily as blissful as it sounds, even in the more exotic locations.

I remember only three things about my first stopover in Goose Bay.

Firstly, I'd never before approached an airfield with the warning, *Beware Moose on the runway!*

Secondly, beyond the cleared tarmac surfaces, there was a good six feet of snow, more where snowploughs had thrown up great banks that towered above our large American crew bus. I'd never seen anything like it.

Thirdly, the heating pipes and radiators in our allocated barrack block warmed the rooms beautifully. But they also juddered, gurgled, rattled and banged in such a continuous, echoing, cacophony that I managed very little sleep.

Sleep or no sleep, the next morning I had to perform my very first overseas leg as a co-pilot. Many of the elements of the flight planning were familiar, although filing a flight plan from Goose Bay to the Canadian capital, Ottawa, more than a thousand miles south near the US border, seemed slightly surreal.

Crewing in had also become more familiar. My instructor was to be the operating pilot, while I was to learn how to handle the radios over unfamiliar territory. Flight time was expected to be three hours forty minutes.

The first two hours took us beyond Labrador and over the province of Quebec. On a day when visibility was unlimited, the blanket of snow stretched from horizon to horizon. Most of the land passing 20,000 feet below seemed completely flat, tundra dotted with meandering rivers and hundreds of white, unblemished, lakes, some little more than pools, others bigger than the biggest Scottish lochs. There were very few settlements, and those I saw were tiny, often no more than a few buildings on the side of a lake, no discernible track leading in or out.

When not drinking in the scenery, I monitored the instruments, made infrequent position reports as we crossed air traffic control boundaries, and dialled up the weather for our destination and diversion airfields.

Weather reports have probably been viewed on in-flight computers for decades now. But for all of my time on the Herc, I spent a fair amount of each flight tuning one or other of the radios to a broadcast of the forecast and/or actual weather conditions for major airfields along the route.

The broadcasts tended to feature about ten airfields. These could be grouped by country or region, such as France or southern France; by geographical region, such as the Mediterranean; or by continent, such as Africa or Australia. Some of the more important airfields appeared on a continuous loop, others at set times, like ten and forty minutes past the hour. Reports were usually updated every hour, more frequently if conditions were particularly severe or changeable.

In areas over which we flew frequently, I came to know the time and order in which airfields would appear, so I could dip into a transmission briefly, just long enough to note the conditions for places in which we were interested. But some reports could draw in other members of the crew, attracted by a particular reader's voice and delivery. It may seem strange, but I still enjoy the rhythm and intonation of the BBC Shipping Forecast today. I guess we found such transmissions calming, unless of course they warned of bad weather ahead.

Female voices were so unusual that, in blokish fashion, we'd try to imagine what the speaker looked like, conferring on them a sexuality merited by neither the tone nor the content of their messages. Geneva Volmet was a particular favourite, especially the way she said zero. *Zayro*. We'd mouth it in imitation, giving the word an erotic quality that I'm sure I'm failing to translate to a wider audience.

Boys will be boys.

From this first flight over the country, I always loved the accent, intonation and rhythm of the Canadian transmissions, something like, *This is the forecast for Labrador, Newfoundland, New Brunswick and the Grand Banks*, and going on to pass reports for airfields such as, *Deer Lake, Churchill Falls, St Johns, Gander* and *Wabush*.

Two hours out of Goose the view began to change, the land dropping away to the east as we closed with a large body of water. It was the St Lawrence River, at this point several miles wide, its covering of snow and ice fractured into a mosaic of white blocks drifting north-east toward the Gulf of St Lawrence. We closed with the river and followed it south east.

As we progressed, the blanket of white became dotted with larger and larger settlements, narrow tracks giving way to metalled roads and highways, the land increasingly given over to cultivation and industry. After three hours, we passed overhead Quebec and, a little later, its larger cousin, Montreal, at which point we began a gentle descent into the province of Ontario.

Ottawa International Airport was only one hundred miles ahead and I felt the pressure ratchet up. It was my first experience of a large international airport, and the chatter on the radio seemed incessant, each aircraft using a callsign based on the international designator of its operating company and a sequence of figures.

The RAF transport fleet's designator was Ascot. For each route, this would be followed by four figures to give a callsign: something like Ascot 4732. We were proud of the Ascot moniker and often dubbed ourselves Ascoteers, natural successors to Alexander Dumas' Musketeers. A crew that gelled and was having a particularly good time would become the Five Ascoteers.

Anyway, on the approach to Ottawa, I had to listen out for our callsign among all the other chatter. I then had to decipher the words that followed, not as easy as it sounds when they were delivered in a strong Canadian or French Canadian accent. The message could be a new radio frequency, a clearance for descent to a new height, directions to a new navigation beacon or approach aid, or any combination of all the above. Clearances had to be read back verbatim.

I often wondered if my Shropshire burr gave controllers a problem. After all, it was a sound rarely heard in most parts of the UK, let alone the rest of the world.

If a change of radio frequency was involved, I had to dial it up and check in swiftly so as not to leave us without a controller for too long; not always easy when several aircraft were trying to speak at once. And finally and most importantly, I had to monitor and help the captain as he set up for and flew the final approach and landing.

After more than three hours with relatively little to do, I struggled to keep up with the new pace of events. And things hardly quietened down when we landed. At such busy airports you had to navigate your way to your parking bay along a confusing and unfamiliar pattern of runways and taxyways by reference to a landing chart.

If you received any help at all from the Ground Controller, it was often by reference to other aircraft - *follow the Pan Am 747* or *pass behind the Canada Airlines 727*.

I dreaded missing or mishearing an instruction and getting us lost, or leading us into a head-on confrontation with another aircraft, delaying its departure. Embarrassing would hardly cover it. So I listened intently to everything the controllers said as they guided us – without mishap - to a distant pan reserved for a Royal Canadian Air Force VIP transport squadron.

I saw nothing of Ottawa beyond the view from the air. I and the other students who'd operated to that point handed over to another trainee crew, who flight planned and flew us straight on to Washington.

Once again, I spent as much time as I could standing behind the co-pilot's seat, looking out, initially at the view of Lake Ontario before the sun sank and we flew on in the dark.

Leaving most light pollution at ground level and climbing above much of the cloud, we often enjoyed an enhanced view of the stars and planets. But I also loved watching the pattern of light and dark below, seeking out settlements and the strings of bright pearls that tended to line the roads linking them. And unlike in the wilds of north eastern Canada, there were plenty of settlements and roads to see as we flew over New York State and Pennsylvania.

But the highlight was passing abeam Washington's floodlit monuments on the approach to Dulles International Airport. I could just make out the Washington Monument thrusting up in the middle of the Mall, book-ended by the Capitol Building and Lincoln Memorial. It was another pinch-me moment.

We landed at Dulles, put the aircraft to bed and boarded a bus that crawled its way to our hotel through twenty five miles of heavy traffic. After checking in, debriefing over a beer, showering and having a light meal, I still had to sort some paperwork and prepare for the next day's big challenge: the return flight across the Atlantic.

With all this completed, I really wanted to head out and see more of Washington. But it was past midnight, there were less than eight hours until the transport arrived to take us back to the airport and, the real clincher, I was just too shattered.

It had been a long day.

A few hours later, after a slow journey back to Dulles, I was preparing to submit a flight plan for the transatlantic crossing.

All aircraft operators, including the RAF, want to minimise costs, and that means burning as little fuel as possible, which in turn means spending as little time as possible in the air. So in flight planning, crews try to find the track and height that will give them either the lightest headwind or the strongest tailwind.

The dominant wind direction across the Atlantic is roughly west to east, so we could expect a tailwind. Just how much of a push we'd get depended on whether we could take advantage of the polar jetstream, a current of air circling northern latitudes at between 23,000 and 40,000 feet.

Several jetstreams circle the globe like massive, flattened, garden hoses a few hundred miles wide and a few thousand feet deep at their cores. In a smallish area near the core surrounded by bands of heavy turbulence, the wind speed often exceeds one hundred miles per hour. The trick is to find and ride these strong winds while avoiding the worst of the turbulence.

The complication is that the actual track, height and speed of the various jetstreams depend on many climatic factors.

For instance, although the polar jet sometimes flows almost

directly across the Atlantic between Newfoundland and Ireland, it's just as likely to arc north over Iceland and into Scandinavia; or dive to the south over the Azores and into Europe via Portugal or Spain. An added twist is that it can form a massive meander, arcing north and south in mid-Atlantic and forcing aircraft that can't fly round or over it to cross its bands of turbulence - twice.

So the actual heights and tracks flown across the Atlantic on a given day usually depend on the path, height and strength of the polar jet.

On the day of my first trans-Atlantic crossing, it must have been blowing strong and straight between the US coast to the south of Nova Scotia and the southern tip of Ireland, because we found ourselves able to complete the flight from Washington to Lyneham in one hop of about nine hours.

I submitted a flight plan on that basis and we set off for the aircraft.

I'd thought Ottawa busy, but as I looked out of the crew transport it became clear that Dulles was in another league altogether. The air was rent by near-continuous jet noise as aircraft approached or departed one of two parallel runways aligned roughly north/south, or taxied to and from them along miles of taxyway. There was a third runway aligned roughly east/west for days when the wind blew strongly from these directions, and as I write this in 2020, there's a fourth runway and plans for a fifth.

With so many aircraft on frequency, my first major task after engine start was to find a way to cut in and ask the controller for our departure clearance, then take down his reply and read it back to him. To reduce the length of such exchanges, the standard routes – several for each runway – were given names and numbers. I had a list with our most likely departure routes highlighted.

The routing we expected that afternoon was JCOBY3 – pronounced *Jacoby Three*, which meant a climb on heading 011 degrees to 820 feet, changing radio frequency to departures on 125.5 for radar vectors to reporting point, RGNIZ, climbing no higher than 3000 feet, then heading 112 degrees via reporting points GRIIN, SOOKI and Swan.

If I was lucky, the controller would give me all that information with the words, 'Ascot 4732, clear Jacoby Three departure'.

But I had to be prepared for another named routing, or maybe even a non-standard departure through reporting points, headings and heights not on the list. The radio log on my knee had a space for whatever clearance was passed. I was poised to write it down and read it back.

Controllers the world over tend to pass clearances - in the local accent - at warp speed. And they expect a prompt and speedy response. There's no room for a Morecambe and Wise approach – all the right reporting points but not necessarily in the right order! My read-back had to give the exact same words in the exact same order or the whole procedure would have to be repeated, to the annoyance of the controller, the crews of all the other aircraft on frequency and, perhaps most importantly, my own crew.

But there's a more important reason for precision than impatience and damaged pride.

The history of aviation is littered with major accidents caused by misunderstandings over clearances. One of the most tragic happened on a foggy day in Tenerife in 1977. A Boeing 747 pilot mistakenly thought he heard clearance to take off and thundered down the runway into another 747 that yet to vacate the tarmac after landing. Five hundred and eighty three people died in the resulting collision.

That day at Dulles, though, my biggest fear was upsetting my instructor. All captains hated having their callsign linked to anything unprofessional. And despite his calm and laid back manner, I knew mine would be no different. So, as you've probably gathered, reading back the various air traffic control instructions was a major test.

In truth, I can't remember whether I was passed a standard or non-standard clearance, but I read it back correctly in whatever form it came. With a few notable exceptions, I tended to be reasonably competent on the radios, but reading back clearances always raised my heartbeat.

Thirty minutes later, I experienced what remains a life highlight. Our departure route took us close to New York. It was a beautiful day with almost unlimited visibility. We were at 18,000 feet and I was excited to see the skyscrapers of Manhattan come into view several miles to the right of track.

I was even more excited when the captain initiated a conversation with the man controlling us for that part of the route. Thirty seconds later, we were given clearance to overfly Manhattan. In the end, we were cleared to orbit and I have a series of snaps of that famous grid layout taken with my little point and click camera.

They include all the major landmarks from Central Park in the north to the Brooklyn Bridge and Battery Park in the south. There were far fewer mega-skyscrapers in 1982, so the Empire State and UN buildings are surprisingly prominent.

Sitting on the flight deck, I was like a dog with two tails. Suddenly all the pain and effort of flying training seemed worth it. There would still be trials and tribulations aplenty, but if there were to be more moments like this – and there were - I knew I'd made the right choice in pursuing my childhood dream so tenaciously.

I feel the same to this day.

There were more amazing sights as we flew northeast over Connecticut, Rhode Island and Massachusetts. The eastern seaboard of the United States and its various islands looked magnificent. Soon though, we set off across the Atlantic and settled down for about three more hours of daylight, followed by four hours enveloped in darkness.

Long flights like this were what led many to see multi-engine flying as boring. After all, beyond staying alert enough to deal with an unexpected problem, making infrequent radio calls and gathering weather reports, there was little to do, certainly nothing physical; the autopilot was doing the flying.

But as I've said, I was always happy just joining in any banter and looking out of the window, on that occasion, at the vast expanse of the Atlantic Ocean, the sky, and then the stars. And, of course, at the end of even the longest transit, I could look forward to stepping onto a foreign land, or returning to Geraldine. Both prospects excited me.

Because of the heights and speeds at which we flew, we received a fair degree of ridicule from those who flew the big jets, both RAF and civilian. They tended to look down on us, not only figuratively, but literally.

Airliners tend to fly at around 40,000 feet, sometimes higher, and fast enough to cross the Atlantic in five hours or so. On any given day, our propeller driven Herc was likely to be one of very few aircraft flying 20,000 feet lower, and much, much, slower. We were also more likely to be flying in and out of cloud, with its associated turbulence and icing. If this was the case, we were obliged to tell the controllers as part of our periodic position reports, providing a warning to aircraft following the same route, or those that might be planning to do so.

I remember one particularly uncomfortable trans-Atlantic flight when we spent several hours bouncing around in cloud at about 24,000 feet. We tried changes of height and direction, but they made little or no difference, and the constant buffeting was becoming tiring, and tiresome. Two thirds of the way across the ocean, I delivered one of several position reports ending with confirmation that we were still experiencing moderate *chop* – aviation parlance for turbulence.

Immediately, the superior tones of a British Airways captain flying high above the weather on the edge of space cut through the ether.

'Ascot 4732, this is Speedbird Concorde Zero Zero Two. Bad luck.'

Our captain needed all his self-restraint not to pepper the airwaves with some ripe Anglo-Saxon, although a few seconds later we were all smiling and shaking our heads at the cheek of the transmission.

In many remote regions, like oceans and the hinterlands of Asia and Africa, the primary means of communication with controllers is High Frequency (HF) radio. We also used it to receive weather reports and to keep our headquarters at RAF Upavon, callsign Architect, updated on our progress. This was especially important if some problem with the aircraft led to a delay or a need for spare parts, even engineering assistance.

Sometimes the clarity of the HF would amaze me. It was as if the person I was speaking to was sitting next to me, not several thousand miles away. But it could also sound as if they were sitting in a broom cupboard with a bucket over their head, in which case it could take the combined efforts of the whole crew to decipher even the simplest message.

The problem is that as they traverse the globe HF signals

are vulnerable to disruption by all manner of atmospheric conditions, even the transition from day to night. To counter this, most stations offer a range of high and low frequencies between two and thirty Megahertz. If I remember rightly, the lower frequencies tended to be better at night, the higher ones more effective by day.

But sometimes, none of the available frequencies seemed to work. We'd lean forward, eyes closed, hands over our headset earpieces, trying to pick out words lost within hissing white noise, whistles, squeaks, or any other form of electronic distortion you can imagine.

This was one of the reasons I was nervous on that first trip across the Atlantic. In the period we were more than two hundred and fifty miles from land – about five hours - I had to maintain HF contact with controllers, initially in Gander, an airfield at the extreme eastern edge of Canada on the island of Newfoundland, then Shannon in the west of Ireland.

If these names aren't well known now, they were very familiar to the pioneers of trans-Atlantic travel.

Right into the jet age, even the largest aircraft carried barely enough fuel to cross the Atlantic in one hop. So airfields were built on either side of the ocean as close as possible to the first available landfall, in places like Gander and Shannon.

For a few glorious years, these airfields grew alongside the expansion in trans-Atlantic air traffic, until tens, if not hundreds of aircraft were landing on their runways each day. Passengers disgorged to shop, maybe even spend the night, before re-boarding and flying on into the heart of Europe or the Americas. They became vast hubs, although, to all intents and purposes, they were still pretty much in the middle of nowhere.

And then, aircraft and their engines became more efficient, enabling flights direct from London to Washington or Frankfurt to New York. Pretty much overnight, places like Gander, Shannon and Prestwick on the west coast of Scotland became surplus to requirements. The airfields remain, used mainly by flying schools, general aviation enthusiasts and smaller aircraft that still need their trans-Atlantic flight to be as short as possible.

They seem unlikely ever to regain their former glory, but there's an echo of it in their continued control of air traffic crossing the Atlantic.

I have one vivid memory of my first eastbound trans-Atlantic flight.

I said in On The Buffet how much I'd enjoyed the limited amount of night flying I'd done. But even after the Finningley course, I don't think I'd flown in the dark above 15,000 feet or beyond the confines of Yorkshire. That night, we were approaching the UK from the western Atlantic at about 25,000 feet.

Night-time satellite pictures are common features of TV weather forecasts now. But I'm not sure I'd seen many, if any, such images in 1982. So on a beautifully clear night, it was a revelation to see the majority of the coastline of Ireland etched in pin-pricks of light, while inland, settlements shone like jewels, interconnected by thin threads.

The volume of radio traffic ramped up as we drew closer to the UK, but I still found time to take in the emerging coastline of Pembrokeshire, the clear outline of Cardigan Bay stretching out to our left, the more populated areas of south Wales shining brightly ahead; and the whole of the Cornish peninsula to our right.

As we descended over Cardiff, Newport and then Bristol, the scale changed until I could see individual street lights and cars running along the roads between Bath, Chippenham and Calne.

My love of flying at night never diminished, and seeing the coastlines, towns and cities of countries and continents was always a joy. I particularly enjoyed approaching Lands End from the south on a clear night, new light sources appearing with every mile until the whole of the south coast of England and Wales stood out. We could sometimes see all the way north into the West Midlands and Greater Manchester, and east beyond London to the North Foreland by Margate. It was never anything other than magical, and often quite moving, especially on the way back from detachments in the South Atlantic.

Six days after the Atlantic crossing, I was on another overseas exercise, this time from Lyneham to the Mediterranean island of Sardinia. We crossed France roughly north to south from the Channel to the Mediterranean, taking in marvellous views of the snow-capped French Alps, the island of Corsica sitting in a blue-blue sea and the rugged cliffs and mountains of Sardinia itself.

When I joined my squadron, I began to follow the standard practice of greeting foreign controllers with a cheery hello in their native language, something like, *Paris, this is Ascot 4123, bonjour*, or, *Rome, this is Ascot 4321, buongiorno.*

But on the OCU we were warned that controllers receiving such a greeting might assume we were native speakers and come back with a staccato burst of French or Italian. I judged the chance of anyone mistaking my Shropshire burr for the accent of a native speaker of any language remote, but on this first foray into southern Europe, I heeded the warning and stuck to English.

As a later episode will demonstrate, it might have been better if I'd maintained this policy on my squadron as well.

Sardinia was home to a weapons range used by NATO air forces for air combat training. Visiting units flew into and operated from Italian Air Force base, Decimommanu - known as Deci, pronounced Dechee - just to the north of the island capital, Cagliari. On this occasion we were delivering personnel and equipment to a detachment of RAF Jaguar ground attack aircraft.

Deci was often the busiest airfield in Europe, with up to four hundred and fifty movements a day as formations of fast jets flew off to practise dissimilar air combat over the Mediterranean before recovering to land.

We witnessed the frenetic pace as we parked at one end of a long dispersal lined with French Mirages, Italian Fiats, British Jaguars and American F-16s. Formations taxied out for their missions from one end of the line while others returned to join at the far end. The air was alive with the sound of jets departing or arriving.

It was the first time I witnessed the highly stylised see-off drills of United States Air Force groundcrew. The tradesmen of other air forces took a more or less casual approach to these duties, but the USAF tradesmen performed a series of highly choreographed movements and hand gestures, culminating in a theatrical salute and emphatic wave as their F-16s taxied away.

Vive la difference!

Although we went off base for a meal in a local restaurant, we were accommodated in a barrack block on Deci, so I gained only a brief glimpse of Sardinian life. The next morning, I stood behind another co-pilot for the flight to RAF Coltishall in Norfolk, the home of the Jaguars, before taking the right hand seat myself for the short hop back to Lyneham.

Following another domestic sortie, I then flew from Lyneham to Keflavik, a US Navy air base close to the Icelandic capital, Reykjavik. As on every other occasion I visited this base, we took off just over an hour later, in this instance, to return to Lyneham. So, although I can say I've been to Iceland several times, I've never spent more than an hour or so there, and never been outside the boundaries of Keflavik airfield.

By now, I'd been at Lyneham for six months, watching aircraft and their crews disappear for days or weeks on end. But strange as it may seem, it wasn't until this third overseas trip in a couple of weeks that it dawned on me that my new job really was to fly the world.

It was an exciting prospect, but events were about to make it more exciting than I could ever have imagined.

THE ARGENTINEANS INTERVENE

On Friday 2nd April 1982, the Argentineans invaded the Falkland Islands.

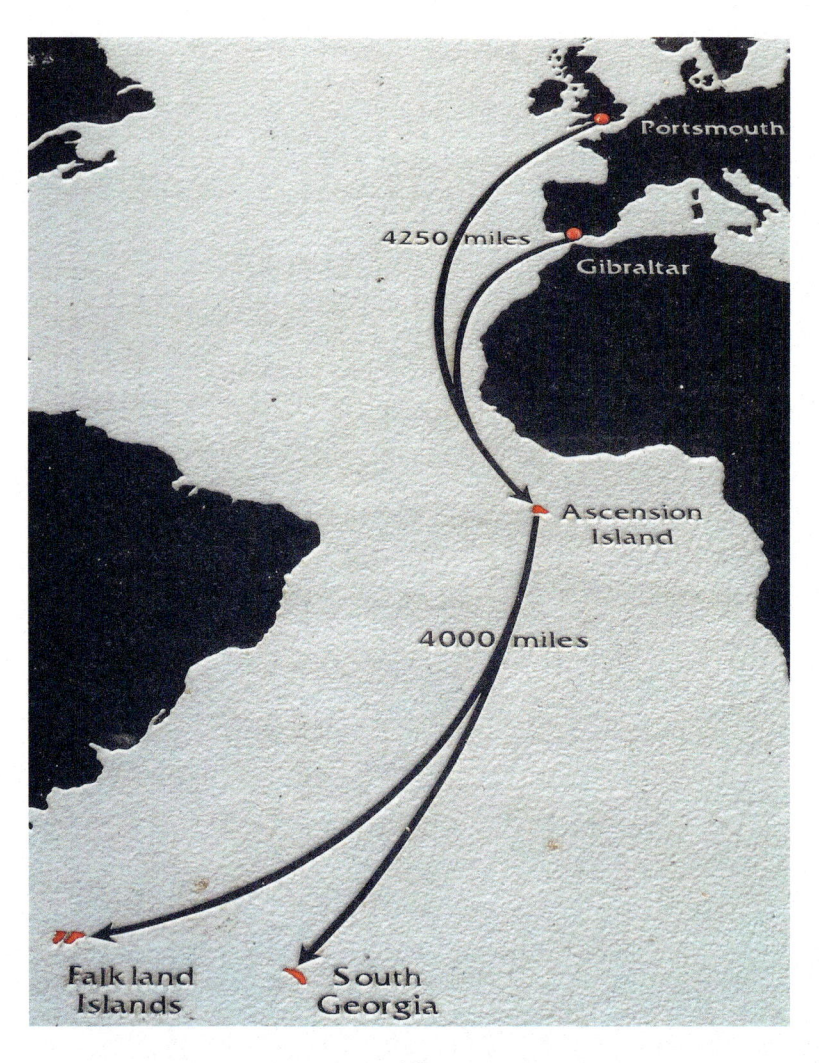

While some wondered why on earth a South American military dictatorship was invading a group of islands midway between Scotland and Iceland - and belonging to Denmark - others began to dig out maps for the Falkland rather than the Faeroe Islands. Improbably, the former belonged to us, even though they were 8,000 miles away, deep in the South Atlantic, three hundred miles east of the Straits of Magellan at the southern tip of South America.

The drama had actually begun two weeks earlier when the Argentineans raised their flag on South Georgia, a British Overseas Territory nearly 1,000 miles to the east of the Falklands. Even at that early stage, signals intelligence revealed the Falklands to be their next target.

Preparations to reclaim South Georgia had begun immediately and the first Hercs flew south on 29th March. But most at Lyneham were as surprised as the general public to hear news of the invasion on the 2nd. Just as surprising given the distance involved was Margaret Thatcher's decision to send a military task force to re-take the Islands.

Whereas the Americans give their military operations punchy names like Rolling Thunder or Desert Storm, we Brits use the next randomly generated title that pops out of some file or computer in the MOD. So the massive undertaking to reclaim the Falklands was given the less than inspiring name, Operation Corporate. Unlikely to have the Argentineans quaking in their boots, we thought, but very British.

Anyway, the opening salvos of Op Corporate saw large numbers of ships set sail and head south, many before they were fully loaded with supplies or personnel; in fact, before it had even been decided what supplies and personnel were required.

In the end, there would be a total of one hundred and twenty seven vessels: forty three Royal Navy, including numerous submarines and two aircraft carriers, Invincible and Hermes; twenty two Royal Fleet Auxiliary, including the Sir Galahad and Sir Lancelot; and sixty two civilian, including the cruise liners SS Canberra and Queen Elizabeth 2, plus cargo vessels like the Atlantic Conveyor. Some sailed immediately from wherever they were in the world, others gathered to load in UK ports or overseas territories like Gibraltar. Some had to be converted for their new use.

A variety of aircraft would support the operation. These included Navy Sea Harriers, RAF Harrier GR3s and an assortment of helicopters: Army Lynxes, Scouts and Gazelles; Royal Marine and Navy Sea Kings, Lynxes and Wessexes; and RAF Chinooks, Sea Kings and Wessexes. Some of the Harriers and helicopters would travel south in the hold of the Atlantic Conveyor.

Over several weeks, ships picked up and sailed south with elements of the Royal Marine Commandos, Parachute Regiment, Gurkhas, Scots and Welsh Guards and the Royal Artillery; plus special forces teams and all manner of specialists.

I don't think you need to be a military strategist to realise that this armada needed a staging post en route to the Falklands, somewhere to pick up fresh provisions, but also equipment and people left behind by its hasty departure. The place chosen was a British Overseas Territory roughly halfway between the UK and the Falklands, and even less well known: Ascension Island.

Once again, maps and encyclopaedias were consulted. What they showed was a tiny dot in the South Atlantic just south of the equator about midway between Africa and South America. Even while this information was being digested, the RAF VC10 and Herc forces were gathering military personnel and equipment from all over the UK and Europe and flying them to the Island, pre-loading it for the day when the Task Force would give it a glancing blow on the way south.

As these early events unfolded, we on the OCU, and especially those of us straight out of training, felt an air of detachment and uncertainty. It was obvious that Lyneham was gearing up for something big. Everyone else was rushing around with a palpable sense of purpose, and the airfield was noticeably busier.

But what about us?

Most were within touching distance of the end of the OCU syllabus. I had three flights left. Would I finish the course, or would training be suspended? And if it was, where would I go, and what would I do?

I think the truth was that even the powers that be didn't really know; and frankly, given the weighty issues unfolding, our fate was small beer. For the time being, Lyneham was focused on planning for operations to Ascension and maybe even the Falklands.

Questions to be answered included, where exactly are these places and what facilities do they have? How would the Herc force get there and back? What loads would they have to carry? And where would they get fuel, food and accommodation?

Some questions were easier to answer than others, and some required radical thinking. Where the resulting ideas were deemed viable, things happened quickly. For instance, so that Hercs could continue to supply the Task Force during operations on and around the Falklands, it was decided to modify eleven Alberts to take fuel in the air.

People talk about planning on the back of a cigarette packet. Well this was one of those instances. From preliminary ideas and sketches to refuelling probes, valves and pipery being sourced, fitted and tested was a matter of days.

To make a wider point for a moment, it's the sort of thing the British military excels at. When faced with a problem, many organisations, public and private, suck their collective teeth and look for reasons to avoid doing anything, whereas the military mindset is to attack the problem until a solution is found, even if, in extreme cases such as war, it may lead to loss of life.

Some recent examples from the less extreme end of the

spectrum are security for the London Olympics, various famine, flood and earthquake relief operations and support to the Covid-19 response, including the building of Nightingale Hospitals and the delivery of vaccinations.

Sometimes, if you want someone to do something and do it quickly, you have to ask the military. One of my hobby horses is that swingeing cuts to the size of the armed forces since the end of the Cold War forget their role as an insurance policy for national and international contingencies beyond armed conflict. Make them too small and they won't have enough bodies to undertake all the tasks required.

And don't say the answer is more reserve forces or civilian volunteers. It is specifically the military ethos that gets things done.

Back at Lyneham, it had been decided that we should carry on with the OCU syllabus. As a result, I flew my seventeenth and eighteenth trips on 6th and 7th April, then prepared for Exercise 19, the final test.

Sometime during Friday 9th April, I was told that this had been postponed. Instead, I was to join Op Corporate as the co-pilot on a flight to Ascension Island departing Lyneham less than forty eight hours later.

I don't want to overplay the drama of the situation. After all, I wasn't a nineteen-year old pilot entering the Battle of Britain after minimal training. Okay, the Argentineans had sent aircraft to reconnoitre Ascension, and there were rumours that at least one of their submarines was in the area. But a serious attack on the Island and those flying into it seemed unlikely.

What was not in doubt was that I was going to the periphery of a war zone before I'd fully completed my training on the Herc.

At least the crew I was to join were all OCU instructors. That should make them sympathetic to my fate – shouldn't it?

To say that the next few days provided a steep learning curve would be an understatement. After picking up the imprest of allowances for the five man crew and checking two large bags of documents containing details of the airspace and airfields along the route, I settled down to complete some prep. For most of Saturday, I annotated radio logs and studied procedures, not only for the airspace and airfields we were scheduled to use, but also those we might divert to in the event of problems.

On the domestic front, it was a more rushed and dramatic introduction to our new life than either Geraldine or I had expected, but she certainly didn't add to my stress levels by being anything other than supportive. She never did.

Ascension was 4,000 miles from Lyneham, so another staging post was needed. The location chosen was Dakar, the capital of Senegal, fifteen degrees north of the equator at the westernmost tip of Africa. It was roughly 2,400 miles from Lyneham and 1,600 from Ascension.

Although a lightly-loaded Herc could carry enough fuel to fly direct to Dakar in eight or nine hours, those aircraft flying south would be far too heavy to do the same. The answer was to jink east at the bottom of the Iberian Peninsula and head for a third staging post, Gibraltar. Fuel wasn't the only reason to visit, though. It had been hosting a large maritime exercise and some of the vessels earmarked for the Task Force were there, so the Herc force delivered additional supplies and manpower for these.

I wasn't sure whether we'd have freight for Gibraltar on the 11th, but it was a fair bet we'd be heavy, so I assumed that our first leg would end there. Depending on the wind, this would add two and a half to three hours to the flying time to Dakar. How much it lengthened our crew duty day would depend on how long we were on the ground in Gibraltar.

Other constraints were also becoming clear.

Even if we'd had the crew duty time to reach Ascension via Dakar, we couldn't. Lack of parking space on the Island meant all arrivals had to unload and fly back to Dakar as soon as possible. So we'd spend at least fourteen hours in Dakar before flying to Ascension and back - a return trip of ten or eleven hours plus time on the ground. We'd then spend another fourteen hours or more in Senegal before flying back to Lyneham.

The time in Dakar explained the large stash of dollars in my imprest, enough to dish out to the crew for their hotel meals. At least I didn't have to pay for the accommodation. This was covered by a contract that must have been negotiated in double quick time at a location more used to seeing American aircraft than British.

Dakar Yoff International Airport was one of several relief landing grounds for the Space Shuttle, which had still only made a handful of launches.

Although I hadn't given it much thought, I'd assumed we'd fly the same aircraft for the entire route. But, the day before our departure, I was given a deeper insight into the way the transport force worked during large scale operations such as Corporate.

When we landed in Dakar and made our way to the hotel, another crew would already be at the airport flight planning. As soon as the aircraft we'd flown in had been refuelled and checked over, they'd fly it on to Ascension and back to Dakar, from where yet another crew would return it to Lyneham - where it would be turned round to repeat the same process a few hours later.

This modus operandi, called a slip pattern, would continue for several months, with aircraft departing Lyneham round the clock. To keep the pattern up and running, there had to be sufficient crews at the two main hubs, Lyneham and Dakar, plus a few at Gibraltar.

If it sounds complicated, it was, even before you added short hops within the UK to pick up or drop off freight, diversions to refuel and pick up loads in Gibraltar, delays due to bad weather or unserviceability, and wrinkles with crew duty time.

For instance, after six days of continuous operation or forty hours flying time in three days, we had to take thirty three hours off. Sometimes, the forty-hour point was met in Dakar or Gibraltar, so we spent thirty three hours there. These were popular locations for an extended stay, but I always hoped I'd reach the limit at Lyneham so I could have some time at home. For a couple of months, though, I seemed to spend more time in Senegal with crewmates than in the UK with Geraldine.

And if you think this could have an adverse effect on relationships, it did. Several marriages crashed on the rocks of Operation Corporate.

Of course, it wasn't only the aircrew that saw a change in the pace of life.

A friend of mine who worked in Eng Ops at the time gave an insight into the effect on the station as a whole. Overnight, staff switched from supporting a relatively low number of routine training and overseas trips, to supporting solely the Northern Ireland and Falkland operations, the latter round the clock. And, of course, when the War ended, the pace of ops in the South Atlantic hardly diminished, while routine flights resumed.

This seems a good point to ask you to discount any instances where I seem to claim I was involved in anything with a high level of danger or hardship.

I'm painfully aware that before, during and after the Falklands War, servicemen of all three services have put themselves in genuine harm's way. Many have shown and continue to show exceptional bravery, often paying the ultimate sacrifice. I don't totally exclude the Herc force from this roll of honour. Some of its crews have always flown extremely hazardous missions.

But I don't claim to have experienced anything like their

levels of danger and sacrifice.

Similarly, other servicemen will have suffered genuine hardship, living in extreme conditions in the Falklands and other wars and operations. In this regard, the most obvious are the bloody infantry, living in the field and carrying everything they need to survive and fight. In comparison with them, I'm all too ready to admit that I lived a pampered existence, either in hotels or with my wife in the UK.

A previous volume included a piece about the differences in outlook between the army and RAF when it came to issues like accommodation. I don't intend to repeat the whole piece here, but the essence is that when the Army dig in, the RAF check in.

So I lay no claim to bravery or hardship. Nonetheless, I want to lay out what I experienced during these *interesting times*, some of which I found very demanding.

I hadn't flown with the OCU crew I was to join before, but thankfully they were sympathetic, especially the captain, a dark-haired Scotsman in his mid thirties, who managed to treat me as a fully paid-up member of the Herc force, whilst also giving extra help and advice in recognition of my inexperience. So, while I felt intimidated by the demands of the route, I never felt intimidated by my crew.

With so many aircraft involved in the Dakar Slip, flights could be at any time of the day or night. But for this, my first true route, a late morning departure meant that Geraldine could see me off with a cooked breakfast – as she always did – at a civilised time. I left the house at about 8.20am to board a crew bus that would deliver me and the other crew members living in married quarters to the Ops block ten minutes later.

Thereafter, although timings and timeliness were of the essence, the time of day ceased to matter. The leg to Gibraltar would be in daylight, but most of the others would be a mix of day and night flying dictated by the slip pattern. As soon as possible, I had to learn to live, eat and sleep to the rhythms of the route, rather than the circadian rhythms my body had experienced during my life to date.

In describing this hectic period, I've decided to give the detail of dates, timings and airframe numbers, partly for serious aviation historians who might be interested, but partly to give a flavour of the rhythm of life for Herc aircrew at that time.

GIBRALTAR AND DAKAR

When we arrived in flight planning on the Sunday morning, I discovered that we would indeed be going to Gibraltar. The captain said he'd fly that leg and then I could take us on to Dakar. After that, he'd take us to Ascension and I could fly both legs back to Lyneham. After all, I was the one in need of practice.

Although we'd expected our allocated airframe, XV302, to be heavy, the actual take-off weight of 165,000 pounds was a surprise, even to this highly experienced crew.

The normal maximum take-off weight for a Herc was 155,000 pounds, or 69 tons, while the normal max landing weight was 130,000lbs, 58 tons. But for operations to Ascension, we'd be complying with a less stringent set of limits known as Military Operating Standards. These allowed max take-off and landing weights of 165,000 and 140,000lbs respectively, 73½ and 62½ tons. As you'd expect, such high weights have a considerable effect on aircraft performance, especially the length of runway required for take-off and landing. But they also affect things such as climb performance, maximum height, cruising speed, fuel consumption and range.

It wasn't until I climbed into XV302 after flight planning that I understood why we were so heavy. The freight bay was crammed floor to ceiling, front to back, with stuff – rectangular boxes and crates that stacked nicely, but also more gnarly items, their jagged edges sticking out to snag the unwary. The odd passenger sat along the side, knees abutting the kit towering over them.

Down route, loadmasters were responsible for the loading

and unloading of cargo, and often helped with the heavy lifting. But at home base, while they remained responsible for the safety of the load, the grunting was invariably done by teams of supply tradesmen and women belonging to the UK Mobile Air Movements Squadron, UK MAMS.

Universally known as *the movers*, their teams were to be found at most RAF air transport hubs, which now included Dakar and Ascension. They also accompanied flights requiring their special expertise or muscle power.

In ideal conditions, the performance tables showed that a Herc loaded to the normal maximum of 155,000lbs could get airborne in 3,600 feet of runway. Now, we obviously wouldn't have been attempting a take off if these tables had indicated that we couldn't take off from Lyneham's 7,800-foot main runway carrying the extra 10,000lbs. But from my seat, the end of the tarmac seemed to be rushing up pretty fast by the time the wheels left the ground that Sunday morning. I sensed I wasn't the only one heaving a sigh of relief as the landing gear and flaps came up and we climbed away.

Gibraltar's runway was 2,300 feet shorter than Lyneham's, so the take off from there was going to be even more interesting. And I'd be doing it.

Located near the southernmost point of the Iberian Peninsula on the eastern shore of a sheltered bay, the British Overseas Territory of Gibraltar juts south into the sea. It's shaped like a spearhead a little less than two miles long and a mile wide at its widest point, and most of its 32,000 inhabitants live in a town beneath the western flank of a towering shark fin of limestone known as the Rock of Gibraltar. This rises steeply to 1,400 feet and dominates, not only the Spanish mainland to the north, but also the sea to the south, where a narrow strait separates Europe from Africa and the Atlantic from the Mediterranean. In ancient times, the Rock and the high ground on the African coast to the south were known as the Pillars of Hercules.

Its strategic position has seen Gibraltar fought over throughout history. But in 1713, to secure British withdrawal from the War of the Spanish Succession, Spain ceded it to Britain. Looking at the map, it's perhaps understandable that the Spanish have contested its sovereignty ever since, although, in a parallel with the Falkland Islands, the inhabitants remain fiercely pro-British.

The simmering resentment means that British aircraft heading to or from Gibraltar are barred from entering Spanish airspace. So to get there, we had to fly south over the Atlantic to just beyond the south-western tip of Portugal, then turn east to stay south of the Iberian Peninsula, before making a non-standard, curving approach to a 5,500 foot runway ranked the most dangerous in Europe by several television channels and websites.

Some of the hazards were obvious. For instance, the curving approaches gave little time to line up with the east/west runway, while an aircraft landing too short or too long would end up in the sea. The western third of the strip actually juts out between two marinas and a major container port, while the remainder crosses a narrow neck of land between the Spanish border, just 500 yards to the north, and the vast bulk of the Rock a few hundred yards to the south. It's also bisected by a public road, Winston Churchill Avenue, running north/south to link the Spanish town of La Linea with Gibraltar town.

In truth, the television programmes and websites overplay the dangers of the runway and its curving approaches. The real danger lies in the way the Rock interacts with winds from certain directions to create fierce up and down draughts that buffet landing aircraft and cause large changes in airspeed known as wind shear. When these conditions are at their worst, the airport closes, sometimes for several days.

The wind on 11th April was a relatively benign easterly, but the need to avoid Spanish airspace still made the approach my most exciting to date.

The Rock towered out to our right as we headed roughly north above the Bay of Gibraltar, Spanish airspace just to our left. We were descending over large cargo ships, tankers and ferries sailing in and out of Gibraltar and the Spanish ports ringing the Bay. The captain seemed intent on ploughing into the Spanish mainland until, a few hundred feet above the waves, when he turned sharp right to line up with the runway. I stared down at the mastheads of several yachts, the tallest seeming to pass no more than a few feet below our wingtip.

During this, my first experience of an approach to a runway in the sea, I was transfixed by the proximity of, not only the water, but also the cranes of the container port to our right and the yachts in the marinas to either side. If you've flown into Gibraltar in a window seat, you'll be familiar with all this, but I was in the front row with a panoramic view.

Immediately after touchdown, with the sea rushing past, our attention shifted to the far end of the runway. The captain pulled the throttles back to a position that set the propeller blades to an angle of minus seven or eight degrees to give reverse thrust and, as a large sports stadium passed down our right hand side, he applied steady braking.

Even at such heavy weight, we stopped with about a third of the runway remaining, but not before we'd crossed the road between queues of cars waiting behind red and white barriers and flashing lights. I wondered what the drivers leaning over their steering wheels thought as a large camouflaged aircraft sped past.

The flight had taken four hours and fifteen minutes, so it was late afternoon. I've always had in my head that, after a stretch of the legs and some additional flight planning, we took off for Dakar that afternoon. However, my log book indicates that we spent that night and most of the next day in and around the Gibraltar Officers' Mess.

A photograph album bears this out, with shots of the Rock alongside others of the Spanish border post and the airfield as another Herc lands.

The photos all seem to have been taken within the small area to the north of the runway, so I suspect there was some doubt about our departure time. Otherwise, I'm sure I'd have attempted to get to the town on the other side of the runway, if not the top of the Rock.

In the end, it was the early hours of Tuesday 13th when we took over an airframe flown in by another crew, XV298. After refuel, it weighed as much as our previous Albert.

There's an old saying in aviation - *runway behind you is as much use as tits on a bull*. And nowhere is that truer than Gibraltar. So the captain taxied through the dark to the western end of the runway, turned through one hundred and eighty degrees and performed a trick most people only see at airshows. He pulled the throttles back and we reversed until the loadmaster, giving instructions from a perch on the very end of the open ramp, was teetering over the water's edge. Then, with the ramp closed and the loadmaster strapped in, he handed control to me.

I took a couple of moments to compose myself, opened the throttles against the brakes then released them. A lighter aircraft would lurch forward at this point, but once again our acceleration seemed painfully slow. And similarly, whereas a lighter aircraft would skip into the air when the nosewheel was raised at the call of *Rotate*, when I pulled the nosewheel off to point into the blackness above the runway lights that night, the mainwheels remained stubbornly stuck to the ground.

I tell people that the only thing that prevented us running into the sea on this and other take-offs in the following months was the whole crew jumping in the air as we reached the end of the runway. It may be fanciful, but it paints a picture. There was little tarmac remaining when the mainwheels left the ground.

Perhaps the few yards the captain had saved by reversing at the other end really had made all the difference.

One thing we all had to put at the back of our minds was the danger of an engine failure in the latter stages of take-off. In such an eventuality, our chances of survival would have been slim. So it was no surprise when, a few years later, I was told that contingency planning for this stage of the operation had included the loss of one or two Hercs at Gibraltar.

Thankfully, it never happened.

The remainder of the leg was more mundane, at least for the rest of the crew. I was still excited to be travelling anywhere near the place names on my map.

During the first few hours in darkness, I looked out to our left at the lights of Tangiers, then cities and towns along the Moroccan coast, Casablanca, Rabat and Essaouira, followed by the Canary Islands, discernible only from the lights of their scattered communities. Looking into the distance to our left, I could see the glow of cities on the coast of Africa. They bore exotic names like Dakhla, Nouadhibou and Nouakchott.

Throughout the night we'd seen the lights of ships below us and I couldn't help wondering whether at least some of them were members of the Task Force heading south.

After four hours, the sky over the coast of West Africa took on an increasingly orange tint until the sun finally rose, revealing a crisp horizon above a thick layer of sand-coloured haze. Concentration levels tend to fall in the early hours and immediately after dawn, but I certainly didn't have to fight to stay alert, especially as we neared the westernmost tip of Africa at Cape Verde and I initiated descent.

Dakar Yoff International Airport sits in an area of dusty scrubland dotted with trees, between Dakar, a city of one million inhabitants, and the coast around the Cape. Although I was busy setting up for the approach, I still found time to delight at the way the deep blue of the ocean gave way to turquoise and then boiled white as rollers crashed onto the coast.

One thing I didn't have to worry about was the length of Dakar's north/south main runway; it was more than twice as long as Gibraltar's. I was desperate to pull off a reasonable landing.

Perhaps the pressure to make a good impression on this trip is understandable. But I was to find it was always there, especially when flying with a new crew, which was the norm of squadron flying. And at no stage of flight did making a good impression seem more important than when performing a landing. Well, as far as I can remember, despite it being an approach to a strange airfield in a relatively heavy aircraft, my touchdown in Dakar was unremarkable.

At this stage of my time on the Herc, that was a good result.

Senegal is a democratic republic that emerged in 1960 from almost three hundred years of French colonial rule. French remains the official language, but the lingua franca is Wolof, the dialect spoken by the largest of many ethnic groups that make up the population of sixteen million. The dominant religion is Islam.

The year before my arrival in 1982, the first democratically elected president had handed over to his successor, Abdou Diouf, who served until the turn of the millennium. Since then there have been two further peaceful transitions of power. During one of my numerous visits to Dakar, I saw the presidential aircraft taxy to the VIP area and President Diouf descend the steps to a guard of honour. On another visit I saw a similar ceremonial for a visiting head of state.

On this visit, the crew door opened and we were welcomed by a blast of air at 25°C, but also a case of cold beer, carried by a squadron leader from the newly-formed RAF detachment. Less than an hour later, we were consuming it in *the party room*. As we did so, we discussed the day's events, and what the morrow might hold.

In total, I visited Dakar twenty five times. Mostly it was for fourteen hours or so, staying in one of two hotels on the coast of Cape Verde close to the airport: the Meridien or the N'Gor.

The N'Gor still exists, but I suspect the Meridien has gone, or at least been renovated beyond recognition and given a new name. Both were large, with hundreds of rooms. In a nod to the country's colonial background, most guests seemed to be French and Belgian, split between businessmen, airline crews and tourists. Apart from the weeks around the arrival of the Paris Dakar Rally, there seemed to be very few Brits, except us.

There were also parties of Americans. These fell into two very different camps.

The first category was African Americans seeking to discover more about their heritage.

Dakar was on their itinerary partly because of the TV adaptation of Alex Haley's novel, Roots, which had aired a few years before. It follows an 18th Century African man, Kunta Kinte, through capture, transportation to the Americas and sale into slavery; and goes on to follow him and his descendants through the ensuing decades and centuries.

The history of slavery in Senegal is complicated and the

subject of ongoing debate. Throughout most of their pre-Colonial history, up to a third of Senegalese had been enslaved by their own countrymen, often as a result of warfare. There was also a flourishing trade in slaves with the Arabs of North Africa. But when Europeans joined in, they *industrialised* the trans-Atlantic trade in West Africans. The main embarkation points were St Louis in northern Senegal, and The Gambia, from where Kunta Kinte was transported.

Dakar, or more accurately, Gorée, a tiny island less than a mile off the beach of the N'Gor Hotel, played only a minor part. And yet it has become an important destination for African-Americans and other descendants of slaves. This is largely down to one man, the curator of a museum opened in the House of Slaves on Gorée in 1962.

Until his death in 2011, Boubacar Joseph Ndiaye so moved audiences with his talks on the horrors of slavery that Gorée became a World Heritage Site and a must see location. Famous visitors have included Pope John Paul II, Nelson Mandela and President Obama.

The second category of Americans was military personnel and NASA civilians. They had a small permanent presence in case a Space Shuttle suffered a problem after take-off and had to make an emergency landing in Dakar. Their numbers were boosted in the run-up to each launch.

The presence of the Americans also drew a few Soviets, and their numbers increased with the arrival of the RAF detachment. In an era when there were few Soviet tourists, I have a photograph of an Aeroflot Ilyushin Il62 -

the Soviet equivalent of the VC10 - sitting on the pan at Dakar. It disgorged tens of *businessmen*, many of whom spent most of their time in and around the hotels within eavesdropping range of us. I didn't feel I had much to offer the Kremlin, but their presence made us a bit more wary than usual about what we said.

On most Dakar stopovers there was rarely more than an hour or so for leisure before getting into flying kit and heading for the airport. So, when not in our rooms sleeping, most crews were to be found sunbathing on the grass by the pool or the sand of the hotel's private beach.

It could be a dangerous business.

That close to the equator, the sun was fierce. For those of us with fair skin, even a few minutes' exposure could lead to sunburn. Cloud cover seemed to offer little or no protection and I found myself prone to burning even when I kept to the shade. Inevitably, some overdid it to the point where donning a flying suit and strapping in became agony. A few ended up in hospital and on drips.

But Dakar had a more insidious and potentially harmful danger than sunburn: malaria. I'd already been injected against most of the world's nastier diseases, but avoiding malaria relied on a daily dose of whatever prophylactic pill the MOD was using at the time. I spent much of the next three years taking them.

The hotels didn't have mosquito nets, so on arrival in Dakar we were given small aerosol *bombs* of insect repellent to set off in our rooms before settling down for the night. The old hands also brought their own homespun repellents, anything from soaps, sprays or creams, to devices transmitting high frequency signals. In the end, nothing was totally effective and we were all bitten, although, as is the way with insect bites, some were bitten more than others, and suffered worse reactions.

On one of my visits, our allocated hotel was full and we were housed in a faux African village of round, straw-roofed, chalets in the grounds. We all woke with many more bites than usual, and the loadmaster was so covered in bulging blisters of yellow pus that he had to receive medical treatment.

It turned out that he – and the rest of us – had been attacked, not by mosquitoes, but bed bugs. After that, the chalets were crossed off the list of suitable accommodation.

I've always thought the best way to get a feel for an area is to walk it. But even on days when I had time to explore, I tended to stay by the pool. The reason is something of which I'm far from proud.

I explained in an earlier volume that I'd grown up seeing hardly anyone who wasn't white. My first few years in the RAF had done little to correct that omission, and I'd certainly never visited a country where the population was overwhelmingly black.

The first time I decided to head out on foot, as soon as I stepped beyond the hotel grounds, tens of men and boys rose from the shade on both sides of the road and headed towards me. Dressed in traditional Jellabiya robes, or jeans and long-sleeved shirts, the first arrivals blocked my way, smiling broadly and asking if they could be my friend or guide, or take me to their taxi, while the youngsters came straight out and asked for money.

I tried, politely, to dodge round and continue walking, but they persisted, always smiling and seeking to engage me in conversation, but making it difficult, if not impossible, for me to advance without pushing a way through, something I was very reluctant to do. In no time at all, I was surrounded.

Statistically of course, I was likely to be French or Belgian. But just as in every other part of the world I'd visit in the coming years, something about my dress and demeanour told them straight away that I was British. So their protestations of friendship were passed in Francophone English, as were the children's pleas for money.

I was torn between sympathy and fear. After all, I was living in a luxury hotel and wouldn't miss the sort of sums that could greatly ease the poverty of their everyday lives. But I'm ashamed to say that I soon found the fear of theft or injury overcoming these more charitable thoughts. I beat a hasty retreat to the *safety* of the hotel. The same happened even when I attempted a short walk along the beach beyond the hotel.

Perhaps if I'd been more worldly-wise, I'd have been able to navigate a way through the situation and carry on with my walk, but at the time, I lacked the confidence. I still can't help wondering, though, whether I'd have been as intimidated by a sea of white faces.

On the other hand, perhaps I was merely being sensible. After all, as I've already mentioned, even walking in the company of his crew, a fellow co-pilot had had his wallet whisked away.

I didn't spend all the time confined to the hotel. If the slip pattern timings allowed an evening meal, my crews often took a taxi or, on one occasion, a colourful wooden fishing boat with a massive outboard engine, to a local restaurant. Seated there, we'd eat swordfish steaks, drink the local beer or wine and watch the sun tracing a golden path over the surface of the

Atlantic until it sank beneath the horizon.

I grew to love the cuisine. For someone who hadn't long ventured beyond chicken and chips – even in Chinese and Indian restaurants – the dishes of fish, rice and exotic vegetables in spicy sauces felt very adventurous.

Invariably the restaurants featured live music, generally a mix of percussion and the kora, an instrument with a large, gourd-like resonator box held on the player's knees, and a long, upright, neck with twenty one strings, plucked with both hands, like a harp. I could only marvel at the dexterity of the musicians, and the beautiful sound they made.

Something similar would occasionally feature among the piped music to be heard in the hotel. There might even be the odd piece by local musicians such as Youssou N'Dour, famous in Africa long before he became an international star with the release of *7 Seconds* in 1994. But more often than not, the hotel speakers would emit the kind of French language Euro-pop heard in the UK only once a year, during the Eurovision Song Contest.

Just after midnight, on Wednesday 14th April, having signed the hotel bill and picked up what was left of my imprest from a safe deposit box, I joined the rest of the crew on the bus for the short drive to the airport. There, we flight planned for a 2.00am take-off in another fully laden airframe, XV307.

In hot weather, shorter runways could limit our take-off weight. The thin air of high altitude could have the same effect. But on even the hottest days, with 11,000 feet of tarmac available, and only a smidgen above sea level, Dakar's main runway offered no such constraints.

The high temperatures did make for sluggish acceleration though, and a shallower initial climb. Bringing the landing gear up reduced drag and improved acceleration a bit, while extending the wing flaps to forty degrees helped the rate of climb. But, on especially hot days, we still barely seemed to clear the chain link fence surrounding the airport. We then had to wait until four hundred feet to raise the flaps. Doing so earlier risked a loss of lift with potentially dire consequences, especially if there was an engine failure.

In the relative cool of the early morning, our take off on the 14th was unremarkable. A couple of months later, though, I flew out of Dakar in another extremely heavy aircraft on a very hot day. At little more than a hundred feet, the captain, a senior officer, asked me to raise the flaps.

I thought he'd probably just forgotten how heavy we were, so, as diplomatically as possible, I replied, 'Waiting for four hundred feet, Captain.'

To my surprise, even though we were still well below two hundred feet and barely climbing, he turned to his right and glowered at me.

'When I say flaps up, Co, I mean *flaps up!*'

I now had a straight choice, disobey an officer several ranks above my own, and with whom I was flying for the first time, or raise the flaps and jeopardise the aircraft.

It was a classic example of what is known in flight safety circles as cross-cockpit gradient; a mismatch in rank, experience and personality that can so intimidate individuals that they obey instructions they know could lead to disaster.

If you think it sounds far-fetched, I have to tell you that aviation history is littered with crashes where the wrong engine was shut down or the aircraft flown into high ground because no-one was willing to challenge the operating pilot. Such case studies are a staple of flight safety courses. Aviation psychologists love them.

Anyway, in this instance, I chose a middle way.

I put my hand on the flap lever and said, 'Flaps up, Captain,' but did nothing until four hundred feet.

I like to think that if the senior officer had challenged me again, I'd have disobeyed him again. But I was never put to the test. He kept his eyes straight ahead and said nothing.

When we were on the ground at Ascension five hours later, the eng took me aside.

'Well done for not raising the flaps,' he said, before adding, 'but just so you know, if you'd tried to raise them, I'd have broken your arm!'

I already knew the senior officer had a reputation for aloofness. But I'd just discovered first hand that he also lacked the humility to acknowledge mistakes. When he also took me aside, it was to offer admonishment rather than praise. I chose not to remonstrate, but he never gained my respect, and I'm pretty sure he knew it.

Whether through coincidence or design on his part, we flew together only once more during his remaining year on the squadron, forty minutes in the circuit at Lyneham. I suspect no other co-pilots were available.

There were no such problems on 14th April.

Out of Dakar, the load included a couple of *Desert Rat,* open-top Land Rovers, and a group of men resembling Roger Moore and his band of mercenaries in the film Wild Geese. The captain seemed to be on first name terms with some of them, and when he went down the back for a chat, we hoped he'd come back and tell us what they were off to do, and where. No chance, although he did make an intriguing throw-away remark.

'Wouldn't be surprised if my next trip isn't as part of the Santiago Slip.'

He'd say no more on the matter, so we were left to wonder whether Hercs really might be heading for Chile, and what they might do when they got there. Maybe fly men like those down the back into the Falklands!

It was years before the fact that RAF aircraft had operated from Chile came into the public domain. And a few weeks after our Dakar trip, my captain really did disappear for a while. I often wondered where he could have been, although, even when I met him years later, he merely smiled and tapped his nose.

He enjoyed winding me up.

ASCENSION ISLAND

Ascension Island sits in glorious isolation in the Atlantic Ocean approximately eight degrees south of the equator. The nearest landfall is St Helena, a small island 800 miles to the south, while Cape Palmas, the closest point in Africa is 1,000 miles to the north. To the east, Angola is 1900 miles, and to the west, it's 1400 miles to Brazil.

Few places on Earth are as remote, and if something like bad weather or a blocked runway prevented us landing there, we'd rarely have sufficient fuel to divert to another airfield. So it was a good job the weather there tended to be benign and Wideawake Airfield little used. This allowed us to carry what was known as *island holding fuel*, enough to hold clear until any fleeting storm passed, or the runway was cleared.

Over the following months and years, the assumptions about both weather and runway availability usually held good. But, on occasion, they were severely tested, more of which later.

The 1,600-mile flight roughly due south from Dakar usually took about five hours. I say usually because the timing depended on more than the direction and strength of the wind.

The boundary where the northern and southern hemisphere trade winds circling the Earth meet is known as the intertropical convergence zone, or ITCZ. Over the ocean to the south and west of Dakar, it meanders north and south between the equator and about ten degrees north with the seasons. On every return trip to Ascension we had to pass through it twice.

Sometimes this was no big deal, with the ITCZ producing nothing more than a few fluffy white cumulus clouds drifting thousands of feet below. But on occasion, we could face a wall of cumulonimbus thunder clouds stretching from horizon to horizon. Climbing from near the surface, they towered, dark and menacing, their tops reaching up to something like 55,000 feet, more than 35,000 feet above our initial cruising height.

The hazards associated with such storms included lightning, severe icing and turbulence, caused by up and down draughts fierce enough to damage any aircraft caught up in them. Nearly three decades after my first encounter with the ITCZ, pilots mishandling problems caused by thunderstorms within it, led to the loss of an Air France Airbus 330 and all two hundred and twenty eight souls on board.

Just in case any of us had been tempted to underestimate the dangers, our OCU training had included the story of a German Herc entering a storm over Turkey and dropping out of the bottom minus its wings. To this, the more experienced aircrew on the course had been encouraged to add their own horror stories of turbulence, icing and lightning strikes that damaged airframes and messed with electrical and navigation systems.

In the early morning darkness of 14th April, these tales came to mind just an hour south of Dakar.

We'd clambered up to 20,000 feet when the sky along the whole width of the distant horizon became peppered with frequent flashes. Fifteen minutes later, the lightning began to outline in silver and gold the sheer walls and anvil heads of a seemingly unbroken line of cumulonimbus clouds. Closer still and they towered above us, beautiful and threatening, each flash making their innards glow like demonic foundries. We even heard the odd thunder-crack above the incessant thrum of the engines.

If I'd thought the stories on the OCU had over-egged the dangers, the tension on the faces of my vastly experienced crew told otherwise. As we speared into cloud on the northern boundary of the ITCZ that night, they knew better than I that we were at a height where the storm cells were most active – and dangerous – and that we might be among them for the next 30 minutes or more.

Even in daylight, once you enter cloud, you're enveloped by an impenetrable fog that makes it impossible to see more than a few yards. And at night, while lightning adds greatly to the drama, it does little to improve visibility. For this reason, the Herc was fitted with a radar dish in its black nose cone. Optimised to spot storm cells with the strongest up and down draughts, its beam scanned the air ahead of us and displayed its findings on a small orange radar screen on the instrument panel between the pilots.

Potentially dangerous cells appeared as bright blobs. Ideally, we'd be able to thread a path around or between these. But the active cells that night were so numerous they melded into an unbroken line stretching from one side of the circular screen to the other.

We bounced in the disturbed air, edging this way and that, peering intently at the display, looking for darker areas between the brightest cells. If we spotted one, the captain turned towards it. Lightning, flashing like strobe lights at a disco, gave fleeting glimpses of my crewmates' faces. We peered out, as if hoping to see evidence of a gap with our own eyes.

Generally though, you just had to trust the radar. And as we threaded through each successive *letterbox* of lighter cloud, we hoped the dark didn't close in or over us, and that we'd find starry skies on the other side, or at least find another gap. You never knew because active cells blinded the radar to what lay behind them.

That night, we flew tens of miles out of our way to find a safe route, jinking this way and that until even the nav was losing track of how far we'd deviated. By the time we emerged into clear air to the south of the ITCZ, we were one hundred miles west of track. But the relief on the flight deck was palpable.

The farthest I ever deviated to avoid storms was one hundred and ninety miles. Such diversions were one reason our southbound journey often took longer than the return, when, being lighter and several thousand feet higher, we rarely had to deviate so far.

A fair few of the thirty plus occasions I transited the ITCZ included moments of high tension, even fear. And yet I always found it exhilarating, especially if we remained clear of cloud as we threaded between the immense storms glowering over us, lightning flashing all around. At night, the images were especially beautiful, moving even.

Clear of this band of storms, we flew on south, the stars above, nothing but darkness below. I was hoping we'd spot elements of the Task Force, but most were still to the north of Dakar and we'd probably be back on the ground there when they sailed past.

At some point the nav mentioned that we were crossing the equator. Had I been on a ship, I and any other newbies would have had some humiliating punishment meted out in the court of King Neptune. On an RAF flight deck, the milestone was merely a point of discussion, for which I was very grateful.

A few minutes later, the sky began to lighten and the sun rose out of the haze to the east. Shortly after this, the nav switched the radar from weather to mapping mode, utilising a more focused beam to search the surface ahead for the appearance of Ascension Island. I for one had no idea what such a target would look like, or when it would appear.

That day, it revealed itself at a range of one hundred and ninety five miles, a tiny bright dot at the very top of the orange screen. Over the next few years, hundreds of aviators would peer at similar screens waiting for that tiny dot to appear. I'd be surprised if any failed to receive a lift when it did, and especially those flying from the direction of the Falklands, many short of fuel.

On the ground at Ascension during a later visit, I met an acquaintance from Linton and Finningley, by then a navigator on Victor tankers. He was waiting to fly home after a couple of months undertaking long missions to the south west of Ascension. During these, they'd refuelled Hercs, Nimrods and other Victors, not to mention the Vulcan bombers that had attacked Port Stanley airfield.

A few years younger than me, in the year or so since we'd last met he'd aged ten, his skin sallow, great bags drooping below grey-rimmed eyes. He said he'd lost count of the number of times they'd returned with little more than fumes in their tanks, eagerly awaiting the appearance of Ascension on the radar screen, then counting down the range, hoping their fuel would last and the aircraft ahead wouldn't block the runway.

Not for the first time, I was glad to be flying Hercs. And although I eventually had my own exciting moments when flying from Ascension in the tanker role, they were nothing compared to those endured by the Victor crews.

In an age when you can conjure up information on any destination at the touch of a screen, you may find it hard to believe that I knew next to nothing about Ascension Island before seeing it *in the flesh*. I hadn't even had time to chase down an encyclopaedia – the Stone Age equivalent of an internet search engine – so I hadn't even seen a photograph. And although the Island was very infrequently used as a refuelling stop by RAF flights to South Africa, none of my current crew had visited either. So none of us knew what lay behind that tiny dot on the radar.

The approach charts gave some clues. They showed an island shaped like an isosceles triangle on its side, the base running north/south for seven miles, the sharp *tip* nine miles to the east. The interior, area thirty four square miles, was studded with contours indicating a number of conical hills, the tallest toward the east rising to 2,817 feet.

The airfield, Wideawake, was located in the south-west corner.

NASA image of Ascension in 2003, twenty years after enlargement of airfield dispersal

The landing chart showed a 10,000-foot runway oriented north-west to south-east on a bearing of 140°. And although the approach chart had indicated it was in an area free of contours, the landing chart told a different story. It showed several conical hills to north and south of the landing surface. It also had several written warnings, including *numerous obstructions up to 921 feet above sea level,* and *Unlighted high terrain immediately south of the runway.*

Much like the Rock of Gibraltar, two hills abutting the southern edge of the runway looked in prime position to disturb the air passing over the landing threshold, so the warning, *Excessive downdraughts/turbulence on approach,* came as no surprise.

The final warning, *possible livestock on the runway,* was similar to the one for Goose Bay in Canada, although I doubted it referred to Moose.

All very intriguing.

Wideawake Airfield was run by employees of Pan American Airlines and licensed to receive a mere two hundred and eighty five visiting aircraft a year, although it usually saw far fewer as most visitors and supplies arrived by ship from St Helena. The only routine air movement was a weekly United States Air Force transport aircraft delivering Iceberg lettuce and other American staples.

As a result, air traffic control was normally manned just a couple of times a week, thirty minutes before scheduled arrivals and departures. Now though, with RAF Hercs and VC10s arriving throughout the day and night, we guessed it would be a 24/7 operation, so I made a speculative call of introduction soon after the island appeared on the radar.

'Ascension, this is Ascot Four Three Two One.'

The response, 'G'morning, Ascot Four Three Two One, how y'all doin?' brought to mind a moustachioed preacher from the deep south with a sixty-a-day Marlboro habit.

'Hallelujah!' chanted the nav.

We were still exchanging smiles when the controller continued, 'Ready to copy weather?'

Friendly – I could sense his smile - but straight down to business.

When I told him to go ahead, the gravelly voice reported wind from a direction of 140° at ten miles per hour with gusts to fifteen, and scattered cumulus cloud at 2,500 feet. In line with American convention, he also passed the temperature in Fahrenheit (80°) and the pressure to wind into our altimeters in inches of Mercury (29.91). These we converted to 27° Celsius and 1013 millibars.

I wasn't to know, but the wind speed and direction, cloud and surface pressure would be virtually the same on every subsequent visit to the Island, whatever the time of day or year. The only thing to show any significant variation was the temperature, but even this rarely changed by more than five degrees, not only between day and night, but between seasons. Highs of 30°C (approximately 85°F) in the peak summer months of January and February, would fall to about 25°C (75°F) in July and August, the depth of the Ascension winter.

Some days, there might be the odd spot of rain on the windward – south easterly - slopes and summit of the highest hill. Less frequently, a few drops might fall a little way down its leeward slopes, but rarely over the rest of the Island. I never experienced rain at the airfield.

Only once did the weather deviate far from the norm, and on that day it was so extreme that it very nearly led to the loss of a Herc full of passengers. A story for later.

And finally, on the subject of Ascension's weather, when I visited for the eighteenth time in 2016, I found daily temperatures a couple of degrees higher, and more rainfall. This had left the island much greener than I remembered, which might sound like a good thing, but is actually a threat to the unique landscape. The accompanying increase in sea temperatures is also a danger to sea life and the birds that feed on it.

The overwhelming consensus is that such rapid and potentially catastrophic change is down to human action. For the record, I agree.

Back to April 1982.

During the descent, the nav adjusted the range of the radar display and the Island began to grow until it took on the triangular shape we expected from the charts. But even when it should have been visible, cloud prevented all but the odd, tantalising, glimpse of reddish earth - until we dipped below 2,500 feet.

The western coast of Ascension Island was about fifteen miles ahead, filling little more than one pane of the flight deck windows. My first impression was of a jagged line of rust-coloured hills, like the erratic peaks on a heart monitor printout. They floated between the contrasting blues of the ocean and a morning sky peppered with fluffy white clouds. The vista was breathtaking, otherworldly, unlike anything I'd ever seen, or thought I'd see.

In hindsight, it was love at first sight.

We levelled at 2,000 feet and aimed for the south-western corner and the foreshortened smudge of a runway. As we approached, in between the odd radio call and set of checks, I took every opportunity to study the landscape.

The Atlantic slammed into the coast, etching it in boiling white, while inland a series of terracotta volcanic cones climbed in height from a few hundred feet near the coast, to the dominant peak, its summit hidden by cloud.

As we'd perused the charts on the way south, I'd resolved to research the Island's origins and history. Now I was even more determined to do so. But, more than anything, I wanted to explore. That opportunity would come, although not for several weeks, by which time I'd done a fair amount of reading.

Some of the information in the following paragraphs comes from that period, some from the rest of my time on the Herc, and the remainder from my visit in 2016.

What I was looking at on that first approach was the top one per cent of a volcano rising 18,000 feet from the ocean floor. It sits on the Mid-Atlantic Ridge, one of the major fault lines in the Earth's crust, running south from the Arctic Circle through Iceland and the Azores, past Ascension, Tristan de Cunha and the Antarctic. Along it, the continents are pulling apart, generating seismic and volcanic activity, even volcanoes large enough to thrust above the surface of the ocean, as Ascension had roughly one million years ago. The last volcanic event on the Island itself is thought to have been in the 16th Century, although there was activity in the ocean a few hundred miles to the north-west in 1838. So, it's probably safer to think of

Ascension as dormant rather than extinct, much like Tristan de Cunha, which erupted unexpectedly in 1961.

As we drew nearer, the coastline revealed several golden beaches, the longest a couple of miles to our left beyond a small settlement of low white buildings, including a picture-postcard white church with a spire.

Between and behind the beaches were a mix of red and black rock shelves and low cliffs. Inland, most of the volcanic cones and the areas between them were rusty red, although some were scarred by fans of black spreading down their flanks, often as far as the sea. Elsewhere were smudges of grey and white, but not a hint of vegetation.

I was witnessing the legacy of Ascension's volcanic past, when explosive cones had shot lava high into the air, or generated pyroclastic avalanches of pumice and ash. Elsewhere, fissures and vents had spewed red and black basaltic lava, and domes of white silica lava had bubbled to the surface and solidified. As the basaltic flows cooled, they bubbled and cracked to produce a tortured landscape of sharp rock riddled with holes, much of it sculpted into wondrous shapes, especially where they reached the sea.

In total, there are forty four vents of one sort or another, and in addition to the volcanic rock and ash, they've left an island littered with lava bombs, pumice, obsidian and all manner of minerals. Inevitably, such a variety of features relatively untouched by water, vegetation or man has made the Island a favourite destination for volcanologists and geologists.

For a moment, the cloud parted to reveal the final few hundred feet of the highest peak. In contrast with the rest of the landscape, it was covered in vegetation, varying in colour from lime to dark green. It was my first sight of Green Mountain.

In the last couple of miles of the approach, I picked out arrays of satellite dishes and radar domes on top of some of the hills, while on a largish tarmac dispersal area to the right of the runway sat a Nimrod, a handful of Wessex and Sea King helicopters and four or five other Alberts.

No time to dwell on what they were doing there. All too soon we crossed the coast above a black shelf of rock abeam a small beach.

As the charts had indicated, the landing threshold of the runway was fifty yards beyond the top of a steep cliff, two hundred and fifty eight feet above sea level. I looked down on its upper rim before the captain flared for landing. As he did so, the far end of the runway disappeared behind a significant hump 1,500 feet in, the tarmac climbing gently to that point before dropping away for the remaining 8,500 feet.

The captain was totally unfazed by the upslope, performing a textbook touchdown well before the peak. It was something I'd struggle to emulate in the coming years, when many of my arrivals were much less accomplished. If I had actually kept a little book of excuses for poor landings, those for Ascension might have included high landing weights, fatigue after long flights and demanding schedules, or turbulence caused by either daytime heating of the tarmac or the airflow over and around the volcanic cones.

And then there was that hump. I found it hard enough to pull off a good landing on the upslope, but if I hadn't put us down before the runway fell away again, we could be left soaring above the tarmac until we lost flying speed and dropped to earth with a bone-shattering crunch.

Excuses aside though, I was just never very good at landing the Herc with any consistency. Only when I became a flying instructor did I really learn to land by reference to visual and other cues, rather than instinct and hope. I often wonder how good I'd have been at landing the beast if I'd returned to Lyneham after my first stint as an instructor. Sadly, I never had the chance to find out.

In the summer months, we've probably all seen hot tarmac deformed by car tyres, or the tyres of heavily laden trucks. Given their higher pressure and the weight they bear, aircraft tyres are even more likely to create damage, especially during sharp turns. As a result, aircraft landing at Wideawake were forbidden to turn through one hundred and eighty degrees before a widened area at the far end of its priceless 10,000 feet of tarmac.

This wasn't a problem for the Herc. We could land and decelerate in time to make a gentle right turn at an exit about 2,500 feet into the runway. Jet aircraft, though, invariably flashed past this point well before they'd braked to a safe taxying speed. They then had to trundle to the end, perform a one eighty and taxy back uphill, a journey of several minutes.

Generally, there were so few arrivals that blocking the runway as you taxied back wasn't a problem. But during the War, there were several hairy moments as formations of Victors returned short of fuel after long missions to the south of the Island. Cool heads and good communication were vital to identify those with enough fuel to loiter while others landed and cleared the runway. On at least one mission, though, four returning Victors were so close to running out of fuel that they had to land one behind the other, hoping none suffered a brake failure and ran into the one ahead.

Things were much more relaxed as we rolled toward the turn-off point. I even had time to admire the landscape.

The volcanic cones to the left of the runway were mostly several hundred feet away, but as the charts had indicated, to the right, the forty five degree slopes of two cones ran right down to the tarmac. The first, just beyond the exit point - Round Hill - rose to two hundred feet; the second – South Gannet Hill - was five hundred feet high and topped with radars.

From the proximity of our right wingtip to the edge of the runway, I guessed we wouldn't have to drift too far right on take-off to scrape those rough slopes. You'd have even less room for error in one of the big jets, both on landing and take-off.

These features alone explained why Wideawake Airfield wasn't licensed for civilian use.

On our left abeam the turn-off was a red and white-checked wooden shack standing about fifteen feet above the stony ground on metal stilts. Behind its large windows, I could make out the silhouette of a man.

'Welcome to Wideawake,' he drawled, giving us a cheery

wave, which we returned as we exited the runway.

After taxying a short distance beneath the flanks of Round Hill, we turned right again onto the tarmac dispersal we'd seen from the air. It was surrounded by a large flat area of what looked like black gravel, much of it already hidden under piles of freight. Beyond this were still more small volcanic cones, some topped with buildings and aerials.

Not long after we'd parked next to the other Hercs, the crew door was opened and a blast of air similar to that in Dakar hit the flight deck. We were greeted by another RAF squadron leader, sadly without beer this time.

While the loadmaster and air engineer did their stuff, the captain, nav and I were led a short distance off the tarmac toward several large olive green canvas tents. The black stones underfoot made a metallic clink. I picked one up. It was much lighter and sharper than gravel.

'Volcanic clinker,' the squadron leader said. 'Plays hell with tyres.'

And jet engines, I thought, looking at the Nimrod and harking back to my Vulcan days, when we'd scoured every surface for anything, no matter how small, that could be sucked into engines. Here, jet exhaust, prop wash and rotor downwash would be bound to blow debris everywhere, and I had no doubt even the smallest piece of clinker could finish off a Nimrod engine compressor.

At least there was plenty of room for everyone to park well away from the edge of the pan – for the moment.

When we re-emerged after flight planning in the makeshift ops tent, our freight had already joined the other piles on the clinker, while Roger Moore and his team had disappeared, presumably to wait for a Task Force ship to board, although the nav wondered if they might be destined to leave on one of the resident Hercs, or even a submarine. Sounded pretty fanciful to me, but then again...

In the few minutes before we boarded the aircraft, I looked

around.

Beyond the runway, the slopes of the volcanic craters also seemed to be covered in clinker, mainly terracotta rather than black, and in a wide variety of sizes up to misshapen boulders the size of a small car. It hadn't looked like it from the air, but there was also some vegetation, thickets of scrubby bushes or prickly pear cacti, and scattered tufts of straw-coloured grass.

On a later walking expedition, I bumped into one of the cacti and spent hours trying to pull vicious hair-like spines from my thigh. The ones I missed snagged my trousers or flying suit and made me wince for days. After that, I made sure I always gave them a wide berth.

From the pan, I could also see that the south-eastern flank of Green Mountain was covered in lush vegetation down to a few hundred feet above sea level. There was even a stand of tall fir trees, Norfolk Pines, grown before the age of steam to replace the masts of sailing ships dropping into Ascension for repairs.

This seems a good moment to say a little about man's involvement with the Island.

For the vast majority of its existence, Ascension seems to have had no permanent residents, and if any intrepid sailors stumbled across it, they left no record or trace.

The first documented visit was by Juan de Nova, a Spanish

mariner in the service of Portugal. He landed in 1501 and named it Concepsion. But he failed to publicise his find, and it was left to a Portuguese sailor, Alphonse d'Albuquerque, to give the name that stuck when he arrived on Ascension Day 1503. Even then, it remained of little more than passing interest for three hundred years. The few visitors noted turtles and large colonies of seabirds, useful sources of fresh meat, but they found no water or edible vegetation.

One visitor also mentions an *ocean letterbox,* a rock crevice on the coast where ships could leave messages for one another. Perhaps in a nod to this, many of the Island's peaks and more remote corners now have wooden *letterboxes* – thirty four at the last count – where modern explorers can stamp books or cards to prove they've reached them.

In 1701, HMS Roebuck pulled in with a leak. Attempts to repair it were botched and it sank, stranding the crew and their captain, buccaneer and explorer, William Dampier. They survived until their rescue six weeks later because he discovered a water source in an area on the north-western flank of Green Mountain, now known as Dampier's Drip.

The most famous visitors were Captain James Cook, who stopped to collect turtle meat in 1775; Charles Darwin, who landed in HMS Beagle in 1836 - and wrote an account of the geology of the Island; and Professor David Gill, who arrived in 1877 to view the opposition of Mars as part of efforts to measure the exact distance between the Earth and the Sun. But long before that, events in Europe had led to a more permanent British presence.

When Napoleon was defeated at Waterloo in 1815, he was exiled and imprisoned on St Helena, 800 miles to the south of Ascension. Despite the remoteness of his prison, it was feared his supporters might mount a rescue and use Ascension as a stepping stone. So it was claimed in the name of King George III and manned by the Royal Navy, becoming HMS Ascension Island.

The sailors set about building fortifications and accommodation at the southern end of the long beach on the western coast, naming their settlement Georgetown. The major problem was finding enough fresh water and something other than seabird and turtle to eat.

Initially, detachments lived at Dampier's Drip, collecting water in casks and carrying it to Georgetown. To provide somewhere to rest out of the sun along the route, small ships were cut in half and placed upright. Later generations of these brightly painted shelters can still be found, one at the appropriately named One Boat, and two close to the main inland settlement of Two Boats.

At some point, donkeys were introduced to carry the casks. About one hundred of their descendants still roam the Island, sometimes wandering onto the airfield; hence the warning about livestock on the runway.

At the same time, the sailors began gardening and farming on the upper slopes of Green Mountain. They introduced a wide variety of plants and seeds, as well as cattle and pigs, even bees. There's still a thriving market garden up there.

When Napoleon died in 1821, the garrison was retained and handed over to the Royal Marines, who often brought their families. Men, women and children continued to die of various illnesses brought on by the hardship, while at least two commanding officers were said to have succumbed to the stress of leading the garrison.

Illness was also brought to the Island. Sailors on anti-slavery patrols off the West African coast who contracted diseases like yellow fever were placed in quarantine in several locations around the coast.

Some are buried in a cemetery to the south of Georgetown, others in one of several small cemeteries on the north-west coast, in an area now named Comfortless Cove.

Over the years, paved catchment areas were laid below the summit of Green Mountain to capture rain and moisture deposited when the south-east trade winds climbed the windward slopes. New springs were discovered and paths, tunnels and pipelines were built to carry the water down the Mountain to Georgetown.

Several garden cottages were also built to exploit the different micro-climates on and around the Mountain. Species such aloe, bananas and bamboo were introduced, as well as the Norfolk Pines. Not all the new flora survived, but much of it did. The downside was that it often went on to supplant the few native species. Conservationists are now working to redress the balance.

Man also had a devastating effect on the wildlife.

Before the garrison arrived in 1815, gannets, boobies, noddies and any number of other seabird species were to be found all over the Island. Colonies could comprise tens, hundreds of thousands of birds, and some, such as the Wideawake Tern and the Ascension Frigate Bird were native to the Island. They were so numerous they could be knocked down with sticks, a practice that soon reduced their numbers markedly, as did the introduction of predators.

The odd rat may have made its way ashore before 1815, but from that year the numbers escalated. Cats were introduced to kill the rats, but found it easier to eat seabirds. Fifty years later, only 11 species remained, and all bar one of these were confined to a few remote cliffs and sea stacks. The exception was the Wideawake Tern. These continued to breed in an area to the south of the current airfield, surviving because they left the Island between each breeding cycle, leaving the predators nothing to feed on and so limiting their numbers.

In 2001, a controversial plan was initiated to eliminate the feral cats. It was so successful Ascension was declared cat free in 2006, at which point birds began to return to the main island. So far, they continue to do so. Work is still under way to control the rats.

Ascension is also the world's second largest breeding ground for Green Turtles. Each year between January and April, females travel thousands of miles to lay clutches of up to one hundred eggs on beaches all around the Island. Six to ten weeks later, the hatchlings dig their way to the surface and make for the sea. Only one or two from each clutch survive to adulthood, the females wandering the ocean until the age of twenty five. Then, once every three years, they return to lay eggs on the very beach where they hatched.

More than a metre in length and weighing up to two hundred and fifty kilograms, the turtles had always provided a ready source of fresh food for visiting sailors, but the garrison began to harvest them, keeping them alive in ponds on the edge of Georgetown to sell to passing ships. An industry developed and they were sent all over the world. This went on until the 1940s, by which time they were an endangered species.

Green Turtles are still hunted elsewhere, but on Ascension they're protected and their numbers have recovered to the point where about 4,000 females visit each year.

In 1899 when the Eastern Telegraph Company laid the first undersea cable between South Africa and the UK, its first landfall was Ascension. A few years later, the Island was at the centre of a spider's web of undersea cables connecting the Americas, Africa and Europe. And when radio equipment began to arrive in 1915, its future as a communications hub was assured.

The last Royal Marine left in 1922, and the men of the Eastern Telegraph Company, by then named Cable and Wireless, became the sole residents. Its senior manager became the Resident Magistrate, while other managers took on roles such as Clerk of the Court and Harbour Master. The population was sometimes swelled by short term visitors and ill-fated enterprises such as harvesting bird guano, but for most of the 1920s and 30s it hovered around the 200 mark, the majority being workers from St Helena, known as Saints.

In 1938, when war with Germany was on the horizon, the

Navy returned, forming a garrison and placing huge guns from the battleship HMS Hood on the hill overlooking Georgetown.

In 1941, as part of the Lend Lease Programme, the Americans were allowed to survey the Island, and the next year they returned to build an airfield. Work started in April 1942 and, despite all the engineering challenges, the runway was finished in just ninety one days, receiving its first aircraft on 10th July.

From then on, Ascension became a base for anti-submarine operations over the Atlantic, and a staging post for the re-supply of North Africa and southern Europe. At its peak, the garrison numbered 4,000 men and 1,000 aircraft a month were passing through. But when the war ended, the military left the Island to Cable and Wireless once more.

This remained the position until 1956 when the United States Air Force returned, setting up radar and satellite dishes to track rockets, missiles and satellites. The BBC arrived in 1963 to build a major relay station for their World Service programming. A year later, more tracking and relay facilities were added when NASA established a base to the east of the Island in an area known as Devil's Ashpit.

It was here that Neil Armstrong's famous, *This is one small step for man,* message from the surface of the Moon reached Earth, to be relayed around the planet.

NASA still has a telescope facility on the Island for tracking space debris, and they've now been joined by the European Space Agency. Finally, Ascension is host to one of only four ground antenna sites for GPS, the Global Positioning System.

And yet, despite the blossoming of organisations, the Island's population in the early decades of the 21st Century rarely numbers more than 1,000. Some are executives, engineers and military personnel on relatively short stays, but the majority continue to come from St Helena. The lengths of their contracts vary, but some have lived and worked on the Island for several decades.

After the Falklands War, the RAF maintained a presence

to service the airbridge to the Falklands. A small tourist industry also developed, with visitors arriving, either by air from RAF Brize Norton, or by ship from St Helena, a more risky business because the Atlantic swell sometimes prevented disembarkation at the one and only jetty in Georgetown.

Unfortunately, wear and tear of the runway led to it being closed to all but emergency users in 2017. My wife and I were lucky to choose 2016 for our visit, because as this book is published in 2022, the runway remains closed.

Back to 14th April 1982. That morning, I was the operating pilot for the leg back to Dakar. We had an empty freight bay and hadn't taken any of Ascension's precious aviation fuel. So when I released the brakes and opened the throttles, we skipped along the runway and into the air before the hump. I'd have to wait for a heavier aircraft to see how close our wingtips came to the clinker of Round and South Gannet Hills. They were well below us by the time we passed them.

As we climbed to the south-east, I looked down on a rugged coastline of lava cliffs falling into the sea, and no visible beaches. The slopes of the easternmost headland looked as if someone had emptied pots of brown and black ink over them, which explained its name, The Devil's Ink Pot.

A few small rock stacks hugged the coast, each circled by sea birds, while to the north of The Devil's Ink Pot a much larger slab of rock thrust hundreds of feet out of the sea.

This was Boatswain Bird Island, the stack to which the vast majority of the Island's birds had retreated to escape the predation of man and the rats and cats he'd introduced. Its thick coating of white guano had been the primary target of those aiming to exploit the deposits in the 1920s. But the stack had proved difficult to reach, and its terrain dangerous. At least one ship and several workers had been lost before the attempt was abandoned.

I turned right and set us up in a climb to the north.

The American controller's final words were, 'Y'all come back and see us now.'

I didn't know it at the time but, in the next three years, I'd take him up on the offer sixteen times.

After a little more than 14 hours on the ground at Dakar, we took off in the early morning twilight of Thursday 15th April to return direct to Lyneham. The flight, in XV209, took eight and a half hours.

Once again, I was the operating pilot, while the captain operated the radios. The fact that I was flying from West Africa to the UK, taking in views of the African coast, the Canaries, Madeira and the Iberian Peninsula was already beginning to seem almost normal. If it was to become routine though, I had to pass my Final Handling Test.

I walked into our married quarter just as Geraldine was returning from work.

I'd been away only four days, but it seemed a lifetime. I'd seen and done so many things that would have been unbelievable, well, right up until I did them.

An old dilemma began to raise its head.

How could I tell family and friends what I'd been up to without seeming to boast, or at least hog the limelight to the point where people began rolling their eyes? It had been difficult enough to curb my natural enthusiasm during my flying training, but I sensed it was going to be even more difficult from now on.

I went into the OCU on Friday expecting to fly my Final Handling Test. But my log book shows that my next flight, on the Sunday, was another with the Scottish captain, a short trip to RAF Binbrook, the home of the Lightning force, to pick up priority freight for Ascension. Although the return flight in XV302 took a total of just one hour and five minutes, a combination of personal preparation, flight planning and waiting for the aircraft to be loaded at Binbrook ate into a fair chunk of the weekend.

On entering the OCU again on Monday, I was told that if nothing else intervened, I'd fly my Final Handling Test the next day. It was a relief, but also a worry.

What would happen if I failed?

One element of doubt had already been removed.

Ever since my two familiarization flights before the OCU, I'd hoped to go to one of the tactical squadrons at Lyneham - 47 or 70. Although they spent much of their time doing the same type of flying as the two route squadrons, 24 and 30, they also flew at low level and dropped paratroops and freight. This modus operandi seemed to offer the best of both worlds, overseas travel with added variety and excitement.

But although I'd maintained a reasonable standard during the course, I already knew I wasn't high enough in the pecking order to grab one of the two co-pilot slots on the tac squadrons. These were going to those of my peers judged to have the best situational awareness and capacity, which turned out to be two of my friends from Finningley.

In the great book of life, it was a minor disappointment. If I passed my Final Handling Test, I'd still be a Hercules pilot in the RAF, a dream come true.

If!

On Tuesday April 20th, I took off in XV207 sitting next to my moustachioed OCU flight commander. The test included twenty minutes of instrument flying, two instrument and several visual approaches, some with engines throttled back to simulate engine failures. We landed after one hour.

The next time I saw the flight commander was on Ascension Island a year or so later. By then on an exchange tour with the United States Air Force, he'd just landed a Lockheed C-141 Starlifter full of supplies from the States, mostly iceberg lettuce, he said. While we were both waiting for our respective aircraft to be unloaded, he proudly showed me round the flight deck of his new *bird*.

A little more than two decades later, we met again when I took responsibility for the first stage of military flying training, including the fourteen University Air Squadrons, one of which he commanded. Even after all those years, I felt grateful to him. My performance in the test was far from flawless, but he'd rated it a pass.

Almost three years to the day after leaving Scampton as a corporal airframe and engine fitter, I was about to join the RAF front line as a Herc co-pilot.

WELCOME TO 24 SQUADRON

After finishing the OCU, I joined the co-pilot section of No 24 Squadron Royal Air Force.

The Squadron had come into being at Hounslow Heath in September 1915, part of the Royal Flying Corps. Six months later it moved to France where it spent the rest of the First World War in either the fighter or ground attack roles, becoming an RAF squadron on 1st April 1918, the birth date of the new service. By the end of hostilities, it had shot down more than two hundred aircraft and counted among its ranks thirty three aces – pilots with five kills or more.

As part of the post-war drawdown, 24 was disbanded in February 1919, but reformed a year later as a communications and training squadron. During the Second World War, it provided transport, postal and courier services and carried VIPs, including Winston Churchill. Post-war it remained in the transport role, operating Douglas Dakotas, Avro Yorks and Lancastrians, Vickers Vallettas and then Handley Page Hastings' - the type I'd worked on at Scampton during its last six months in service.

In 1968, 24 moved to RAF Lyneham and converted to the C-130 Hercules.

The Squadron badge – on which it appears as XXIV Squadron – was granted by King George V in 1937. It bears an image of a blackcock, chosen for its speed, agility and ability to turn and fight. The motto, In Omnia Parati, translates as Ready For Anything, although the Squadron also had a more informal motto – Hit the Floor, It's 24.

Unlike most other units in the RAF at the time, Herc squadrons didn't have their own groundcrew and aircraft. Lyneham operated a system of centralized servicing, so crews merely signed out whichever aircraft they were allocated from a maximum of 35 CMk1s and 31 CMk3s - although on any given day, there tended to be significantly fewer. Some would be undergoing servicing in the hangars at Lyneham, others at the contractor, Marshall of Cambridge.

Financially, centralised servicing made sense. It saved on some duplication of posts, and it seemed to make no practical difference in terms of aircraft availability. But as an ex-tradesman, I think it greatly diminished the bond between aircrew and groundcrew. Even on a Vulcan squadron with hundreds of personnel, we had contact with the aircrew, not only before and after flight, but also at the odd beer call.

At Lyneham, I don't remember meeting the same

groundcrew on more than a handful of occasions. There was no social interaction and no real bond beyond the professional desire of both aircrew and groundcrew not to let anyone down. How you convince bean counters of the added value of close proximity and camaraderie is one of the dilemmas military leaders face. On the transport force at least, the financiers had won the argument.

24 and 30 Squadron aircrew each occupied half of a utilitarian single storey brick building with a flat roof of thick concrete slabs. A single wide corridor ran the entire length, doors to offices off to left and right. Halfway was the door to 30 Squadron, which my ex-Nimrod mate had joined.

I don't remember ever going through that door, and I rarely met him or any other 30 Squadron aircrew except down route, in happy hour or at functions in the Mess. And throughout my three and a half years at Lyneham, I remember only one visit to 47 or 70 Squadron on *the other side* of the airfield, and that was to see a member of my apprentice entry who was by then a captain on 47.

Even stranger perhaps, on a daily basis, I met few of the aircrew on my own squadron.

Fast jet squadrons tend to be small, about fifteen or sixteen pilots on a single-seat squadron, twice as many with the addition of navs on a two-seat unit. While this small group might attend briefings and plan sorties among aircrew from other squadrons in a separate ops block, between short training flights that invariably landed back at base, they'd spend their time together in their own squadron offices, often located along the side of a hangar that also accommodated *their* groundcrew and *their* aircraft. And if they went away from base on a domestic or overseas detachment, they invariably went as a squadron. They even tended to socialise as a squadron.

All this helped to form them into a tight knit band of

brothers.

The dynamic on the Herc force was different.

Even without our own groundcrew, we numbered about one hundred and thirty people on each squadron: twenty to twenty five on each of the captain, co, nav, air eng and loadie sections, a handful of flight commanders and ops clerks, and the CO and his PA. A fair proportion of the aircrew would always be flying, often on long routes thousands of miles from base. And while there might be room for those that were left to attend a specific briefing or training event in the crewroom, there just wasn't enough office space for most to hang around.

Apart from the executives – section leaders, flight commanders and the CO - the majority of us tended to spend our time at home, be that a private house off base, a married quarter or a room in the Sergeants' or Officers' Mess. Unless we were called in for some other reason, we usually only visited the Squadron offices to find out what we were doing next, be that a domestic or overseas route, training flight, simulator detail, standby duty, some form of ground training on base or a professional development course somewhere else.

Standby duties meant spending twenty four hours once or twice a month ready to fly unexpected tasks, anything from support to civil emergencies or terrorist incidents, to short notice troop or freight movements and medical evacuations. This could mean staying on base ready to move at a moment's notice when on Quick Reaction Alert, known as Q; or being prepared to take off within six hours as a member of one of two crews, known as 6A and 6B. There was also a Duty Working Crew who picked up any task that didn't fit into the other categories, such as air tests.

In the co-pilot's office, a large whiteboard divided into columns and rows filled one wall. Down the left hand side were our names and along the top about thirty days worth of dates. The resulting grid was filled with movable magnetic plaques detailing the various tasks each co-pilot had been chosen to undertake. Other boards detailed when we were due for specific training or tests, even when our inoculations were due or when our passports expired. We had two passports just in case we had to visit a country that denied entry to people with stamps from certain other countries, a particular problem in the Middle East.

The captains, navs, air enges and loadies all had similar boards in their offices.

When I visited the co's office, I might also nip into the squadron ops room to see the master-board, or the crewroom for a cup of coffee and a chat with whomever else happened to be about. Otherwise I'd be elsewhere, flying or preparing to fly.

Since Geraldine and I had moved into married quarters, the sight and sound of aircraft had made it all too plain that RAF Lyneham was a 24/7 operation. But in truth, the vast majority of take-offs and landings had occurred within daylight hours.

Now though, the Falklands War meant there was frenetic activity at all hours of the day and night.

In more normal times, I could have expected a fairly measured squadron arrival process, a few days of admin followed by the odd, well-spaced route, giving plenty of time for planning. I might even have had some dedicated co-pilot training flights leading to a squadron acceptance check, a chance for the squadron to see what they were getting. But with Op Corporate in full swing, life was too hectic for such niceties.

I joined the Squadron on Thursday 22nd April. I must have completed at least some arrival admin, but the next day was spent preparing for another Corporate sortie - as far as Gibraltar, via Edinburgh on the way out and back - leaving early Saturday morning. The captain was one of the squadron training captains, a tall, slim, fair-haired man in his mid-thirties. Patient and helpful, I grew to respect him greatly.

It turned out to be quite an introduction though.

About fifteen minutes into the flight to Edinburgh, a red light shone out on the overhead panel and an alarm sounded.

Fire in No 1 engine!

The captain initiated the engine fire drill, which included shutting down the outboard left engine and discharging its extinguisher system. The Herc carried no parachutes and getting on the ground before a fire destroyed the airframe or made it uncontrollable was a priority. So at the same time as we carried out the emergency drills, we commenced a descent toward the nearest suitable airfield.

Again, it's a cliché, but our training kicked in, even mine. In fact, as a recent graduate of the OCU, I'd probably carried out fire drills more recently than any of the rest of the crew, including one on my final test four days earlier. But I'd seen only one demonstration of an actual engine shutdown, so it was quite something to look out on a stationary prop, the leading edges of its four blades facing into the airflow to reduce drag.

With the immediate drills complete, we discussed what to do next. As it turned out, there were no signs of fire, either through the window, or on the instruments. So the captain elected to return to Lyneham. I made the necessary radio calls and we landed thirty minutes after take-off, to be met and escorted to dispersal by a handful of fire engines, foam cannons at the ready.

Excuse the pun, but despite the crew's assurances that this was an unusual occurrence, it seemed like a real baptism of fire.

While XV290 was inspected – it turned out to be a problem somewhere along the fifty five feet of firewire in and around the engine – we transferred to another aircraft, XV220, and headed for Edinburgh, where we picked up troops and equipment bound for one of the ships sailing from Gibraltar.

As we approached the Rock, it was clear that something had changed since my first visit two weeks earlier. Every building was adorned with red, white and blue bunting and Union Flags. Most impressive were the apartment blocks, tens, hundreds of windows alive with colour. Those that didn't have a Union Flag had painted the design on a bed sheet and hung that out.

If there'd ever been any doubt, the loyalty of the Gibraltarian people was now plain to see. I can honestly say that it brought a lump to my throat.

After all the initial excitement, and flags aside, it turned out to be a routine couple of days, if returning to Gibraltar in the right hand seat of a Herc could now be called routine. The captain let me fly the leg to Edinburgh and the return to Lyneham.

With a much lighter aircraft than on my first visit, even the take off from Gibraltar seemed no big deal.

We landed back at Lyneham late Sunday afternoon, at around the time the Argentinean forces on South Georgia surrendered to a small force of Royal Marines.

Less than twenty four hours later, presumably having found time to return one imprest and pick up another, check the route bags and do some route prep, I took off in the early afternoon of Monday 26th April on another trip to Ascension. In the captain's seat of XV305 was my flight commander, a larger than life, ruddy-faced, squadron leader with a reputation for blowing his top spectacularly.

It was another memorable route.

In the thirteen days since I'd last visited Ascension, individual ships and the carrier battle group of the Task Force had struck the Island a glancing blow on their way south, the majority on and around 18th April. But even before that, as soon as they'd come within helicopter range, the men and supplies we'd pre-positioned at Wideawake were being flown out to them. These ferry flights continued, not only as most of the ships anchored offshore, but also as they sailed away again toward the Falklands.

The Royal Marines even practised an amphibious assault, while troops from the other units also spent time ashore. Having spent days confined to marching round and round the flat decks of their ships, they took the opportunity to complete gruelling route marches all over Ascension's varied terrain, in high temperatures and full kit.

They'd already put a high premium on fitness, but it's said that this short period on Ascension was instrumental in preparing the British foot soldiers to cross the unforgiving terrain of East Falkland to Port Stanley. It also helped some survive injuries that may have killed lesser mortals. More of which later.

When the ships were out of helicopter range again on the voyage south, Hercs took over the re-supply task, dropping materials and sometimes men, but always mail, seen as vital to morale. Soon, the distances were such that drops could only be completed by Hercs hastily fitted with probes, their crews newly-trained in the art of air-to-air refuelling behind the Victor tankers. Initially, one refuelling slot was enough, but as the ships dispersed around the Falkland Islands, the missions became so long and complex that they relied on several Victors passing fuel between one another as well as the Hercs.

The longest Herc sortie on record over this period was twenty four hours forty five minutes. Once Nimrods were fitted with probes, they notched up sorties of similar length. One was flown by a man I worked alongside on my first instructor tour.

And of course, the whole shebang relied on the Victors, and more importantly, their crews, the Tanker Trash.

After a stopover and change of airframe in Dakar, we were approaching Wideawake in XV190 at about 8.30pm on 27th April when we picked out the lights of several ships, still anchored off Ascension or sailing away south. Closer still and we could see the blinking anti-collision and navigation lights of numerous helicopters. Some were flying loads out to the vessels, others returning to the Island, a process that continued for the rest of April and into May as more ships arrived, anchored briefly and then sailed on south.

It was quite a sight, as was the dispersal area.

On my last visit on 14th April, there'd been a Nimrod, a couple of Hercs and a few helicopters. Thirteen days later, even from a few miles out, I sensed that something remarkable had happened. Within a large area of pan and clinker illuminated by a myriad of bright lights were tens of aircraft.

Only when we taxied onto the dispersal did we realise just how many. It seemed as if half the RAF was represented. There were three Harriers and three Phantoms for Island defence – supported by a radar unit that had been placed on Green Mountain; three Nimrods for anti-submarine ops, maritime reconnaissance, surveillance and search and rescue; several Hercs, some now fitted with refuelling probes; a VC10, like us, visiting to deliver freight; and tens of helicopters: Chinooks, Sea Kings and Wessex.

There was also a United States Air Force Starlifter and, more surprisingly, a Short Belfast, a wide-bodied, four-prop, aircraft that had gone out of RAF service six years earlier.

The Belfast was in the livery of a company called HeavyLift. They were rumoured to have been going out of business before the Argentinean invasion. Now the need for an aircraft to fly outsize loads the RAF could no longer carry had revived their fortunes. On another occasion, I saw a United States Air Force C5 Galaxy, one of the largest aircraft ever built, and an indication of the overt and covert assistance we received from the US.

But by far the most impressive sight as we taxied in was the Victors. Fourteen ringed the western end of the dispersal area. Given the constraints of the runway, getting them in must have been quite a feat, but parking had also proved a challenge. Most were backed onto the clinker.

For a couple of days around 18th April, Wideawake was the busiest airfield in the world, with five hundred movements a day, more than airports like Chicago O'Hare and London Heathrow. And by the end of the Falklands Campaign in mid June, it had seen 2,500 fixed wing and 10,600 helicopter movements, not bad for an airfield licensed for two hundred and eighty five movements a year.

There was a palpable air of purpose and activity. The lights – portable masts with four powerful lamps and their own chugging generators – illuminated, not only the helicopters flying in and out, but also men and vehicles criss-crossing the pan and bustling about the resident aircraft. On the clinker just within the ring of lights stood tens of large tents, the new technical accommodation, and beyond them, hidden in the darkness, tents in which the majority of the 1,100 military personnel on the Island lived.

There wasn't much time to stand and stare. They wanted us gone. By the time we'd updated our met forecast and done our planning, the aircraft had been unloaded, so we started up, taxied onto the runway and took off again at about 9.30pm.

We'd been welcomed to the Island by the same American I'd heard on my first visit. He also bade us farewell. I couldn't help thinking he sounded a bit less chirpy this time, and he no longer said, *y'all come back and see us now* as we headed north. After all, nothing was more certain.

After a flight of four and half hours we landed at Dakar in

the early hours.

I'd wondered if I'd see my flight commander live up to his fiery reputation. But not on this route. It had run so smoothly that he remained fairly placid. He'd hogged the flying though, granting me only the final leg as operating pilot.

I discovered that some captains did this. In this case, it was because he was a squadron executive and tended to spend more time in his office than the cockpit. So, when he did fly a route, he needed all the operating time he could get to maintain his skill levels.

Other captains might monopolise the flying for a variety of reasons. Some were just selfish, stealing all the best legs for themselves. Some sought to dominate the crew, and especially the co-pilot, part of which was achieved by hogging the flying. And some seemed to lack confidence, so just in case their co-pilot put them in a difficult situation, they flew any legs they thought might prove tricky.

Flying too often with any of these characters could hamper a co-pilot's development. Generally, I was lucky in this regard. Others were not so fortunate.

My last memory of this route was approaching Lands End in XV300 just before midnight on the 28th. It was one of those beautifully clear nights when the coastlines of southern England and south Wales were etched in pinpricks of light, and every major road and settlement as far as the Midlands shone out.

I found it quite emotional, another pinch-me moment.

With minimum time on the ground and no need to go to Gibraltar, we were home just into the first hour of Thursday 29th, having flown eleven hours forty minutes in daylight and fourteen hours fifty minutes by night. We'd been away little more than forty eight hours.

THE PACE CONTINUES

The next day, Friday, I had a two-hour simulator sortie to practise emergencies, and in the late afternoon of Saturday 1st May, flew to RAF Waddington, the home of the Vulcan bomber force. There, XV187 was loaded with men and material bound for Ascension. We took off in the dark for a return to Lyneham.

Until that day, I don't think many people had any inkling that Vulcans were to play a part in the war. They were due to be retired in July and as far as the South Atlantic was concerned, they seemed to have been well and truly upstaged by their V-bomber cousins, the Victors from RAF Marham.

But on the evening of 29th April, a little less than 48 hours after I'd visited Ascension for the second time, two Vulcans landed there, giving those responsible for allocating parking slots another headache. And a little more than 24 hours after that, one of them - XV607 - completed one of the most audacious and demanding bombing raids ever undertaken, before or since.

Like most of the world, I found out over breakfast that Saturday morning, in my case from The Today Programme on BBC Radio 4, which informed me that a Vulcan had attacked Port Stanley airfield.

I don't intend to go into details of the Black Buck raids. The full story is related brilliantly in Rowland White's book, Vulcan 607. But in brief, to get a Vulcan to Stanley and back required a minimum of eleven Victors plus a Nimrod for search and rescue cover.

To give a margin for unserviceability, two Vulcans and thirteen Victor tankers took off from Wideawake late on Friday 30th April. The mission plan was immensely complicated, requiring a succession of fuel transfers from Victor to Victor and Victor to Vulcan until one Vulcan was left to fly on to Stanley, drop its bombs and take fuel from another Victor on the way back, a return journey of nearly 8,000 miles.

Soon after take-off, the first choice Vulcan became unserviceable and returned to Ascension, leaving the reserve and its crew to take over. Later, a couple of Victors also had to pull out, so the formation was down to the minimum required for completion of the mission.

Over the course of the night, one and a half million pounds of aviation fuel were passed during nineteen air-to-air refuelling operations, five of them Victor to Vulcan, often in foul weather. As they flew south, they were all burning far more fuel than expected. To keep the mission on track, several Victors gave away so much fuel they jeopardised their return to Ascension. Even then, the Vulcan remained low on fuel. Disaster was only averted when additional tankers were launched from Ascension to meet the returning jets.

Despite all these dramas, using bombing kit developed from and little better than that used in the Lancaster during the Second World War, the Vulcan crew managed to drop twenty one 1,000 pound bombs across Port Stanley airfield. One smashed into the runway roughly two thirds along, leaving a crater one hundred and fifteen feet across and eighty four feet deep.

The raid made the Argentineans so fearful of Vulcan attacks on their mainland that they withdrew fighter cover from the Falklands for the duration of the campaign. And although the damage to the runway was repaired, the surface remained so unstable that it couldn't be used by fast jets. These were forced to carry their bombs and sea-skimming missiles from the mainland, limiting their time over the Islands and the seas surrounding it. Had they been able to fly from Stanley, their effect on the Task Force and its ships could have been even more devastating than it was.

As an aside, the final Victor, which was also a reserve, had given away so much fuel that its crew were resigned to ditching in the sea well before Ascension. They'd performed minor miracles and shown great bravery throughout, and they all received awards, including the co-pilot, who received a Queen's Commendation for Valuable Service in the Air.

Seven years later, I was on the staff of the Central Flying School when he was training to become a Bulldog flying instructor. During the flying phase of the course, I was his instructor and we flew together twenty times. As a sign of his modesty, I don't think he ever mentioned his involvement in the Black Buck raids. I only found out when I read Vulcan 607 a few years later.

Back at Lyneham, it was decided that given the pace of events, it would ease the programming task if the same five people flew together on every mission as constituted crews, much like other multi-engine fleets.

I've already said that constituted crews had their good and bad points. For co-pilots specifically, being crewed with a good captain could be a boon, while ending up with a bad one could be a disaster. When I saw the crew I was to join, my heart sank. The names of the air eng and loadmaster meant nothing to me, but I recognised the other two.

The captain had been a qualified flying instructor at Linton. He hadn't been on my squadron, but I had a clear picture of a slim man of medium height in his mid to late 30s with jet black hair and a very loud voice. He'd been known for an abrasive manner and a cruel line in banter, invariably directed toward students.

My co-leader confirmed that this captain still had a reputation for being hard on some individuals, especially his co-pilots. Apparently, the only way to get him to back off was to stand up to him.

I could also picture the nav, another slim man in his early

30s, but with slightly receding sandy hair. He'd been Linton's combat survival and rescue instructor, in which capacity he'd supervised our dinghy drills and survival exercises. Perhaps it's unfair to base an opinion on someone you only see when you're wet and cold, but he seemed to take great pleasure in our discomfort, while also being quick to ridicule and chastise.

Since arriving at Lyneham, I was still nervous before flights, but not in the way I had been at Linton and, to a lesser extent, Finningley. Now I was worried that joining a crew with these two characters could lead to a downward spiral, even a return to those dark days. But happily, I discovered that although both could be sarcastic and unsympathetic, they could also be understanding and helpful.

And I don't remember having to *stand up to* my new captain. We just seemed to get on, even on occasions when I did, through inexperience and deficiencies in skill, manage to make a fool of myself. His criticism was robust, but both he and the nav seemed keen to push me toward greater knowledge and skill in a constructive rather than destructive manner.

The other two on my allocated crew were just fantastic. The air eng, a tall, dark haired sergeant in his mid to late 20s, was fairly new to the Squadron, but was building a solid reputation as a good engineer and crew member; while the loadie, a master aircrew of medium height and build in his early fifties, was a man of vast experience, skill and integrity.

All four were also good fun and I had some of my best moments on the Herc force – of my life - in their company. At the time, this element seemed the most important, but of course their positive effect on my early development as a co-pilot was also vital, not least because, in a top pocket of my flying suit, I carried a tiny blue hardback book, the 38 Group RAF Transport Aircraft Aircrew Categorisation Card. I still have it.

The Cat Card provides a record of my proficiency in four areas: Basic Handling, Operating, Route Flying and Operational Efficiency. The categories awarded could be anything from A, walks on water, to E, below the standard required, effectively a fail.

Like the vast majority of those fresh from flying training, I came out of the OCU as a D in all four categories. If things went to plan, I'd have a chance to confirm or upgrade my Basic and Operating cats during Periodic Refresher Training on the OCU six months after joining 24, and annually thereafter. The timelines for changes of my Route Cat were more ad hoc, but usually wouldn't be too far out of step with the other two.

The final cat, for Operational Efficiency, was awarded by the Squadron and was a rough amalgam of the other three, although not an average. Someone with three Bs could be seen by the squadron as operating below that level and merit only a C overall, whereas someone with a C in one or more of the other categories could be awarded a B Cat. My ambition at the outset of any test was to avoid making such a mess of things that I dropped to an E Cat.

There were some notorious examples of this, including one where a co-pilot flying down the west coast of Italy was asked by his route-checker, a blunt Yorkshireman, where he'd divert if there was a catastrophic problem with the aircraft. He looked at the map on his knee, panicked and spouted the first place name he saw.

'Ponza.'

The route checker drew himself up and, in a thick Yorkshire accent, bellowed, 'Fuckin' Ponza! Fuckin' E Cat!'

Unfortunately, Ponza has no airport.

Achieving success was much easier if you completed your training on time, if your day to day flying comprised mainly busy European routes relevant to the testing regime, and if the majority of the captains you flew with set a good example.

I suffered from delays to my training and a small amount from the time I spent in the South Atlantic, especially later in my tour. But some of my contemporaries were unlucky on all counts, missing training, spending months in the South Atlantic, and ending up with captains that gave them little flying, set a bad example from which they learnt little beyond bad habits, and made their lives a misery.

Crew categories were far from my mind, though, when I set out on another Ascension route with my new crew.

On Sunday 2nd May - the evening after my trip to Waddington – we were allocated another extremely heavy aircraft that would necessitate a jink into Gibraltar. The nature of the load meant there was some doubt as to its exact weight. Potentially, it exceeded 165,000lbs. When I climbed the crew steps of XV305 and looked to my right, I could see why.

At the front of the freight bay sat a lorry, or, to be more precise, a fuel tanker. What we called a bowser. Behind it were sundry items of kit, once again stacked floor to ceiling. And although some if not all the freight was classified as dangerous air cargo and would normally preclude the carriage of passengers, the odd body was sitting in the shadow of the load.

Just like my first experience of a heavyweight take-off from Lyneham three weeks earlier, when the captain opened the throttles, the acceleration was sluggish and we ate up much more runway than usual before we lurched into the air. I'd brought up the gear and flaps and we'd established in the climb when he announced that he'd seen the Station Commander standing next to his car on the taxyway adjacent to the far end of the runway.

'Do you think he came out to see if we made it into the air?' he mused aloud.

'Not sure why else he'd be there at seven o'clock on a Sunday night,' the nav replied, adding, 'probably wanted to make sure he didn't have to chair the subsequent board of inquiry.'

The same sentiment was voiced whenever a group of aviators gathered to watch anything involving risk. If you witnessed a crash you could only be a witness at the board of inquiry, not a member or chairman of the board.

Of course, it was more likely the Station Commander was

visiting one of the sections on the other side of the runway than trying to side-step a board of inquiry. Whatever the reason, we laughed at the nav's analysis.

We coasted out and flew across the Bay of Biscay in daylight, but the sun dropped below the horizon as we carried on south and east around the Iberian Peninsula. I sat back to enjoy the lights along the Portuguese and north African coasts, followed by those ringing the Bay of Gibraltar. The night approach over the sea to the runway beneath the vast bulk of the Rock was another spectacular experience.

We were scheduled for a night-stop and it would have been nice to pop out for a meal and a drink. But it was past midnight when we arrived at the Officers' Mess, so, after a quick beer, it was off to bed.

Unbeknown to us, a few hours earlier, the Royal Navy Submarine, HMS Conqueror, had sunk the Argentinean cruiser, General Belgrano, with the loss of three hundred and sixty eight lives.

When we heard about it the next day we were cock-a-hoop. I doubt whether the number of deaths would have been known at that stage, but harsh as it sounds now, I also doubt we'd have been too perturbed if we'd heard that the entire ships' complement of more than a thousand had died.

The overwhelming sentiment was that *they shouldn't have started it.*

And as to subsequent arguments about whether the ship was sailing within, outside, toward or away from the Total Exclusion Zone around the Falklands, we didn't care. The Belgrano was a threat to British servicemen and was therefore a *legitimate* target. I believe it to this day, although I find the loss of life more regrettable than I did at the time.

Whatever the morality of the Vulcan and Conqueror attacks on 1st and 2nd of May, two swift blows had greatly reduced the effectiveness of the Argentinean air force and caused its navy to head for port, never to return to the fight. They'd also provided a tremendous psychological blow, not only to the Argentinean leaders and people, but to the young conscripts preparing to defend the Islands. Already suffering through poor leadership and lack of supplies, they now knew they'd have to fight a determined and ruthless enemy.

The next day, Monday 3rd May, we wandered Gibraltar town until it was time to return to the Mess and prepare for another night leg to Dakar. Flags and bunting still fluttered from every building.

My third heavyweight take-off from Gibraltar was more dramatic than the others. The darkness seemed to mask what acceleration there was and, once again, it felt as if we were barely airborne by the time we lurched into the black void beyond the runway lights. I wouldn't have been surprised to hear that our wheels had skimmed the water before we climbed away.

After a flight to Dakar of six hours twenty five minutes, we left XX305 and its fuel tanker to be taken to Ascension by another crew, and spent what was left of the night and most of the next morning in and around the N'Gor hotel.

On a personal level, the next day, Tuesday 4th May, was memorable for several reasons, starting with the ferocity of the afternoon storms on the ITCZ. Flying XV213, this was the day we had to deviate one hundred and ninety miles from track to find a way through cumulonimbus clouds towering tens of thousands of feet above us, their dark interiors lit by frequent flashes of lightning.

But as we were doing that, more than 4,000 miles to the south-west, an event of much greater importance was taking place.

At about 11am, HMS Sheffield was hit by an Exocet Missile off the Falklands. It snuffed out twenty lives and left twenty six wounded. After four hours trying to save the destroyer from the resulting fire, the captain gave the order to abandon ship. She didn't actually sink until six days later, during attempts to tow her to South Georgia, becoming the first British warship to be lost to enemy action since the Second World War.

If there'd been any complacency in our minds, or among the general public, this event swept it away. Both sides now knew how serious and capable their opposition was.

Twelve years later, at a drinks party in Whitehall, I met and chatted with Commodore Sam Salt, the captain of Sheffield on that fateful day. Even in the short time we had together, it became apparent that it was the defining moment of his life, and that he still felt the loss of his ship and its crew members very deeply.

I'm not sure exactly how and when we would have heard news of the action, maybe on the BBC World Service during the flight back to Dakar later in the day.

We often tuned one of the HF radios in to the BBC, and to this day, nearly forty years later, the sound of the tune, Lilliburlero, can take me back to the flight deck during long sorties over the South Atlantic. Following the words, *This is London*, it was played before the World Service's news bulletins.

Most often, these bulletins were the means by which we found out how the war was going, for good or ill. And sometimes we were amazed at the speed with which the MOD and/or the media broadcast to the world what seemed to us to be quite sensitive military stories. For instance, they trumpeted the success of the first Black Buck raid while several of the aircraft were still struggling to make a safe return to Ascension. And once Argentinean aircraft started to bomb our ships, they let slip that many bombs were failing to explode because they were being released too low.

A free press is one thing, but sometimes, as in this latter instance, we couldn't help thinking British lives were being jeopardised in support of the principle.

Back on the personal scale, my strongest memory that day is not of performing my first landing on Ascension, but of seeing

Vulcan XM607 taxying in following the second Black Buck raid on Port Stanley airfield.

It had missed the runway but destroyed facilities and aircraft, killed several Argentineans and sent another very strong message of British resolve.

It was almost exactly three years since I'd left Scampton after two years working on these aircraft, beetling away, spanner in hand, on their airframes and engines. Seeing one under these circumstances was quite emotional. Later, I found the time to go and stand in the shade of its delta wings and talk to the groundcrew. The Olympus engines were ticking, components still cooling after their 8,000 mile mission. The Vulcan had always looked menacing, capable of anything that was asked of it. But it had to wait until the very end of its career to prove it.

The next two Black Buck missions were cancelled because of bad weather and Victor problems respectively, but three others went ahead, one more on the facilities at Stanley airfield, and two against the air defence radars there.

It was quite a last hurrah.

The retirement of the Vulcan bomber force was delayed, but only until December of that year, by which time six had been converted to the tanker role. These remained in service until March 1984. During their final few months, I'd be lucky enough to see them up close and personal when taking fuel in the skies around the UK and Ascension.

Following another night-stop in Dakar, we arrived back at Lyneham in the early hours of Friday 7th May, having flown twenty eight hours fifty minutes over the course of the two and a half days we'd been away.

My next route was on Sunday. I assume I picked up an imprest and checked the route bags on Friday afternoon, because on the Saturday we went to the christening of a nephew in Shropshire. It was the day the Task Force had sailed so far south that Hercs from Ascension had to commence air-to-air refuelling to deliver supplies and mail.

About 6am on Sunday 9th May, I was back in flight planning for a day route comprising four legs: Lyneham-Antwerp; Antwerp-RAF Gütersloh, the Harrier and helicopter base near the East German border; Gütersloh-Brussels and Brussels-Lyneham.

Each leg was relatively short, but busy, great training for a new co-pilot. Over the course of the day I had to file four flight plans, communicate with domestic, foreign, military and civilian air traffic control agencies and fly the approaches and landings at Gütersloh and Brussels, a busy international airport.

That evening, after three hours thirty minutes in the air, and a crew duty day of about ten hours, I returned to our married quarter.

CYPRUS

While Geraldine was at work the next day, Monday 10th, I picked up an imprest, checked the route bags and planned for another European route, this time over three days. The farthest point was RAF Akrotiri on the island of Cyprus.

Sitting in a strategic position at the eastern end of the Mediterranean south of Asia Minor, north of Egypt and the Suez Canal, and just one hundred and sixty five miles east of Lebanon and the Middle East, Cyprus has, at one time or another, been occupied by most of the great civilizations and empires. It came into the British sphere of influence at the end of the 19th Century, but gained its independence in 1960.

Four fifths of the population are of Greek origin, and one fifth of Turkish descent. Nevertheless, Turkey claims the whole Island as part of Anatolian Turkey. The resulting tension between the two communities worsened after independence when the new government sought closer ties with Greece. Things came to a head in 1974, when the Turks invaded and seized a large part of the north of the Island.

I was undergoing apprentice training at RAF Halton at the time and, in a display of teenage naivety, was one of several who volunteered for sniper duties with the British forces on the Island. Our only qualification, marksman badges earned firing Self Loading Rifles on a twenty five yard range. I don't remember anyone laughing uproariously, but neither do I remember anyone praising us for our bravery. Thankfully for all concerned, we heard no more about it.

In 2022, despite on-going international condemnation, Turkish forces continue to occupy northern Cyprus. The Turkish and Greek areas are separated by a Green Line buffer zone monitored by the UN.

In 1982, the south of the Island still hosted a number of British military bases, including two Army garrisons and a large RAF station, Akrotiri, the airhead for forces on the Island, and a staging post for British units deploying to East Africa, the Middle East, South Asia and the Far East. It also hosted frequent detachments by air defence Lightning and Phantom squadrons taking advantage of the good weather and uncluttered airspace to practise air-to-air combat and live missile firing. The weather also attracted the Red Arrows for a month in the spring of each year to complete their winter training in preparation for the new display season.

As a result of all this activity, Herc aircrew could expect to fly to Cyprus at least once every three months or so. Conforming to that pattern, I visited twelve times in my three years on the front line. It was a popular destination, although one of its major attractions arose out of a significant debit point.

To reduce the numbers of personnel having to work in the full heat of the afternoon sun, Akrotiri airfield was open for visitors only between six in the morning and one in the afternoon, although they liked us to arrive between 7.00 and 9.00am Cyprus time (GMT +2). So, as the 2,000-mile flight to Cyprus took about six and a half hours, we generally departed Lyneham shortly after midnight UK time and flew through the night.

Once we arrived though, because we didn't have enough crew duty hours to swop loads and fly straight back to the UK, we were guaranteed a night-stop, and a relatively civilised departure time the next morning. A rare luxury.

Of course, if you had to drop into somewhere else on the way to Akrotiri, the start time at Lyneham tended to be that much earlier, making for a long night on the flight deck.

We were supporting a Phantom detachment, so our trip in XV207 on 10th May included an interim stop at RAF Wildenrath, the fighter base on the Dutch/German border. As a result, I left the house for flight planning a couple of hours after Geraldine arrived home from work.

Given the preparations I'd had to undertake during the day, I doubt very much whether I'd had ten hours rest before entering flight planning at about 8.00pm. I probably had a go at nabbing some sleep, but while others may be able to nap at will, I discovered that I couldn't. So, setting out for most night departures, I probably wouldn't have slept since the night before. It was just the way it was.

That Monday, much of the one and a quarter hour flight to Wildenrath was in the dark, as were the first few hours of the leg to Akrotiri, by which time it was early Tuesday morning. I was the operating pilot and our track took us south over Germany, the Swiss Alps and northern Italy, then down the Italian west coast. Between discussions on the flight deck, I enjoyed watching the lights of the coastal cities and, out to my right, the islands, including Corsica, Sardinia and Sicily.

Even when such flights became routine, I was still too keyed up to nod off, as some of my fellow crewmates were prone to do. But as we turned onto an easterly heading over the town of Crotone on the instep of the boot of Italy, even I shut my eyes tightly, although for a reason other than tiredness.

The Crotone Death Ray!

No matter what time we left Lyneham, the turn over Crotone invariably pointed us at the sun just as it rose above the horizon like the brightest of theatrical spotlights. Sunglasses did little to diminish its intensity, and as I blinked under its onslaught, my eyelids felt as if they were coated with sandpaper.

This may seem a cruel way to describe one of the most beautiful of nature's wonders, but for those first few minutes heading out over the Mediterranean from Crotone, the sunrise could be an exquisite form of torture. Of course, as it rose higher and moved round to the south, it became a great reviver, bathing the flight deck in softer tones.

It also illuminated the wonders of the Mediterranean.

Our initial track took us to the south of Corfu, a beautiful island sitting a few miles off the coast of Albania. While admiring the scenery, we had to be on the alert for a Cold War ruse known as *meaconing*, that is, shifting the apparent position of a navigation beacon to lure aircraft off course and over an unscrupulous rival's territory.

The resulting violation of national airspace could be used as a pretext for anything from intercepting the target aircraft and forcing it to land for ransom or propaganda purposes, to, at the more extreme end of the spectrum, shooting it down or using its incursion as an excuse for military action against a neighbour.

Perhaps the most famous instance of meaconing was in 1983, when Korean Air Fight 007 flying from New York to Seoul via Alaska was shot down by a Soviet fighter over Sakhalin Island to the north of Japan, with the loss of two hundred and sixty nine passengers and crew. Prior to the firing of the fatal missiles, the crew of the 747 had either made a catastrophic navigational error or, more likely, been lured into a prohibited area above the Kamchatka Peninsula by a rogue beacon. Twenty minutes later, they were shot down when briefly transiting Soviet airspace for a second time over Sakhalin. After initially denying responsibility, the Soviets alleged Flight 007 had been targeted because it was on a spying mission.

Well, the Albanians had been known to try meaconing, so while heading past Corfu, we, and especially the navigator, had to ensure we weren't tricked into entering Albanian airspace. We thought it unlikely we'd be shot down, but we didn't want to be responsible for handing the Communist regime of Enva Hoxha a propaganda coup. That would have been very embarrassing.

Further south and east over the Mediterranean, as the captain made the radio calls and checked the weather, I revelled in the views of a turquoise sea and rocky islands dotted with white villages.

Our track took us southeast across the Peloponnese to the south of the Greek mainland, then over islands such as Milos and, my favourite, Santorini, all-too-easy to identify as the caldera of a gigantic volcano. Its eruption in 1600BC had devastated the Minoan civilization, not only on the Island, but also in the coastal settlements on Crete, 60 miles to the south.

Beyond Santorini, we passed over the Dodecanese Islands, including Rhodes, before flying the final two hundred miles over the sea to the south of the Anatolian coast of Turkey.

On a clear day, Cyprus could be picked out not long after it appeared on the radar. As we approached, I began a descent that took us round the rugged south coast in sight of the evocatively named Mount Olympus, on which there was an RAF radar installation.

RAF Akrotiri sat between two bays on a flat stubby peninsula at the southernmost tip of the Island. Its 9,000 foot runway was easy to spot, almost bisecting the peninsula to the south of a large saltwater lake. We approached it over the deep blue waters of Episkopi Bay, Akrotiri Bay shimmering beyond, the resort of Limassol flanking its northern shore. As far as I remember, I pulled off another unremarkable landing.

My first impression as I stepped from the aircraft and looked around me was that Cyprus was hot and dusty.

With variations, I'd had the same first impression of most of the places I'd visited in the preceding weeks. Perhaps that's not so surprising though. All of my early life had been spent in the UK, with a yearly day trip to Borth on the west coast of Wales. The highest temperatures I'd experienced were during the heat wave of 1976, but they'd been little warmer than the norm in Dakar, Ascension, Decimomannu and Akrotiri; while the harsh landscape in those places was nothing like the luscious greens of Shropshire, mid-Wales and the English counties I'd lived in as an airman and trainee pilot.

That doesn't mean I wasn't appreciative of the rugged beauty of each new location. On the contrary, I was smitten with each and every one. They were just way outside anything I'd experienced up to this point in my life.

Anyway, Cyprus was certainly hot, dusty and rugged.

The look and feel of RAF Akrotiri was such that it could have been constructed in the UK and dropped fully formed at the eastern end of the Mediterranean. We were generally accommodated on base, not in the standard-pattern Officers' Mess, but in one of several red-brick barrack blocks – usually Block 101 - of exactly the same design as Cheshire Block, where I'd lived during my two and half years at Scampton. At least the block in Cyprus comprised mainly single rooms.

Having dumped our bags, we'd settle on white plastic chairs at the back of the building, look out at the blue skies and scrubby ground and drink wind-down beers – Keo, in large brown bottles. It may seem strange that anyone should settle down to drink beer at 10.00am, but for us it was the end of a long working day. We did the same everywhere we went, whatever the hour, except when we arrived back at Lyneham, although even there, some went to the bar if it was open.

And if the length of our stay and the local time of day permitted, after freshening up, we'd go for a meal, accompanied by more beer and/or wine. I'm fairly confident in saying *we*, because I struggle to remember anyone who didn't conform to this pattern of alcohol consumption. People may have drunk different amounts, but pretty much everyone drank.

Once again, I was an enthusiastic supporter of this culture, and remained so for the rest of my career. I doubt there was a week over the next twenty three years when I didn't drink significantly more than the maximum recommended weekly alcohol intake.

I'm not saying it was big or clever. It was just the way it was for me and others like me. Our only constraint was a regulation forbidding the consumption of alcohol within ten hours of our next flight. All very well, but even if I didn't realise it at the time, I now know that ten hours wouldn't have been long enough for the alcohol to clear the systems of the heaviest drinkers, who would undoubtedly have been caught out by the random breath and blood tests introduced in the late Noughties. By this time, though, societal changes meant many aircrew had already begun to moderate their consumption.

For my generation, a few drinks seemed to add to the ambience of occasions like that morning in Cyprus. Vocal cords lubricated, we'd sit around and exchange advice, stories, jokes and banter. Given my limited time on the front line, I'm not sure I'd have had that much to offer. The rest of my crew, on the other hand, had all travelled the world and were a fund of information and amusing anecdotes.

One of the loadie's stories has stayed with me in a way many others haven't.

His first tour in the early 1950s was as an airman in Malta. For young men like him, one of the main attractions of the Island's capital, Valletta, was The Gut, an area of bars, clubs and – at that time – brothels. They all used to visit the bars and clubs, but our loadie told the story of *a friend's* first visit to one of the brothels.

He arrived behind a Maltese man riding a push-bike, bicycle clips round the bottoms of his suit trouser legs to stop them flapping against the machine's oily chain. The man leaned his bike against the wall, and the loadie's friend followed him inside, finding himself in something akin to a dentist's waiting room, chairs spaced around whitewashed walls. After a few minutes, a woman descended the stairs.

Following a brief exchange to decide who was at the front of the queue, the man in the suit followed her up. Other local men appeared and sat. While the airman blushed and avoided eye contact, the newcomers seemed unperturbed, either at being seen in a brothel, or at the sounds wafting down from the floor above.

When, after several minutes, the man in the suit descended the stairs again, he still had the bicycle clips round the bottom of his trousers!

I – we – would spend the majority of the time laughing at such anecdotes. It was another reason sight-seeing sometimes fell by the wayside. It was all too tempting to crack open another beer and carry on with the stories.

Great times.

On the morning of 11th May, I limited myself to a couple of beers. While some of the others settled down to sunbathe and carry on drinking, I went to my room to prepare for the next day's flying before trying to catch up on some sleep. In the end, I did little more than doze fitfully, defeated by a combination of a baking hot room with thin, ill-fitting, curtains and echoing footfalls, voices and slamming doors, plus the scream of jets taking off or returning to land.

I also spent time wondering why the rest were so looking forward to that evening. We were going *for a kebab*. Perhaps there was something magical about what I pictured as nothing more than a few cubes of meat on a skewer, but if there was, I was blowed if I knew what it was.

In the early evening, after meeting behind the Block for another beer, we took a taxi to a small, unassuming, taverna-style restaurant just outside the station: Chris's. The eponymous owner greeted us with a smile and led us into a large room with closely packed tables draped in thin plastic and laid out for parties of anything from two to twenty.

About half the tables were occupied, and the room was alive with animated chatter and laughter. All the diners seemed to be British servicemen. I was told it was far too early for the locals. They probably wouldn't arrive until after we'd left, at about the time more well-lubricated Brits would begin to appear after a night in the clubs and bars of Limassol. As we sat, my companions exchanged greetings with some of those on other tables.

The owner stood over us, waiting patiently, and the captain asked, 'Red, white or beer?' Noting the hands raised for each selection, he then said, 'Full kebab, two Kokkanelli, a Pandemonium, a Keo and a Sprite.'

It seemed that you could have either a half or a full kebab, although why anyone would want half a skewer of meat was another mystery. Kokkanelli was the local red wine, Pandemonium – actually Panteleimon – the local white. Among the many things I discovered later was that other wines were available, but at extra cost, whereas the ones we'd ordered came free with the meal. The Sprite was for anyone who wanted to take the edge off the Kokkanelli.

Kokkanelli was an acquired taste. Strong and acidic and said to contain any number of poisons, it had a fearsome reputation and was one of several wines affectionately known as Chateau Brain Damage. Well, despite that, I liked it, or should that be, I liked it when I drank it with a kebab in Cyprus. On the few occasions I was tempted to buy a bottle and return it to the UK, it seemed barely drinkable, as if it had become rancid sometime during the flight.

Several years after we left Lyneham, Geraldine and I ate at a Greek restaurant in St Ives, Cambridgeshire. To my delight, Kokkanelli appeared on the wine list. When I ordered a bottle, the waiter looked taken aback, as if he'd forgotten they sold it.

'Would you like that chilled or at room temperature?' he asked.

At the time, I'd never heard of chilling red wine, so I went with room temperature. When the waiter returned I asked why he'd given us a choice.

'Because,' he said, as if addressing an ignoramus, 'drunk at room temperature, Kokkanelli has the strength of whisky.'

Perhaps that explained the wine's fearsome reputation. And if true, during my twelve visits to Cyprus, I'd drunk a heck of a lot of whisky.

The wine in the St Ives restaurant had travelled well and was very enjoyable. It also came in a bottle with a smart label and a plastic seal encasing a well-fitted cork. In Chris's and similar establishments on Cyprus, if not already opened, the bottles would have no more than a cork stopper with a red or blue plastic cap. And if they bore a label, it was invariably streaked with wine, as if the bottle had been filled from a container round the back of the restaurant, which of course it had. Vintages of Kokkanelli and Pandemonium were measured in days or weeks rather than years.

I watched in surprise as some poured Sprite into their Kokkanelli. Apparently it took the edge off the strength and the bitter taste, but my one and only sip of the result convinced me to continue drinking my wine *neat*, whatever the risks.

Given my previous scepticism about what might be on offer in terms of food, when the kebabs arrived, I was impressed. As well as the skewers of lamb, the waiters had filled our table with bowls of mixed salad, plates of pitta bread, saucers of olives and dish upon dish of dips of various textures and colours.

All bar the salad were new to me. Nonetheless, having eaten nothing more than a few salted peanuts with my beer that morning, I dug in with gusto, selecting a kebab for my own plate, which I went on to pile with salad, slices of pitta and spoonfuls of the really, really, tasty dips. The others looked on, smiling and nodding as I returned for second and third helpings of the trimmings. I noticed they were eating far less, but more fool them.

As everyone finished their kebab, I was pleasantly stuffed, with just enough room for dessert, if that was part of the deal. Then a couple of waiters appeared and laid down another plate, this one holding six long skinless *sausages*, known affectionately as horses' willies. I raised my eyebrows in surprise and there were peals of laughter.

Learning the true nature of a Cyprus kebab was another rite

of passage, an introduction to one of the most enjoyable facets of life down route.

On that first occasion, I managed to no more than pick at the remaining courses, watching in amazement as signature dish after signature dish arrived and the salad, dips and wine were replenished at regular intervals. I'd blown it on this occasion, but on subsequent visits, I too would learn to pace myself.

Just as well, because with minor variations, a full meze at Chris's comprised kebabs of lamb, pork and sausage; then Loukanika – Cypriot sausage; Keftedes – Greek meatballs; Sheftalia – sausage shaped meatballs; Loutza – pork fillet in red wine; pork chop; grilled fish; grilled halloumi; feta; and Dolmades – vine leaves stuffed with mince meat and rice. The accompanying dips included: Tahini – a creamy sesame paste; Tallatouri – yoghurt flavoured with mint, cucumber and garlic; Taramosalata – creamy fish roe with lemon juice, chopped parsley and onion; and Hummus, which seemed to come in endless varieties.

At the end of the meal, there was never any discussion or argument over the bill. Including a generous tip, it would amount to no more than about four or five Cypriot pounds per head, about seven or eight pounds Sterling. Whatever the cost, it was tremendous value for money, especially as the bill was accompanied by complimentary glasses of Cypriot brandy, ouzo or Filfar, an orange liqueur.

I'd discovered that the Cyprus kebab was a feast rather than just a meal. And it was invariably accompanied with lashings of laughter, perhaps the most important ingredient. I consumed it with relish on every subsequent visit to the Island.

The next day was meant to see us return some of the Phantom detachment to RAF Wildenrath, pick up freight and personnel from RAF Gutersloh, the Harrier base further to the east, and drop into RAF Northolt, the home of the Queen's Flight in northeast London, before returning to Lyneham.

But that morning, a Phantom en-route to Cyprus had developed a problem and diverted into Brindisi, a joint military/civilian airfield halfway up the eastern coast of the heel of Italy. In a quick change of plan, it was decided that we'd land there on the way past and deposit some ground tradesmen. If they could fix the broken jet, or start fixing it pending the arrival of more manpower and spares, we'd leave them to get on with it. If there was nothing they could do, they'd re-board and we'd take them on to Wildenrath, from where another team would be sent out. Either way, we didn't expect be on the ground for more than about forty five minutes.

The captain flew us across the Med to Brindisi, landed and taxied over to the military site, where we parked on a large pan next to the Phantom, its pilot and navigator and a few Italian Air Force personnel. The engineers disembarked with their kit and, while we stretched our legs, they spoke to the Phantom aircrew and took off a few panels.

They were confident they could fix the jet, but less sure how long it would take, so we started up and left. As an ex-tradesman, I couldn't help wondering how long they'd take to repair the defect and how and when they'd get back to base when they had. But as was often the case, I never found out.

I flew the leg to Wildenrath and then to Gutersloh, where the captain took over again to fly us to Northolt and Lyneham. It was a busy day of high training value, with plenty of flight planning, radio work and short flights with little time between take off and landing. Overall, we were airborne for eight hours and thirty five minutes, but I should imagine that meant a thirteen or fourteen-hour crew duty day, maybe more.

The highlight for me was flying low over Central London during the approach to Northolt. Seeing so many familiar landmarks laid out no more than a few thousand feet below was another wonderful experience. And once again, when I walked in the door of 86 Eider Avenue at about 9.30 that Wednesday night, so much had happened it was hard to believe I'd been away no more than forty eight hours. In fact, the whole period since I'd taken off for on my first Ascension trip had been a complete blur. Perhaps nothing says more about the pace of the period than my logbook.

In seven months of basic flying training on the JP, I'd flown a total of one hundred and eleven hours thirty minutes. But in the thirty three days between 11th April and 12th May, I'd flown one hundred and fifteen hours thirty five minutes.

ASCENSION AGAIN – AND AGAIN

While we'd been flying across Europe on 12th May, 8,000 miles away in the south Atlantic, an Argentinean Skyhawk had hit the destroyer HMS Glasgow with a bomb that passed through the engine room. Luckily it had failed to explode, but it had caused enough damage to the fuel system and engines to put the ship out of the war.

Then, on Saturday 15th, we heard the first indication that ground forces were becoming engaged. In an action reminiscent of their operations in the North African desert in the Second World War, the SAS had carried out a raid on an Argentine Air Force forward operating base on Pebble Island, off the north coast of West Falkland. The forty five men in the raiding party destroyed several aircraft, damaged the rest and escaped at a cost of one man wounded by shrapnel from an explosive device set off by the Argentineans. They'd assumed they were being over-run by a much larger force.

We sensed things would happen quickly now. But as it turned out, before we heard anything else from the Task Force, I had time to make another quick dash to Ascension and back with my constituted crew.

We departed on the afternoon of Sunday 16th May and with no intermediate stop in Gibraltar were back by Wednesday lunchtime, having flown a total of fifteen hours by day and eleven hours twenty minutes by night in three airframes: XVs 297, 193 and 211.

The 8,000-mile route included another spectacular night transit of the ITCZ, but was otherwise unremarkable.

On my return to Lyneham on Wednesday 19th May, I'd flown one hundred and seventeen hours and forty minutes in twenty eight days. Another two hours twenty minutes would see me exceed the limit.

Now I don't want to plead any hardship, certainly not compared with those in and around the Falklands, and I was keen to carry on, but I'd had precious few days off in the preceding six weeks, and no leave since Christmas. So although I may not have wanted it, I was told to disappear for a few days.

Photos in an album indicate that Geraldine and I visited a few places in the Cotswolds and were able to celebrate our second wedding anniversary with a meal at a local restaurant. But while it was good to spend some time with her, I can't believe I didn't feel guilty.

It had been a deadly few days in the South Atlantic.

On Friday 21st May, much of the Task Force entered Falkland Sound and headed for the coast of East Falkland at San Carlos Water and Ajax Bay. There, while the troopships and freighters landed a force of four thousand Commandos and Paras, their support units and equipment, the warships made ready to defend the force against surface or air attack.

The plan beyond that was for 2 Para to secure the southern flank of the beachhead by taking the Argentinean positions at Darwin and Goose Green, while Special Forces and Commando units secured the northern flank and Argentinean strongholds en-route to Port Stanley. This would allow the bulk of the troops to be airlifted toward the capital by helicopter, where they'd be joined by an infantry brigade that was yet to arrive.

One of the warships in the air defence screen that Friday was the frigate, HMS Ardent. She was hit by several bombs dropped by three waves of Argentinean Skyhawks and Daggers. Twenty two men lost their lives and many more were wounded, either in the raids or the attempts to put out the resulting fires and save the ship. It sank the next morning.

Her captain, a man I met several times, was Commander Alan West. He went on to become First Sea Lord and enter the House of Lords as Admiral Lord West.

The same day, the frigate, HMS Argonaut was hit by two bombs, also dropped by Skyhawks. The bombs failed to explode, but killed two of the crew and took several days to defuse. Another frigate, HMS Brilliant, was damaged by gunfire.

The area around San Carlos Water became known as Bomb Alley, and while the Argentinean Air Force suffered losses to Royal Navy ships and Sea Harriers, they continued to notch up successes.

Two days after the hits on Ardent, Argonaut and Brilliant, another frigate, HMS Antelope, was also hit by two bombs dropped by Skyhawks. Neither bomb exploded but one had pierced the hull and was thought to be particularly dangerous. The other was inaccessible, hidden among the wreckage it had created.

Antelope was towed to more sheltered waters and two Royal Engineer bomb disposal experts attempted to defuse the single bomb they could reach. At the fourth attempt it exploded, killing one of the Royal Engineers and severely wounding the other.

I think it takes a special kind of courage to approach and work on something likely to explode at any moment. My respect for who do it knows no bounds.

The explosion that killed the Royal Engineer started fires in both Antelope's engine rooms and caused so much damage that the ship had to be abandoned. Five minutes after the last man, her captain, had stepped over the side, the fires set off a series of explosions in her magazines. These ripped through the ship all night and she sank the next morning.

The following day, Tuesday 25th May, there were further losses.

After the sinking of HMS Sheffield and the damage to HMS Glasgow, the only remaining destroyer in theatre was HMS

Coventry. She and the frigate, HMS Broadsword, were part of the air defence screen in Falkland Sound when they were attacked by two pairs of Skyhawks. The first pair damaged Broadsword, before the second hit Coventry with three bombs that caused her to capsize and sink within twenty minutes. Nineteen men were killed and thirty injured.

Another Argentinean success that day was perhaps the most crucial of the whole operation.

The roll-on roll-off container ship, MV Atlantic Conveyor, had sailed to the Falklands with a cargo of Harriers, Sea Harriers and various helicopters, including the four Chinooks needed to ferry the majority of troops and equipment east from San Carlos Water. On the 25th, she was sitting to the north of East Falkland when she was hit by Exocet anti-shipping missiles fired by two Super Étendard fighters. Twelve merchant seamen including her master were killed and she sank three days later.

Fortuitously, the Harriers and Sea Harriers had already been flown off, but most of the helicopters - six Wessex, one Lynx and three of the four Chinooks - and their associated spares were lost in the fires that engulfed her.

The surviving Chinook, *Bravo November*, became famous for the work she carried out during the rest of the campaign, not least in the casualty evacuation role. But she couldn't be everywhere at once, so most troops were left to cross the difficult terrain of East Falkland on foot.

Several years later, I completed Staff College and a tour at RAF Benson alongside the co-pilot of Bravo November. He never talked about it much, but I heard some very sobering stories when he did.

Thursday 27th May saw the first large scale land battle when 2 Para attacked Darwin and Goose Green. By the next morning, they'd taken both objectives with the loss of forty seven Argentinean and seventeen British lives, including Lieutenant Colonel H Jones, the commanding officer of 2 Para, who was awarded a posthumous Victoria Cross.

This attack cleared the way for the Marines and Paras to begin their advance across East Falkland, while Special Forces and Commando units were airlifted forward to secure the northern flank and clear Argentinean positions threatening them.

Following that, my contribution to events seems vanishingly insignificant, but I'm going to continue anyway.

Having returned to work on the 28th, the Friday the Argentineans at Goose Green surrendered, I spent two hours fielding emergencies in the simulator and an hour in the air flying XV307 on my first dedicated co-pilot training sortie on the squadron. I should have flown at least one training sortie a month, but, after five months on 24, this was my first. The flight included circuits and an instrument approach at the home of the VC10 fleet, RAF Brize Norton in Oxfordshire, a few minutes flying time from Lyneham.

That experience came in handy just two days later, Sunday 30th May, when my next route started with a short transit to Brize Norton in XV202 to pick up freight and passengers, before flying on to Gibraltar, then Dakar, Ascension, Dakar and back to Lyneham, where we landed in the early hours of Thursday 3rd June.

From my logbook I can only guess that the system of constituted crews had been abandoned, because I began to fly each trip with a totally different crew. The captain on this occasion was a specialist aircrew squadron leader in his early fifties, a real character with a fund of stories from his long career starting in the 1950s as a co-pilot on the Hastings, the piston-engine aircraft I'd worked on at Scampton during their final six months in service.

The final leg was memorable because, in XV222, we flew the crew of Black Buck 1 from Dakar to Lyneham. At that time, we knew little of what they'd done, but just flying to the Falklands and back in a Vulcan was enough to earn our respect and admiration, a point the captain made when he addressed them over the PA as we neared Lands End.

During this route, we'd heard that an Argentinean Herc had been shot down by a Sea Harrier. In contrast with the elation we'd felt at other Argentinean losses, this one was greeted with sympathy, if not sadness. It was impossible not to conjure up images of the Harrier hovering and tracking dear old Fat Albert as it flew past, teasing it like a cat playing with a mouse before firing the fatal missile.

There were also a further two Black Buck raids, several ground engagements and the Gurkhas and the Scots and Welsh Guards began to take up positions around Bluff Cove to the south of Port Stanley.

On Monday 7th June, I flew another trip to Decimommanu in Sardinia, via Wattisham - in XV305. It was the day the RFAs Sir Galahad and Sir Tristram were bombed in Bluff Cove. Thirty two Welsh Guardsmen were killed and one hundred and fifty of the survivors suffered burns. They were treated in a field hospital run by Surgeon Lieutenant Commander Rick Jolly, an amazing character I'll mention later in this volume.

Also on the 8th, HMS Glamorgan, another ship that had joined the Task Force from Gibraltar, was hit by an Exocet missile while supporting the ground assault on Two Sisters. The explosion and resulting fire led to fourteen deaths and many more injuries, although the ship stayed afloat and eventually made it back to Portsmouth for repairs.

On the 9th, I completed another three hours in the simulator practising various emergencies, and just before midnight on Friday the 11th, took off for Gibraltar in XV188, returning in the same airframe the next morning. As we flew, bloody battles were being fought for the high ground around Port Stanley, places like Mount Tumbledown, Wireless Ridge, Mount Harriet, Two Sisters and Mount Longdon. By the night of the 13th all these objectives had been taken and British troops were advancing on Port Stanley itself.

Back at Lyneham on the 14th June, we were greatly surprised to hear that the Argentineans had surrendered. The short, bloody, war was over. It had lasted seventy four days and resulted in the loss of six hundred and forty nine Argentinean and two hundred and fifty five British servicemen, including one Gurkha. Three Islanders also lost their lives.

I've given only a snapshot of the major milestones during those seventy four days. In historical terms, it was a small conflict. But of course it was a huge milestone in the lives of those most closely involved, and their families. And although my involvement was peripheral, the conflict continued to influence the rest of my time on the Herc fleet.

The day after the surrender, Tuesday 15th June, I set off on my sixth visit to Ascension, this time with the senior officer captain whose ire I attracted for not raising the flaps when he told me to on our climb out of Dakar. But the trip proved memorable for a much more striking event.

Flying XV183, we landed at Ascension on Thursday morning an hour or so before sunrise and parked near the centre of the pan, surrounded by numerous Victors, Vulcans, Nimrods, Hercs, a VC10 and all manner of helicopters. As the captain, nav and I walked to the Ops tent to update our met reports and flight planning, the rear ramp and door were being lowered to the horizontal so the three pallets down the back could be rolled out onto waiting flat bed trucks.

Twenty minutes later, we ducked out of the Ops tent into the night air.

'What the fu..!'

Under the glare of the arc lamps, XV183 sat at a crazy angle, its nosewheel several feet in the air, the tip of the ramp on the ground, held down by a fully loaded pallet that had run into, rather than on to, a flat bed truck.

Everyone working on or around the pan had stopped to stand and stare.

We recovered from the initial shock and set out toward the

aircraft. The loadie, an experienced flight sergeant, spotted us. He made his way over, intent on intercepting the captain, who was working himself into a fair old lather. The NCO stopped, barring our way and, before the senior officer could get started, held up a hand and began to explain what had happened.

'I watched the unloading of the first couple of pallets, sir, then nipped up to the flight deck to collect some paperwork.' He waved a few sheets of paper. 'I'd just climbed down onto the tarmac when the nose reared up.'

He turned to point at the aircraft. 'Scared the life out of me!'

'Right,' the captain said, wringing his hands and setting off to crucify someone.

But the loadie made another calming gesture. To my surprise, the senior officer allowed himself to be restrained a second time.

'As you know, sir, when the pallets are rolled out, the Elephant's Foot' – a strut pushed in under the tip of the ramp – 'supports the weight.'

He paused, looking at me for a nod of understanding.

'Well, today, the two pallets at the back of the freight bay rolled off fine. But then, we think the front pallet forced the nose down enough to lift the end of the ramp clear of the Elephant's Foot. Perhaps it happens all the time, but if it does, the ramp always settles back onto it when the weight of the next pallet comes on.'

'Well not always!' the captain responded tartly, pointing at XV183.

'No, sir,' the loadie acknowledged sheepishly. 'Today, the Elephant's Foot must have toppled for some reason, and unfortunately, no-one noticed. Without it, as soon as the pallet rolled beyond the centre of gravity, it forced the ramp down, and down, until the bottom skin hit the Elephant's Foot and the pallet slammed into the flat bed.'

He finished with an expressive crashing sound.

As he did so, a young man was being given a leg-up onto the crew steps, still several feet off the tarmac. He disappeared into the freight compartment and re-appeared a few moments later at the top of the ramp, holding a cable. Under the gaze of the air eng and a crowd of movers, he walked down the ramp and attached the cable to the rear of the pallet, then climbed back into the freight bay.

Realising he could delay us no longer, the loadie moved aside and fell into step as we walked toward the aircraft. At least he'd achieved something. The captain had calmed down. We were still about fifty yards away when the pallet began to edge back up the ramp, pulled by a winch on the forward freight bay bulkhead.

It hadn't moved far before there were shouts of, 'Stop!'

A couple of men stepped forward to inspect the front of the flat bed. After only a few seconds, they gave the driver a thumbs-up and he reversed it clear. The pallet began to move again, shepherded by a couple of movers. As it entered the freight bay, the airframe groaned, and the ramp lifted a couple of inches.

More shouts of, 'Stop!' brought things to a halt.

The air eng knelt and looked underneath the ramp. He too gave a thumbs-up and the pallet resumed its journey. Creaks and groans rang out as the pallet rolled into the freight bay and the aircraft began to right itself, the ramp rising and the nosewheel lowering until it rested on the tarmac. People looked at one another as if they could hardly believe what they'd witnessed.

I suspect that if we'd been at Lyneham, or anywhere else during more normal times, the aircraft would have been grounded for all manner of checks, while those responsible would have been subject to a disciplinary process that would have made their eyes water. After all, who knew what the unusual stresses and strains had done to our Herc and its components.

But Wideawake airfield was as busy as ever. The last thing it needed was a dead aircraft taking up pan space. The only visible damage was a tear a few inches long where a sharp edge on the base of the Elephant's Foot had punctured the skin of the ramp, and the air eng soon covered that with some good old bodge tape.

After that, I don't remember much debate. While we crewed in, the Elephant's Foot was re-inserted and the pallet unloaded. The ramp seemed to close normally, so we started up and flew back to Dakar. The crew waiting there were told what had happened and decided to fly XV183 on to Lyneham.

I have no idea what the outcome of the engineering investigation was, nor did I hear whether those responsible were punished, either at Ascension or on their return to Lyneham. I'd have been likely to hear about the latter, so I guess no formal action was taken. In the end, I think we all, including the senior officer captain, realised that everyone had been – and still was - under immense pressure. So perhaps, in this one instance, even the movers deserved to be cut a bit of slack.

After an eventful few days, I arrived back at Lyneham in a different airframe, XV188, on the late evening of Friday 18th.

Forty eight hours later, I set out on my seventh trip to Ascension, this time via Gibraltar.

A few miles south of Lands End on the southbound journey, I broke a tooth biting into a Mars bar. It was one along from the three I'd lost to a rugby prop forward's elbow a few years earlier. Over the next few months, the dentist at Lyneham designed and fitted a complicated bridge that he documented as part of his professional portfolio.

At the time, while I ran my tongue over the damage, there were jokes about applying for a Purple Heart when I returned to base.

We arrived back on Thursday 24th. It was to be my last flight of that calendar month, during which I'd flown ninety six hours, most of them during three visits to Ascension Island. I'd become very used to this level of activity. After all, it was all I'd known. But although I was to fly some memorable trips over the next several months, the pace of life seemed to slow a little, and I certainly began to see more variety.

OP BANNER AND BERLIN

After ten days leave, my return to work on Monday 6th July included two hours of emergencies in the simulator. The next day included a forty five-minute air test in XV300 plus route prep for a flight to Gibraltar on the Thursday. My logbook contains no record of a return flight, so this must have been one of the few occasions during my time on 24 Squadron when I had to travel down the back of a Herc as a passenger.

On Sunday, we joined several other Alberts flying to Southampton to pick up Royal Marines that had just returned from the Falklands by ship. In XV301, we delivered them to RAF Leuchars, a Phantom base near St Andrews, from where they'd go on to their base in Arbroath. We returned to Lyneham.

On the TV news that evening, I watched film of the ships docking in Southampton, where the Marines had been greeted by military bands and thousands of well-wishers waving flags, cheering and singing. After such a welcome, a few hours down the back of a Herc must have been quite a come-down.

My next trip, in XV176, was the first of many I'd fly in support of Operation Banner, the codename for the British military involvement in Northern Ireland. For Herc crews it generally meant a day or two ferrying troops between bases on the British mainland, Germany and Northern Ireland.

This day we flew from Lyneham to Aldergrove, the joint military/civilian airport serving Belfast, then to RAF Gutersloh in Germany, before flying back to Aldergrove and returning to Lyneham. The trip was fairly typical, with about six hours spent in the air. But adding in pre-flight prep and time on the ground at each location, Op Banner days could be long, even if they were completed without a hitch, which was far from guaranteed.

Beyond the nagging fear that the IRA may one day target a Herc with a shoulder-launched ground to air missile, mine was a cold war. I only ever viewed the more dangerous and dramatic events in Northern Ireland at a distance on the TV news. It wasn't until nearly two decades later, when I flew around some of the fortified bastions in the Ulster countryside in a support helicopter, that I gained a deeper insight into the day to day risks and pressures some of those based in the Province faced.

I'd always been interested in history and current affairs, but now, involvement in events like Ops Corporate and Banner made keeping up with the news something of an obsession, one I retain to this day.

My next route provided a host of vivid memories and experiences. It was my first flight with another training captain I grew to like very much. Like many at Lyneham, he was not a typical military man, being far too laid back to impress anyone in the Army, or many in the Royal Navy or RAF. But he was a very able pilot who did his job without fuss and was adept at passing knowledge on to the likes of me.

The five-day route began on Monday 26th July with a leg in XV176 from Lyneham to Leuchars, where we spent the night before flying a Phantom squadron's personnel and equipment to an Armament Practice Camp at Decimommanu in Sardinia.

From there we flew north to Ramstein in Germany, a United States Air Force base and the headquarters of NATO Allied Air Forces Central Europe. Here we picked up a large party of squadron leaders and wing commanders, part of the 1982 intake of the RAF Advanced Staff College at RAF Bracknell. They were mid-way through a ten-month course designed to prepare them for command and staff appointments in higher rank. We were their transport for the final few days of a tour taking in political and military venues on the continent, including historic battle sites.

Our last duty that Tuesday was to fly them from Ramstein to RAF Wildenrath. The Staff College party must have taken all the accommodation in the Officers' Mess, because we were sent to a small hotel in the local town of Goch. The next day, while they visited Second World War battlefields, such as Arnhem and Nijmegen, just over the border in Holland, we wandered the town, stopping for coffee and sussing out restaurants for lunch and dinner.

Thursday was spent ferrying the Staff College officers from Wildenrath to Berlin, flying back and forth along the City's central air corridor before a final landing at RAF Gatow, the air base I'd visited in a Jetstream at the end of my flying training, just one year earlier.

That evening, several small groups set out from the Officers' Mess for a night on the town. The captain, nav and I met up with our air eng and loadie outside the Sergeants' Mess and set out to do the same, starting with visits to some of the tourist sites. As we progressed, we kept bumping into one or other Staff College group, firstly at the Brandenburg Gate, and then at various viewing points around the Wall. We even met some at the restaurant we chose for our evening meal, and in the bars we visited afterward. On each occasion, we'd wave a friendly greeting but otherwise keep our distance, each group happier to keep its own company.

Inevitably, as the night wore on, we gravitated toward the nightclub district and a club the loadmaster said he knew well. To my amazement, it turned out to be the one I'd visited with my Finningley course mates: The Mon Cherie.

The centrepiece was still a bubble bath, in which the *dancers* cavorted before encouraging members of the audience to join them. On my previous visit, a group of soldiers had been only too keen to take a dip. This time, much to my surprise, it was members of the Staff College in the spotlight at the front of the room.

I still had the naive notion that senior officers were above such things, so this was quite an eye-opener - in many ways. It seemed that when they thought they were free of prying eyes – we were lost in the cigarette smoke at the back – some were every bit as likely to make fools of themselves as the humblest airman. They were certainly prepared to party that night, and they were still going strong when we decided to call it a day.

The next morning, Friday, there were some very pasty faces at breakfast, but I was full of beans. I'd just been told that rather than hang around while the Staff College drove through Checkpoint Charlie to visit East Berlin, we were being allowed to join them. We'd been granted dispensation to wear our No 2 uniforms – all we had with us – which led to a few strange looks from the Staff College party, resplendent in their No 1s.

I'd grown up watching films like The Spy Who Came in from the Cold, but never dreamt I'd see the Berlin Wall - twice. On a foggy night a year earlier, it had been all I'd imagined, eerily atmospheric, straight out of Le Carré, but also sinister in its design and purpose, to corral its own population. I'd wondered ever since what life was like on the other side. Well now I was being granted the opportunity to find out.

Before we boarded one of two buses waiting outside the Mess, we late additions were given a hurried briefing. The gist was that we were likely to be tailed throughout our visit, so we should stick together; be ambassadors for the West; be wary of unsolicited contacts; and avoid situations that could provide the Soviets with either an immediate propaganda opportunity, or material for some future attempt at exploitation. To my surprise, we were allowed to take cameras, but were told to use them only when cleared to do so. To be caught taking unauthorised photographs was one of the quickest ways to get arrested.

We took most of the warnings with a pinch of salt. After all, the chances of being caught in a honey trap when surrounded by fifty-plus senior officers seemed remote. That said, we realised we had to be on our guard.

At Checkpoint Charlie a year earlier, the fog had shrouded everything beyond the small American border post and its attendant military policemen. But that morning, as we passed these and a sign warning that we were *Leaving the American Sector*, the weather was beautiful. A few yards further on, just as I'd seen in countless war and spy movies, an East German soldier, rifle slung over his shoulder, raised a red and white barrier for us to drive beneath.

The American wooden hut had a pitched roof and windows, but it seemed determinedly makeshift and casual, as if to make the point, *we're only here because you are*. The Soviet post was also single storey, but a larger, more substantial affair, overlooked by large concrete barriers and goon towers. It meant business.

The surveillance started early. As the bus stopped by the building, we held our passports up at the windows. They were scrutinised by the unsmiling eyes of armed border guards, some taking photos. I wondered if my face and passport details would end up in the file I'd been warned the Soviets probably kept on me.

The vetting process was drawn out, I guess in an attempt to intimidate. If so, it didn't work. It just seemed petty and, frankly, pathetic. But then, we were on an official visit and unlikely to be detained. If I'd been an ordinary citizen re-entering the Eastern Bloc by this route, I suspect it would have had a more chilling effect.

Beyond the checkpoint, other differences quickly became apparent.

By the end of the Second World War, Berlin was a city of rubble. Few buildings had escaped the combined efforts of Allied and Russian bombers and artillery. But apart from a few sites kept as reminders of the period, the western sectors of the city bore little sign of damage. The Marshall Plan had seen buildings and infrastructure either renovated or rebuilt, the architecture a mix of pre- and post-War styles, including large areas of modern concrete and glass.

But beyond Checkpoint Charlie, close to the Wall in the Russian sector, the views to both sides of the bus were of old apartment blocks and buildings pock-marked with bullet and shell holes. There were also large, rubble-strewn, areas, and even where rubble had been cleared, nothing had been built. It was as if nothing had happened since 1945.

The bus set off to tour points of interest, our guide a member of the Staff College who'd served in Berlin and knew his way around. We drove past the site of Hitler's bunker, a place both the Soviets and, several years later, the unified German government, were keen to keep out of the limelight to prevent it becoming a shrine to Nazism. We also visited an imposing monument to the Russian war dead, before finally ending up at the Brandenburg Gate.

Here, we left the buses and wandered about among hundreds of other tourists. We'd been told they were likely to be a mix of East Germans and citizens of other areas of the Eastern Bloc, all eager to visit a city meant to showcase the benefits of Communist society more clearly than anywhere outside Russia.

If I'd expected them to be walking round shouting, *Help, help, I'm being repressed*, I'd have been disappointed. Their very presence indicated a certain level of privilege and wealth, or at least that they were well connected. As a result, they dressed and behaved pretty much as Western tourists would on a sunny day in June. And confronted with 50 plus strangers dressed in unfamiliar uniforms, they were also perfectly civil, exchanging friendly smiles, muted greetings and apologies when our paths crossed as we milled around the sights.

This turned out to be the only area where photography was allowed and two of my four photographs are of the Brandenburg Gate, topped by its iconic statue, a female figure representing peace on a chariot pulled by four horses. Viewed from the west of course, you saw only her back – and the backsides of the horses. At least I could now see her riding toward me, straddling Unter den Linden, the wide thoroughfare that runs east/west beneath her feet for several miles in either direction.

For centuries it had been the City's main processional route, used by political protesters and triumphant armies alike. That is until 1961, when it was blocked a few hundred yards to the west of the Gate by a tall, smooth-sided, concrete wall that went on to encase the entire western half of the city.

It seemed an affront to me, so how Berliners felt I could only guess.

One of the strangest sights was the heads of those standing on the viewing platform on the western side of the Wall. There they were, staring across and taking photographs of us, staring back and taking photographs of them.

My other two photos are of a short guard-changing ceremony outside one of the nearby buildings. The crowd stand two or three deep, forming a three-sided square within which half a dozen East German troops in plain grey uniforms, calf length black boots, steel helmets and wooden-stocked rifles can be seen marching. The ceremony itself was unremarkable, except in one regard.

When the soldiers marched back and forth, they performed an exaggerated goose step. In another country it might have had a comedic quality. But in Berlin! The performance could hardly fail to bring to mind images of German troops goose-stepping through countless European cities, and often under arches similar to the one by which we were standing.

When we discussed it later, it was apparent that I wasn't the only one to find the cultural insensitivity, not only bizarre, but chilling.

We parted company with the Staff College shortly after this. While they went off to some official function for the remainder of the morning, we were dropped in Alexanderplatz, a large square beneath one of the tallest and most distinctive buildings in Europe, the Berlin TV tower. Standing a little over 1,200 feet tall, it still dominates the city skyline, as the Soviets intended when they built it in 1969.

This was one area where there'd been a lot of development, most of the architecture similar to many a western city's 1960s shopping streets and precincts. But if the architecture was similar to many places in the West, the shopping experience was very different.

From the outset, we were surprised at the poor variety and standard of the goods on offer. This covered everything from food to electrical goods. Take clothes, for instance. The limited ranges were muted in colour, if not dowdy, and years behind the styles you'd find in similar western shops and department stores. Any counter selling more modern, colourful and stylish items seemed to attract long queues, none longer than that snaking back fifty yards from the single counter selling blue denim jeans.

We hadn't really come prepared for shopping, but the loadie said he was looking for a new set of golf clubs, so we headed for the sports' departments. Having seen the prices of everything so far, he was excited. Even with an exchange rate of two West German marks for one East German, he was confident of getting a bargain. But the sports kit was another eye-opener.

For a start, there were no golf clubs. What there was was lots of school PT kit for adults. In fact, nothing but school PT kit for adults: plain white or light blue t-shirts, navy shorts and black or white slip-on or lace-up pumps. Perhaps there was more variety elsewhere, but not in the stores we visited.

The items that have really stuck in my mind are the badminton rackets. These all had blue or red plastic handles and plastic strings. They looked and felt identical to those we'd bought in seaside shops as children heading for the beach. If there were any higher quality options for sale, they were well hidden. The few tennis rackets were similar, and we never saw a squash racket.

Again, none of this exactly shouts repression. But if this was its showcase, you had to wonder what the shopping experience was like in the rest of the Eastern Bloc. And as we walked from shop to shop, I gained the strong impression that the locals were only too aware of their poverty of choice. Even in the summer sun, they looked anything but a band of happy shoppers.

Having wandered around fairly aimlessly for the last half hour of our allotted time, we were picked up and driven back through Checkpoint Charlie and across the west of the city to Gatow. I couldn't quite put my finger on why, but I'd found the atmosphere behind the Wall oppressive – claustrophobic. And while I was extremely grateful to have visited, I was relieved to be getting out.

There was one more treat in store.

Before flying back along the central corridor and on to Lyneham, we were authorised to fly the senior officers above the city within the Berlin Control Zone. Not only would we be exercising a right laid down by the Joint Powers at the end of the War, but also giving some of our future leaders a valuable overview of one of the major potential flashpoints on the planet.

So, after take-off, we levelled at 1,500 feet and the loadie opened the rear ramp to the horizontal and placed cargo nets over the resulting gaps. Then, while we flew above the city, he allowed small groups of senior officers onto the ramp to look out - without the danger of falling to their deaths.

I spent much of the time on the radios gaining clearance for our next manoeuvre, but I also had time to take in the sights. I even managed to take a couple of photographs. From the air, some of the disparities between the western and eastern sectors we'd noted on the ground were less evident, although the East of the city was ringed with far more high-rise apartment blocks, arranged in vast estates.

The one thing that stood out all too clearly was the Wall. Straight or meandering, it stretched for miles, often following the lines of water courses or roads, but always wrapping round to encircle the western half of Berlin. It was also easy to distinguish east from west. In the western sector, buildings sometimes came close to the Wall, and cars ran along roads adjacent to it. But on its eastern side, there was a wide, cleared area, devoid of movement.

The Killing Zone.

After an uneventful flight through the central corridor and across Western Europe, we landed back at Lyneham on Friday evening. While I went home to Geraldine, the Staff College members boarded buses for their return to Bracknell. I'd spoken to a few of them. The course sounded interesting, full of things I'd probably enjoy studying. I'd also noticed how much fun they seemed to have, and their camaraderie. They were a band of brothers.

Perhaps this planted a seed, a latent desire to undertake a similar route some day. But it was very definitely latent. At the time, such aspirations seemed total pie in the sky. After all, it was only a couple of years since I'd been a corporal technician on a Vulcan squadron.

And yet, twelve years later I completed the same course.

And twenty years after that, Geraldine and I spent four nights in a hotel in the old East Berlin. We were able to roam the whole city at will. And we did. Highlights included walking along Unter den Linden, under the Brandenburg Gate and on into the west; spiralling up the glass dome of the Reichstag at night; and standing on the viewing gallery at the top of the TV tower to see the prospect from a loftier perch.

Rarely have I felt such a sense of freedom, or realised what a precious commodity it is.

Even Checkpoint Charlie had lost its menace, unless you find the golden arch of the adjacent MacDonald's burger bar sinister.

NEW ZEALAND

October included an early boost to my confidence, followed by the trip of a lifetime, which provided some of the highlights of my time on the Herc, but also some of my lowest moments.

Before all that though, August and the first three weeks of September were relatively quiet. I completed my eighth visit to Ascension and my second to Akrotiri.

The Ascension sortie was much as before, although big changes were planned as Wideawake airfield was becoming the airhead for regular Herc airbridge flights to the Falklands in support of its new garrison troops, ships and a mini air force of Phantoms, Harriers, Hercs and helicopters various.

Like my first trip to Akrotiri, the second was via Wattisham on the way out, and the night-stop included another enjoyable kebab. The return was different though, featuring stops in Souda Bay on Crete, Pisa in north-western Italy, and Binbrook, the home of the Lightning force in Lincolnshire. On the climb out from Pisa, I was lucky enough to see the leaning tower, beautifully framed by a gap in the clouds.

Alongside the flying, I completed several standby and QRA duties and a couple of simulator trips. But I also picked up something deeply unpopular with the vast majority of officers, and especially aircrew. Not a disease, but a secondary duty.

As you'd expect, soldiers, sailors and airmen all have primary duties to perform based on the major role of their unit. On 24 Squadron, the primary duty of the vast majority of us was to fly, as pilots, navigators, air engineers or loadmasters. And in this effort, we were supported by everyone at Lyneham, their primary duties ranging from engineer to supplier, administrator to medic, cook or bottle washer.

But like any town or village, military units have all manner of clubs and societies, anything from sports and adventure clubs, to hobby groups covering a vast array of interests from stamp collecting to amateur dramatics. These had to be run by someone as a secondary duty, the completion of which invariably fell outside the normal working day. And much like any town or village, it was generally people with a personal interest in the sport or hobby that volunteered to run it as a secondary duty. For instance, I was in charge of the volleyball teams on several stations until I stopped playing at the age of 38.

But many more secondary duties were thrown up by the regulatory requirements surrounding any activity, such as health and safety and finance. These tended to be more onerous and less fun. As a result they were less likely to be filled by volunteers, even though doing them was a way to stand out from the pack in the race for promotion.

More than that.

You were highly unlikely to be promoted if you hadn't performed well in one of the more demanding secondary duties. It was only when I sat in on promotion boards much later in my career that I found out just how important they were. If two officers of equal merit in their primary duties were going for a single promotion slot, a good or bad performance in one of the weightier secondary duties was often the deciding factor.

As a result, some ambitious officers volunteered for the meatier duties, while some deemed to have promotion potential were encouraged to *volunteer* for a duty deemed *good for their career*. But in truth, such were the number of secondary duties that most officers were merely given a duty and told to get on with it. And on small units with few officers, you could end up with several.

For instance, three months after becoming a qualified flying instructor on the University of London Air Squadron in late 1985, I had five: War Plans and Home Defence

Training; Combat Survival and Rescue; Health and Safety at Work (Ground); Student Log book checker; and Fire Officer, responsible for both the airfield buildings and a town headquarters in London – a large building a few hundred yards from Harrods that sold for fifty four million pounds in 2015.

All six junior instructors on ULAS had a similar number of secondary duties. Some were more onerous than others, but they all had to be fitted in around flying four times a day when the weather allowed. So it was no wonder we sometimes prayed for rain, or that some officers, but especially pilots, became so fed up with secondary duties that they chose to leave the Service. After all, you could work for an airline and have no duty beyond flying the aircraft.

In contrast with ULAS, 24 Squadron had so many officers and senior NCOs that not everyone had a secondary duty. So, as a relatively new co-pilot, I was surprised to be given one of the more demanding ones: OIC - Officer in Charge – Squadron Fund, a fund that everyone on the squadron paid in to through their Mess bills.

Day to day, my duties included ordering and selling squadron memorabilia, such as Hercules prints, squadron plaques, engraved tankards, T-shirts, sweat shirts, cravats and Christmas cards. When I was away on route, the Squadron Commander's PA, a sergeant administrator, would mind the shop and keep a record of what he sold, but otherwise, it was all my responsibility.

Squadron flying suit badges and red and black cravats were *presented* to every new member –although they also had to pay for them – while those leaving at the end of their tours could choose a departure gift, a squadron plaque, print or tankard, which would be paid for by the Fund and handed over at some more or less elaborate ceremony in the crewroom.

As an aside, I also stocked and sold something very popular at the time - squadron zaps. Zaps were small, glossy, sticky-backed, squadron badges or cartoonish adaptations of them.

All squadrons had them and the idea was to stick them in a prominent position wherever you went to show that you'd been there, a bit like graffiti.

I suspect they're a slice of history that no longer exists, overtaken by the immediacy of social media posts and videos. But back in the day, zapping could be very competitive, squadrons vying to get their zap on other units' signs, buildings, crewrooms and aircraft. You'd find zaps everywhere you went all over the world, adorning not only other military units, but also tourist attractions and accommodation.

One of the greatest challenges was to stick them on high ceilings where they were both prominent and difficult to remove. To perform the feat, you had to lay the zap, sticky side uppermost, on a wallet and throw it up to hit the ceiling, leaving the zap stuck there for all to see, while the wallet fell back to its owner, ideally without shedding its contents on the way down. It was quite a skill, and not many could do it consistently.

Such fun!

Anyway, on a daily basis the Fund could take up quite a bit of my time, and then there were monthly stock checks, reconciling the accounts and preparing them for audit, plus involvement in the planning and financing of squadron events, from parties and barbecues to open days. In addition to flying, it could be a real pain.

So why had my flight commander decided to test me so early in my life on the squadron?

Of course, I'm not entirely sure, but from my own later experience, there were probably several factors. For a start, he'd have wanted the job done by someone capable of doing it, and he must have judged me that. And although it could be several years before I became a serious contender for promotion to squadron leader - if I ever was – he was already looking that far ahead, as well as assessing my potential for other, more demanding positions on the squadron and beyond.

Senior officers do that.

In the fourth week of September, I completed two one-hour co-pilot training sorties in the local area, an attempt to make up for the dedicated training I'd missed in the previous six months. And then, on the 28th, I set out on my ninth trip to Ascension, via Gibraltar and Dakar.

The sortie was fairly standard until we arrived in Ascension, where we were joined by a route checker. He was going to assess my performance as non-operating pilot on the leg to Dakar, and as operating pilot on the leg to Lyneham. This came as quite a surprise. It was only four and a half months since I'd joined 24 and I hadn't expected to be considered for a route check for at least another six weeks.

As a result, I'd have been happy to come out with my D Cat intact, but my 38 Group Category Card shows that I was awarded a C Cat. I think I was lucky to be examined on what had become a familiar route. Had I been checked on a European or North American sortie, I suspect I might have struggled to impress. But hey, it was the first building block to an overall C Cat, and a welcome boost to my confidence.

Early in September, my name had appeared on the programme board in the co-pilots' office alongside a route to New Zealand, due to depart in early October. When the co-leader had convinced me it wasn't a joke, he told me a bit more about it.

The destination was Royal New Zealand Air Force Whenuapai – pronounced fenoo-uh-pi – near Auckland, in the north of New Zealand's North Island, where two RAF Nimrods were taking part in a maritime reconnaissance competition, the Fincastle Trophy. We'd be one of several transport aircraft ferrying men and equipment to and from the base.

The outbound journey was planned via Akrotiri in Cyprus, Muscat in Oman, Colombo in Sri Lanka, Tengah in western Singapore, Darwin in north Australia and Richmond, near Sidney, in south-eastern Australia. The return was via

Richmond, Darwin, Hong Kong, Colombo, Bahrain and Athens. Overall, there were fourteen legs, and we'd spend at least fourteen hours on the ground everywhere except Tengah and Richmond, which were brief refuelling stops. We'd be away for two weeks.

It was the kind of route that came to a squadron rarely, perhaps only once every couple of years, so I was a source of envy among some of the more experienced co-pilots. Heck, even I felt it was unfair, especially when at least one of my peers was already doing his first detachment in the Falkland Islands.

It wasn't going to be plain sailing, though. A route with so many legs crossing multiple time zones would normally see the doubling up of each crew position. This allowed individuals to operate alternate legs, ensuring adequate time for rest and planning. But I was to be the only co-pilot on a crew of two captains, three air enges, including a squadron leader examining officer, two sergeant loadies and two ground engineers. The navigator was also on his own, but he was a very experienced flight lieutenant in his late forties or early fifties. At my level of experience, everyone agreed it would be a demanding two weeks.

The scale of the admin burden crystallized when I picked up the imprest, more than twelve thousands pounds worth of US dollars and pounds sterling in a mixture of cash and travellers' cheques, plus a sheaf of related forms.

By far the easiest and safest thing for me would be to hand a large proportion of the cash to each crew member as soon as we left Lyneham. But one of the captains wanted me to hold the money and trickle feed it as we approached each new location. This complicated the paperwork and left me carrying wads of cash for most of the route.

Checking the contents of the route bags was another sobering task. We were flying over so many countries that there were several bags, each stuffed with maps and charts for tens, hundreds of airports. Digging out the right documents as each leg unfolded was going to be a bit of a nightmare. Additionally, once beyond Cyprus, everything would be new to me, and without anyone to share the burden, I'd have little time for the kind of detailed pre-planning I'd relied on hitherto.

It was going to be quite a test.

In my short time on the Herc force running up to the New Zealand trip I'd discovered that, if a crew gelled, you could have an absolute whale of a time on the most mundane and unpromising route. And up to that point, I'd been lucky enough to avoid the flip side, a route that looked great on paper but failed to live up to its billing because the crew didn't get on.

Way before his interference in the running of the imprest, I'd been warned that the captain who'd laid down the imprest rules, let's call him the Grinch, liked to undermine less experienced crew members, and especially his co-pilots. His favourite weapons were sarcasm and ridicule. I hoped not to provide him with too much ammunition, but over such a long route, it was hard to believe I wouldn't make mistakes - probably several. It gave me an uneasy feeling.

The other captain was my flight commander, the excitable squadron leader I'd flown with to Ascension and on a couple of other occasions. Although far more amenable than his opposite number, he could be very intense. On this route, I was to discover that he'd give interminable debriefs, all in the name of preparing me for eventual captaincy. After a mere six months as a co-pilot, it often seemed as if he was trying to make me run before I'd learnt to walk. I'd leave the party room long after everyone else, my head spinning with advice he wanted to see me implement the next time I was operating pilot.

As an added complication, my two captains didn't really get on, so we rarely joined together as an entire crew, even for a wind down beer.

The navigator was a pleasant enough chap, but any hope that he might provide companionship on the ground was dashed. He tended to stay in his room, perhaps struggling to keep up with his own high workload, or maybe counting his allowances. Either way, I saw little of him away from the flight deck.

The two air enges were also far from unpleasant, but they were busy trying to impress their squadron leader route checker in the air - and steering clear of him on the ground. So they tended to keep themselves to themselves, as did the two ground engineers.

As for the two loadies, between loading and unloading at either end of the route, they had little other than crew rations to worry about. Beyond that, they seemed determined to party their way round the trip of a lifetime. Perhaps I should have taken the initiative and off-loaded some of my peripheral duties onto them, things like booking morning calls and running the crew drinks kitty. But frankly, as a newbie, I'd have needed the support of at least one of the captains, and neither of them was interested.

That leaves the squadron leader air eng, a quiet, studious man in his early fifties. I suspect he too was feeling a bit lonely - a part of the route, but not of the rather peculiar crew. We seemed to hit it off, and on the longer stopovers, he and I would meet up for a meal or a bit of sight-seeing. His calming presence was a valuable safety valve.

The tone of the route for me was set on the first leg to Akrotiri, or rather, in the subsequent debrief.

We took off from Lyneham at 0635 on Monday 4th October, with the Grinch, a slim, fair-haired flight lieutenant in his mid-thirties, in the left hand seat. With good weather and a later departure for Akrotiri than normal, I'd seen the snow-capped Alps and the west coast of Italy in daylight. We'd also avoided the Crotone Death Ray on turning east and heading across the Mediterranean. I'd made all the radio calls as we passed through French, Italian and Greek airspace, apparently without mistakes. But the Grinch had seemed singularly unimpressed, tetchy even. I didn't find out why until we were taking a wind-down beer outside Block 102 with the nav and a couple of the NCOs.

He began a very public debrief with, 'You're a c**t, you know that?'

Now I'd been in the RAF for nine years by then, so I'd heard the word before. In fact, the insult had been directed at me many times, but invariably in jest, as a form of mild rebuke, as in, *you stupid c...!*

But the man spat it with such venom that, frankly, I was shocked.

'You have no idea, do you?' he continued, warming to his task.

Only when I expressed my ignorance did he give an explanation.

It seemed that from the moment we entered Greek airspace, I'd greeted a succession of controllers with what I thought was a hearty good morning in their native language, *Athens, this is Ascot 4246, kaliméra* (kaleemaira). But apparently, the word I'd used was *kalamári* (kalamahree).

So, as you may know, the captain was accusing me of saying to each controller in turn, *Athens, this is Ascot 4246, squid!*

He finished his explanation with, 'So you've made a complete twat of yourself.'

Of course, if what he said was true, it was far from my finest hour. Now, if he'd pulled me up after the first occurrence, I'd have merited his rebuke and plenty of jokes at my expense. After all, it was pretty funny. But why on earth had he let me make the same mistake again and again, and left it until now to tell me? It could only be, as I'd been warned, to maximise the ridicule and humiliation.

Later, the nav pulled me aside and said it was what this captain did, and not just to his co-pilots. And such was his reputation that others were reluctant to intervene or rein him in. The nav also pointed out that, in reality, the joke was on the Grinch, not me. After all, it was his callsign that was forever linked to the mistake, which, incidentally, none of the other crew members had noticed.

This did little to cheer me up at the time, although I took on board a couple of immediate lessons. Don't try to be too clever on the radios, and never emulate this man's captaincy style.

I still think he was wrong in so many ways. But on the day, it hardly seemed to matter. After a period of steady progress and the boost of a C Cat on my route check just three days earlier, he'd struck a terrible blow to my confidence. He'd also cast a shadow over the remaining two weeks. I now dreaded the other legs, all to be flown over territories that were totally new to me.

With the benefit of hindsight, I doubt whether I'd actually greeted a controller with the word squid more than once. That was enough, of course, but if I'd carried on doing it, I'd have noticed the rest of the crew laughing behind my back. More than that, other aircraft or the controllers would have been unable to resist making a joke of it. British Airways crews were always keen to butt in and point out any error you made on the R/T.

The next morning, the flight commander was in the left hand seat for the leg to Muscat Seeb airport in Oman, a flight time of six hours forty minutes.

My most vivid memory of this largely uneventful flight was the vastness of the Saudi Arabian desert, almost four hours of reddish rock and sand.

But there was also the contrast between the dusty land and shimmering blue waters of the Arabian Gulf as we passed over Bahrain, Qatar and the United Arab Emirates, the Straits of Hormuz and Iran a hazy presence in the distance.

I'd done nothing more than co-pilot duties again, but all really had seemed to go well this time. And yet, even though it was late evening when the party room began to empty, the flight commander couldn't resist regaling me at length on how to be an effective captain. By the time he'd finished, I still needed to eat, catch up on admin and plan the next leg before putting my head down, so there was no time to venture outside into Muscat itself.

As we continued to head east, the difference between Greenwich Mean Time (Z) - effectively UK time - and local times became more pronounced. No matter how much I tried to align my routine solely with local time at each location, on this route, I struggled to counter the cumulative fatigue. To give a flavour of the problem, I'll continue to mention GMT and local for the rest of this chapter.

Take-off for Sri Lanka with the Grinch was at 0305Z, or, taking account of the four time zones we'd transited, 7.05am local. Twenty odd minutes later, we passed over the coast of Oman and headed southeast over the Arabian Sea. Shortly afterwards, I spotted an island out to the right, a sixty-mile strip of terracotta surrounded by the bluest of blue seas. It was Masirah – pronounced, in the RAF at least, Muhzeeruh.

While I was completing my apprentice training at Halton, Britain withdrew from everywhere east of Suez except Hong Kong. So I'd assumed I'd never see Masirah, or any of the other exotic places mentioned by more experienced airmen. And yet, here I was, looking down on the place. It seemed surreal. I watched it disappear behind us as we crossed the Arabian Sea then the Indian Ocean, passing the southern tip of India and approaching Sri Lanka, the large, tear-drop shaped island separated from the Sub-continent's southeast coast by a narrow strait.

After the Akrotiri leg, I hadn't been looking forward to flying with the Grinch. Once again, he wasn't a barrel of laughs, aiming the odd barb at me and the less experienced NCOs. But as the leg progressed, I began to realise something that came into sharper focus as the rest of the route unfolded. At least some of his unfortunate manner was a defence mechanism, a shield against his own shyness and lack of confidence.

With the hindsight of almost three decades, I think he'd probably be placed somewhere on the autistic spectrum now, like many other military types I met. And while we're at it, I'm pretty sure I served alongside a fair range of sociopaths, if not psychopaths. As for me…!

Such excuses didn't generate much sympathy at the time though. On subsequent routes, he and I forged a working relationship short of friendship. But on this trip, his behaviour just made life difficult and unpleasant, especially as I was never sure whether the debrief would include a vicious slap-down for something I'd done hours earlier. It played on my nerves, especially as we crossed evermore time zones and fatigue began to take hold.

After a flight time of five hours thirty five minutes, we began our descent to the airport serving the Sri Lankan capital,

Colombo, situated on the south-western coast. The scenery was spectacular.

From the city, just visible in the haze about fifteen miles to the south, to as far as we could see to the north stretched a narrow, seemingly unbroken, strip of golden sand. It was sandwiched between the bluest of oceans and a lush green forest that stretched to the landward horizon in every direction. The runway itself was just beyond the waters of a large lagoon full of native fishing and pleasure craft.

I'd never seen anything like it.

We drove into the city on roads fringed with the greenery we'd seen from the air, a mix of tall palms and broad leaf trees of countless species. Much of the time, we were alongside a swollen, muddy brown river.

This and the clusters of wooden buildings lining the road had been invisible from the air. Everywhere, there was the bustle of Sri Lankan life. Men in shirts and sarongs and women in colourful saris sat outside their houses, many tending stalls selling food and all manner of wares, from household cleaning products to ironmongery. Other women washed clothes in the river, while laughing children jumped and splashed about in the water.

Our taxi crawled along the dusty roads, the driver leaning on the horn as he weaved around pedestrians, people riding rickety old push bikes loaded with produce, motor bikes and mopeds bearing several generations of the same family, cars similarly laden and, most surprisingly, brightly decorated carts pulled by one or two large white cows with prominent shoulder humps and fearsome horns. More cows were to be found slumped in the middle of the road, chewing the cud and gazing about, unperturbed by the surrounding mayhem.

Our driver's attempts to cut a path through the chaos often led us on to the other carriageway, where we'd find ourselves head-on to a colourful truck, its horn thundering as it bore down on us. It was one of the slowest journeys of my life, but also one of the most terrifying, surpassed only by the return to the airport thirty six hours later.

I'm not sure why we had so much time on the ground so early on the route, but I wasn't going to complain. I remember Colombo as a mix of modern and colonial buildings and temples, but also of exotic smells, from fragrant spices to less pleasant odours generated by the heat and humidity and a drainage system struggling to cope. Sad to say, though, the thing that has stuck in my mind is the poverty.

I know I mustn't keep blaming the lack of internet for my ignorance, especially when we did have encyclopaedias, documentaries and travel programmes. But while these had given me an idea of the geography and architecture of the various places we were to visit, they had not prepared me for sights like those beyond our large international hotel.

The streets were lined with beggars, many minus limbs, often several limbs. Their begging bowls and plaintive cries were unnecessary. Their need was all too clear. I was overwhelmed, didn't know what to do, whether to give or not to give. And if I did give, who should benefit from my generosity? What measure should I use and how much was appropriate?

Older hands advised against giving anything. If I did, they

said, I'd be swamped by more beggars, and anyway most of them were run by criminal gangs. When I was with others I took their advice. But when I ventured out alone, on my return to the hotel, I put money in the bowls of several of the beggars closest to the door, reasoning that it would minimise the chance of being surrounded before I reached *safety*.

My meagre generosity didn't stop me feeling mean and cowardly. After all, competition for pitches closest to the hotel was bound to be fierce, the prize probably going to the *fittest* rather than the most deserving.

Even after all these years, I still never know whether or not I should give to people on the street.

Following another terrifying taxi ride, this time in the dark, we departed Colombo for Royal Singapore Air Force Tengah at 0100Z (6.30am local) on Friday 8th October, the flight commander in the captain's seat.

I'd spent a fair bit of the time in Colombo preparing for this day. Tengah was just a brief refuelling stop on the way to Darwin, and while the captains were flying only one leg each, I'd be on duty for both. The leg to Darwin would be my first as operating pilot - with my favourite captain in the other seat.

The scenery flying out of Colombo was just as spectacular as that flying in. Crossing the south of Sri Lanka, I had the ocean to my right and, to my front and left, an undulating sea of trees, wisps of mist rising from the canopy like smoke from thousands of chimneys. Every so often, a tower of sheer, reddish, rock would climb hundreds of feet above the foliage to a small plateau covered in more trees. Most of these pillars looked unattainable, potential lost worlds. Other breaks in the trees revealed terraced slopes of ruddy earth and light green vegetation. These, the old hands told me, were the tea plantations.

At one point, we passed to the south of cliffs rising several hundred feet above the foliage to a large plateau covered in a blanket of fog. In several places, the fog slipped over the edge of the plateau and cascaded down the cliffs like huge, wispy, waterfalls. Whenever I hear anything about Sri Lanka, this is the image that comes to mind. It was truly awe inspiring.

After three and a half hours flying southeast across the Indian Ocean, we passed over a string of what I can only describe as archetypal desert islands. Large or small, each was ringed with golden beaches and had a hinterland of lush vegetation. Beyond lay the larger island of Sumatra, and beyond that, the Malacca Strait, a waterway taking the bulk of sea trade travelling to the markets of the Far East, including China and Japan.

One of my dad's oft-repeated stories from the Second World War was of passing through the Malacca Strait when he was a film projectionist on a troop ship bound for Singapore, the British territory at the tip of the Malay Peninsula. Singapore was also a frequent topic of conversation for another, much darker reason.

As recounted in Preparation For Flight, my dad's younger brother, the uncle after whom I was named, had been captured when the territory fell to the Japanese in 1942. He was held captive and mistreated for the remainder of the War and, on his release, was so haunted by his experiences that he spent the rest of his life in hospital, where he died in 1986.

It would have been nice to share this personal story with the crew. But the lack of chemistry on the flight deck, and the prospect of the Grinch, who was on headset, making snide remarks, meant I kept my thoughts to myself.

After only one hour fifteen minutes on the ground at Tengah, during which I didn't get beyond the shade of the aircraft wing, we took off for Darwin at 0745Z – 3.45pm local.

If it was possible to become bored looking at desert islands, this was the leg. Before the light faded three hours in, we'd flown over the South China and Java Seas, passing to the north of Sumatra, Java and a string of beautiful islands with exotic names like Batam, Rempang, Sebangka and Belitung, none of which I'd heard of before, and none of which I've heard of since.

It was dropping dark as we neared Bali, so I saw only the lights of settlements on the islands dotting the Flores, Savu and Timor Seas. They included Komodo, one of the few names familiar to me, from the dragon of the same name, seen in childhood on Zoo Quest, a David Attenborough nature programme.

After a flight of six hours and twenty five minutes, we touched down in Darwin just before midnight local time. Thankfully I pulled off a decent instrument approach and a landing not even the Grinch could moan about.

Our greeting in Darwin was a surprise that would be repeated in New Zealand and on return to Australia a few days later. As soon as the crew door opened, a man with an aerosol can in each hand climbed the crew steps and without introduction began spraying what I later discovered was a mixture of disinfectant and insecticide, first onto the flight deck and then along the cargo bay, which he walked up and down spraying liberally.

It turned out it was standard procedure when landing in Australasia, but it seemed to take us all by surprise. And what was more, those in the habit of taking food off the aircraft to eat in the hotel soon found that it was confiscated, even a birthday cake the loadies had bought as a surprise for one of the air enges.

Welcome to Australia!

I'd like to say I spent several hours exploring Darwin, but it was past 1am by the time we reached the hotel, so after a fifteen and a half hour crew duty day, I settled for a quick wind-down beer then headed for bed. And with only fourteen and a half hours on the ground, by the time I'd woken up, had a meal, caught up on admin and planning for another day of two legs divided by a quick refuelling stop and a change of captains, it was time to board the transport.

We took off at 0440Z - 2.10pm local – on Saturday 9th October.

Now I knew Australia was big, but it still came as a surprise that the flight from Darwin to Richmond, an Australian Herc base within spitting distance of Sydney and the New South Wales coast, took five hours twenty minutes. I also knew that a fair proportion of the land beneath us would be wilderness, if not desert. After all, I'd grown up watching Skippy, an Australian TV series about a kangaroo that solved crimes and rescued people from their own stupidity, often when they'd become lost in the Outback.

But I just wasn't prepared for the reality. From the moment we departed Darwin until the light faded four hours later, there was almost nothing below but ruddy brown earth, from horizon to horizon, for hour after hour. Almost nothing. Every twenty miles or so, there'd be a dark pinpoint on the ground. Each would have several thin lines, tracks, radiating straight out from its heart to the horizon, like sunbeams in a child's drawing. These dark *suns*, which we assumed were wells or watering holes, were seemingly independent of settlements, while the tracks seemed to run nowhere other than the next well.

As I study an atlas now, we must have passed above towns and smaller communities connected by metalled roads, but memory being a tricksy thing, I don't recall anything other than these pinpoints and their radiating tracks.

There must also have been vegetation down there, because about an hour or so out of Darwin a great plume of smoke appeared in the distance just to the right of track. As we approached, we could see that it rose from the ground like a shimmering grey curtain tens of miles wide. The wispy tops reached up to not far below our level, something above 20,000 feet. Closer still and we could smell smoke, although I don't remember seeing any flame.

During my planning, I'd found an HF frequency on which bush fires could be reported. So, armed with lat and long coordinates from the nav, I duly reported it. The response was, to say the least, underwhelming. The voice on the other end acknowledged the message without enthusiasm, in a tone that shouted, *'Tell me something I don't know!'*

Undaunted, but feeling increasingly like an over-enthusiastic boy scout, I continued to report the bigger fires that popped up every few hundred miles, some stretching from horizon to horizon. And each response was as flat and unencouraging as the first.

I suspect that if the Grinch had been in the left hand seat, he'd have told me to stop making the reports. Or maybe he'd have waited until we'd landed and called me a c**t for making them. But the flight commander encouraged me to continue, so I did.

When we approached and passed directly over a curtain of smoke, it generated enough turbulence to have us bouncing uncomfortably for several miles before we cleared the plume of heated air. If there were any airliners flying a similar route, we never heard from them, but they'd have been 20,000 feet above us, unperturbed by smoke or turbulence. And if there were any more fires in the one hour twenty minutes we flew on in the dark, they didn't generate enough flame to be seen, or enough smoke to be smelt.

In the early decades of the 21st Century, we hear much more about, not only bush fires, but wild fires in general, mainly because they've begun to endanger the richer suburbs of our ever-expanding cities. But when watching newsreel of flames threatening Sydney or Melbourne, I can't help wondering just how much more devastation is being wrought in the thousands of square miles of Outback.

We were on the ground only one hour ten minutes at Richmond before taking off for Whenuapai with the Grinch in the left hand seat. After climbing above the lights of Sydney, our track took us straight out over the Tasman Sea toward New Zealand's North Island.

On a moonless night, the ocean below was pitch black, but above, the stars shone brightly, a magnificent, but also a puzzling sight.

I'm far from classing myself as an astronomer, but I can recognise at least some of the major constellations in the northern hemisphere, like the Big and Little Plough (Dipper), Cassiopeia, Taurus and, of course, Orion the Hunter. But although there seemed to be more stars in the sky this night than I'd ever seen, I recognised none of the patterns, that is, until I finally located the Southern Cross - much smaller than I'd expected.

During the three hours between periods of intense activity on the radios, I sat back, admired the view and wished I'd included a study of the southern constellations in my route prep.

We picked out the orange glow of Auckland long before we began our descent. There were a few small areas of light to north and south of it, but not many, an indication of the paucity of habitation beyond New Zealand's most populous city. It rings a large natural harbour - Waitemata - and sits astride a narrow isthmus linking the rectangular bulk of North Island to a thin peninsula thrusting three hundred miles northwest into the Pacific.

By day, the harbour was busy with yachts, ferries, passenger liners and freighters, but as we descended over it in the early morning, it was nothing but a ten-mile diameter black hole surrounded by the lights of the city's various districts and suburbs. The Grinch located the lights of Whenuapai's main runway close to its northern shore and we landed at four in the morning local time on Sunday 10th October.

While the loadies earned their keep helping to unload kit for the Nimrod detachment, the rest of us were driven around the western shore of the harbour to the hotel, a Travelodge, which daylight would reveal was close to the city's main passenger shipping terminal. And daylight wasn't long appearing. The sky was already lightening as we downed our first beer at about 5.30am.

Despite my determination to adhere to local time, the twelve-hour disconnect with GMT was now causing me some difficulties. I should have stayed awake for the rest of the day, ensuring that I'd be tired enough to get a good night's sleep before our early morning call just under twenty four hours later, at 5.40am on Monday 11th, or 1740Z on Sunday 10th. But when I blinked, it was as if my eyeballs were being scraped with sandpaper. So I decided to put my head down for a couple of hours – and no more. After all, in and around the necessary paperwork and planning for the following day, I wanted to see some of the city.

In the end, I didn't wake until 3.00pm, nine hours after my head hit the pillow. I'd obviously needed the sleep, but I was put out that I hadn't set an alarm. I'd left myself very little time – or daylight - to see any of Auckland.

As it turned out, it hardly mattered.

I met up with a couple of the NCOs who'd also over-slept and we set out from the hotel. Everywhere was shut. Everywhere had been shut all day. And it was raining. So, somewhat crestfallen, we wandered round the waterfront and business district in the wet.

I know Auckland has changed out of all recognition in the interim, but that day it was a bit like walking round my county town, Shrewsbury, on a wet Sunday afternoon in the 1980s. Nowhere to go and nothing to do. Eventually, with hunger pangs driving us on, we set out to find a restaurant. Again, almost everywhere was closed, and I'm ashamed to say we ended up at a Macdonald.

Had I really travelled to the other side of the globe to eat somewhere I rarely, if ever, visited at home? Disappointment would be an understatement. It felt more like a defeat. Anyway, transport was at 6.10 the next morning, so after the burger and a couple of beers in the hotel bar, I headed to my room to prepare for the following day.

Before I settled down for the night at about 10.00pm, I rang Geraldine. For her, it was ten o'clock in the morning. Luckily, she was in, and we spent a few minutes catching up on one another's news.

This call was an oddity for us. We'd decided early on that when I went away, I wouldn't ring routinely in case she didn't answer, which would worry me, or I was unable to call, which might worry her. Every time I left the house on route, she had a rough idea of when I was due back and that was it. If I was delayed significantly, someone on the squadron would let her know. Otherwise she got on with life until I showed up.

I was to discover that not all wives could cope with this. A small minority needed a daily call from their husbands or they'd become distressed, fearing the worst. They'd ring the squadron or, out of hours, the section leader or his wife to ask what was going on. Generally, the squadron or section leaders were unable to help. Unless they'd heard something to the contrary, the assumption was that the route was progressing as planned. Beyond the offer of sympathy for the lack of news, there was nothing else to be said or done. This often made these wives even more anxious, but the bottom line was they had to wait for their husbands to get in touch.

I'd witnessed a similar situation in flying training, when one of my friends had had to ring his wife every time he landed to reassure her he was safe. If he didn't ring, she'd be on the phone to the squadron. It made life miserable for her, and put him under added pressure, especially as there was little sympathy for his plight.

Over the years, I suspect e-mail and mobile phones will have done much to eradicate the problem, although probably not completely.

The sense of disappointment at not seeing more still nagged as we departed Whenuapai for Richmond. But there was no time to dwell on it. I was operating pilot for only the second time on the route, this time with my flight commander in the captain's seat.

There must have been strong headwinds over the Tasman Sea that morning. A flight that had taken three hours forty minutes eastbound just over a day earlier, took an extra hour westbound. Otherwise it was uneventful until the clouds opened during the descent over Sydney Harbour to give me a wonderful view of the bridge and opera house.

After an hour and a half on the ground at Richmond, we took off for Darwin, the Grinch in charge. As I'd guessed, after an unenthusiastic response to the first couple of fires I reported, he told me not to bother reporting any more.

We landed in Darwin at 0820Z – 5.50 in the evening of Monday 11th. We'd had a crew duty day of just less than twelve hours. Having slept well in Auckland, I wasn't as tired as after some of the previous legs and, having watched the sun set from the hotel, I thought I might explore the city. But this was one of the few occasions the captains decided we should have a crew meal, and I didn't want to let the side down. I have a dim memory of eating crocodile steak, but I may have made that up.

At 9.30 on the morning of Tuesday 12th – midnight GMT on the

11th - we took off for the seven hour fifty minute flight from Darwin to Hong Kong.

The next five hours were spent passing above the Arafura, Banda, Ceram, Malucca, Celebes and Suvu Seas. Once again, the names were new to me, and each expanse of translucent blue was dotted with islands and chains of islands big and small, most forested, with their fair share of beaches, and all stunningly beautiful from 25,000 feet or so.

The two-hour transit of the South China Sea was boring in comparison. But as we approached Hong Kong, radio traffic intensified and it became apparent we were to fly an approach for which we'd begun preparing three weeks earlier.

Before the handover to China in 1997 and the opening of a new airport in 1998, Hong Kong had made the most of an increasingly cramped and unsuitable airfield on the north-eastern shore of the Kowloon Peninsula about twenty miles south of the Chinese border. Ringed by rugged mountains and increasingly encroached upon by high-rise buildings, its single runway had been extended over the years until it was 11,000 feet long, the vast majority built out into the waters of Kowloon Bay on a bearing of 130°.

We dug out our approach charts for Runway 13.

They showed a dog-leg descent between the surrounding peaks, some more than 4,000 feet high. The penultimate leg was infamous among pilots. It was a non-standard instrument approach that led aircraft down, not toward a runway, but a huge red and white checkerboard on the lower slopes of a line of hills 2,000 feet high.

A few hundred yards short of the checkerboard at a height of six hundred feet or so, we expected to pass over a beacon known as an inner marker and hear a tone in our headsets. At that point we hoped to be beneath cloud and able to see both the checkerboard ahead and the tarmac of the runway out to our right. If so, the captain would turn sharp right through about fifty degrees to make a visual approach and landing.

If we couldn't see the checkerboard and runway, though, he'd have to initiate a missed approach procedure and climb between a series of radio beacons to avoid the surrounding high ground.

As a result of all its idiosyncrasies and hazards, Herc aircrew couldn't fly into Kai Tak unless they'd practised beforehand.

So back at Lyneham on 21st September, we'd spent one hour forty five minutes flying Kai Tak approaches and missed approaches in the simulator, mostly to Runway 13, and mostly with various emergencies necessitating the shutting down of one or two engines. Only when we'd completed this exercise satisfactorily were we cleared to fly into Hong Kong.

Of course, the simulator lacked visuals for Kai Tak, and it would be many years before YouTube videos of the checkerboard approach appeared, so I had no idea what it would look like on the day.

I was about to find out.

Despite its inadequacies, Kai Tak was a busy international airport, especially at 3.30 in the afternoon. With radio calls and changes of frequency coming thick and fast, we were slotted into a continuous stream of airline and cargo traffic, all flying much faster than dear old Fat Albert. As a result, every new controller asked us to keep our speed up at 240 knots, 60 knots faster than our normal speed in an instrument pattern. This, allied with a brisk southerly wind, meant the calculation of rates of descent and headings between radio beacons was a tad different to usual.

We tried not to deviate too far from the ideal track and descent profile when approaching any airport. But Kai Tak was one of those places where an accumulation of fairly small errors really could lead you into high ground, especially when, like today, we were spearing into the flanks of scattered cumulus clouds that covered some of the taller peaks.

I sensed that I wasn't the only one working hard to stay on top of things.

When we were clear of cloud, I had glimpses of wooded hills, blue waters and heavily built up areas. But I lacked the capacity to take much more than peripheral interest. And then, shortly after the squadron leader had captured the beam of the Instrument Guidance System, we popped out beneath the cloudbase.

The tension on the flight deck eased immediately. I was still busy on the radios, and we still had to fly the checkerboard approach, but I sensed a collective sigh of relief as we finally felt able to take in our surroundings.

Even though I'd seen Hong Kong on television and the big screen, the view elicited an unbidden 'Wow!'

We were flying east over the sea just beyond Lantau Island - where the new international airport would be built – heading directly toward the wooded flanks of a line of hills. I couldn't make out the checkerboard, but I could see Runway 13 out to our front right, thrusting into the water. A Boeing 747 was just touching down, towering skyscrapers a few hundred yards to its north and the blue waters of Victoria Harbour and Hong Kong Island to the south.

In anticipation of this moment, I'd put my little camera on top of the books in the nav bag down to my side. But now it came to it, I was so busy on the radios I knew I wouldn't have time to pick it up and take any pictures. There was a tap on my shoulder. I looked round and the squadron leader air eng's bespectacled face smiled down from where he was standing behind my seat. He held up the camera, his expression saying, *shall I?* I nodded in gratitude and turned back to my duties.

To our right, Discovery Bay held tens of ships, large and small, many moored in the open water or alongside numerous jetties. They included junks ploughing this way and that, distinctive sails billowing in the strong southerly wind. These added to the sense of flying into a Bond or Kung Fu movie, a feeling heightened by the architecture.

Most of the flatter land on the Kowloon Peninsula below and to our right was occupied by tall apartment blocks and skyscrapers crammed tightly together to form vertiginous canyons. The few open spaces contained cranes and buildings in various stages of construction, presumably more apartment blocks and offices. Even from 1,500 feet, I sensed energy and bustle, as if the city was a giant ant colony.

And then I saw the checkerboard. It didn't actually sit on the mountainside, but about a mile closer, on a small, wooded, hill surrounded by tall buildings. Short of it was an even smaller hill on which I guessed the tone-emitting beacon was sighted. Down to our right was a sports stadium, while on the runway another 747 was starting its take-off run.

We were still barrelling along at 240 knots and whether being chased down by airliners or not, with little more than six hundred feet left to descend, we had to slow down if we were to have time to lower the landing gear and flaps before the runway. So the squadron leader pulled back the throttles. The props on the Herc make great airbrakes and our speed was already reducing nicely as the tone rang in our headsets and he turned right.

We were pivoting about the stadium. Stan snapped a groundsman marking white lines on the football pitch a few hundred feet below.

The captain rolled out of the turn, keeping the right wing low to counter the strong crosswind from the south. As the jet ahead rose from the far end of the runway, he called for the landing gear. I responded and lowered the handle as we descended through a gap between apartment blocks, passing just above TV aerials on the stubbier buildings below. A few moments later, with the gear down and locked, I lowered the flaps as we passed low over a busy multi-lane highway, vehicles in the middle lanes climbing towards us on a flyover.

And then we were down and running along the tarmac into Kowloon Bay, ships of every size from liners to tugs in the water to our right. The captain braked relatively hard to take advantage of the first available turn off to our left. The reason became clear when I glanced back to see a Boeing

707 beginning its turn a few hundred yards short of the checkerboard.

There was another collective sigh as we cleared the runway to point at more skyscrapers, a line of jagged hills beyond them. I changed to the ground frequency and we followed instructions toward a pan brimming with aircraft in the distinctive green and white livery of Cathay Pacific Airlines.

Welcome to Hong Kong.

The last RAF aircraft based in Kai Tak had left four years earlier, but there was still an RAF office there. After parking in a far corner of the pan, we were met by the squadron leader who ran it.

It was just after four in the afternoon when the crew door opened and he climbed aboard, accompanied by a blast of heat and humidity. We were to be on the ground for two nights and a full day before an early morning departure thirty six hours later. The break was a rare luxury, and in one of the most famous cities in the world.

The squadron leader escorted us to the hotel where, much like a tour rep, he gave us a briefing on the best places to go for various activities, including shopping, and those places best avoided. He even gave us a card with an official stamp entitling us to a ten per cent discount in some of the recommended shopping areas. It was a nice touch, especially as I hoped to surprise Geraldine with a smart ladies watch.

That evening, after a wind down beer, shower and shave, we went out for only our third crew meal.

The hotel was in a business and shopping district toward the south of the Kowloon peninsula. October was one of the less oppressive months in the city, but as we stepped out of the air-conditioned lobby into the fading light it was still about 25°C, 77°F, and very humid. It wasn't long before sweat prickled my armpits beneath my short sleeved shirt.

In a nod to those who'd never visited the city, we walked to the southern end of the peninsula to look across Victoria Bay. The whole experience was an assault on the senses. There was the sight of thousands of people walking, cycling and driving between the closely packed skyscrapers; the sounds of the traffic, raised voices speaking a strange language and music with unfamiliar pitch and intonation seeping from shop doorways; and so many smells, from food and spices, to drains and poor plumbing.

When we reached the shoreline it was dark. Two miles south, beyond the lights of the many boats plying the Bay was Hong Kong Island, a dense forest of skyscrapers, stepping up from tens of storeys near the shore to hundreds a few blocks inland. Each building was covered in tiny yellow squares, the light streaming from thousands of windows. It was a picture postcard sight I returned to in daylight, when it was no less impressive.

The meal was another incredible experience. A sort of Chinese meze, more banquet than meal, although don't ask me to list the dishes in the way I did for the Cypriot equivalent. As I've said before, it wasn't long since I'd been eating chicken and chips in Chinese restaurants at home, so the dishes stretched my comfort zone to its limit, beyond in a couple of instances. I drew the line at anything with tentacles or a segmented body sprouting spindly legs and claws.

Almost two decades later, I was treated to a real banquet in Beijing, one consisting entirely of duck. That time, in the name of diplomacy, I had to eat everything put in front of me, including the feet and beak, parts I haven't been tempted to ask for when ordering crispy shredded duck from my local Chinese takeaway.

After the meal, we toured a few bars that highlighted the more western, ex-pat, side of Hong Kong. The only ones I can remember were Australian, Ned Kelly's Last Stand and the Waltzing Matilda, or Wally Mat's. From the latter, I still have a little rectangle of orange card that could be hooked over the rim of your beer glass. On one side it proclaims *Wally Mats, The World Famous Pub, Offering Homely Atmosphere, Draught Beer, Meals, Dominos and Darts*, and on the other side it reads, *PLEASE DON'T TOUCH, Gone to Wee Wee*!

With thirty six hours on the ground, we were due allowances for two breakfasts, a lunch and two dinners. But by this stage of the route, I had little currency left, so I intended to change some travellers' cheques into Hong Kong dollars in the hotel and give the crew their entitlement. But the Grinch complicated things again. He wanted me to issue everyone just enough cash for dinner that evening and find a better exchange rate for the travellers' cheques the next morning, then give everyone the balance of their allowances in Hong Kong dollars before lunch.

I should have told him to fuck off, but once again, I bowed to his demands, although some of the crew expressed incredulity at the plan.

Throughout my time at Lyneham, I never understood the desire to wring the last cent out of an allowances system that seemed pretty generous anyway. But quite a lot of my time as a co-pilot seemed to be spent doing just that. So here I was on my first morning in Hong Kong, touring various banks and bureaux de change to try and find the best exchange rate. In the end, I probably gave the Grinch and the others a few pounds more in local currency than I could have secured in the hotel. It seemed a poor return for my time and effort, but it kept him off my back for a while.

Most annoyingly, it had scotched my plans to explore beyond Kowloon as I still wanted to buy Geraldine that watch, an endeavour I expected to eat up most of the afternoon.

There were shopping opportunities everywhere in Kowloon, anything from small independent shops lining every street, to department stores and enormous indoor markets, food, much of it live, on the ground floor, other goods of all types spread over the floors above. There was even a large duty free shopping complex, Tsim Sha Tsui.

I'd decided before leaving the UK that I wanted a particular Seiko ladies watch and a fair proportion of the outlets we visited stocked it. But even armed with how much the genuine article would cost in the UK, how did I avoid being sold a fake at an outrageous price?

Luckily, the squadron leader air eng offered to help. I had no idea how to haggle, still don't, but he turned out to be a Jedi Master. And although I began the afternoon thinking I was imposing on him, it quickly became apparent that he was having a whale of a time and probably wouldn't have wanted to be anywhere else.

We visited a range of jewellers where he was greeted like a long lost cousin. The vendors immediately realised that although it was my money they were after, it was the squadron leader they had to impress. I was very happy with this state of affairs, and after a couple of hours of watching him haggling and playing one shop off against another, I bought Geraldine a watch at a discount considerably greater than the ten per cent voucher I had in my pocket.

As I watched the air eng in action, I began to realise why he enjoyed such shopping. It was the thrill of the chase. But much like ducks' feet and beaks, I never gained a taste for it; although I met many over the years just as passionate, or more so. I particularly remember the wife of an attaché in Beijing who took a group of us shopping for gifts for our wives. Whenever we spotted something we liked, she intervened, nostrils flaring as she haggled over the cost of every single item. She seemed to epitomise the term *shopping addict*.

Of course, even after all the assurances from the trader and the squadron leader, I couldn't be sure the watch I chose was genuine, or that I'd gained a bargain. But Geraldine was delighted with her gift, so who cares?

In the ensuing decades, several jewellers have assured us of its provenance. But a couple of years ago we found that new parts are no longer available for that model. It didn't really matter. The face and hands are so small that Geraldine hadn't been able to see them for several years.

I spent what remained of the afternoon wandering round Kowloon soaking up the atmosphere before meeting some of the NCOs in Wally Mat's for a few beers and a meal – something less exciting than the Chinese banquet of the previous night. Then it was back to the hotel for a bit of admin and planning.

After an early morning alarm call, we checked out, drove to Kai Tak, flight planned, crewed in and took off for Colombo at 7.40 local on Thursday 14th October. The Grinch was captain and I had my third stint as operating pilot. The take-off and climb above the water of Kowloon Bay was a little tame after the checkerboard approach, but the views were still spectacular.

Had we been allowed a straight line track from Hong Kong to Sri Lanka, I suspect the flight time would have been less than six hours. But, British military aircraft weren't allowed into Chinese or Vietnamese airspace, so we had to fly roughly south past Hainan Island and down the South China Sea to the east of the Vietnamese coast before turning onto a westerly heading. The result was a flight time of eight and a half hours.

Much like when flying past Albania, for the first few hours, we had to be awake to attempts to lure us into hostile airspace – meaconing. This was a possibility when passing

Hainan Island, but more likely as we passed Vietnam. For years afterwards I thought the practice was spelt Mekonging, presumably because I conflated Vietnam's penchant for it with the name of their major river.

As I looked down from the flight deck that day, I was blissfully unaware that in defiance of international law and the legitimate territorial rights of other countries in the region, China had laid claim to several of the island groups and reefs we passed, places like The Paracels, The Spratleys and Discovery Reef. My ignorance was brushed aside two decades later when I became the MOD desk officer responsible for our military relations with China. These same names were pretty near the top of my in-tray then, and they remain potential flashpoints for a major conflict now, with China pouring vast quantities of concrete into the ocean around islands and reefs to turn them into military bases, ports and airfields. They also claim the surrounding seas and airspace, so had our flight taken place in the 21st Century, it might well have been considered hostile. Whether anyone will have the stomach to face up to Chinese aggression in the future, we'll have to see, but it will remain a dangerous area no matter what.

In 1982, once past the southernmost point of Vietnam, we were able to turn west to cross the Malay Peninsula to the south of Thailand and set out across the Bay of Bengal. After another descent over Sri Lanka's beautiful forested terrain, we landed in Colombo at 2.10 in the afternoon – 0840Z.

By the time we reached the hotel it was early evening. With a 1.30am wake-up call booked, I don't think anyone ventured out. I settled for a couple of wind down beers and a meal before heading to my room for a bit of prep and a few hours' sleep.

The next morning, the leg from Colombo to Bahrain turned out to be my fourth and final as operating pilot, the flight commander in the captain's seat.

We took off at 4.25am on Friday 15th October – 2255Z on the 14th – the first two hours being flown in the dark, thus denying views of anything beyond the lights of the Sri Lankan coast and the tip of India. The next five and a quarter hours were in daylight though, so I feasted on the contrasting colours and terrain of the Arabian Sea, Oman, Qatar and the Persian Gulf before I landed in Bahrain from an instrument approach at 9.10 in the morning – 0610Z. Greenwich Mean and local times were converging again.

Once again, it sounds madness, but I saw nothing of Bahrain. As other people made their excuses and left the debrief, my flight commander chose to give me one of his longest talks on the subject of captaincy. Again, it was useful stuff, and I know he had my best interests at heart, but by the time he'd finished there were nine hours until transport, just enough for me to have a meal, do some paperwork and hit the pillow.

At 11.00pm, thirteen hours fifty minutes after we'd landed, we departed Bahrain with the Grinch in the captain's seat. For the next six and a half hours we flew in the dark over Saudi Arabia and into Egyptian airspace above the Sinai Peninsula, up the Gulf of Suez and across the Mediterranean, passing above Crete and the Greek Islands to land in Athens.

Highlights included the contrast between the almost total darkness of Saudi Arabia and the Sinai and the near-continuous strip of orange light marking out the snaking progress of the Nile in northern Egypt, and then the lights of the Greek Islands and Peloponnese on the descent into Athens.

The difference between GMT and local time was now down to two hours, so as we touched down in the Greek capital at 0230Z it was 4.30am on Saturday 16th. I was desperate for some sleep, but I was also determined not to make the mistake I'd made in Auckland. For once the itinerary was on my side. We had thirty hours on the ground.

I'd been very careful not to say squid to any of the Greek air traffic controllers, and the Grinch didn't spring any other surprises during his debrief so I was in bed by 6am, this time with my alarm set for four hours later.

I was out of the hotel by 11.00am, on my own as far as I can remember. In perfect sightseeing weather, I explored central Athens and its temples including, of course, those on the Acropolis. Standing next to the Parthenon and overlooking the city was magical.

My photos include one of the guards outside the Presidential Palace. What it doesn't convey is that much like the East German soldiers in Berlin, they marched with an elaborate goosestep. But whereas the effect in Berlin had been sinister, the Greek equivalent elicited a totally different reaction.

To my eyes, their uniform of dark tunic, white tights, bright red cap and black slippers with fluffy black bobbles seemed more suited to a ballet dancer than an armed guard. Had I visited in summer, the outfit would have been even more theatrical, the dark tunic becoming a white mini-dress with voluminous sleeves and a pleated skirt. And when they marched, it was a slow motion parody of John Cleese goose-stepping in the *Don't mention the war* episode of Fawlty Towers.

At the risk of being disrespectful to a fellow NATO nation, I thought it was pure comedy magic.

On almost any other crew, the last night before returning

home after a long route would have been an excuse for a final get-together over an evening meal. Such events offered a chance to reminisce about our experiences and create a group narrative before we went our separate ways after landing at Lyneham. Some of us might fly together again, some might not, but we would always share this bond. With this crew though, there was no final gathering. I can't even remember where I ate or with whom. Sad really.

The Sunday morning seemed positively civilised compared with some of the preceding days. Our call wasn't until 08.45 local – 0645Z - and we didn't take off until 12.10.

After an uneventful flight of five hours twenty minutes across the Ionian Sea, up the east coast of Italy and over Switzerland and France, we landed at Lyneham at 3.30pm, thirteen and a half days after we'd left. I'd spent most of the quieter periods of the flight reconciling the remaining cash and travellers' cheques, then completing each crew members' imprest form and getting them signed ready to hand in to the Accounts Section the following morning.

I walked into my married quarter at about 5.00pm and Geraldine and I carried on with our lives. The pattern of frequent separations and reunions was now a normal part of our marriage.

Over the preceding two weeks, I'd seen some wonderful sights. I'd also learnt a lot about human nature and enjoyed moments of professional fulfilment. I shall always be grateful to the RAF for the opportunity to fly to the other side of the planet. And yet, I can't help thinking that, with a different crew, it could have been so much better.

Luckily, during my three years on 24, there were very few occasions when a crew failed to gel, and this was by far the worst example. It reinforced a valuable life lesson.

Enjoyment depends not on where you go and what you do, but who you're with.

BREAD AND BUTTER

Never dwell on the past. Look ahead and prepare for the next challenge. This philosophy is instilled during military training and emphasised at points throughout your career. If followed to the letter it means no time wasted basking in the glow of a success, or beating yourself up over failure.

Sometimes, of course, it's easier said than done, but I did my best to put the disappointments of the New Zealand trip behind me. The pace of life helped.

When I visited the co-pilot office after handing in the imprest on the day after our return, the programme showed a two hour simulator sortie that afternoon and an Ascension trip, my tenth, two days later. By the time I'd returned from that on Saturday 23rd, I'd already flown more than one hundred and twenty hours in October, the normal limit for a rolling thirty-day period. In fact, I'd flown one hundred and forty hours in the last thirty days, so I had to spend several days on the ground.

Highlights on my return to flying in the second half of November were a flight to Oslo and back and another Akrotiri trip. In between there was a quick dash to RAF Coningsby, a Phantom base in Lincolnshire, a co-pilot training sortie, two sims, various standby duties and, for some reason, three air tests, short flights to see whether some engineering fix or new component worked as advertised.

I also planned a flight to Thessaloniki in northern Greece as part of a large multinational exercise on NATO's *southern flank*, Apex Express. But it was cancelled at the last minute. Turkey had raised objections arising out of its territorial disputes with Greece.

That a fellow NATO country should cause such wilful disruption to the Organisation's activities seemed strange at the time, but the more I encountered Turkey over the years, the stranger its membership of the Alliance seemed.

With my Squadron Fund hat on, I'd commissioned and selected a new design for a squadron Christmas card, a pencil drawing of a Herc in the snow by an artist on the station. I ordered two hundred and fifty and they proved so popular I was unable to sell the remaining stock of old designs.

I write about this not to crow about a success, but to give an idea of the range of activities in which an RAF officer could be involved. I was as surprised to be selling Christmas cards as you probably are to be reading about them.

I'd also been tasked with finding a replacement for the Squadron's black and red cravat. These distinctive strips of material - tied at the neck and tucked into the flying suit - were universally unpopular, seen as outdated, untidy and uncomfortable, especially in hot climates. As a result, many had taken to removing them as soon as the wheels were up on departure from Lyneham. When I canvassed opinion on an alternative, most people seemed to favour a flying suit badge. I took that as my starting point.

Early in my research, I discovered that before, during and after the Second World War, the tailfins of 24 Squadron aircraft bore a distinctive chevron badge, like sergeant stripes, alternating red and black. I decided to work up a design based on that.

Over the next couple of months, in between flying and other duties, I drew a range of red and black chevron badge designs – some with no embellishments, some with RAF eagles or crowns, and combinations of these with backgrounds of different shapes and colours. I carted the alternatives round the Squadron seeking opinions until I'd whittled them down to three.

In the end, the Squadron execs and, ultimately, the

Boss chose the original red and black chevron without a background, eagle or crown. I went ahead and ordered hundreds, handed them out and watched them appear on the right breast of everyone's flying suit.

The whole process had been a pain – and again not something I'd expected to do when I joined the Herc force. But I have to say, I thought the finished article looked mighty handsome. Four decades later, 24 Squadron aircrew still wear the design, and I always get a buzz when I see it.

Of course, at the time, feedback on the new badge was far from universally positive. Almost everyone moaned about having to pay for it, while inevitably some, and often those who'd been most vociferous about getting rid of it, now said how much they missed the old red and black cravat. I suspect a few were just trying to wind me up. At the time, they succeeded.

Having discovered my reader base, in this volume, I decided to concentrate almost exclusively on my professional life. But life at Lyneham was also busy on the social front. As an example, November included a dining-in night in the Officers' Mess, a couple of visits from friends and family, an *At Home* - a drinks party with nibbles - at my flight commander's married quarter, and a trip to see Welsh folk singer and comedian, Max Boyce, at the Oasis Leisure Centre in Swindon. Most months were similar.

The first half of December was relatively busy with a day return flight to Gibraltar via RAF Lossiemouth in northern Scotland; a day route to Hanover, Gutersloh and Northolt; and another Ascension sortie, the one during which we spent a night in *chalets* in the grounds of a hotel in Dakar and were badly bitten by mosquitoes and/or bed bugs.

But then I didn't fly for the rest of the month, although I completed a couple of standby duties and two sim trips. I also volunteered to be Station Orderly Officer on Christmas Day.

As explained in On The Buffet, every day of the year, a junior officer becomes the first point of contact on the station for any problems deemed to require an officer's input outside normal office hours. If I felt unable to deal with anything referred to me by the Orderly Corporal and Orderly Sergeant, I could pass it up the line to a Duty Executive, a squadron leader or wing commander, who could deal with it themselves or pass it on to the Station Commander.

On a station like Lyneham with hundreds of junior officers, Orderly Officer didn't come round that often, but 24 Squadron co-pilot section had been told to provide *a volunteer* for Christmas Day. Against the advice of my father – *never volunteer for anything* – I put up my hand. With my saintly hat on, the self-sacrifice would allow those who lived away from base to go home to their families, and those living on base with children to spend the day with them.

My reasons weren't entirely altruistic though. Firstly, if all was quiet, I could expect to spend most of the day with Geraldine in Eider Avenue anyway, and secondly, doing such a duty on Christmas Day would gain me enough smarty points with the other co-pilots to guarantee I wouldn't be Orderly Officer for a very long time, probably for the rest of my tour. I wasn't.

My only routine duties were saluting the RAF Ensign as it was lowered outside Station Headquarters at 4.30pm and again when it was raised at 8.00am. I might also have to inspect people on *jankers*, that is, airmen who'd been found guilty of ill discipline or some minor criminal offence. As part of their punishment, they had to report to the guardroom in their No 1 uniform at 7.00 each evening to be inspected by the Orderly Sergeant and then the Orderly Officer. Either could decide the miscreant hadn't put enough effort into their appearance and send them away to smarten up and return at a later time. It was one of the irritants for those on jankers, but could also be a bit of a pain for the duty staff.

I was lucky. There was no-one on jankers and there were no crises during my twenty four hours on duty, although it was a bit of an alcoholic obstacle course. I decided to visit as many of the sections where people were working as possible, just to see how they were and say Merry Christmas. But it seemed that almost everyone else in the chain of command was doing the same, Duty Execs, squadron commanders, the Station Commander, even the padres. And most seemed to have presented the sections they visited with mince pies and alcohol, a proportion of which I was offered everywhere I went. Had I succumbed I could have been very full - and very drunk.

Lyneham was an RAF Regional Detention Centre, meaning the guardroom had a suite of cells for airmen remanded in custody to appear before a military or civilian court, or serving a short period of custody for a crime that didn't merit a term in the Military Prison at Colchester. One of my duties was to visit the inmates to see if they had any problems or complaints.

On the day, I was surprised to find several airmen in residence. Having no idea what their alleged or proven crimes were, I adopted a sympathetic approach, which wasn't that difficult as they all looked pretty crestfallen. Who wouldn't be, spending Christmas in a cell?

The first two weeks of January included a day ferrying troops between Northern Ireland and Germany in support of Op Banner; and three flights to northern Norway, where Harrier, Jaguar and Royal Marine units were taking part in exercises to prepare them for winter operations on NATO's *northern flank*.

The first and third Norwegian visits in support of Exercise Clockwork were to Evenes, an airport and Norwegian Air Force base near Narvik. The second, in support of Exercise Timber Thorn was to Bardufoss, an airfield a little further north, near Tromso.

I discovered that approaches to most locations in Norway could be more demanding and, in many ways, more exciting than the checkerboard approach to Runway 13 at Kai Tak.

While the Norwegian airfields were nowhere near as busy, they tended to be located on what little flat land there was close to the sea in the mouths of steep valleys or fjords. And while a descent and landing from over the sea was all very routine, approaches toward the sea meant flying much closer to high ground than on any approach to Kai Tak. The terrain also tended to hamper or prevent the use of radar, so approaches were largely procedural, that is, timed spiralling descents centred on radio beacons.

The few approaches I flew in daylight were spectacular, descending toward jagged, snow-capped peaks and high plateaus dotted with lakes and glaciers, before spiralling down into the steep-sided valleys for the final approach. It highlighted the need to fly accurately, because when flying in cloud or poor visibility, all that rock was out there just waiting for you to make a mistake. I also loved descents in good visibility at night, when the rock walls slowly blotted out more and more stars, as if you were sinking into a black hole or a canyon on the Death Star.

Very atmospheric.

Both Evenes and Bardufoss were well within the Arctic Circle, and with most arrivals and departures carried out at night, I thought I might catch a glimpse of the Northern Lights. Unfortunately, it was not to be. It would be the late 80s before I saw them for the one and only time in my life so far – from outside a bar in Aviemore, Scotland, in the wee small hours. But that's another story.

Another disappointment was that I spent no more than one and a half hours on the ground on any trip to Norway. It would be nearly four decades before Geraldine and I enjoyed a wonderful week walking in the Sognefjord area, north of Bergen.

February saw me embark on another transatlantic trip, this time to Calgary in Alberta, western Canada. We flew via Keflavik and Goose Bay on the way out and Ottawa and Gander on the way back.

Although there were three night-stops, Goose Bay, Calgary and Gander, each allowed the minimum time on the ground, so it was a busy few days, not least because I was once again the only co-pilot alongside two captains, neither of whom I'd flown with before. On the face of it, it had all the potential pitfalls of the New Zealand trip.

I was told one of the captains was very affable and easy to get on with, but the other, a portly pipe-smoker in his early fifties, could be a bit of a tyrant. He thought he was a lovable rogue, whereas he was, in fact, just a rogue, prone to making everyone's lives a misery if anything angered him. On the other hand, my informant added, as long as everyone humoured him and all went well, things would be okay.

Luckily, on this route and the few other occasions I flew with him, the worst I suffered was the reek of pipe smoke and stale tobacco rising from him and his flying clothing. He'd light up soon after take-off and a few minutes later be humming contentedly, while the rest of us coughed and flapped our hands in front of our faces. Mentioning the fug was one of the things guaranteed to set him off, so crews tended to put up with it.

Even if he'd been less content, this route would have been nothing like New Zealand because the rest of the crew gelled. The young, moustachioed navigator and I struck up a relationship that would stand us both in good stead a few months later when we embarked on one of the most demanding training courses in the RAF.

This was my first trip with one of the few female loadmasters on the Herc at the time. She was very professional and there was no reason to rail against her competence, or even her very presence, as a minority were prone to do. I never witnessed her receiving overt intimidation, but I doubt her life was easy, not only when flying with the misogynists, but also because of the backdrop of sexist banter that would be unacceptable now.

As on previous forays to Canada, my main recollections are of the Atlantic ice and the endless expanse of tundra and lakes across northern Canada. But there was also Alberta, thousands and thousands of square miles of flat farmland dotted with isolated settlements. Everything was hidden beneath a covering of snow, so it was hard to imagine the same landscape turning gold with ripening grain. And just when you thought the plains would go on forever, Calgary appeared, a dense thicket of skyscrapers thrusting out of the ground like shimmering crystals. Beyond that, poking above the haze in the distance, the snow-capped peaks of the Rocky Mountains.

I was operating pilot for the legs into Calgary and Gander where, despite, or perhaps because of, the several feet of snow surrounding the operating surfaces, we were asked to do a crash drill. This meant being shepherded off the runway and followed to our dispersal by several fire tenders, then *rescued* from the *wreckage* of our aircraft by the stereotypically beefy and moustachioed Canadian fire-fighters. Perhaps it's sexist to say that the loadie seemed more excited by this than the rest of us.

Anyway, we were all glad to oblige.

In addition to various standby duties, February finished with day trips to Wildenrath and Jever in Germany and a night-stop at Deci in Sardinia, while March began with a long-delayed week of Periodic Refresher Training - PRT - on the Operational

Conversion Unit.

I should have completed the course of four sim and five flying sorties five months earlier, six months after joining the squadron – and annually thereafter. But OCU instructors had been needed to support the effort in the South Atlantic and training schedules had slipped. For the same reason, Herc pilots filling instructor posts away from the front line had been dragged back to Lyneham. This was to have an unexpected effect on my cohort of co-pilots when our tours ended.

In contrast to squadron flying on long routes with few landings and, hopefully, few emergencies, the week of refresher training was a chance to hone pure flying skills on short flights with multiple approaches and plenty of practice emergencies, most simulating the loss of one or more engines. I'd done some of this on squadron Co-Pilot Training sorties, but these had been few and far between during the Falklands War and its aftermath.

Had I completed my PRT in October, maintaining the D Basic Category I'd been awarded by the OCU the previous April would have been the most likely outcome. But in the intervening five months, I'd been awarded C Cats for both Route flying and Operational Efficiency. So although a D Basic Cat would still be acceptable, the pressure was on to upgrade to a C, making me a C overall, good progress for this stage of my first operational tour.

Without blowing my own trumpet too loudly, since joining 24 Squadron, things had been going well, certainly better than my performance in flying training would have predicted. I think this was largely because I'd relaxed into the demands of squadron life, to the benefit of both my general well-being and my flying. But as soon as I entered the more formal regime of the OCU again, my performance dipped.

Much of this was undoubtedly down to lack of skill when being pushed harder on more demanding flights. But some was also down to a recurrence of the old nerves. I seemed to revert to my flying training persona, struggling to eat and sleep. And on the flight deck, it was back to swimming through treacle. Even though I recognised the paralysis of my thoughts and actions, I was unable to *snap out of it*.

After a difficult week, I did secure a C Basic Cat, and therefore an overall C Operating Cat, but my adverse reaction to such a short period of formal training was a worry.

It was to be a recurring problem, making every flying course or test a major obstacle, whether it should have been or not. I was not unique in this. The same trait was evident in some of those I'd completed flying training alongside, and it would be evident in many of the young men and women I went on to train as pilots or instructors in the following decades. Otherwise capable, some fell by the wayside solely because of their inability to cope with the pressures of training.

With one exception to be covered in the next volume, I managed to more or less hang on in there during most courses. But it was always a painful process.

CAPE CANAVERAL

The week after PRT, at short notice, I became co-pilot for a route that would not only restore my confidence, but take it to new heights. Known simply as the Patrick-Andros, it came to the Herc force when Britain needed underwater equipment tested at a specific American facility. On this occasion, we were to be one of three crews from different squadrons supporting a test programme lasting a little more than six weeks. For me, it meant two weeks flying between Patrick Air Force Base in Florida, Andros Island in the Bahamas and Cape Canaveral, a few miles to the north of Patrick.

The mere mention of Cape Canaveral was enough to make my mouth water. The name was synonymous with all the US space missions I'd followed as a youngster, including the Apollo moon landings. Now, it was the home of the Space Shuttle programme, another I'd watched with interest – and awe – from the outset. To think that I'd be flying into the place where such magic happened was unbelievable.

And it was all to be done with a crew I knew well and looked forward to flying with again: my original constituted crew during the Falklands War. With the addition of two ground engineers, we quickly became the Seven Ascoteers. It was to be three weeks of unrivalled camaraderie and, well, fun.

On Wednesday 16th March we took off for Gander in XV219. On board was freight for several destinations and a team of movers to load and unload en-route and during our two-week stint at Patrick. As usual, the captain was meticulous in allowing me to fly every other leg, so after he'd flown into Keflavik for a refuel, I flew us on to a very snowy Gander for a night landing, by which time it had been a sixteen-hour crew duty day. Just over twelve hours later, we took off for Patrick, where we landed in the late afternoon.

Before we relieved the first Herc crew, we had another short task to perform. At 6.30 local the next morning – Friday - I took off to fly us on to Bridgetown in Barbados, where some of the freight was to be handed over to the crew of a Royal Navy ship before we flew on to Belize in Central America to offload spares for the resident garrison and its supporting Harrier detachment. After a night stop in Belize, we were due to return to Patrick the next morning. Five movers accompanied us.

About three hours into the five-hour first leg, during which I'd enjoyed wonderful views of the Bahamas and the Turks and Caicos islands, we discovered that the Navy had mixed up their GMT, ship and local times. The upshot was that their vehicles couldn't be at Bridgetown airport until at least five hours after we'd landed. Even if they arrived no later than that, with Belize more than six hours away, we were suddenly looking at a minimum crew duty day of eighteen hours. And while this may have been necessary in war or a relief operation of some sort, it was hardly merited in our current circumstances.

So, as I flew us on past beautiful islands – Guadeloupe, Dominica, Martinique and St Lucia – the captain contacted 38 Group on the HF to work out a revised itinerary. By the time he'd finished, we were night-stopping Barbados and flying on to Belize and Patrick the next day. The British Consulate, Belize and Patrick had been informed.

After a flight of five hours five minutes, I flew over surf breaking onto a reef just off a rocky shoreline dotted with sandy beaches and landed in Barbados. It was 12.50pm local time and the sun was shining. The freight was unloaded and the movers hung around to hand it over to the Navy while a member of the British Consulate staff escorted the rest of us to our hotel.

You'll just have to take my word for this, but the Consulate had been able to find only one of their contract hotels with a dozen rooms available at such short notice: the Barbados

Hilton. We were beaming even before we discovered that it occupied a prime beach-front spot on a picturesque headland in the south west corner of the Island.

After a couple of wind down beers and a promise to meet up in the early evening for a crew meal, I showered and set out to explore the headland, Needham Point. There, I watched turquoise waves break onto the beach in front of the Hilton, before heading off to a colourful lighthouse and 18th Century fort, its cannon pointing out to sea, ready to rake any passing pirate ships with powder and shot.

It was all very pleasant, but my strongest memory is of stopping every few yards on the way back through the hotel gardens to watch hummingbirds. Near every flower bed, there'd be a flash of colour before the tiny creatures, most no bigger than the top of my thumb, came to the hover, their wing-beats a whisper within a hazy mirage of shimmering air. And there they'd stay, motionless except for their tongues, darting into the trumpets of red, yellow and blue hibiscus, or other exotic flowers I couldn't name. The birds' primary colours varied from green to blue, purple and black, but the plumage of most seemed alive, rippling with vivid spectra, like oil on a puddle.

I was mesmerised, so mesmerised I was almost late for dinner.

Had we been paying for the meal from allowances, we'd have found somewhere cheaper than the Hilton to eat. But we were on what was known as *Actuals*. This meant the Consulate would pick up the tab for not only our accommodation but also our meals, which had to be taken in the Hilton. All we had to pay for was our drinks. So, after a meal in unusually plush surroundings featuring plenty of laughter, we retired to our rooms for a good night's sleep and a morning call at the civilised time of 7.00am.

The captain flew us across the Caribbean to Belize, a Central

American country bordered by the Guatemala to the south and west, Mexico to the north and the ocean to the east. The majority of its hinterland is dense jungle, but its coast is fringed with golden beaches and thousands of tiny islands that make tourism a vital part of its economy.

Britain had granted Belize – formerly British Honduras - independence in 1981, but Guatemala refused to recognise the new country and laid claim to its territory. As a result, a garrison of fifteen hundred British troops, RAF helicopters and a flight of Harriers stayed to guarantee its survival. The Harriers remained until 1989 and the bulk of the troops withdrew in 1994, leaving behind a training team to support the Belize Defence Force.

In 1988, while on the staff of the Central Flying School, I helped train a Belizean pilot to become a flying instructor.

Back in 1983, I'd have loved to have had time to visit some of the Mayan sites in the jungle, but less than two hours after landing we climbed away for the return to Patrick AFB. The two and three quarter hour flight took us roughly north along the Belizean and Mexican coasts and into the Gulf of Mexico to the west of Cuba. Once past the Communist island – another place to be on the alert for meaconing – we flew northeast toward our destination.

Patrick Air Force Base sits halfway up the Atlantic coast of Florida toward the northern end of a thin ribbon of land running just offshore for one hundred miles from Palm Springs. The ribbon varies in width from a few miles to a few yards where narrow causeways and bridges bear a four-lane highway that runs its entire length.

For most of its northward journey the ribbon is separated from the mainland by The Indian River, a lagoon a few miles wide crossed by numerous bridges. Just to the north of Patrick, it splits, one arm continuing north, the other curving northeast round The Banana River and widening into a large, flat, triangular headland: Cape Canaveral.

Even in the 1980s, both shorelines of the Indian River and the Atlantic shore were fringed with unbroken lines of hotels and apartment blocks – or condominiums – and marina after marina. I'd never seen so many small boats, or so many miles of beach.

The last four days had included visits to Iceland, Canada, Barbados and Belize, and now our second landing in Florida. It seemed like a lifetime of experiences.

But the best was yet to come.

Sitting about ten miles south of Cape Canaveral, one of Patrick's primary roles was supporting the space programme. In the run up to and during space shuttle and rocket launches, its reconnaissance aircraft scoured the ocean and airspace down-range for aircraft or vessels that could endanger the launch or put themselves in danger from discarded booster rockets or any other falling debris. If necessary, other aircraft and helicopters from Patrick could shepherd away or engage a threat or, should the worst happen, mount search and rescue operations.

So as we taxied in that Saturday evening, we passed dispersals lined with tens of Hercs, C141 Starlifters, P8 Orions, F16 fighters and helicopters various.

One afternoon, we were shown round a Herc gunship by its proud crew, members of the Air National Guard. As a last resort, they were prepared to blow out of the water any vessel deemed a danger. To emphasise that it was no idle threat, the captain pointed to an enormous multi-barrel gun where most Hercs had a rear side door for disgorging paratroopers.

He explained that when it was fired, its barrels rotated like a giant Gatlin Gun, spitting thousands of high-velocity cannon shells a minute. While the rest of his crew nodded, he went on to boast that a two-second burst at a football field with a dinner plate on each square yard would break every plate.

Chatting amongst ourselves afterwards, it turned out that we'd all considered asking if there was much prospect of finding a football field covered in crockery down-range of a space shuttle launch. But we'd all decided against it, realising that neither the captain nor his crew would have appreciated the humour. More earnest and intense than any Harrier pilot, they saw nothing funny in the analogy chosen to illustrate the potency of their weapon system.

Absurdity aside, we had to admit that, whether you were on a football pitch or not, you wouldn't want to be fired on by that gun, or its mate on the other side of the aircraft.

Anyway, that first Saturday, we parked XV219 at the end of a long line of USAF Hercs and had a brief chat with the crew we were replacing. An hour or so later, with their movers down the back, they took off, heading for home via Gander.

By that time, the captain was driving the fifteen miles or so south to our hotel in a hire car that was ours for the duration of the detachment. It came with a daily mileage allowance of sixty miles, enough for us to commute each day and make the odd visit to local shops and amenities for supplies. The ground engineers had a separate car as they often had to stay on at Patrick after we'd landed to fix snags.

To any readers who spent their military detachments confined to tents or holes in the ground, I can only apologise and say that as far as I know no-one had bribed the USAF to say they couldn't provide us with transport, or accommodate us on base at Patrick. And I'm sure the bean counters would have done their utmost to secure a good deal for the taxpayer, both when choosing a hotel and when opting for hire cars rather than daily taxis.

But it has to be admitted that the cars gave us a degree of unimagined freedom when planning our days off - and that we found ourselves living in a large resort hotel. It wasn't so much in Melbourne Beach as on Melbourne Beach. I was able to watch the surf break onto the sand less than one hundred yards from my room. And by making two of their number double up, the movers had even created a permanent party room – more of a crewroom really, where members of the detachment could chew the fat before heading to one of several hotel restaurants or cheaper alternatives a short drive away.

I grew to know the young flying officer in charge of the movers reasonably well. A few years younger than me, he was a thoroughly decent and sensible young man, far more responsible than most aircrew officers of the same age. He had to be in order to lead and manage the dozen airmen under his command.

He and I met infrequently for the rest of our careers, and every time we did he'd advanced at least one rank above me. The last time I saw him, I was a group captain and he was an air commodore. As we relived some of the experiences of that short period in Florida twenty years earlier, he still seemed a thoroughly decent and sensible young man. That said, we spent a lot of time shaking our heads at memories of the amount of beer we'd consumed most evenings, the last few in Mr Tease, the hotel nightclub, more of which later.

There was little partying that first Saturday night though. I had to prepare for our first Patrick-Andros day starting early next morning.

A Patrick-Andros run consisted of a one-hour flight to an airstrip halfway up the east coast of Andros, the largest of the Bahamian Islands. The airstrip was a couple of miles from the US Navy's Atlantic Underwater Test and Evaluation Centre – AUTEC, from where we'd pick up British torpedoes that had been test-fired and retrieved from the ocean. Once they were loaded, we delivered them to Cape Canaveral Air Force Skid Strip. There, they'd be unloaded and driven away to be studied while we flew back to Patrick.

Each working day began at 7.30am in Patrick Base Ops, where the captain, nav and I would receive a personalised met briefing for our route from a USAF sergeant. Over the course of the detachment, we were briefed by several different NCOs, but they all finished with the same warning.

'There is a fifty per cent chance of cumulonimbus activity along your planned route today and we would advise against taking off on your mission.'

The first time we heard the words we were more than surprised. Met men at RAF stations – in aviation in general – provide forecasts outlining the conditions that might be encountered over the duration of a route. And while they might suggest things such as the best height to avoid icing or turbulence, they *never* strayed into advising a crew on the conduct of their mission; nor would they dare.

So on that first day there was a lengthy pause while the captain, never the most even-tempered of men, digested the information and decided how to respond. Had we been on an RAF station, he'd probably have blown his top and given a speech littered with expletives making it clear that the met man should stick to weather forecasting and let him decide how to fly the aircraft. But, that morning, he channelled his inner Zen and merely thanked the young man, before turning and leading us to a table in the corner of the room.

It was all a bit perplexing. I doubt there's a day in that part of the world when there isn't a fair chance of meeting a thunderstorm. So, if we'd taken the NCO's advice each day, we'd never have flown to Andros, and if we'd heeded such warnings elsewhere in the world, things like flying through the ITCZ to Ascension Island would have been unthinkable. Similarly, the tens of aircraft out on the pan at Patrick would rarely have moved, and US military aircraft worldwide would have spent most of their time on the ground.

But even on that first morning, the noise and activity outside our window indicated that USAF aircrew were, like us, taking the warning with a pinch of salt and getting on with their missions. And of course, despite the warnings, we flew each subsequent day. We saw the odd storm, but not once did we have to deviate from track to avoid one.

So what was going on?

We might have understood if the Met man had been wearing

the logo of some contractor trying to cover its ass should we end up in the Atlantic as a result of bad weather. But he was in the military. All very strange!

Anyway, each day, having submitted flight plans for the outbound and return journeys, we'd depart Patrick at 9.00am, head south down the Florida coast for Palm Beach and turn south east across the ocean for Andros Town International Airport.

The word international in the title was over-egging it a little. Even the word airport was something of a misnomer. Andros was – and still is - a fifty-foot wide, 4,000 foot long strip of sun-bleached tarmac running east/west two miles inland of the coast. The landing surface and adjacent dispersal area are surrounded by a dense forest of scrubby trees, there are no airfield buildings, and facilities such as customs turn up only if requested on a flight plan.

There was also no air traffic control. At top of descent on the way in, we'd say goodbye to Miami Flight Services and contact AUTEC Ops. They'd give us an idea of the weather and despatch a couple of large yellow fire trucks – Rescue 4 and 5 – to meet us. If asked, the crew of Rescue 5 would let us know if there were any other aircraft in the area. There rarely were.

Perhaps visitors were deterred by the wrecks in the bushes to either side of the strip, or the battered light aircraft sitting on its nose in the corner of the dispersal.

The length of the runway limited our take-off and landing weight to 125,000lbs, several tons below maximum. Even so, there was little margin for error if you landed long, or failed to get airborne in time to climb above the encroaching vegetation. These constraints did little to curb our captain's enthusiasm though, as he demonstrated during our first arrival.

Diving down over the surf-fringed beach and flashing above the trees, he descended to about fifty feet over the eastern threshold of the runway before closing the throttles and pulling up and left in a tight wingover. As the speed washed off, we carried out the landing checks, lowering landing gear and flaps just before he lined us up on short finals for a textbook landing from which we stopped a little over halfway down the tarmac.

The captain, beamed. I don't think he'd performed a run and break like it since his time on the JP at Linton a few years earlier. I hadn't seen one since then either, and I certainly hadn't expected to experience one from the flight deck of a Herc. It must have been quite a sight for the crews of Rescue 4 and 5.

Every day thereafter, we came up with a different name for our arrivals – a Beach 7 or a Lagoon 5 – but, whether flown by the captain or me, all involved rorting in toward the runway at fifty feet or so and performing a run and break to land.

I'm not going to pretend that my performance was as polished as my captain's, but I somehow pulled off all the landings I flew from such unstructured approaches. It was not only great fun but also a great boost to my confidence.

After landing at Andros on the first morning, in a sort of *I'll show you mine if you show me yours* exchange, we gave the crews of Rescue 4 and 5 a conducted tour of our Herc and they showed us round their fire trucks. They'd seen us doing our stuff, so they were keen to show off their kit and explain their capabilities, and to assure us that should anything go wrong, they had our backs. On each subsequent day, we had a brief chat with them before taking transport through the town of Andros to AUTEC.

And here I feel I have to apologise again.

We didn't bribe the test team and our movers to take their time. It was just that preparing the torpedoes for flight and loading them always took at least four hours. After all, they were the very definition of dangerous air cargo. And while all this was happening, we'd be forced to lounge on the beach, popping up only to go for a swim in the turquoise water, to join in the odd game of beach volleyball, or to nip into the adjacent café for a drink and/or a bite to eat.

My only duty was to find a phone on arrival and ring Miami to confirm that they'd received the return flight plan I'd submitted at Patrick Base Ops. On about half of occasions, they hadn't, so I'd pass the plan verbally – then head to the beach.

Sometime during the early afternoon, the movers would call to say they were nearly finished. We'd return to the aircraft and, in the shade of a wing, plan for our departure.

Take-offs were always interesting. Our wings stretched well beyond the edges of the narrow runway and, as we accelerated, the forest rushed past just beyond the wingtips. But it also rushed towards us as we neared the end of the tarmac. On the hottest days, we seemed to clear the tree tops by a very small margin. I imagined the fire crews holding their breath as we did so.

Following a reverse routing via Palm Beach and north up the Florida coast, the leg to Cape Canaveral Air Force Skid Strip took an hour and five minutes. Once established in the climb, I'd get on the HF and contact either George Smith or Bill Johns in Skid Strip Operations to give our estimated time of arrival and ask them to pass this and our passenger and load details to the test team waiting for us.

My excitement mounted as we approached the Cape, not only that first Sunday, but on every subsequent visit. It was such an otherworldly place, eerily familiar, yet totally defying expectation.

I'd grown up with television images of rockets nestled alongside launch towers, but appearing out of the haze a little to the north of our flight path as we descended toward the otherwise featureless swamp-land of the Cape were tens of such towers, and a few isolated buildings, including the Saturn V Assembly Building. The towers varied in height, but most were hundreds of feet tall, red oxide skeletons of steel on large concrete hard standings linked by a network of chalky roads.

On more than one occasion, I had to force myself to look away, scared I might miss a distant rocket rising on a pillar of smoke and flame.

And I really did need to look away and concentrate for our landings.

The contrast between the runways at Andros and Cape Canaveral could not have been greater. Whereas our wingtips overlapped the former, we positively disappeared into the latter, an expanse of tarmac three hundred feet wide and ten thousand long that seemed to wrap round and swallow us as we touched down.

I mentioned visual illusions as an excuse for poor landings in an earlier chapter. Well, at Canaveral, your brain tended to struggle with the scale, tempting you to round out far too high in an effort to make the runway aspect look normal. And while

I don't remember having to make excuses for any of my five landings there, I did have to fight the illusion, especially as the last runway I'd seen on each occasion was the tiddly strip at Andros.

Unloading the torpedoes at Canaveral took much less time than loading them, and no more than thirty minutes after landing, we'd be requesting take off again. Then it was only a short hop down the coast to Patrick, a leg that took no more than five minutes.

It was rarely later than 5.00pm when we arrived at the hotel, time for a wind down beer or two before deciding where to eat and when.

Over the fifteen days operating from Patrick, AUTEC's working pattern gave us two forty eight-hour breaks. During these we used some of the mileage allowance we'd saved over the working week to visit two places I'd never expected to see *in the flesh*: Disney World and the Cape Canaveral Space Centre and Museum. They lived up to their hype in a way so many other things in life don't.

Fifteen years later, I returned with my family. I've been such a lucky man.

That luck was evident again in 1983.

Over the previous two years I'd watched as much of the first five space shuttle missions on television as work and sleep would allow. I'd certainly caught all the launches. So I was familiar with images of the large white vehicle pointing skywards attached to an enormous fuel tank and two thin, tubular, booster rockets. I'd followed the countdowns to calls of *engine start* and *lift off*, then waited for that distinctive shape to rise from billowing clouds of liquid oxygen, smoke and steam and climb clear of the tower on jets of flame. I'd watched it roll onto its back a short time after launch and accelerate away until the call, *go with throttle up*, a minute into the flight. A minute after that, I'd seen the booster rockets cutting out and separating to drop away and land in the ocean, followed by the fuel tank.

The date of the sixth shuttle launch, April 4th, had stuck in my mind because it was my 28th birthday. And for a moment when the Patrick-Andros trip appeared against my name in the co-pilots' office, I thought I might get to see it. But our tenth and final Andros run was due on the 2nd, after which we'd be handing over to a replacement crew and setting out for home on the 3rd.

So near, and yet so far!

And then, in the early hours of Sunday 27th March, an overnight storm verging on Hurricane force swept the Bahamas and the Florida coast. Patrick returned to normality fairly quickly, but AUTEC took the rest of the day to clear up. The torpedo test planned for that day was cancelled. We awaited a revised itinerary from 38 Group HQ, expecting to be ordered home as planned, having completed nine rather than ten Andros runs.

But when we received our Revitin the next day, it had us doing a tenth run on our original departure day, the 3rd, and handing over to our replacements on the 5th.

I was going to be in Florida for the launch of space shuttle Challenger. What a birthday present.

As the day approached, it became apparent the Americans were still very much in love with the space programme. During the drive to Canaveral each morning, the car parks of hotels and motels began to have fewer and fewer spaces, and more and more Winnebagos set up camp on either side of the road. By Friday, there were no spaces in the car parks or on the roadsides, but the cars and vans kept coming.

Looking down as we flew along the coast to the south each day, every road for tens of miles was the same, and it was hard to believe there wouldn't be similar scenes to the north of the Cape and inland toward Orlando.

It was a miracle the weight of vehicles and people didn't

make Florida snap off and float away.

Each afternoon we landed at Canaveral I kept my eyes peeled for Challenger being transported to a launch pad, or nestling against a tower attached to its fuel tank and booster rockets. And then, on the afternoon of Friday the 3rd, I saw it in the haze, on a pad near the triangular apex of the Cape.

It was due to launch at 1.30pm the next day.

My excitement jumped another notch. But it was tempered with a tinge of disappointment.

By Thursday, the roads had become so busy that we'd begun to wonder how close we'd be able to get to the launch. And looking down as we approached the Cape on Friday afternoon, the traffic heading north was gridlocked. We weren't even sure we'd be able to drive south from Patrick to the hotel. We managed, but after a painfully slow journey along roads clogged with space tourists, we came to a decision.

Rather than risk getting stuck in traffic and missing the launch behind an impenetrable screen of hotels and winnebagos, we'd watch from the hotel beach.

It had been a point of discussion all week. The hotel staff said that the curve of the coast meant we'd have an unrestricted view of the launch, just ten miles away over the ocean. The captain said they just wanted to sell more beer and he doubted we'd see much.

Under the old itinerary I'd have arrived home in time to spend a few hours of my birthday with Geraldine. But that morning, as I watched the build-up to the shuttle launch on the TV in a hotel room 4,300 miles away, I have to admit that excitement soon overcame any feelings of homesickness. Alongside footage of VIPs and families gathering on grandstands a mile or so from the launch pad were helicopter shots of mile after mile of beaches thronged with people drinking beer and tending barbecues.

The party had started early.

The seven Ascoteers gathered a little later, meeting for

brunch and carrying a cool box of beer onto the beach an hour before the launch. We found a spot with nothing and no-one between us and the Cape to spoil our view on a clear blue day with almost limitless visibility. The captain lay on his towel, put a cap over his eyes and told us to wake him up when it was all over. The rest of us clinked beer bottles and settled down to wait.

I too doubted there'd be much to see from ten miles, but, as the minutes ticked by, my excitement mounted. By the time the countdown - just audible on the radio of a couple of nearby sunbathers - reached sixty seconds, everyone but the captain was standing and peering into the north-east.

Shortly before the voice on the radio said zero, a smudge of billowing white appeared low on the horizon. From it emerged a small, sun-like, ball of bright light. It climbed slowly, trailing a yellow jet of flame that expanded and dimmed seamlessly into a long tail of white smoke.

I still find it hard to believe, or explain, but although it would be tens of seconds before any sound made it to us – if indeed it ever did – I sensed a crackle in the air, as if static electricity was sparking over and around us. My heart soared and my skin tingled.

It was at this point that the Americans began to jump up and down and whoop in wonder and delight, while we Brits emitted a more restrained series of *Wows!* I glanced to my left to see the captain, standing, open-mouth, as awestruck as the rest of us. Even from ten miles, it was a magnificent sight.

From about fifty seconds, a faint rumble could be heard, a whispering echo of the air being ripped apart by the fury of the launch itself. After that, we watched in silence as the jet of flame climbed and dwindled to a pinpoint, while the trail of smoke lengthened, its base already dissipating to a misty haze. I was amazed that we could still see the glow of the booster rockets burning, even more amazed when, at the two-minute point, two small pinpoints of light diverged and began a slow descent, dimming until they disappeared.

Amazingly, it was the booster rockets separating and falling away at a height of thirty four miles and a range of forty eight miles. Shortly after, the glow of the shuttle engines also disappeared.

It had been a magical two minutes. I could see why people travelled hundreds of miles to experience it.

On a more sober note, it also gave me an inkling of the horror onlookers must have felt in 1986 when Challenger exploded seventy three seconds into its tenth flight, killing all seven crew members.

There were so many elements that made the Patrick-Andros route one of the highlights of my time in the RAF – of my life.

The flight across the Atlantic to Canada, down to the USA, across the Caribbean to Barbados, Belize and back to Florida had provided memories aplenty. That it was followed by fifteen days flying to a beautiful island and one of the most iconic places on the planet barely seems believable. And to top it all, although the working days weren't entirely free of frustrations and problems to overcome, they were relatively short. We invariably returned to the hotel in time to eat, drink, be merry and get a good night's sleep before repeating the process the next day.

I found the variety of flying stimulating and rewarding and the captain was always pushing me to improve. The crew gelled brilliantly and I never felt I received anything other than their full support. I was the most content I would ever be on a flight deck and it did wonders for my confidence.

But despite all we experienced, the true highlight was the camaraderie of a crew that, on the ground, expanded to include the ground engineers and the movers.

I – we - drank far more alcohol than modern health and professional guidelines would recommend, or allow, but beer was an important part of the bonding process then. We'd meet for a wind down beer in the party room before drinking with a meal and moving on, usually to the hotel nightclub, where we'd finish off most nights drinking more beer.

Maybe the alcohol clouded my judgement, but we seemed to forge a great relationship with the bar staff and regulars in Mr Tease. They enjoyed our antics – like the night after our visit to Disney when the Seven Ascoteers formed a line and shuffled into the bar on our knees, rocking from side to side and singing as much as we knew of, *Hi ho, Hi ho, it's off to work we go*, from Snow White and the Seven Dwarfs.

I relished the opportunity to meet *ordinary* Americans and to discover that they had a totally different world view, if indeed they had a world view. A surprising number seemed to have little interest in anything beyond the borders of the US, or even Florida. In their eyes, they had everything they needed, and what they had was bigger and better, so why look elsewhere.

Such conversations were always fascinating and I had many of them.

Our final night – the night of the shuttle launch – was particularly enjoyable. The bar staff presented me with a birthday cake. Everyone had great fun watching my surprise when, after puffing my cheeks and blowing them out, the candles burst back into life. It was the first time I'd seen something that, a decade later, seemed to become a staple of every birthday party.

Ever a people watcher, I loved observing the other guests in Mr Tease, acting out the mating game and dancing to disco classics of the time, like Beat It and 1999. Each evening included a rendition of the club's signature tune, Mr Bojangles. It produced an earworm that lasted long after my return to Lyneham.

During a conversation toward the end of the final night, the vastly experienced loadmaster, soon to retire, said I should do the same, because I'd never have another experience to match the previous three weeks.

In the end, I was lucky enough to go on and enjoy many other highlights, both at Lyneham and later in my career. But on one point, the loadie was right, nothing ever surpassed the fulfilment and sheer enjoyment of that Patrick-Andros route.

As is the way in Service life, I never met any of that crew again after leaving the Herc. If I met any of them now, though, I can guarantee that, within thirty seconds, we'd be saying, *do you remember the time we...*

VOLCANOES, MEDEVACS AND CRACKER BOXES

The next highlight came in mid-May, just a month after the return from Patrick-Andros.

Following a couple of standby duties and sims, and three days flying between various bases in the UK and Germany, I found myself sitting next to the pipe-smoking captain for another trip in support of the Nimrod force. This time, they had two aircraft detached to the island of Sicily to take part in a NATO exercise in the Mediterranean. So on Saturday 14th May we picked up personnel and equipment from the Nimrod base at RAF Kinloss in northern Scotland and headed for Italian Air Force Sigonella, which sits about 25 miles south of Mount Etna, an active volcano near the eastern coast of the island.

Etna often smokes, grumbles and spits ash and rock, but during the period between late March and August 1983, it was particularly active. None of it had made the British press, though, so during our approach, I was excited to see wisps of vapour rising from its 11,000 foot summit and upper slopes.

The distance masked the significance of those wisps. As we landed and taxied onto a pan brimming with maritime patrol aircraft from several countries, up on the mountain, explosives were being used to divert lava flows threatening settlements. We were still ignorant of this when, an hour or so later, we boarded a blue US military bus and headed for a hotel on the coast to the east of Catania, a large town at the base of the volcano.

The streets were incredibly busy, vehicles scattered haphazardly across every junction, horns blaring as they nudged their way through the chaos. Lambretta scooters weaved in and out, squeezing through impossible gaps. Behind many of the male riders, women sat side saddle, some young and smartly-dressed, handbags on their laps, others older, nursing shopping bags or boxes of vegetables.

Hardly anyone was wearing a crash helmet. When someone pointed this out, the nav, an ex-Rhodesian policeman with a dry sense of humour, said, 'Why bother with a bloody crash helmet when a thousand tons of molten rock might land on your head at any minute?'

He was right of course. If you lived within spitting distance of an active volcano, other threats were likely to seem trivial.

Every so often we caught a glimpse of the summit through gaps between the tall buildings lining the roads. It had belched a taller, darker, pillar of billowing cloud. The captain pointed up and asked the driver whether the weight of traffic was in any way linked to this.

'No,' he said in an Eeyore'ish southern US drawl. 'Catania's like this every day.'

The volcano was certainly making the local news. As I

changed for dinner, excited voices issued from a TV showing wide lava channels advancing slowly through vegetation and toward buildings. And after dinner, a few of us waited for darkness and walked south, hoping to see the summit and upper flanks of the mountain. What we saw instead was a shroud of vapour, the heart of which pulsated with a ruddy orange glow, like a cartoon depiction of hell. It might have been the wine, but we thought we could make out thin orange lines within the glow.

The next morning, the traffic on the return to Sigonella was just as bad, but the volcano was worse. Overnight, it had shot a huge pillar of ash five kilometres into the sky. By the time we emerged from flight planning and prepared for take-off, this had formed a sooty grey plume drifting tens of miles to the south-east on the prevailing wind. My photo album from the time has several snapshots of this, taken as we climbed a few miles west of the summit.

Ascension had kindled an interest in volcanoes, and now I'd

seen one erupting. Five months later, Geraldine and I would stand amongst the sulphurous fumaroles on the summit of Vesuvius, and three decades after that we'd return to Etna, which was performing again. We walked to fresh lava fields on the upper slopes beneath a summit wreathed in smoke – and were caught in a blizzard on the way back.

On the same trip, we visited the Aeolian Islands to the north of Sicily and walked trails on the flanks of Lipari and among sulphur clouds on the rim of Vulcano, the island and peak that gave the geological features their name. We even spent twenty four hours on the small island of Stromboli, Italy's most predictable active volcano.

Approaching the cone-shaped island by passenger hydrofoil in the afternoon, we could see smoke rising from the 3,000-foot summit. And when we landed and walked away from the noisy ferry, we heard the first echoing boom of an eruption, just out of sight of the port and the white village wrapping round its lower slopes. The boom would be repeated every twenty five minutes, a dramatic backdrop to our stay in a hotel on the extreme upper flank of the village.

That night we joined a group of about thirty for a guided walk up the mountain, initially to a vantage point just below the summit. We settled down and ate a snack as the sun set over the ocean and the light faded. Then, about half a mile away, chunks of molten rock shot out of the slope to our front, followed a few seconds later by a resounding boom. Mesmerised, we watched the red missiles fall and roll down the mountainside, slowly fading from sight as they cooled, until all that remained was the sound of them cascading further down the slopes.

We'd watched four eruptions before our guide rang the summit to check on the sulphur dioxide levels, then ushered us on up the rough slope. Travelling by the light of our head torches, Geraldine and I felt quite intrepid, until a ten year old girl sped past us. The summit was shrouded in a foul-smelling mist, but it was worth the odd cough to look down into the main crater. Its floor was obscured by the fumes, which pulsed with a demonic, fiery, glow similar to the glow on the flanks of Etna that night thirty years earlier.

The Monday after I returned from Sigonella, I was part of a six-hour standby crew. At a little after 5.00pm we were called out for a Medical Evacuation – Medevac – task. In Ops, we found out we were to collect a pair of premature twins from Gibraltar and deliver them to Heathrow Airport for transfer to one of the London hospitals.

After flight planning and a short wait for an RAF medical team to load their equipment, we took off from Lyneham in XV301 at 7.40 in the evening, with me as operating pilot.

I soon learned that our discrete Medevac callsign opened doors normally closed to us. Most importantly, the French and Spanish air traffic controllers cleared us to overfly Spanish airspace rather than take the normal oceanic route round the Iberian Peninsula. This allowed us to shave about twenty five minutes off our normal flight time to Gibraltar, where I landed at a quarter to midnight.

The twins, born in a Royal Navy hospital to the wife of an Army private, weighed two and two and a half pounds respectively. In the 1980s, the survival prospects for babies with such low birth weights could be poor, and each of the twins had a number of complications requiring specialist medical care not available in Gibraltar.

Speed was of the essence, but so was meticulous preparation. In the end, readying the patients and their incubators for flight took nearly four hours and we didn't leave the Rock behind us until 3.40 in the morning. Because the aircraft had to be maintained at sea level pressure, we couldn't climb above 15,000 feet, although we opted to fly even lower than that, just in case we suffered a pressurisation failure.

At every opportunity, Spanish and French air traffic helped us save precious minutes and I passed each updated arrival time to our headquarters for onward transmission to the hospital. Curiosity took me down the back a couple of times, but the incubators were surrounded by attentive medics and I didn't attempt to get close.

The sun had long risen as we were handed over to the UK controllers shortly after 7.00am. They immediately gave us direct routings for a westerly approach to Heathrow, moving us straight to the front of a continuous stream of passenger aircraft approaching to land at that time in the morning.

Airliners hate being told to hold off. It leads to grumpy passengers and the burning of extra fuel. But on this occasion, there were no complaints as we passed above and below aircraft forced to adopt holding patterns across the whole of the south-east of England. On occasions, we had one Jumbo Jet orbiting one thousand feet above us, another one thousand feet below.

To minimise the disruption, each new controller encouraged us to keep our speed up and the wheels were hardly down before we passed over Heathrow's runway threshold and touched down. Even then, Heathrow was a sprawling complex of tarmac and buildings spread over several square miles. Hundreds of aircraft in a tremendous array of airline liveries were parked around the various terminals, and tens were taxying to and from the parallel runways.

I had a landing chart on my lap, but frankly, when we turned off the runway – as early as possible to leave it clear for the jets chasing us down – I was finding it hard to work out where we were, never mind where we were going. Thank goodness for the ground controller. He immediately began a running commentary, instructing us to follow, cross behind or cut in front of one colourful aircraft after another until we found ourselves at our allotted parking slot.

Phew!

The easing of stress was short-lived. There were no ambulances!

Whether my updates had failed to be passed on to the ambulance drivers, or the vehicles were stuck in traffic, we never found out. But they didn't turn up for forty minutes. It was an agonising wait, although things happened quickly once they had arrived. Within a few minutes the incubators had been unloaded and the ambulances driven away.

We watched their departure from the flight deck windows, took a few seconds to wish the twins well, then prepared to start up and call for departure clearance. Returning to the runway at Heathrow took longer than the twenty-minute flight to Lyneham.

It was a very quiet, contemplative, journey, not without its dangers. We'd used up our reserves of adrenaline, it was the end of a fifteen and a half hour crew duty day and we'd all been awake for more than twenty four hours. I for one was bushed. Classic conditions for mistakes to creep in, so we knew we had to be on our guard. In the event, we landed safely at 9.20am on Tuesday morning.

As we were leaving the Ops building, we were told that one of the twins had died. I suppose it would have been possible to look at it the other way, that is, that one of them had survived. But such is human nature that it seemed a devastating blow. And I couldn't help wondering if I'd had a part in the ambulances arriving late.

No time to dwell on it though. The next day, I flew a day trip to RAF Gütersloh in Germany.

A few days later, a story appeared in the national newspapers:
> *A huge RAF Hercules aircraft has helped to save the lives of two tiny twin boys with a special flight from Gibraltar to London.*

The article, which I'm looking at now in a scrap book, goes on to explain more about the twins and our flight. But most importantly for me, it finishes:
> *Last night, the twins were under special care to beat breathing problems at Louise Margaret Hospital, Aldershot.*

I don't know the date of the article, but it certainly post-dated the news of a death I'd been given. At the time, it was a great relief, and as I sit here now, I hope the twins have gone on to lead happy and healthy lives.

Early in the morning of Tuesday 31st May, I was crewing one of several Hercs flying troops and equipment to Incirlik Air Base in south-eastern Turkey, one hundred miles from the Syrian border. We were to spend ten days participating in Exercise Adventure Express 83, which, unlike its Greek counterpart six months earlier, was actually taking place.

The exercise was designed to test NATO's ability to withstand a Soviet assault on its south-eastern flank. So transport aircraft from several NATO air forces were ferrying men and equipment between Incirlik and Erzerum Airport, a joint military/civil airfield 100 miles west of the Soviet border near what are now the independent states of Armenia and Georgia.

Incirlik was operated by the United States Air Force under a similar arrangement to USAF bases in the UK, like RAF Mildenhall. And as with all such bases, once inside the perimeter, everything from the buildings and equipment, to the personnel, vehicles and aircraft was identifiably American, right down to the trading and food outlets. It was as if you were in the USA.

Tens of USAF transport aircraft, bombers and fighters called the base home, and it was well used to hosting NATO units flying in for short detachments. But as I landed at Incirlik after a seven hour flight, it was positively brimming with transport aircraft, including several other RAF Hercs. Aircraft were taking off or arriving every few minutes, slaves to a tight timetable of exercise movements designed to keep supplies flowing to Erzerum.

But, unbeknownst to us that Tuesday afternoon, the flying programme was proving impossible to maintain, disrupted by an age-old problem: disease, or at least illness. Crews and groundcrew that had been in Turkey for a few days were going down with severe bouts of diarrhoea and vomiting, a malady that had already been named Ataturk's Revenge.

The RAF Herc crews were accommodated in the nearby town of Adana.

I remember it as a sad and careworn town, far more Middle Eastern than European, and a far cry from the image of Turkish resorts and cities portrayed in magazines and travel programmes. Many of the buildings lining the dusty streets and the businesses occupying their lower floors seemed on the verge of collapse. There were more hand, pony and donkey carts than cars, and the leathery, wrinkled, faces of those escorting them made it all too apparent that life was hard.

The animals, especially, seemed to suffer. They were invariably thin and dishevelled, bowed down as much by undernourishment and harsh treatment as by their burdens. At that point in the country's history, both men and women wore Western dress, the colourful headscarves of the older women being a nod to secular tradition rather than the patriarchal interpretation of Islam the country has adopted today, when women are increasingly likely to be fully covered.

I also gained a lingering impression of the harshness of military life, especially for young conscripts. Those we saw at Erzerum seemed slim to the point of emaciation. They also seemed excessively tense around their superiors, like dogs expecting a blow, although I saw no evidence of physical punishment.

I'm sure some of the foregoing is coloured by conversations with a young man on London University Air Squadron who'd been a Greek conscript. He'd witnessed at close quarters the cruelty meted out to his Turkish counterparts. His progress into the RAF is quite a story, and the last time I met him he was a group captain.

Having said all the above, the Turkish civilians of all ages we met in Adana were never anything other than courteous and friendly. Our presence, in a town away from the regular tourist track, offered great possibilities to the local carpet, furniture and knick-knack shops. I came away with just a fireside rug, but others returned to Lyneham with enough wares to furnish a palace.

Back to the start of the detachment. After checking in to the Buyuk Sermeli Hotel on the first evening, we headed to the pool to meet the resident Herc crews and find out more about what to expect. The pool was empty except for a few inches of slimy green water at one end, but the crews were still there, sunbathing and drinking beer. We soon discovered that the major, indeed the only topic of conversation, was the illness and how to avoid it.

Local food and/or water were deemed the most probable cause, with at least half the early arrivals spending twenty four hours or more unable to travel further than a few feet from the nearest toilet.

In an attempt to avoid the malady, everyone had taken to drinking only bottled water – and beer of course. When it came to food, things weren't quite as clear cut. The in-flight meals were almost certainly okay, so you could eat with confidence when airborne. On the ground, however, there was a difference of opinion.

Some had decided to stick with the Herc fleet's standard practice of eating in local hotels and restaurants. But others had decided to eat only on the USAF base, taking taxis to dine in its Mess halls if they could talk their way in, or at the likes of Macdonald or Burger King if not. At first, their strategy appeared to work, but soon, even these ultra-cautious folk began suffering Ataturk's Revenge, and at the same rate as those eating the local fare.

With the greater knowledge of such things now, I guess the illness was as likely to be picked up through contact with people and surfaces as through the things we ate and drank. But whatever the cause, in the short period we spent by the pool we witnessed some of our fellow aircrew clutching their stomachs and excusing themselves to make a dash inside. They'd appear fifteen minutes later, looking pale and drawn, but preferring to spend at least a little time in the fresh air, rather than closeted in their stifling rooms. Once they'd identified themselves as sufferers, though, we gave them a wide berth.

On the plus side, although a few people had ended up in the Incirlik medical facility on a drip, most people seemed to recover in about twenty four hours. And most of these had not suffered a recurrence.

Our captain decided we'd take the risk of heading into town to eat. We had a delightful Turkish meze washed down with local beer and wine and went to bed prepared to get up and do our first Erzerum run the next morning. This we did, but shortly after take-off for the return to Incirlik, the young nav began to feel unwell. He spent most of the last hour of our ninety-minute flight down the back, either sitting on or leaning over the Elsan – the chemical toilet, affectionately known as the cracker box.

No-one liked using this contraption at the best of times, and this was far from that.

The cracker box was stowed high against the rear left fuselage wall near the ramp and door. It was released by a handle, which could then be used to help take the weight as it was lowered into position above the freight bay floor. I seem to remember that users could gain a small amount of privacy from those in the freight bay by pulling across a short curtain on something like a shower rail.

When passengers were aboard, the loadies would sometimes lower the cracker box. When there were no passengers, they wouldn't. I remember one captain relatively new to the Herc going down the back to use it in the early stages of a thirteen hour flight in the South Atlantic. He returned to the flight deck in civvies. He'd released the box but failed to slow its descent. It had crashed down and, *badoosh*, sent a tsunami of Elsan toilet fluid over him and his flying suit. Luckily, he'd been the first to use the contraption, so it was only chemicals that hit him, not something less savoury.

Despite the change of clothing, he smelt of toilet fluid for the remainder of the sortie.

At the risk of being overly graphic, I can't resist another Elsan story, again from the South Atlantic. After using the cracker box, one of my captains hefted his flying suit back up, only to feel something soft and wet splat against his back. Instead of hanging down below his knees, the top of his flying suit had caught on and draped over the cracker box.

The loadie helped clean him up - or should that be washed him down - and he'd returned to the flight deck in civvies, looking sheepish and knowing he had to confess.

Anyway, on that first return flight to Incirlik from Erzerum, the nav had risked leaving the cracker box to return to the flight deck and help with the approach. But after landing, he rushed straight down the back and resumed his perch as we taxied in. At least the freight bay was empty, so there was no-one to see him squatting there. That is, until the loadie opened the ramp and door.

As we entered the pan and taxied toward our parking slot, groundcrew and movers from several nations began to nudge one another and turn to laugh at the nav as he passed. There was nothing he could do but grin and bear it, giving a royal wave from his throne.

The loadie had had her fun, but she spent most of the next thirty six hours sitting on the throne herself. The engineer suffered for a similar period of time. I was relatively lucky, suffering for just a day. The only member of the crew not to succumb then, or for the rest of the detachment, was the captain. He said he was so pickled in whiskey that he was impervious to bugs. It seemed he was right.

The upshot was that we had three unscheduled days on the ground, taking off for our second Erzerum run at 5.15 on the morning of Sunday 5th June.

From a few miles north of Incirlik, our flight path was entirely over mountainous terrain, initially the eastern Taurus Mountains and then the Anatolian Highlands, some of the peaks reaching up to 10,000 feet. Such high ground tends to produce towering cumulus clouds and, during the hotter months of the year, vast cumulonimbus storm clouds reach up beyond 30,000 feet.

I've already mentioned that a Herc had fallen out of such a storm minus its wings in this very area. So we listened to the pre-flight brief from the USAF met men at Incirlik intently. And every day, they warned us of thunderstorms, although, unlike their peers at Patrick a few months earlier, they didn't advise us not to fly.

Some days we wished they had.

Taking off from Incirlik we were invariably fully loaded, which limited our height to around 20,000 feet, well below the tops of the bigger cumulonimbus clouds we encountered. And just as when passing through the ITCZ between Dakar and Ascension, we spent hours peering at the weather radar, looking for the most active cells and deviating tens of miles off track to avoid them.

An added complication was that, unlike when flying over the ocean off the coast of Africa, the weather radar over Turkey suffered interference from the mountains, known as ground clutter. This made the active cells harder to spot. And whereas we were likely to meet few other aircraft in the South Atlantic, the airspace over eastern Turkey had plenty of transport aircraft weaving about in an area of intermittent or no radar coverage. We just hoped those coming the other way were able to maintain their designated heights to ensure separation.

Although Erzerum sat on a plateau about 6,000 feet above sea level, it remained remarkably clear of the worst of the weather. The airport occupied an isolated and largely treeless area 11 miles from the city, so its tall buildings and 12,500 foot long parallel runways were easy to spot from several miles out.

At 5,965 feet above sea level, it was the highest airfield I'd operated into so far, giving me at least one other thing to consider on landing.

The wheels of aircraft are limited to a maximum touchdown speed to prevent blowouts caused by stress and excessive temperatures when the tires spin up on contact with the runway. The limiting speed for Fat Albert's nosewheel was 139 knots – 160 mph. At sea level, this was rarely a problem. But changes in pressure with altitude mean that for every 1,000 feet a runway is above sea level, the true air speed, and therefore the groundspeed, on touchdown increases by roughly two knots. So for a landing at Erzerum, we'd be touching down about twelve knots – fourteen mph – faster than at sea level and twelve knots faster than the speed displayed on the cockpit instruments.

The minimum touchdown speed of a Herc is subject to many variables, such as weight, temperature and air pressure, but it's likely to be well in excess of 100 knots. And if, as was often the case when going into Erzerum, we were being asked to keep the speed up, it could be significantly higher. Whatever the pressures to land fast, though, I had to make sure I didn't touch down at an indicated speed in excess of 127 knots.

I remember only one major problem during our seven round trips to Erzerum.

To save time, we tried to offload cargo with at least one engine running, enabling a quick re-start and taxy away. On one occasion though, our number 3 engine, the inboard one just to my right, refused to start, probably because its starter drive shaft had sheared.

Normally, such a snag would have meant hours, maybe days, on the ground while new parts were delivered and fitted. But such was the pressure to vacate our slot on the pan at Erzerum that novel solutions were considered, like carrying out a three-engine departure and transit to Incirlik. Before attempting that, though, it seemed there was one other thing to try: a buddy/buddy start.

After some hasty radio calls to another RAF Albert just about to take off, we outlined our plan to air traffic and were given clearance to taxy onto the runway behind him. This we did, edging forward until our flight deck was about ten yards back and to the left of the tip of his left tailplane. This positioned our number 3 propeller about twenty yards behind and between his port engines, so that we'd get maximum effect from their combined propwash.

I had yet to experience flying in formation with another Herc, so being so close to the rear end of one on that occasion was quite something. In fact, over the many months of formation flying in the South Atlantic during the following year, I never ended up as close to another aircraft's engines or tailplane. If I had, it would have been alarming.

Truth-be-told though, that afternoon, even safe on terra firma, I found it alarming.

With the other Herc at low power, we were rocking in

the smoky mixture of his exhaust gases and corkscrewing propwash. And then he advanced his throttles. By the time he reached 80% power, we were bucking and bouncing so violently I wondered whether our wheels were actually leaving the ground. Allied with the screaming jet and prop noise, it was a terrific assault on the senses. But what really grabbed my attention was the sight of the other Herc's tail assembly out to my right, almost within touching distance.

The tips of his tailplanes were rocking violently up and down, the whole rear end twisting about the base of the towering fin. And the fin itself was slamming from side to side, moving by several inches, if not feet. It was a shocking sight, especially when I realised it was the norm for every Herc I strapped into, on the ground and in the air.

It reminded me of when I used to find cracks up to nine inches long on the exhaust cones of the Olympus engines powering the Vulcans on 35 and 617 Squadrons at Scampton. I couldn't help wondering whether similar cracks were being generated somewhere within that madly thrashing Herc tail assembly.

It hardly bore thinking about. So, just as I had all those years ago, I decided not to think about it and get on with my job. I looked back over my right shoulder just as our number 3 propeller began to rotate. Soon it was turning fast enough for the engine to go through a fairly normal start sequence - and save us from a three-engine transit.

We thanked our compatriot and heaved a collective sigh of relief as he acknowledged our call and throttled back, allowing a slow return to the gentle rocking with which the whole operation had started. Soon, he taxied a safe distance ahead of us, opened his throttles, accelerated away and rose into the air, his engines leaving a trail of brown smoke – similar to the one we'd been sitting in a few minutes previously. We spent another five minutes on the runway checking everything was as it should be and letting him get well ahead of us, then flew an uneventful take-off and returned to Incirlik.

The high excitement of the buddy/buddy start had lasted little more than a minute, but it remains one of the strongest memories of my time on Fat Albert.

BEIRUT AND THE RED ARROWS

Ten days after my return to Lyneham from Incirlik, I flew into Beirut with my new squadron boss, a tall, silver-haired, man in his early 40s that I grew to respect greatly. He was far from the stereotypical image of a military leader prevalent at the time.

Many were larger than life characters, loud, aggressive and prone to displaying extremes of emotion – from joyful guffaws to angry bellows. Such behaviour was taken as a sign of strength, and as a result some aspiring leaders at all levels within the Service adopted a similarly loud and hectoring persona. And because it was what they were used to, many subordinates favoured such a *no-nonsense* approach. If it sometimes verged on or slipped over into bullying, so be it. Not that anyone talked of bullying at that time.

In contrast, the new boss, although professional, determined and able to be firm when required, was generally even-tempered and quietly spoken, traits that some, used to the more traditional model, interpreted as weakness. I've already said that I liked him, but I also liked his leadership style and his sense of humour, which seemed, more than most in authority, to be based on things other than making fun of or belittling people. Whether consciously or subconsciously, I watched and learned. He was influential in my later approach to leadership and it started on the trip to Beirut.

Just before I leave the subject of leadership though, I acknowledge that different situations require different approaches and, in times of crises or war, leaders have to make sure their orders are heard loud and clear, and then acted on without hesitation or question. But even then, I'm not sure bullying is required. In the areas and situations through which my career meandered, I always found the more bombastic characters wearing and, in the end, less effective than their more measured contemporaries.

Another reason for distrust, if not antipathy, toward the new boss was that he wasn't a Herc mate. His previous type was the Andover. Some felt this might make him a less effective operator and, almost worse, might lead him to challenge and change the Herc way of doing things. And finally, there were those who thought Herc executives should be drawn exclusively from the Herc force, so any interlopers were bad news whatever their strengths.

In contrast with these sceptics, the way he mastered the twin challenges of operating a new, larger and more sophisticated aircraft, and running a large squadron, only added to my admiration. He could have locked himself in his office and concentrated on the command bit first, but he set out to fly regularly and encouraged his executives to do the same. This commitment was amply demonstrated by his captaincy of a Beirut trip so soon after taking command.

He would also go on to set the same example in the South Atlantic, more of which later.

Lebanon seemed to be in a near-continuous state of civil war and, in June 1982, it had been invaded by Israel in retaliation for the Palestine Liberation Organisation's attempted assassination of the Israeli ambassador to London. After seven weeks besieging Beirut, the Israelis signed a deal under which they and the PLO would withdraw. The resulting ceasefire would be monitored by a Multi-National Force (MNF) of US, French and Italian peacekeeping contingents, who would also train elements of the Lebanese Armed Forces.

The deal fell apart in September when the Lebanese President-elect was assassinated. Lebanon returned to civil war and the Israelis moved back into Beirut. The MNF was sidelined and chaos reigned, a period culminating in militias massacring Palestinian civilians in the Sabra and Shatila refugee camps while they were under Israeli control.

This led to a beefing up of the US and French contingents, and in February 1983 they were joined by a small British force from the 1st Dragoon Guards cavalry regiment, equipped with Ferret armoured cars. The RAF also provided a detachment of twin-rotor Chinook helicopters operating from RAF Akrotiri on Cyprus, a little more than 100 miles away across the Eastern Mediterranean. Hostilities between various factions continued, with the MNF often caught in the crossfire.

In April 1983, a suicide bomber attacked the US Embassy, killing sixty three people. A new accord was signed, but hostilities continued with Shia and Druze militia shelling the airport. The US retaliated, mainly by firing on militia positions from warships off the Lebanese coast. This was the situation when, carrying supplies for the British contingent, we made the forty minute flight from Akrotiri to Beirut Airport on Monday 21st June.

It was the only time I flew into a hot war zone.

We'd already had some excitement. On the way into Akrotiri the previous day, we'd been intercepted by a Lightning from a Binbrook squadron on an armament practice camp. The rocket-like, twin-engined fighter flew a series of attack profiles, all of which ended in him *shooting us down* with his

Firestreak missiles. But whether we were attacked from above or below, from ahead, behind or the side, each assault ended with him flashing past our flight deck. It was a great display.

As an aside, that he shot us down every time makes it sound as if Fat Albert was an easy target. But he only did so because we did nothing to evade him. On this occasion, aggressive manoeuvring would have upset the passengers and maybe damaged the cargo. During regular dissimilar type combat exercises with the fast jet detachments in the Falklands, however, there was often a very different result, with Hercs evading fast jet attackers for long periods, if not totally. A single Phantom - or later, Tornado F3 - would often struggle to get any sort of weapons lock, and even a pair had to be good to nail their adversary in a reasonable period of time.

Planning and receiving clearance from the various agencies controlling access to Beirut airport was quite a task. We had to be sure to contact the right frequencies, transmit the right codes and fly the authorised approach with great accuracy.

We were particularly concerned about flying near warships of any nationality. Their gunners were notoriously trigger-happy, prone to shoot first and ask questions later. And at a time when few if any Hercs had anything resembling a defensive aids suite, there was also the danger of attack by shoulder-launched missiles and small arms during our approach to and climb away from Beirut.

Thankfully, our transit, approach and landing were trouble-free, and we parked on a pan close to the airport air traffic control tower. Puffs of smoke rose from the hillsides a few miles to the east of where we sat, the only aircraft on the pan. We'd received no notification of US warships firing, so we assumed they were the result of the various militias targeting one another. I suppose I should say how concerned I was about the civilians suffering under the bombardment, but in truth, I was hoping the shelling stayed where it was and didn't edge closer. If it had, we were very poorly placed to do anything about it.

A single Ferret armoured car appeared and positioned itself close to the tip of our right wing, pointing its turret-mounted, 7.62mm, General Purpose Machine Gun at the hills. Frankly, it looked unlikely to deter any serious attacker.

I unstrapped and, feeling unusually lonely and exposed, walked over to air traffic to confirm the details of our departure and return flight. As I did so, I heard the unmistakable *wocka wocka* sound of a Chinook helicopter.

We'd shared the pan at Akrotiri with several, surprised to see both sides of their high rear rotor pillars painted with enormous Union Flags. These seemed to offer an ideal aiming point for any potential marksman, and as I watched this one fly north to south mid-way between me and the artillery bursts on the hills, my concern for my own welfare melted away. At that moment at least, he was much more vulnerable.

After one hour twenty minutes on the ground, our climb away from Beirut airport and return to Akrotiri were also uneventful, as was the return to Lyneham the next day.

I'd really enjoyed flying with the new boss, and my first trip with him had gone much better than the same milestone with his predecessor.

My next major route a couple of weeks later was in support of the Red Arrows. It was the kind of trip each squadron picked up just a handful of times a year, so I was lucky to get it. Even so, when it appeared on the board, some of my fellow co-pilots felt I should have been disappointed. The dream ticket was to support one of the team's extended tours of the Americas, Europe or the Far East, whereas I was due to spend four days flying their kit and groundcrew around England.

Nightstops in Darlington, Oxford and Lincoln don't have quite the same ring as New York, Rome or Kuala Lumpur, but I wasn't that worried. It was an unexpected opportunity to get closer than most to the best fast jet display team in the world, and one of the inspirations for me joining the RAF in the first place.

I still have the movement order for the route, which started with another personal milestone.

When I left Scampton and its Vulcans to commence officer training in April 1979, I wouldn't have dared hope that my next visit would be at the controls of an RAF aircraft. But just over four years later, here I was on a sunny Friday afternoon, landing a Hercules at my old base.

The Red Arrows had been there for just a few months, arriving a year after the last of the Vulcan squadrons had left. Now, as we taxied toward the line of red Hawks outside one of the hangars, it felt really strange to be looking out on dispersals and buildings where I'd spent two and a half years working as a Junior Technician and corporal.

Strange also to be marshalled up to and parked on the end of the line of distinctive red jets. Each was attended by a small team of groundcrew in equally distinctive blue overalls that gave them their name, the Blues. There were ten Hawks, nine for the display pilots and one for the team supervisor, a squadron leader known as Red 10. The aircraft gave him a method of accompanying the team between their main display locations, but it was also a spare, ready to be used if one of the other nine became unserviceable.

Red 10 had to be on the ground for each display to make on-the-spot assessments of the safety of the venue and weather before calling in the team and providing commentary, while also meeting as many dignitaries and members of the public as time allowed. For more remote locations, he'd fly or be ferried around by RAF light aircraft or helicopter. On a busy day, he could have to dash between four or five displays.

For most transit flights, the rear seat of each Hawk was occupied by specially selected members of the Blues, known as the Flying Circus. Their task after landing was to carry out routine servicing and replenishment of the jets while the pilots prepared for the next flight, be that a display or another transit.

That afternoon, loading the kit took a couple of hours. In the meantime, we ambled over to the hangar and were invited into the Reds' crewroom for a coffee. Team members came and went, exchanging a few pleasantries with us before disappearing to get ready for what was, for them, just another display weekend.

On first meeting, they seemed as normal as any RAF officer walking round in a bright red flying suit could be. But I felt a bit in awe, like a third-former in the sixth form common room. After all, they'd reached the pinnacle of their profession, while I'd barely made it into the foothills.

Did I try and act as if I was their equal – which of course in terms of rank and most other areas bar skill, I was – or assume they were superior and act accordingly?

Even the more experienced members of the crew didn't seem to know quite how to react in their presence, whether to be aloof or over-familiar. It was strange, and over the course of the weekend I became fascinated by how their *celebrity* affected both them and the way people reacted to them.

Over the years, I came to realise how fleeting their fame was, with very few of them being remembered outside the tiny circle of people that took a wider interest in the team than most. Even having met all nine of the 1983 Reds, I remember only two, and those because I crossed paths with them again later.

The first was Red 4, Tim Miller. I met him only fleetingly that weekend, but when I arrived at Scampton to join the staff of the RAF Central Flying School in February 1988, he was in his first year as team leader. And as they worked up toward that summer's display season, he was having a baptism of fire.

During a practice close to the airfield in November of the previous year, one of his pilots had collided with him. Both ejected successfully, but while Tim sustained only minor injuries, the other pilot suffered a broken leg that ended his time with the Arrows. More tragically, just two months later, one of the team's new pilots, Duncan MacLachlan, was killed in a practice over the airfield.

Thankfully, the rest of Tim's time as leader was less dramatic. I saw him around the station daily but met him only a handful of times at various functions. He was always smiling but I sensed wariness, his eyes scanning his surroundings as if looking for the next challenge. Later, I'd recognise the trait as a function of command, a by-product of the situations he'd experienced and the pressures he faced.

After handing over the team to his successor, he left the RAF to become the personal pilot of Nigel Mansell, the world champion Formula One racing driver.

My second acquaintance from the 1983 team was Red 9, Chris 'Curly' Hirst, a lively, approachable character I probably chatted to more than any of the others that weekend. A few months later, in March 1984, he was involved in one of the more memorable Red Arrows incidents. While practising in Cyprus, he hit the ground at the very bottom of a loop. Luckily, the impact fired his ejection seat and he survived, although it was the end of his time on the Red Arrows.

Like many ex-Reds, he went on to become a pilot with the airline Cathay Pacific, based in Hong Kong. Fifteen years later, he had a house in the Forest of Dean and our daughters went to the same school in Gloucester and became friends. He spent a lot of his time in Hong Kong, but on one of the occasions he was home, our families enjoyed a memorable Bonfire Night in his garden, where he set off enough Chinese fireworks to rival many a municipal display.

Anyway, back to 8th July 1983.

Just before 3.00pm, a small number of spectators, including their families, watched as the Blues and Reds performed their choreographed start routine. Largely unnoticed at the far end of the line, we also started our engines, and when Reds 1 to 10 checked in on the radios, we adopted the unofficial callsign we'd use for the rest of the weekend: Mucky Brown Eleven.

The Blues waved away the Hawks and boarded our Albert for the twenty minute flight north to RAF Leeming, an airfield sitting just to the east of the A1, The Great North Road running between London and Scotland. At the time, it was home to the RAF Central Flying School and one of four bases that hosted major displays on different weekends throughout the summer, the others being Abingdon in Oxfordshire, St Athan in Wales and Leuchars in Scotland.

That Friday, the Reds closed the first afternoon of the Leeming show. It may seem strange, but over the four days of the route, this was the only display I saw. All the others were flown at locations remote from the airfields into which we flew.

That evening, the weather was beautiful, the crowds large and the display, which we watched from the flight line adjacent to our Herc, superb. Afterwards, we shared the team's transport to Darlington, twenty miles north up the A1, where we were to spend the night in a pub-style hotel on one of the town centre streets.

We were treated to an immediate insight into what made the Reds' job so different from any other in the RAF.

On the bus, they conducted a preliminary debrief of the display, which would be followed up with a more detailed analysis from video footage in the hotel later. This event was short and brutal, with pilots owning up to or being challenged for mistakes none of us had seen from the ground. It was an indication of the professionalism and attention to detail that made them so good at what they did.

No sooner had it finished, than we followed them off the

bus and up to the wide entrance of what looked like a former Georgian coaching inn. Now I can't remember the exact choreography, but I'm pretty sure that checking in had to wait, because just inside the hotel entrance, by a sign welcoming the Red Arrows, was a line-up of local dignitaries, including the mayor, there to greet the men in red suits. While we, in our less stylish green bags, sneaked past and hovered in the background, the Reds had to switch roles, from pilot to diplomat.

The only time I'd had to do anything vaguely similar was at Battle of Britain cocktail parties, where I'd had to make small talk with local worthies directed to one of several groups in the Officers' Mess anteroom. But of course that was for a couple of hours once a year. I suspected the Reds had to do this everywhere they went, and on the evidence of this weekend, they did.

Beyond the line-up were waiters offering glasses of champagne and buck's fizz from silver trays, and a large bar area full of more smiling people waiting to meet the team. We took the proffered drinks and followed, once again staying in the background. The resulting reception lasted about an hour. We weren't left totally out in the cold, but there was no doubt about the centre of attention. And even when we were approached by individuals, there was only one topic of conversation: how wonderful the men in red suits were.

Watching the pilots in action, I was impressed at the energy they put into each individual encounter and at the grace and style with which they answered even the most inane questions. Okay, so it hadn't been too taxing a day – it was an unusually sedate weekend by their standards - but I was pretty sure they'd have tried as hard to please at the end of a busy weekend, or on day twenty of an overseas tour.

I was also impressed at how level-headed they seemed amidst all this adulation. This was partly because I'd been primed to expect each one of them to be arrogant and vain. Now, over the years I certainly met some who were both these things, obnoxious even, but they couldn't all be tarred with the same brush, and some accusations said more about the accuser than the Reds. Plus, appearing normal would be hard for any of us to achieve when wearing that colour flying suit.

That said, there have been instances where their elite status has gone to their heads and caused them and the RAF problems, but I didn't witness any of that on this first close encounter.

As the reception wore on, I noticed groups of young women in their Friday night finery walking past the hotel. A few caught sight of the sign by the entrance, or even the young men in their red flying suits. In a comical tableau imprinted on my memory, moments later they'd reappear from the opposite direction and look in to confirm that they hadn't been seeing things. And then, following the briefest exchange of conspiratorial glances, several groups stepped inside and headed for the bar. By the time the reception ended, there must have been thirty or more of Darlington's finest, all eying up the Arrows like hyenas appraising a herd of gazelles.

I suspect that if it hadn't pre-dated mobile phones and social media, there might have been hundreds.

Now if I had any tales of Red Arrows pilots wallowing in drink and debauchery, I probably wouldn't share them. But the truth is that I don't have anything racy to relate. Of course we weren't with them all weekend, so they could have been up to all manner of things, but what I saw with my own eyes was nothing more than a bit of mild flirting, some moderate drinking and all the team heading upstairs for their debrief.

If someone had pushed temptation my way, who knows how I'd have reacted, but without a red suit, I remained invisible, my virtue unchallenged.

As the reception ended, those of us in green flying suits went upstairs to shower and change before heading out into the Darlington streets for a meal and a few beers. The crew had already gelled and we enjoyed a night filled with laughter that couldn't have been bettered had we been in Kuala Lumpur.

We didn't see the Reds until breakfast the next morning. They looked better rested than us.

Saturday was another relatively quiet day, especially for Mucky Brown 11.

Fitting in around the flying programme at Leeming, the Reds departed for a 1 o'clock display over Barnard Castle then returned. Thirty or so minutes later, they took off for RAF Brize Norton and after a short delay while we loaded their kit and the Blues, we followed. This time, they had no display commitments, so we went straight to a hotel in Oxford, where once again there was a sign in the foyer, a line-up of worthies and a reception, albeit smaller and shorter than the one in Darlington.

Afterwards, for the one and only time that weekend, I heard one of the Red Arrows cash in on their name.

It seemed as if playing golf was a pre-requisite for selection to the team, and their clubs travelled everywhere with them, including this weekend. When I was checking in after the reception, one of the Reds happened to be on the phone at the far end of the desk.

'We were hoping to play a few holes this evening,' he said.

The person on the other end of the line obviously delivered bad news.

'Oh that is a shame' the pilot said, pausing for effect, then adopting a tone that could leave the golf club employee in no doubt that they were turning up a golden opportunity. 'Because, you see, we're Red Arrows pilots, and we're only here for one night.'

After a lengthy pause, the pilot smiled, 'Oh that's marvellous. Thank you so much. We'll see you just before six then.'

I wondered if the person at the other end had also offered to sacrifice their daughter!

While the team played golf, we had another pleasant meal

and a night on the town.

The Sunday was busier, at least for the Reds.

It was several years before I found out just how many requests for displays and flypasts they received, so many that they have to be sifted and considered by a special committee. So I wouldn't have known that there was a fair chance every transit had been planned to pass over as many events as possible, from village fetes and town shows to funerals. I was aware of only one flypast that weekend.

They departed Brize Norton at 11.32, flew over an event taking place on Horse Guards Parade in central London and on to RAF Mildenhall, an airfield in Suffolk about twenty miles north-east of Cambridge, arriving at 11.55. We landed fifteen minutes later, but the Reds were off again within forty minutes, this time for a display at Chelmsford.

Both the Hawks and our Albert had been parked close to a restricted area overlooked by armed guards in sentry towers. They were protecting a hangar housing an aircraft that, officially at least, didn't exist, and certainly not on British soil: a large, futuristic-looking dart of a reconnaissance plane, the SR71, Blackbird. I say this with the benefit of hindsight. At the time, we had no idea what the hangar held.

As an aside, a few months later, I was lucky enough to see a

Blackbird pass beneath us as we crossed the North Sea at dusk. In an indication of why the aircraft was so special, we were descending from 28,000 feet, while he'd set out from above 50,000.

That Sunday afternoon, the Blues were playing football while they waited for the Reds to return. All was well until someone lost control of the ball and it rolled over the line and into the restricted area. No-one was sure what to do, but in the end one of the Blues went over to the line, held up his hand like a naughty schoolboy and pointed at the ball. The two goons in the tower chatted and eventually one of them nodded and gestured with his gun. Trusting that he'd read the body language correctly, the young tradesman crossed the line and retrieved the ball.

Just like warships, armed guards at US facilities had a reputation for shooting first and asking questions later. I often imagined the conversation that might have taken place if there'd been a fatal misunderstanding.

'He was within the Restricted Zone, sir.'

'But he was only retrieving his ball.'

'He was within the Restricted Zone, sir.'

Just as well that everyone was on the same page because it happened several times during the course of the football game.

The Reds returned from the Chelmsford display for a quick turnaround and a transit back to Scampton. We followed, landing there for the second time that weekend at just after 3'o'clock.

Once again, the Reds had little time to relax. An hour after their arrival, they took off to display over RAF Cranwell, about twenty miles to the south. On their return at 4.20, they disappeared into the hangar for another debrief, followed by a night with their families, while we boarded transport for a hotel in Lincoln.

Sadly there was no sign welcoming the crew of Mucky Brown Eleven. There wasn't even a reception party, although there was a moment of mirth when the hotel receptionist said, 'Ah, the Red Arrows,' as we carried our cases over to her desk.

If only!

The next morning, Monday, we followed the Reds to RAF Fairford in Gloucester, their base for a lunchtime display over Royal Naval Air Station Yeovilton, about 50 miles to the south west. On their return, they debriefed while their aircraft were replenished and then we chased them back to Scampton. By the time we landed, they'd headed away for a well-earned day off with their families. We spent an hour on the ground while the Blues unloaded their kit and then returned to Lyneham, where we landed at just before 6pm.

For us, it had been a very quiet, at times, boring weekend. Between the transits we'd spent long periods on the ground while the team flew off to their displays. They often flew four or five displays a day during the summer, so it had been relatively quiet for them too. Even so, they'd flown thirteen transits, who knew how many flypasts, including the one over Horse Guards Parade, and five displays, all requiring meticulous preparation, precise navigation and supremely accurate formation flying and timing.

And of course, the weather had been kind. Navigating nine or ten aircraft between flypasts and displays in bad weather was a different kettle of fish altogether. Even when the weather wasn't bad enough to merit cancellation, they had to decide whether the combination of cloud and visibility were suitable for a full display, or would limit them to a sequence of flat or rolling manoeuvres.

The pressure to perform could be enormous. It was bad enough disappointing the public, but when flying the flag in front of foreign political, military and industrial leaders, the team were all too aware that cancellation could have serious reputational or commercial consequences for the UK as a whole.

It's very easy to say flight safety is paramount and such

pressure should be resisted. But aviation in general, and display flying in particular, is littered with examples of pilots feeling the need to fly in unsuitable weather, and paying the ultimate price. The Red Arrows have not always been immune to the dangers, but in comparison with similar teams, their safety record is good.

Blissfully unaware of such issues while growing up, I'd admired them simply for what they did. Now, armed with a little more knowledge and a weekend of following them around in Mucky Brown 11, I admired them even more.

Over the following decades, I'd be lucky enough to operate from the same airfield as the team for two years, to share an office with their headquarters staff officer, have a hand in selecting and training some of them, and finally to fly as a passenger during a full display practice over RAF Scampton, an episode described in the introduction to Volume One of this memoir, Preparation For Flight.

The next few months consisted mainly of short domestic and European routes, but also a trip to Nairobi, via Cyprus, with the pipe-smoking captain. Highlights included stunning views of the Great Rift Valley, the Nile and even the Giza Pyramids.

In Nairobi, I was fascinated by a tall tree outside a café. Surrounding its trunk at a height of about ten feet, and projecting out by about three feet, was a square sloping *roof*, tiled like a Roman villa. Shielded from the sun and rain beneath it were four large rectangular notice boards, to which people had pinned business cards, brochures and small handwritten notes in many languages. Those in English said things like, *Mike, meet you in Cape Town on 7th, Tom*; or *Sally, meet me in Khartoum on 12th September, Jeremy*. Not many included specific addresses, as if you could just walk into Cape Town or Khartoum and bump into one another. Perhaps you could.

I presume such boards were scattered all over Africa, but I doubt they've survived into the internet and mobile phone eras, which is a shame. Even in 1983, the one in Nairobi seemed to belong to a more innocent and romantic age.

A few weeks later, Geraldine and I enjoyed our first ever foreign holiday, a week in Sorrento, Italy, booked with Cosmos Holidays at a cost of £618, including flights with Monarch Airlines, a room, breakfast and dinner in a large hotel perched above the town.

It wasn't as adventurous as driving across Africa, but as we stood on the hotel terrace and looked at Mount Vesuvius across the blue waters of the Bay of Naples, it seemed like another milestone, another departure from the lives our parents had lived.

The only other trip farther afield over this period was to Istanbul and back. It started with a squadron leader appearing in flight planning and announcing that he was joining the crew to give me and the captain a route check. That surprise was memorable enough, but it's an episode while attempting to return to our aircraft at Istanbul Airport that has stayed with me ever since.

Approaching a barrier after flight planning, the captain, nav, route checker and I were halted by two burly armed guards, one of whom took our passports and disappeared into an adjacent office. We shuffled under the gun barrel of the other guard until a burly man with a large moustache and masses of gold braid stepped out of the office. He walked up to the route checker and commenced an earnest conversation. After a brief exchange, the squadron leader beckoned me over.

It seemed the only way to get our passports back without a fuss was for someone to buy the guards four hundred cigarettes. And guess who was going to do it?

Feeling very conspicuous, I walked back to the nearest duty free shop and bought the cigarettes. As I returned under the watchful eyes of the armed guards and their imposing boss, scenes from a film I'd seen not long before came to mind. Caught smuggling, the chief protagonist in Midnight Express had gone on to endure years of hellish conditions in a Turkish prison.

Okay, in his case the contraband was hashish, while I was merely carrying tobacco. But technically it was still smuggling. What if it was a sting operation designed to create a diplomatic incident or, more likely, for these characters to extort money from the crew by threatening to arrest me for a crime they'd initiated?

There were all manner of possibilities, most of which seemed likely to see me spending time in a Turkish slammer while it was sorted out.

Fanciful perhaps, but the possibility seemed real enough for me to be on edge as I handed the duty free bag to the guard commander. He looked in and paused, just long enough to ramp up the tension. Then he nodded at me, smiled and handed over the passports. Only when I looked at the faces of my fellow crew members did I realise that they too had been on tenterhooks.

You read about institutionalised corruption in some

countries, but this was the only time during my career that I experienced it – and in a fellow NATO country.

After landing back at Lyneham, the route checker said I was operating as a solid C Cat - what was expected of me at this stage of my co-pilot tour - and signed my Categorisation Card accordingly. It was a relief not to have stumbled under test conditions this time.

As he walked away, I couldn't help wondering if my performance as a smuggler had been taken into account.

COMBAT SURVIVAL AND RESCUE

I've already mentioned that when not flying or involved in other duties, those aircrew not in executive positions were often to be found at home. At least that was the case before April 1982. Since then, I for one had been fully stretched, either flying or preparing to fly. As 1983 progressed, however, unless you were on detachment in the Falkland Islands, activity returned to pre-invasion levels.

When not down route, I still had the Squadron Fund to run and I made the occasional outing for the Station football and volleyball teams. I also went running and played almost any sport for the squadron in events like the Station Commander's Cup. But with Geraldine at work, I sometimes found myself at a bit of a loss.

One answer was to apply for external training courses.

During many lessons and practical exercises in flying training, I'd developed an interest in the subject of combat survival. So I applied to become a Combat Survival and Rescue Officer, a CSRO. To gain the qualification, I had to complete a twelve day course at the RAF Combat Survival and Rescue School at RAF Mountbatten, the base on the outskirts of Plymouth I'd visited for sea dinghy drills eighteen months earlier. The course was acknowledged to include some of the toughest physical challenges in the Services, certainly in the RAF.

Many of the exercises during my apprentice and officer training had been physically demanding, as were later undertakings, like London Marathons and running up

Vesuvius. But they were over fairly quickly, a matter of hours, whereas the more physical elements of the CSRO course were rumoured to last a week. I say rumoured because the course was surrounded by a cloak of secrecy, partly to prevent future course members knowing too much about the course, but partly for genuine national security reasons. Elements of the syllabus had to be cleared at the highest political levels. As a result, even after the passage of nearly forty years, I still have to be careful what I say – although we all know the things I seek to protect will undoubtedly be in the public domain somewhere on the internet.

Anyway, all this meant there was a fair amount of tension in the air when fifteen aircrew met in a classroom at Mountbatten at 0830 on Monday 26th September 1983. A couple were in their 30s, but most of us were in our mid to late twenties.

Twelve were officers, nine a mix of RAF pilots and navigators from the Herc, Nimrod, Phantom and Jaguar fleets. One of the navs was from my own squadron. We'd flown together a few times and got on well. The other three officers were a French Jaguar pilot and two helicopter pilots, one from the Royal Marines, the other the Army Air Corps.

The three NCO aircrew were a Herc loadmaster, a Nimrod Air Electronics Operator and an American helicopter crewman from Arizona who'd only recently arrived in the UK.

He was the youngest and least experienced course member, and about as far from the stereotypical brash American as you could imagine. Quiet and introverted, he rarely contributed to lessons or, despite our best efforts, attended social events, preferring to sit on the shoreline of the Mountbatten peninsula watching the sea, which he'd only ever seen from the air. Unlike the rest of us, he was also a pressed man rather than a volunteer, which may go some way to explain his lack of enthusiasm.

The syllabus he was handed at the start of that first morning could have done little to ease his trepidation. It certainly didn't ease mine.

Although most of the first week was to be spent in the classroom, I couldn't help but notice periods set aside for *Single and Multi-seat Sea Dinghy Drills*, one at 11 o'clock at night. My one and only sea drill in broad daylight had been bad enough. I dreaded doing something similar in the dark. Another teaser was *Night Navigation*, again not starting until 11pm.

But the second week was even more intriguing. After Monday 0800 - *Brief Moorex, Hand in Valuables and depart for Dartmoor* - the rest of the programme was blank until 0800 the following Monday, when we were scheduled to *Debrief Moorex*.

It seemed to me that a lot could happen in that missing week.

The course started with a quick introduction to the role of a CSRO, which was to impart the knowledge and skills we gained to our fellow aircrew. And because we'd be expected to maintain the role beyond our current tours, and maybe on a different aircraft, we were to be taught the general principles of combat survival equipment and techniques, then relate them to whichever aircraft type we operated in our own time.

The lessons were delivered by staff or visiting lecturers utilising the mix of professionalism and ribald humour I'd become used to on other courses. Most focused on how to survive after a forced landing, crash or ejection in deserts, jungles, the arctic wastes or the sea, and in any climate zone from the equator to the arctic.

The priorities in each case are fairly similar: Protection, Location, Water, Food, Maintaining Morale and, from the outset, Planning how these priorities can be achieved with the manpower and materials you have available. Of course much also depends on whether you land on Oxford Street, the Russian Steppes, the Amazon Rainforest or the Sahara; or in the sea a few yards from Brighton Pier or the open ocean, not to mention whether you find yourself in friendly or hostile territory.

Protection on land begins with getting away from immediate hazards and administering first aid before finding or building a shelter, something to protect you from the elements in friendly territory, or to conceal you if you're behind the lines.

Ideally you'd be able to shelter in your aircraft, a dinghy or a nearby building or cave. But in most survival situations, you're probably going to have to build something from whatever materials you can find. In the jungle you want to be above ground to avoid insects; in the desert, above or below ground to keep cool; and in the arctic, if you can't build an igloo, you may need to dig a snow hole.

Over the duration of the course, we had plenty of practice at building different types of shelter for temperate climates. Sometimes they gave us parachutes or military ponchos from which to fashion our grand designs, but at other times, we had to forage material for frames, cladding and flooring.

An early priority is building a fire. As well as warmth – even in the desert, where it can get very cold at night - they can be used for cooking and signalling to would-be rescuers. And as anyone who's been camping will testify, they're also good for morale. So after the theory of fire-lighting, we had plenty of practice.

Who knew how much time and energy it takes to gather enough tinder, kindling, small and large logs to keep a fire going for even a few hours, not to mention how long it can take to create a spark to light the damn thing if you're not armed with matches, a lighter or a flare?

I discovered that some people only have to look at a pile of kindling for it to burst into flames. But as Geraldine would testify from my attempts to light fires in our various married quarters, I lack the caveman gene. So my fires were usually among the last to burst into life, although I always seemed to get there in the end.

In enemy territory of course, any fire would have to be

shielded and we were taught how to build a Dakota Hole Fire, essentially an underground fire with ventilation to disperse smoke before it can be seen. And on snow or ice you'd have to light your fire on a *raft* to keep it well clear of the surface.

One result of taking part in such exercises was the acquisition of a tobacco tin, which I filled with survival goodies, including a Swiss Army Knife, wire, string, water-purifying tablets, safety matches, cotton wool and a flint and steel. Alongside a compact first aid kit, I carried it in a lower pocket of my flying suit for the rest of my career. Even now, I always have something similar in my rucksack when walking the hills.

Location in survival situations tends, initially at least, to prioritise attracting would-be rescuers. Finding out where you are and where you want to go will rise in importance if no-one turns up. Generally, the principle is to stay where you are for the first few days on the assumption that rescuers will make for your last known position.

In enemy territory though, it's about getting away from your landing point as quickly as possible, then attempting to attract help while remaining hidden from hostile eyes - a delicate balancing act. Ideally, you'll have been briefed on safe areas and escape options. But in the end, you might have to survive for long periods while evading detection and heading for a border crossing.

In friendly territory, giving away your position is the priority, and this means placing aircraft and personal locator beacons as high as possible, so their signals beam as far as possible. Personal beacons can also be used as radios, but that facility drains the battery very quickly and should only be used when rescuers are close and other methods of attracting them to your exact location have failed.

In 1983 these beacons were the cutting edge of technology and a Search and Rescue satellite had just been launched. There are many more satellites now, of course, not to mention mobile phones and GPS.

Back in the day though, we relied on much less sophisticated location devices, including whistles, heliographs or any shiny metal surface, torches and smoke. To make a location stand out from the air, you could also lay out colourful items like your parachute or dinghy, and symbols – the bigger the better – from the Ground/Air Emergency Code: V – require assistance, X – require medical assistance – and, if you'd set out to find help, arrows to indicate your direction of travel.

Water is vital to survival. The average human body contains eighty eight pints of the stuff, but in temperate climates you lose about a pint a day to breathing, another to urine and variable amounts when sweating, depending on the temperature and how much effort you're expending. You can also lose vast amounts if suffering from vomiting, diarrhoea and injuries such as burns. Even eating consumes water, so if you're short of it, don't eat.

Without water, if in good health and not having to expend too much effort, you could expect to last between ten and fourteen days, again in a temperate climate. But you go downhill fairly quickly. The loss of four pints leads to symptoms such as dizziness, sleepiness and headaches; the loss of five to nine to shortage of breath, a swollen tongue and blueness of extremities as the blood thickens; and finally, the loss of ten to eighteen pints leads to such things as delirium, deafness, dimming of vision, painful stiffness of the joints, coma and death.

Unfortunately, if you land in the sea, you shouldn't drink sea water. The human body can cope with about two per cent salt in water, but most seawater contains about three and a half per cent, which can be fatal. Neither should you drink blood, fish juices or – damn it – alcohol. All take more water to digest than they provide.

So, hopefully, there are sources of fresh water nearby to add to the limited amounts you may have in any survival packs.

Otherwise, you have to fashion things to capture moisture from the air – if there is any. In the jungle, some may be available in plants. In other areas you may be able to dig for it and in arctic conditions you should aim to melt ice rather than snow. Wherever you are, with water in short supply, the principal is to take none for twenty four hours, then a pint a day, unless injured or suffering from the aforementioned vomiting and diarrhoea. Even when available, most water collected should be treated as suspect and be boiled or treated with water purification tablets.

Of course, in the desert, all this becomes somewhat academic. Even at 95°F, the body requires nine pints of water a day to keep dehydration at bay, so you should drink when you're thirsty and hope for rescue. Rationing will only lead to more rapid deterioration.

Luckily, there was generally plenty of water around us on Dartmoor – sometimes too much – but we also experienced how difficult it is to find something practical to carry it in when you need to travel. One answer, we discovered, was to include non-lubricated condoms in your personal survival tin. Placed in a sock to limit their expansion, they could make a handy water carrier. Most of the time on Dartmoor, though, we were able to use rigid plastic bottles, and the water we collected was always boiled or treated with purification tablets, on the assumption that there was a dead sheep somewhere upstream.

Food is the fourth survival priority.

Much like water, downed aircrew could expect to have at least a small amount, things like biscuits and boiled sweets, in their survival packs, enough to last until rescue in most situations. But once that was gone, in remote locations, we'd have to try and live off the land – or the sea.

Without food, the average person can last for about thirty days. But although the deterioration in health is slower than from lack of water, the initial symptoms of low energy and muddled thinking can be felt after a surprisingly short period, especially when working hard. I know because we went for long periods with little or no food during our week on Dartmoor, when there was lots of walking and scavenging for materials to build shelters and fires.

One day we'd been split into five groups of three – in my case, with the Herc nav and loadmaster. We spent the morning building an encampment of five makeshift shelters and fashioning fishing nets and animal traps comprising a mix of nooses, nets and heavy rocks released by various trigger mechanisms. Having not eaten for more than a day, we laid our traps and spent the rest of the afternoon eating hawthorn berries, foraging for plants, fishing and imagining the local wildlife queuing up to be caught.

As you can probably guess, there was a general air of disappointment that evening as we huddled round our fires listening to our stomachs growl and watching a thin soup comprising mainly nettles come to the boil. The fish and game had evaded us.

Our instructors had a habit of turning up at odd times to set us off on some more or less unpleasant task or adventure, so there was a collective groan as they drove up and walked over. They were carrying a live chicken and rabbit.

I suspect it wouldn't happen now, and I won't go into too much detail, but in 1983, they proceeded to show us how to despatch both creatures, pluck or skin them and prepare them for cooking. The meat was distributed and while they went back to their vehicle, we added it to our pots, grateful that our soup had turned into a much heartier stew.

But there was another surprise. Rather than drive off, the instructors returned with five more live chickens.

We looked at one another as the chickens were distributed, one to each group. Now I guess I'd have despatched the bird if I'd had to, but the loadie seemed keen so the nav and I stepped aside. One by one, and I have to say, with the minimum of fuss or suffering, the five birds had their necks stretched.

It was a brutal introduction to an aspect of meat eating few of us like to think about, but I actually think it was less cruel than the industrialised transport and slaughter I'd witnessed at the frozen chicken plant I'd worked in briefly before joining the RAF. And the resulting meal was very welcome, much more appetising than the worm curry we sampled a day or so later.

There were many salutary lessons from the week on Dartmoor, but one that really has stayed with me is how difficult it would be to find food in this or any other country if the shops suddenly ran out.

To my mind, Morale is a bit of a catch-all phrase for attitude of mind in its widest context. In essence, as in so many areas of life, it's much easier to cope with the day if you're busy and motivated, not to mention warm, dry and well fed. And while not all these things can be guaranteed in a survival situation, the motivation to get up and make things happen is vital. The very act of striving can be good for morale.

It goes without saying that in a lone survival situation you have to be self-motivating, while in a group, the leader takes some of the responsibility for keeping people busy. But there's still a large element of personal responsibility, not least in not letting yourself or the team down. Of course, if your efforts come to nought, sitting, cold, wet and hungry in front of an unlit fire can be a real test of mental resilience, but the boost if even some of your labours bear fruit can be enormous.

Over the week on Dartmoor we had plenty of opportunity to experience the ups and downs of trying to survive in the wild, sometimes while being hunted. And although we knew we were never far from rescue if things went badly wrong, there was a real air of jeopardy as we were pushed toward our physical and mental limits over an extended period. Much of the time was spent in groups, and I can attest that most of us worked hard and tried to remain upbeat. But I also witnessed others finding things more difficult.

The young American crewman was the most extreme example of someone struggling to cope with the conditions. Despite our best efforts, it didn't take long in the cold and wet for him to suffer a mental collapse that saw him retreat into a near-catatonic state.

There had been signs of inner turmoil in the classroom and the night navigation exercise in the first week, when he'd struggled with the difficult conditions and terrain, even over a relatively short period. But the second week saw a more rapid and dangerous deterioration in his morale.

I've worked with plenty of Americans I'd want by my side in a sticky situation. But this young man's heart had never been in the course. Less experienced than the rest of us, he'd found himself among a strange group of people in a strange country where the weather was vastly different from his native Arizona. This was all exacerbated by his status as a non-volunteer.

In my opinion, he should never have been exposed to the course, or at least not at that stage in his career. Perhaps his superiors were trying to get him to *man-up*, but it didn't work. His morale collapsed.

The upshot was that he left Dartmoor with the instructors one evening and didn't come back. I've often wondered how his life panned out afterwards.

On paper, Planning is the sixth and final priority. But in reality it needs to be front and centre from the moment you hit the ground, when you need to be working out how you're going to protect, feed and water yourself while attracting help and maybe evading capture.

Unless you land somewhere like Central Park, the initial plan will probably involve staying put for a period to allow rescuers to find you. And although you'll have to move a reasonable distance after a landing behind enemy lines, you may be able to head for a pre-planned recovery area where you can rest up and await rescue.

Even when you reach the point where immediate rescue seems unlikely, factors like the distance to be covered, terrain, weather, injury or the physical condition of you or your team could complicate the decision to travel or not, especially if you're already in an area with adequate shelter, water and food. And of course before setting out, you'll want to have a fair idea where you are and where you want to go, and the safest route to get there. Finally, if and when you do decide to travel, you're not going to be able to carry much, so you need to be meticulous in planning what to take and in packing it.

No-one said it would be easy!

In the classroom, among the many tips we were given was how to work out direction and time without a compass.

With clear skies, depending on time of year, the sun rises roughly in the east and sets roughly in the west, but in the northern hemisphere it's always due south at its highest point at noon. At other times of day, you can point the hour hand of your watch at the sun and, again in the northern hemisphere, south will be the point between the hour hand and 12 o'clock. On a clear night, the Pole Star will be due north and a line through the horns of a crescent new moon will give the north/south axis, while on gloomy days and nights, you may be able to use clues like moss and lichen, which tend to grow on the north side of tree trunks and rocks.

If you don't have a watch, but plenty of time, a stick in the ground can be turned into a sundial, with the longest shadow marking not only midday but also the south/north axis.

The lessons on the varying priorities were backed up by others on survival in different areas of the world. These were all equally fascinating, but I'll home in on just one example.

In the jungle, the very environment is hostile, potentially deadly. If the spiders, ants, hornets, scorpions, leeches, crocodiles, poisonous frogs or snakes don't get you, falling deadwood, dysentery or infected, bites, cuts and sores might. To minimise at least some of these deadly threats, it's vital to stay meticulously clean and store all food and human waste at least one hundred yards from your campsite, which also has to be cleared of vegetation, especially beneath the raised sleeping quarters you'll have to construct.

If, like me, the thought of a large hairy spider crawling up your leg makes you shudder, the instructors' advice to stay calm and stroke it off with a Wilkie survival knife sounded, at best, optimistic. I knew I'd be much more likely to give in to panic and start hacking at the beast. And sure enough, wounds resulting from people doing exactly that were so common in the jungle they were known as Wilkie bites.

Diving in to thick undergrowth or water to avoid angry hornets also sounds easier said than done, although I was relieved to discover that cutting the skin and then sucking out the poison from a snake bite is not recommended outside Hollywood.

Unsurprisingly, travelling at night is also discouraged. Not only can it be near impossible to clear a path, but every brush with vegetation tends to induce heart-stopping panic as the mind conjures images of an attack by nightmarish creatures hidden in the darkness. Travel simply becomes too physically and mentally demanding.

Dartmoor sounded positively benign after such lectures. And yet, soon after returning to Lyneham, I volunteered for the Jungle Survival Course, which was held a couple of times a year in Brunei. Unfortunately, or perhaps fortunately, other priorities led to my application being rescinded a few months later.

Among the practical exercises in the first week were multi- and single-seat dinghy drills in the choppy waters of Plymouth Sound – by day and night.

Although darkness added a whole new dimension, the multi-seat drills were similar to those described earlier in this volume. But the single-seat drills were nothing like those performed in a nice warm swimming pool during my flying training. The numbing cold, the violently pitching swell and the unpredictable waves filling my mouth, nose and eyes with salt water made the whole exercise much more physically and mentally demanding.

It wasn't long before I couldn't feel my fingers. Actions like dragging myself in to the dinghy, finding and deploying the drogue, turning over, inflating the floor and canopy and baling became so difficult it would have been easy to give up. And that was before I'd been tipped out by a rogue wave and had to repeat the process, which happened a couple of times.

Even in daylight, with safety personnel and rescue close at hand, I felt incredibly apprehensive, close to panic. But, in darkness, all the difficulties were greatly amplified, while intense feelings of loneliness and claustrophobia also crowded in.

I couldn't help thinking of the young Spitfire and Hurricane pilots in their late teens or early twenties who ended up in the Channel during the Battle of Britain. Many were so badly wounded or burned that they could barely inflate their Mae Wests, let alone climb aboard a dinghy – if they had one. And they'd have been all too aware that unless they were in sight of land or a passing ship, rescue was unlikely. There was no search and rescue organisation.

Going into battle over the Channel several times a day knowing that ending up in the sea was likely to lead to a lonely, lingering, death is one of the many things that, in my eyes, marked these young men out as heroic.

My own ordeal was much less dramatic and prolonged. Nonetheless, at the end of the day drill, I was very glad to see the big yellow Sea King come into the hover above me. Being winched from the water and into its belly is another life highlight.

Classroom tips on navigation and the best ways to attract or avoid detection when travelling were driven home during Moorex, when we were invariably being hunted.

Travelling at night was particularly memorable.

The night navigation exercise in the first week involved trekking between manned checkpoints several miles apart while being hunted by the staff and various volunteers. At each checkpoint, our team of three – the Herc aircrew again - were to meet a friendly *agent*. He'd provide instructions to reach the next objective.

If you really want to stay undetected at night, you have to travel slowly and pause often to look and listen. But the need to reach each checkpoint in a reasonable time meant we had to strike a balance between moving at pace and maintaining at least an air of stealth. Not easy, especially for the loadie, who was six foot five and almost as broad as he was tall!

On a dark, moonless night, the Moor was pitch black. As we stumbled over tussocks and across ditches, we were rarely able to see more than a few feet in any direction. It could be very disorientating, making it difficult to keep in contact with one another, let alone navigate between checkpoints. And if the friendly agents hadn't been deliberately *careless* and shone their powerful torches heavenwards every now and then, I doubt we'd have found any of them.

For reasons that escape me now, the loadie was map reading. At one point, we came to a body of swiftly flowing water several yards across. Our torches had red filters to protect night vision and make them less easy to spot. But this made them useless at illuminating anything more than a few feet away. We spent a few minutes fumbling around vainly for a shallower, narrower or slower section of stream, before shrugging our shoulders and stepping into the torrent.

As recommended, we'd armed ourselves with stout sticks with which to prod the ground ahead for hazards, like holes, barbed wire fences or leats – the name for Dartmoor's steep-sided irrigation channels, a couple of yards wide and several feet deep. Now, they had to brace us against the force of a rock-strewn river about fifteen yards across and three feet deep. Without them, we'd have been swept off our feet, with who-knows what consequences.

Eventually, we flopped down on the far side, panting and wet, but grateful the experience was behind us. A few moments later, though, the loadie coughed.

'Ah,' he said. 'Slight navigational error! We actually need to be back on the other side. Sorry.'

Teamwork is sometimes about accepting that people make mistakes - especially when they're six foot five and as broad as... So, having established that it wasn't some cruel joke, we took a few moments to compose ourselves and tottered back across.

At the time, it was pretty scary, but if the three of us ever met up again, we'd soon be crying with laughter as we relived the episode.

The stout sticks didn't always work as advertised.

Another night, the nav and I were several hours into a walk across the Moor to our next bivouac site. It was dark and misty, and we'd spent several hours walking in line astern, prodding the ground ahead of us. When we reached a relatively flat area, against advice, we began walking side by side.

One moment we were striding out, the next we were falling.

After a drop of several feet, we landed on soft earth at the base of a peat digging area. Miraculously, neither of us suffered anything beyond wounded pride, so we sat there, laughing at our stupidity - and our good fortune. It's another episode I'll always remember.

As to the sticks, we'd become so lulled by the rhythmic sound and feel of them hitting the ground in front of us that we failed to notice when they met nothing other than fresh air and followed them into the abyss.

And finally on the issue of night navigation, I've already said it could be disorientating, but on a couple of occasions I found myself move beyond this vaguely unsettling feeling into hallucination, once when leading the nav on the night of the peat digging incident and once a few nights later, when walking the Moor on my own.

Both instances occurred when tiredness, monotony and lack of visual cues combined to make me feel as if I was walking an extremely narrow path with a vertiginous drop to either side. The fact that I knew it to be nonsense didn't prevent me suffering a form of dizzying vertigo, on occasion severe enough to make me stagger, at which point my heart raced because I momentarily believed I'd stepped into thin air.

It was all very bizarre and unsettling, but as it turned out, not that unusual. Several of my fellow course members admitted to having the same sensation during their own nocturnal treks. Thinking about it later, I suspect the mechanism at play is not dissimilar to the disorientation suffered when flying in cloud or poor visibility. When that happens, though, you're strapped in and unable to stumble.

Thankfully, none of the many walking expeditions I've undertaken since has included a combination of factors that caused hallucinations, although strangely enough, I almost wish they had.

One of the wider aims of the course was to give an insight into the realities of war, and three of the visitors in the first week had fascinating tales to tell. Two were Harrier pilots.

The first, Squadron Leader Bob Iveson, a large avuncular man with a bushy black moustache, had been shot down on 27th May 1982 by small arms fire when making his third pass over Argentinean positions near Goose Green on East Falkland. He ejected at about one hundred feet and 450 knots, suffering spinal compression and wind damage to his eyes. Under his parachute for no more than a few seconds, he landed close to a large house he'd seen from the air.

In flight, he'd spotted no Argentineans nearby, and after watching the building for a short period, he headed for it and let himself in. It was unoccupied, but with a stock of food and blankets, so he spent the night there. Knowing it would be one of the first places the Argentineans would search if and when they reached the area, the next morning he set out to walk toward British positions, but was forced back by a storm. On his second morning in the house, he heard prolonged gunfire, actually the Battle of Goose Green. When it quietened, he gambled that the British had won and set off his Personal Locator Beacon. It attracted a Royal Navy helicopter, which initially disappeared, but returned later to pick him up.

His was almost an object lesson in what *not* to do. He'd flown over the same position three times, hidden in the most prominent feature in an area very close to where he'd ejected, and he'd set off his locator beacon when he had little idea who it would attract.

And yet he'd got away with it.

As he and the staff of the School readily admitted, sometimes you needed luck on your side.

The second Harrier pilot, Flight Lieutenant Jeff Glover, was nowhere near as lucky, becoming the only British serviceman in the Falklands War to enter captivity.

He was on a reconnaissance mission over Argentinean positions on the coast of West Falkland on 21st May when, flying at about 600 knots, his aircraft received a fatal hit from a surface to air missile. With the right wing detaching, it had completed 360° of roll by the time his ejection seat shot into the airflow, the force of which knocked him out and broke his collar bone and his left arm in two places. Contact with the waters of Falkland Sound added a black eye and further damage to a face already severely swollen by wind blast. He may have drowned had he not been picked up immediately by Argentinean soldiers.

After a short period receiving medical treatment on the Falklands, he was transferred to Argentina. Overall, he spent seven weeks in captivity, and although twelve days were in solitary confinement, he was never mistreated. They never even interrogated him with any vigour, either when he was at his most vulnerable and useful – straight after his ejection – or later.

Six years after his ordeal, I was to serve alongside him at Scampton when he became a member of the Red Arrows.

For us, the major lessons from both stories were just how discombobulating it would be to be sitting in a warm aircraft one minute and dangling under a parachute or waking up under water the next, and how much mental fortitude was required to stop yourself descending into panic, closely followed by complete physical and mental collapse.

Jeff Glover had had most of the decision-making taken from his hands, but he'd still had to maintain his composure, and his will to survive; while Bob Iveson had galvanised himself into immediate action and spent forty eight hours making difficult decisions, any of which could have turned out badly for him.

The third visiting lecturer gave one of the most fascinating and thought-provoking talks I'd heard in my life to that date.

Another large exuberant man, Surgeon Lieutenant-Commander Rick Jolly had deployed to the Falklands as medical officer to 3 Commando Brigade and landed with them at Ajax Bay on the north-west coast of East Falkland. Here he set up a field hospital in the only vaguely suitable buildings, the leaky ruins of an old refrigeration plant. Initially at least, most patients were either Paras or Royal Marines, which is why the hospital became known as the Red and Green Life Machine, a reference to the colours of their respective unit berets.

Over the course of the war, despite dire conditions, inadequate lighting and air raids leading to the presence of two unexploded bombs, Rick Jolly and his team operated on and treated five hundred and eighty men, many with life-threatening injuries. They gave no preference to British over Argentinean lives, always treating the most serious cases first, regardless of nationality. Perhaps the greatest testament to their skill and dogged determination to help everyone is that not one man died while under their care.

This was all the more remarkable because some casualties were picked up having lost so much blood that they should have been dead, of shock if nothing else. But somehow, what little blood they had seemed to shuttle between their brains and their hearts to keep them alive long enough to reach the hospital. No-one really understood exactly what process was at work, but Rick was sure the effort British troops had put into improving fitness during the voyage to the Falklands had played a large part.

Among many striking things Rick Jolly explained was that the damage caused by high velocity bullets was greatly exacerbated by the pulverised fabric, dirt, flesh and bone they sucked into the wound to contaminate it. Images of medical and forensic procedures are more commonplace now, but back then, seeing such images on the large screen at the front of the classroom was, for many of us, quite shocking.

Rick explained that a number of the Argentinean casualties were caused by the callous disregard their officers had for the health and welfare of their young conscript soldiers, a situation worsened by the incompetence of their logistic arrangements.

This was exemplified by the case of a young man who, forced to move positions at short notice, lost his boots. Although there were containers full of such things in Stanley, they were never emptied and there was no way of getting a pair to him – even if anyone had taken the slightest interest in his plight. After days and nights in the wet and cold, during which he'd been reduced to trying to warm his feet in penguin nest holes, the skin had progressively peeled off until they were down to the bone. The images will stay with me forever.

I knew I wasn't the only one in the classroom feeling a bit cold and clammy after looking at the damage bombs and bullets could do to a human body. So when the skeletal feet appeared on the screen, the scrape of a chair followed by the thud of something large hitting the ground came as no surprise. I looked round, bracing myself to receive vicious banter from the Army and Royal Marine pilots because one of us soft RAF types had fainted.

But no, it was the Royal Marine on the classroom floor. He was just rousing himself, face ashen, eyes open, trying to work out where he was and what had happened. He never lived it down.

I was lucky enough to hear Rick Jolly speak several times over the years and to sit next to him when we were both guests at a dinner of London's University Royal Navy Unit, by which time he was a Surgeon Captain and the author of several books about the Navy's distinctive language and customs. He was great company.

The majority of Moorex would be spent role-playing the aftermath of a parachute landing behind enemy lines. In preparation, we were given advice on escape and evasion, conduct after capture and resistance to interrogation.

In the case of war, it was assumed that those hunting us and taking us into captivity would be Warsaw Pact forces. So the lessons were based on the experiences of those who'd fallen foul of the various puppet states behind the Iron Curtain. Forgive me if, as I said earlier, I have to draw a veil over some of it.

When it came to escape and evasion, the advice was to travel at least five miles from our landing site before going to ground. Hilltops, ridgelines and valley bottoms were to be avoided, as were road, rail and river bridges. We should seek an area of natural cover, like a wood, unless it was the only such feature for miles around. And unlike Bob Iveson, we were advised to shun isolated houses, barns or caves. They'd be sure to attract search parties.

If we were lucky enough to find a wood or area of thick undergrowth to shelter in, we should aim to make it more difficult for trackers by taking a meandering path round its boundaries before entering from an unexpected direction. And if we needed to cross roads, rail lines or rivers, we should observe them for several minutes before crossing, all at once in line abreast if part of a group.

Things would be much more difficult if the enemy had a dog. We could try masking our scent with things like pepper or strong-smelling liquids if we had them, by passing close to livestock if there was any, and by crossing rivers, wading downstream for some distance before climbing out on the other side.

The final resort fitted very much into the easier said than done category. It was to kill the dog!

When it came to hiding ourselves, even in wooded areas, it was deemed better to dig down or construct a camouflaged shelter at ground level than to climb into the treetops, which risked not only falls during the climb or later, due to lapses of concentration, but also motion sickness and hypothermia.

I found the lectures on conduct after capture and resistance to interrogation particularly fascinating.

The point of capture would be one of the most dangerous moments. If we were caught by civilians or soldiers not subject to strong discipline and leadership, we were likely to be beaten or even killed on the spot. This risk was even more acute if we were captured in a region NATO aircraft had been bombing or strafing

I immediately thought of a particularly chilling scene in Len Deighton's novel, Bomber, in which German civilians find a Lancaster crewman dangling from a tree in which his parachute has snagged.

Deighton states merely, *They killed him with their spades*.

That phrase was enough to convince me the best I could hope for in a similar situation was capture by forces who knew my value to Warsaw Pact interrogators. But hey, during Moorex at least, we were fairly confident our captors would skip the beatings and move straight on to interrogations.

I say fairly confident, because the instructors had planted a scintilla of doubt with the revelation that the hunter force would be members of the Parachute Regiment undertaking their own training on the moor. Reminders of how much they hated officers, and especially aircrew officers, ensured that I wasn't the only one to feel real trepidation as they circled my hiding place a week later. But I'm getting ahead of myself.

If we survived the first few hours after capture, our priority was to avoid being selected for interrogation. This wouldn't be easy. Several factors were against us.

Firstly, aircrew, and especially officer aircrew are particularly attractive to interrogators. In addition to being a source of time-sensitive tactical information linked to our mission and the forces involved in it, our captors would assume our lofty perch during flight had given us a wider perspective of operations on the ground. RAF aircrew are also notoriously nosy, so there'd be an assumption that even if we hadn't heard NATO's wider aims, tactics and equipment through official channels, we'd have done so on the rumour network.

Secondly, because someone not in uniform faced summary execution as a spy, we were likely to be in flying kit at the point of capture, even if we'd tried to hide it under civilian clothing. This would immediately mark us out from other soldiers, sailors or airmen.

But there could also be factors in our favour.

The files the Warsaw Pact were said to have kept on us since flying training were unlikely to be available initially, so our captors would be denied this method of selecting people of particular interest. Also, interrogation is labour intensive, each interrogator having to spend significant periods questioning each prisoner.

Of course, if we were the only aircrew, or part of a small group, there was little to be done to avoid selection. But if we were in a large group, we had to make ourselves as invisible and unattractive as possible. Basically, we had to keep a low profile and act dumb.

Easier for some of us than others!

One tactic that proved remarkably successful in gaining information from captured German aircrew during the Second World War was to house them in groups after capture. It wasn't long before some were chatting away about what they'd been doing before their captivity, and bringing those who'd been prisoners for longer up to date on the war in general. Of course, their cells were bugged and some of the other *prisoners* weren't captives at all. The chattier prisoners were not only divulging information, but marking themselves out for interrogation.

So the lesson was to keep schtum and avoid doing anything that could draw attention.

Throughout all this, although the likelihood of serious maltreatment was said to be low, it was made plain that the enemy would do as much as they could to *soften us up* and break our will to resist questioning, a process that would begin long before we set eyes on an interrogator.

As Bob Iveson and Jeff Glover had found, being shot down was traumatic enough in itself. But add the trauma of capture – probably when cold, wet and hungry after days trying to evade - and almost anyone bar Superman would be at a low ebb. Our captors would seek to exploit this, and any character and cultural traits that might be turned to their advantage.

As a generalisation, aircrew are gregarious, keen to bond with, impress and please those with whom they come into contact. Being among people who not only dislike, but actively hate us, would be a profound shock to the system.

Before and between interrogations, we could expect to be dealt with *firmly*. This was likely to mean being kept cold, hungry and thirsty and deprived of sleep and sensory information, probably through the use of hoods and white noise. We were also likely to be forced to maintain unnatural kneeling, squatting or leaning stances for long periods, what were known as stress positions.

Other softening up methods would rely on our cultural conditioning. For instance, most of us have been taught to maintain high levels of personal hygiene. A period on the run would have made this difficult, but after capture an enemy would take things further by denying us washing and toilet facilities. Worse, we could be shackled and left to soil ourselves. I was all too willing to believe that such treatment could push some to a much darker place, even cause a complete collapse. At the least, it would induce humiliation, another useful way of breaking down the will to resist.

Women could be especially effective at heaping humiliation on men, and were likely to be used in this role. Again it wasn't too hard to believe that having a woman see us naked when at our lowest ebb could cause distress, while having them ridicule our physical attributes and likely sexual prowess could be a powerful weapon in breaking us down.

I was subjected to many things after capture on Moorex, but thankfully I wasn't denied visits to the toilet, nor was I humiliated by any women. And in the end, no matter how good we were at making ourselves seem poor subjects for interrogation, we all knew we were going to be interrogated.

It sounds like wishful thinking, and the treatment of captives in the first Gulf War would expose it as such, but the perceived wisdom until then was that we were unlikely to be physically tortured during interrogation. The reasoning was that we'd be prepared to say anything, true or false, to stop such treatment, so any information gained was likely to be untrustworthy. What we could expect instead was long sessions of questioning designed to persuade, bully or trick us into divulging the accurate information the interrogators wanted.

Our aim was to survive long enough for our time-sensitive

tactical knowledge to pass its sell-by date. After that, we were to protect in-depth, strategic, information for as long as we could. So, from the point of capture, we were meant to reveal only three things: our full name, Service number and date of birth. All other questions were to be answered with the words, *I cannot answer that question, sir*, a wording based on the assumption that the interrogator held a rank one above our own.

It would be an uneven contest.

Our interrogators would be well fed, rested and fully prepared for what was about to unfold, whereas we'd be tired, hungry and plagued by doubt. And despite assurances that torture was unlikely to be part of the process, it would only be natural to be fearful of physical abuse. Even on Moorex, uncertainty about exactly how far our captors and interrogators were likely to go generated a certain amount of fear. So it wasn't difficult to imagine how much worse it would be in reality.

As to the interrogators, descriptions of some of those we might face would be familiar to anyone with an interest in crime literature or films. They included the bully and the good cop/bad cop combination, plus those who were well-informed, who'd hide what they knew and seek to catch us in a lie, or display their knowledge and say, *why hold out when we know everything anyway*? But there were others, like the monotonous one who'd try to lull us into a trance-like state from which we'd reveal things before realising it.

There were even interrogators who'd play for sympathy, appearing to bungle everything, while saying they had to get something to show their bosses or they'd be punished. Hard to believe that a captive would fall for such a ploy, but there are well-documented cases of just that.

One category of interrogator I didn't meet was a woman. They can be extremely effective. For a start, men – and especially aircrew – were usually keen to impress a woman, and there were precious few opportunities to do this in an interrogation room beyond telling her how important you were and how much you knew.

It was emphasised that we'd slip up at some point and reveal more than we should, but we weren't to let that undermine our resolve, no matter how much our interrogators tried to exploit or reward our error.

On the subject of reward, we were taught to accept any unconditional offer of kindness, but to turn down anything linked to the disclosure of information beyond the basic three items. Over the course of my captivity, I remember receiving nothing more than a few pieces of bread and some thin soup.

And finally, it was acknowledged that, for most of us, there'd come a point when we'd break down completely. Even this was not to be taken as a failure. Everyone has their limits. What we had to do was delay that point for as long as possible so that the information we divulged was as out of date as possible.

And so to Moorex itself.

After the briefing on Monday morning, we were driven onto Dartmoor where, for the next four days and three nights, we moved between bivouac sites, the size of the groups diminishing as the week wore on. Increasingly the moves were at short notice, forced by the need to stay ahead of the enemy.

Following the rabbit and chicken stew, we began to receive less food and managed far less sleep, partly because of the conditions, partly because of the need to travel at night. Most of the time on the high moor seemed to be spent in drizzle and/or fog, but a couple of nights were cold enough for air and ground frosts.

That was the case on Thursday night, by which time I was bedding down on my own. In the early hours, I was told to move to and hide in a different area, several miles across the moor. Once there, I should expect the Paras to search for me from 10.00am. If I hadn't been captured by 2.00pm, I'd hear whistles being blown, the signal to leave my hideout and hand myself in.

The only reward for those who remained undiscovered would be a sandwich. Doesn't sound much, but by that stage it was motivation enough. I really wanted that sandwich.

I reached my wooded refuge area a couple of hours before dawn and tried, with little success, to snatch some sleep, wrapped against the cold in a poncho beneath the trees. As dawn approached, I could see that I was in a forest of mature pines. Nearby, the trees were bisected by a grassy firebreak about twenty feet wide, down the middle of which ran ruts up to a foot deep caused by the wide tyres of heavy vehicles.

Heeding the advice of our lecturers, I shunned the idea of climbing into the tree tops, although it looked as if I'd have been largely invisible from the ground if I had. Instead, I began looking for somewhere and something from which to fashion a shelter good enough to conceal me from the Paras. It was a frustrating time. Beneath the lowest branches of the trees, four or five feet up, there was no vegetation, just a carpet of golden pine needles and fir cones. There was also a clear field of view, at least as far as the next firebreak, so searchers would find any structure above ground hard to miss.

Although I never saw any of my course mates, I could hear the occasional bang and scrape of wood, which I interpreted as evidence of others working away in the same plantation. At about 8.00am, an instructor dropped by to see if I was still alive and happy to continue.

We'd had the right to pull out at any stage before this, but he reiterated that from the moment of capture, if we decided to throw in the towel, no-one would think any the less of us. This was hard to imagine, so I was sure none of us would be keen to give up.

Soon after he disappeared, I decided my only option was to enlarge a wheel rut in one of the tracks and cover it with a roof of twigs coated in moss and grass. With a knife and bits of wood, I excavated a refuge similar in size and shape to a coffin. The camouflaged *lid* I fashioned from twigs, moss and grass wouldn't bear the weight of a Para, but I hoped it would conceal me from anything less than a close inspection.

Before sliding into the gap I'd left at one end, I weaved a smaller cover to pull in over me. When I'd finished, the hide looked pretty good, although I had no idea whether its camouflage would survive me squeezing in.

At about 9.30am, having made sure my bladder was empty, I laid my poncho and trusty stout stick in the rut and, dressed in every item of clothing I possessed, wriggled in and pulled the cover over me. I reasoned that if I damaged anything while sliding in, I'd have time to get out, make repairs and get back in again by 10 o'clock. All seemed to go well though, so I lay there taking in my new surroundings, senses heightened by the near total darkness, the silence behind my own rustling and breathing, and the peaty smell of the earth encasing me.

The next four and a half hours were purgatory for many reasons.

For a start, although I'd chosen a track that looked as if it hadn't seen a vehicle for many months - hence the grass - what if the Paras drove down it? More importantly, what if I missed the sound of their approach? It was going to make for an anxious few hours. And if I did hear a vehicle approaching, to avoid being turned into mush, I'd have to burst out, which seemed to negate the idea of hiding in the first place.

Not very clever, but it was too late to move.

Secondly, although I could just about shuffle onto one side or the other, my coffin was so snug that I couldn't bend my legs more than a few degrees. And when I did move to subject a different bony bit to the hard ground, my shoulders inevitably brushed the lid, causing dirt to fall in my eyes, nose and mouth, and raising fears for my camouflage. As a result I spent most of the time on my back looking up at pinpoints of light where the earth, moss and grass had shifted. If my limbs hadn't been so numb from the cold, I'm sure I'd have been writhing with cramp, but perhaps the incessant shivering gave my muscles all the exercise they needed.

One of our lecturers had covered the science behind shivering. His warning that stopping shivering was a serious warning sign on the road to death came back to me that morning. I needn't have worried though. I shook uncontrollably for the entire duration of my interment.

Although it was difficult to sneak a look at it, my trusty aircrew watch had maintained its luminosity. So as I lay there trying to minimise noise just in case anyone was creeping up on me, I was able to confirm just how slowly time passed. Every so often, I heard raised voices. And on a couple of occasions, the kerfuffle made me think one of my fellow evaders had been discovered.

As the hands swept round to 1.50, I dared hope that I'd survive to claim my sandwich. But, moments later, I heard footfalls and whispering. Light suddenly flooded my coffin and I was blinking up into the faces of several men in purple berets. They were all shouting at once.

Despite the warnings during our lectures, the shock of capture was very real.

The Paras glowered down on me, snarling in anger. I was pulled from the ground, dragged a few yards and searched. There was no way of telling what had alerted them to my presence. The shattered remains of the lid were scattered across the clearing. All my possessions, such as they were, were confiscated. And then the lights went out. From this moment on I saw very little, except during my interrogations, the first of which wasn't for several hours.

I was frog-marched for several minutes to a vehicle and shoved into the back of it. Judging from the shouts all around, there were other captives. Almost immediately, I heard the shrill blasts of several whistles. I actually have a piece of paper in a scrap book giving my time of capture as 1400 hours, but I know it was 1.50, A, because I'd seen my watch before it was taken from my wrist, and B, because I didn't get my bloody sandwich.

So close and yet so far!

I later found out that the only people who hadn't been captured were a handful that had taken to the treetops. None of them had fallen during the climb, and they'd all managed to tie themselves securely to the upper trunks. But, as the instructors had warned the combination of their weight and the wind cutting through them set the treetops swaying alarmingly, causing severe discomfort, fatigue and motion sickness.

Their most vivid memories, though, were of hallucinations. One, who estimated he was about thirty feet up, became convinced he was just a few feet above the ground. He spent much of the time resisting an overwhelming urge to end his discomfort by untying from the trunk and just stepping away from it. Another suffered the heart-stopping sensation of falling, over and over again. And one, safely hidden in thick foliage among hundreds of other trees, imagined he was in the middle of a clearing atop a bare pole, searchers circling beneath him with murderous intent. He had to fight the incessant urge to untie and run away – despite the fact that he too was thirty feet above the forest floor.

All this reinforced the unsuitability of hiding in trees. But the fact remained that those who'd done so had evaded capture. The message seemed to be that if you ploughed your own furrow, like Bob Iveson and the tree huggers, you might just succeed. Those who, like me, had stuck to the guidelines had all failed.

I've always pictured the place we were driven to and detained in for the rest of the exercise as an old fortification of some sort, or at least a large derelict building with draughty, echoing, passageways and rooms. Whatever or wherever it was, this was where, between interrogations, I was subject to some of the softening-up processes described earlier.

It was, to say the least, a cold and uncomfortable experience, during which I grew to welcome the respite offered by the interrogations themselves. Even being frogmarched there and back by my Parachute Regiment guards gave a chance to stretch out my aching muscles and use my legs.

Again, I'll draw a veil over my actual interrogations, except to say that I experienced a variety of techniques, and to relate one episode.

Even before the internet and social media, our instructors had made clear just how much personal information an enemy could harvest without ever resorting to *spying*. All of us were likely to have generated local press cuttings about our various graduations and other achievements in the RAF. I had such things in scrap books, so I knew they included details of my family as well as my Service history, from my apprenticeship to officer and flying training, even my work on the Vulcan and my posting to the Hercules fleet.

Well, this particular interrogator made it plain that he knew all that. But things took a surreal twist when I intoned my name in answer to one of his questions. He paused for a moment then accused me of hiding behind a false identity. The crux of his argument was that no officer would pronounce the name Powell in the way I did - as in owl. Someone of the officer class would say *pole*.

Twenty years earlier he could have been right, witness the novelist, Anthony Powell – pronounced pole. But by the 1980s, my pronunciation of my name had become standard in all but the highest echelons of society.

Nevertheless, on this flimsy fabrication he threatened to have me taken out and shot as a spy – unless I could prove I was who I said I was. And the only way to do that was to reveal more than my name, number, date of birth and the other personal information he already had.

As tired, cold and hungry as I was, the episode was too ridiculous to be taken seriously. I gave him nothing. But once again, had my captivity been genuine, who knows how effective this and the many other tactics the interrogators deployed might have been.

Following my experiences on the CSRO Course, I went on to give presentations on conduct after capture and resistance to interrogation to all the units on which I served – right up to the First Gulf War in 1991.

Then, overnight, the images of John Peters and John Nichol, two of the Tornado aircrew captured by Saddam Hussein's forces, blew away the naive idea that captivity was unlikely to include extreme brutality. Their bruised and bloodied faces made my qualification to talk on the issue obsolete.

I never did so again.

After something less than twenty four hours in captivity, we were put on vehicles and driven to Mountbatten, where we emerged into the light of a Saturday morning. We were given a quick once over by a doctor and a chance to say if our experiences had caused any problems, physical of otherwise, before settling down to a hearty breakfast and, I seem to remember, the odd beer.

Just in case any of us had been tempted to drive off to see loved ones, or even just go shopping, we were confined to base and forbidden to drive until 8am the next morning. After a week of disrupted sleep and at least twenty four hours with none at all, the risk of falling unconscious at the wheel was just too great.

Over the meal, we interrogated one another about our experiences. As you can imagine, these were remarkably similar, although some had faced interrogation styles I hadn't, and vice versa. Our instructors joined us, but remained determinedly tight-lipped about where we'd been imprisoned. And as to whom our captors had been, the only faces I'd seen, apart from those I'd glimpsed when pulled from my hiding place on the Moor, belonged to my interrogators.

Before they disappeared, the staff reiterated that while we were free to chat about what had happened amongst ourselves, the detail of our final hours was not to leave Mountbatten.

Hence my reluctance to reveal all, even after the passage of forty years.

I couldn't resist driving home to Lyneham on Sunday morning and spending a few hours with Geraldine before driving back to Mountbatten again in the evening. Even after such a short period of captivity and interrogation, I felt changed, somehow different from the people around me, going about their normal weekend activities. In my case, the feeling didn't last long, but it gave me an insight into how difficult, if not impossible, it must be for prisoners of war and hostages like Terry Waite and John McCarthy to return to normality.

And finally, my renewed freedom made me realise just how precious a commodity it is.

Monday included a review of Moorex and the lessons we should take from its various elements. On the Tuesday, in preparation for presentations we'd be expected to give to our units, we had to research and deliver an illustrated ten-minute talk on a survival topic. Most of us gave fairly dry, forgettable, presentations about survival drills or equipment. But the talk by one of my peers has always stayed with me.

It was about how useful blow-up sex dolls could be in a range of survival situations.

Over the course of his ten minutes, he outlined how they could be used as flotation aids in the case of a landing on water, or as comfortable mattresses on land. And wherever you were, they could be both a striking location aid, guaranteed to grab the attention of any passing rescuers, and a source of exercise, providing stimulation and a boost to circulation. But perhaps most importantly, they could provide companionship, benefitting the survivor's mental health and easing the passage of time.

Unless it's happened since I left the Service, I'm not sure his recommendation that such dolls be included in survival packs was ever taken up.

A certificate to mark completion of the course sits in my scrapbook. It states that I have *with fortitude and dexterity met the rigorous requirements of the School of Combat Survival and Rescue.*

For a piece of paper marking such a short period of time, the certificate means more than almost any other award I gained during my service. It's certainly the one I went through most pain to earn.

TACEVAL AND FLIGHT SAFETY

When I returned to work on the Monday after my CSRO course, Lyneham was gearing itself up for a major exercise known as a Part 2 Tactical Evaluation, or Taceval. A week later a team of NATO specialists would descend on the station and spend several days assessing it in three main areas: bringing its manpower and aircraft to readiness; defending them from attack, including by nuclear, biological and chemical weapons; and mounting operations under the same forms of attack.

During the Cold War, Tacevals were seen as important ways of measuring the effectiveness, not only of a base, but also its senior officers, and especially the Station Commander. It was a major test of his leadership. If it went badly, his period in command was unlikely to be judged a success. So his keenness to succeed filtered down to anyone likely to be involved, and I returned to memos directing me to ensure everything from my firearms training to my medical and flying qualifications were up to date.

In the week leading up to startex, the station received *exercise intelligence* setting the scene. By the time the team arrived, mounting tension with the Warsaw Pact had turned to open hostility.

I'd participated in a few Part 2 Tacevals before, one as a corporal at Scampton, where I'd been part of the guard force, and one at Linton while in pilot training, when I'd had a similar role. They'd both had their moments, but most of the time had been spent sitting around waiting for something to happen. This time, as a front-line pilot, I thought things might be more exciting. But guess what? I still spent long periods sitting around, either on the squadron, or in a centralised aircrew facility. Only a few hours were spent on the flight deck.

In the case of war, most of the Hercs would have been flying, and most of those that weren't would have been dispersed to other bases to prevent a strike on the station destroying the bulk of the fleet. But during Taceval, those of us not involved in normal routes or exercise tasks were likely to do little more than disperse to the far side of Lyneham. And this is what happened.

Just a couple of hours into the *war*, we joined other crews climbing into the Hercs on the line. When the dispersal order came – in code – we joined a stream of about twenty leaving the pan. I don't know what it looked and sounded like to an outside observer, but from our seats it all seemed a bit shambolic, smoky engines filling the air with the reek of burnt aviation fuel and crews not quite sure where anyone bar themselves was headed.

Anyway, we reached our allotted parking area safely and there we sat – and sat, the monotony broken only by the odd coded message that rarely gave any idea of what was happening. I remember only one thing of note.

After a couple of hours sitting there, an aircraft transmitted. 'I'm bored.'

There was a lengthy pause before an angry voice responded. 'Aircraft transmitting, state callsign?'

There was an even longer pause, before the original voice replied, 'I'm not that bloody bored.'

I imagined flight decks all over the airfield ringing with laughter. Ours certainly was. The rogue crew had, of course, demonstrated reprehensible ill-discipline. But that didn't make it any less funny. Over the years, I heard many similar stories from other exercises and other aircraft fleets.

The only other things to break the monotony were warnings of impending air raids, at which point we donned respirators and tin hats. There was no shelter to run to, so there we sat, dressed like extras in a sci-fi movie. We could have made a much more striking impression, though.

In a soft-skinned green case about the size of a rectangular violin case, we each had a bespoke aircrew respirator assembly, an AR5, designed to protect us from nuclear, biological and chemical threats. It resembled a black rubber deep-sea diving hood with integral eyepieces and oxygen mask. The rubber hood extended down over the neck, shoulders, upper chest and back, fitting under our special, charcoal-impregnated, flying suits. Coming unawares on someone wearing the full kit and caboodle could be quite startling, like meeting Darth Vadar ambling toward you.

When walking out to the aircraft, we'd plug the oxygen and comms tubes dangling from the oxygen mask into a portable ventilator similar to that carried by Apollo astronauts making their way to their Saturn V rocket. In the air, we'd plug them into the aircraft systems.

I'd completed one simulator sortie dressed in AR5 and discovered it was far from comfortable, or compatible with flying. The head shroud and umbilicals were so cumbersome they restricted movement and, despite a circulating air system designed to prevent it, we tended to overheat. Then, a combination of evaporating sweat and exhaled breath made the eyepieces - which greatly reduced peripheral vision anyway - steam up. Wearing it for long periods was very tiring, which further degraded performance.

The few aircraft trials to date had been closely supervised, even when they involved only taxying. So, during the Taceval, although we all practised putting our AR5 kit on to sit around in the aircrew facility, very few wore them on the flight deck. I was glad I wasn't one of them. Of course, none of the drawbacks would have mattered if we'd needed to wear them in a real war. We'd have just got on with it, as many Herc aircrew did in later conflicts.

While the exercise went on for the rest of the week,

my involvement finished on the Tuesday lunchtime when I was sent to get some rest on the squadron before entering flight planning for a genuine route to Cyprus, via Leuchars in Scotland. We took off late that night and, after a routine Akrotiri nightstop, returned via Leuchars again late Thursday evening.

I spent Thursday night on the squadron trying to sleep on a camp bed in the co-pilots office while also reacting to exercise alerts and air raids. Speaking to my fellow co-pilots, it seemed I hadn't missed much during my absence. The rest of the week had been pretty similar to the day and a half I'd experienced. The news made me very glad I'd escaped, and the Taceval had effectively finished by the time I handed in my imprest on Friday morning.

During the final two months of 1983, I flew routes to Belgium, Norway, Iceland, Sardinia, Gibraltar and Cyprus. I also completed numerous standby duties and five sim trips, three in the week before Christmas for some reason. But looking at the names of the crews and the timings in my little blue book brought no stories to mind.

Once again, as part of my Squadron Fund duties, I helped plan the Squadron Christmas Draw. And once again, it all seemed to go well on the night.

There was one other thing of note before the year ended.

The CSRO course must have whetted my appetite for knowledge beyond the confines of the flight deck. And although I didn't know it at the time, it was a hunger that would stay with me, leading to participation in many more courses. None were anywhere near as physically demanding as the combat survival course, but many were just as interesting.

The first, undertaken in the second week of December 1983, was the RAF Flight Safety Course, held in the central London offices of the RAF Inspectorate of Flight Safety.

Efforts to prevent aviation accidents and incidents all come under the umbrella term, flight safety. Unsurprisingly, it is something of paramount importance to an organisation with flying at its heart. Almost every stage of RAF training included flight safety lectures and films, while the Service also produced a monthly magazine, Air Clues, dedicated to the subject, plus tens of other publications, posters and flyers. Perhaps most avidly read were abridged versions of the board of inquiry reports into every flying accident.

Those responsible for implementing flight safety policy and keeping the subject at the forefront of people's minds were known as Flight Safety Officers (FSOs). They were to be found at all levels of the RAF structure, from the Ministry of Defence and other HQs, where there'd be a flight safety staff under a senior officer, to stations, where it would be a full-time role for a junior officer. Individual squadrons or sections also had junior officers or NCOs performing the role as a secondary duty.

I don't think I gave any thought to the fact that completing the course might leave me open to another secondary duty. I just thought it would be interesting.

So, on the Monday morning, I joined a class of four members of the Army Air Corps, a USAF engineer and twenty two RAF officers, mainly aircrew but including a smattering of engineers and air traffic controllers. Over the course of the week, complementing lessons on the various responsibilities of an FSO were others on subjects as varied as Structural Integrity, Equipment Development, Bird Hazards and the Pathology of Accidents. Almost every lesson involved a case study of an accident relevant to the subject at hand.

Of course, the causes of accidents could be many and varied, from failures of aircraft structures or equipment to human failings, often exacerbated by sloppy procedures, poor supervision or downright negligence. But it quickly became apparent that few accidents came totally out of the blue. The vast majority were the final link in a chain of events that could, and probably should, have been severed at some point.

So the RAF encouraged all its personnel to report anything that didn't look quite right, no matter how trivial, be they an admin clerk spotting something unusual as an aircraft taxied past, or an engineer noticing a more technical problem. It even rewarded people for such reports with certificates and prizes. More difficult was getting people to report their own failures and near misses, especially if this could lead to disciplinary action or ridicule. This problem was attacked from several directions.

Firstly, the RAF sought to encourage an atmosphere in which mistakes could be reported without fear of immediate retribution, partly by distancing flight safety and disciplinary processes, and partly by recognising that there was such a thing as a genuine mistake. But it also set great store on personal integrity, encouraging people to report anything from a missing screwdriver to a heavy landing, all in the hope of preventing an accident further down the line. Finally, there were avenues to report things anonymously, a process that proved invaluable over the years.

One of the most interesting, and sobering, days on the course was spent at the Air Accidents Investigation Branch at Farnborough. After being given an overview of the accident investigation process, we walked among the remains of wrecked aircraft laid out on the hangar floor, some retained as training aids, some the subject of ongoing investigations.

Military aircraft of the time lacked black boxes. They also had few if any electronic diagnostic tools and nothing digital. So, in addition to gathering evidence from the crash site, witnesses, radar printouts and the like, investigators spent a lot of time sifting through wreckage by hand, like detectives in the Sherlock Holmes mould. Scrapes and dents could point to crash parameters, while such things as corrosion, explosive residue or evidence of fuel starvation could point to cause. I was to witness this process first hand during the inquiry I presided over fourteen years later.

Throughout the course, I found the importance of psychological factors in accidents especially fascinating.

Some, like the reaction to visual illusions, are near universal. Others though, are linked to personality, things like over or under-confidence, and the reaction to pressure generated by the task or external factors, such as marital problems. And once again, there were examples of how such psychological factors could contribute to accidents. Perhaps most importantly, we were given an idea of how to spot warning signs in individuals and act on them, something that would be increasingly important as we moved into supervisory positions on the ground and in the air.

The examples came from across the full range of RAF trades and branches, but inevitably, those I remember are from the aircrew world.

For instance, why would a crew knowingly let their pilot shut down the wrong engine, or fly them into the ground?

Well, as in so many cases, there were all sorts of nuances. Even when faced with imminent catastrophe, some personalities, through a combination of under-confidence and timidity, are unwilling to challenge others, especially superiors. But such reluctance can also be exacerbated by organisational or cultural norms that discourage, even forbid, challenging those of higher rank, age or experience. The catch-all phrase for this phenomenon is cross-cockpit gradient.

I already had an inkling of it from my experience of refusing to raise the flaps when asked to do so by a senior officer on climbing away from Dakar a year or so earlier. But as my career developed, I'd hear of many more examples leading to accidents and near misses.

And why would someone on a routine training sortie push on in a combination of terrain and weather that was bound to lead to catastrophe?

The answer was generally pressure, either from within or without, or both.

An experienced pilot could overestimate his abilities, while the inexperienced could fail to recognise a deteriorating situation. But both could be tempted to push on because of reluctance to show *weakness* by turning back. This reluctance could be triggered internally, but also externally by supervisory chains and HQs that elevated the importance of task completion above all else, whatever the circumstances. Such organisations tend to promote those espousing the same values, while those who favour caution are assessed as lacking drive. They may even be seen as cowardly.

Now, in war, a can-do spirit verging on recklessness can be useful, essential even. But in training, I believe you need to temper determination and drive with common sense and a sense of perspective.

Is this particular sortie worth the risk?

In training, the answer is quite often no, but some leaders lose sight of this in the quest to impress their superiors and headquarters staff.

I believe that at least a proportion of the high RAF accident rates in training in the decades following the Second World War can be attributed to a misplaced emphasis on a war-time ethos of mission completion. I had to confront individuals that danced to this beat several times later in my career, some vastly superior in rank. For a non-confrontational character like me, it wasn't easy and my final flying tour was a bit of a nightmare in this regard.

Another story for a later volume.

Pressure could affect even the very best, leading experienced display pilots to continue a manoeuvre they knew was going to end with them hitting the ground. Occasionally, the pressure came from organisers, but more often it was internal, an ultimately fatal desire not to disappoint the public, or to be seen to fail in front of knowledgeable spectators, including their fellow pilots.

I've known at least two display pilots who succumbed to such internal pressures and died as a result. One of them lectured on display safety.

As I'd hoped, the Flight Safety Course was immensely interesting. And although I never became an FSO at any point, the lessons I learnt were invaluable for my remaining time on the Hercules. More than that, augmented by later courses, they stood me in good stead for the rest of my career, especially when it came to presiding over my own board of inquiry in 1997.

The course had also made me keen to apply for more. I'd already applied for the Jungle Survival Course in 1984, and I'm sure I'd have applied for others. But the squadron had other ideas. I was about to undertake two new challenges. One I already knew about. The other would come as a surprise.

NEW YEAR, NEW CHALLENGES

The first challenge, the one I knew about, was becoming a Hercules tanker co-pilot.

Frankly, it was about time.

After my initial flurry of visits to the South Atlantic in the spring and summer of 1982, I'd rarely returned. In the meantime, the Herc airbridge had become the primary means of moving people and priority supplies between Ascension and the Falklands. There were several flights a week, each requiring the ability to take fuel in the air. Many of my fellow co-pilots had qualified in this receiver role and flew regular airbridge sorties. Some had been doing it for 18 months.

At the same time, the Herc had also become the primary tanker in the South Atlantic, with 24 and 30 Squadrons providing tanker crews in Port Stanley and Ascension. Some of my fellow co-pilots had done four-month stints at Port Stanley, where their duties included refuelling the resident Phantoms and Harriers. Others had done several detachments of up to three weeks on Ascension, refuelling the southbound airbridge and providing search and rescue cover for its northbound journey.

I have no idea why I hadn't been put on a course before, but the second week of January finally saw me sitting in a classroom at the home of the Victor tanker force, RAF Marham in Norfolk, for three days of tanker groundschool.

For the tanking task, we formed constituted crews, and mine included an experienced nav, eng and loadie, while the captain was my squadron commander. I hadn't flown with him since our trip into Beirut the previous June, but I'd seen a fair bit of him on the ground and I continued to like him and his leadership style. I was also impressed that he wanted to subject himself to the tanking course when he was still relatively new to the Herc. Even some experienced captains struggled with air-to-air refuelling. He could easily have hidden in his office and accepted less demanding challenges.

The course started with a brief history of air-to-air refuelling.

There are basically two methods of passing fuel between aircraft.

The US military tends to favour a *flying boom* system, in which an operator in the tanker flies a rigid fuel pipe into a coupling on the receiving aircraft, which merely has to stay in position while fuel is pumped into its tanks.

The RAF, on the other hand, favoured a *probe and drogue* system in which the tanker unwinds a fuel hose into the airflow. It's up to the receiver pilot to plug in and stay in contact long enough to take the fuel he needs.

Buccaneers had a little-used capability for buddy-buddy tanking, but, until the Falklands War, Victors had effectively been the RAF's sole tanker asset. They dispensed fuel to Lightnings and Phantoms intercepting Russian Bears probing

UK airspace, and any fast jets exercising around the UK or heading for deployments overseas. Almost overnight, from 2nd April 1982, their list of customers expanded to include Fat Alberts, Nimrods, Vulcans and other Victors ranging over vast areas of the South Atlantic. To help the venerable tankers out, six Hercs and six Vulcans had been converted to the role.

The Vulcans would only serve until the summer of 1984 when their tanking equipment was removed to be used in the Victor replacement, the VC10. This proved a lengthy project. The Victors remained in service beyond the First Gulf War and only reeled in their hoses for the last time in 1993.

By early 1984, when we were sitting in the classroom at Marham, almost all tanker tasking in the South Atlantic had passed to the Hercs. We still had to learn how to take fuel from the other two types though, not least because they were the ones we'd meet most often during training.

The lessons moved on to describe tanking equipment and procedures.

All three types had probes through which they could receive fuel.

The Herc's thrust a couple of yards into the airflow from a rough fairing bolted to the outer skin above the co-pilot's head. Fuel entering through it was piped into the aircraft fuel system.

All the tankers also had additional fuel tanks from which fuel could be pumped to a receiving aircraft through an 80-foot long black hose, the majority of which wound into the airflow from a Hose Drum Unit, like a large garden hose reel, universally known as a hoodoo.

On the end of the hose sat something resembling a large shuttlecock, its silver metal spokes spreading out to form a funnel with a circular opening about two feet in diameter, known as a basket. A delicate balance between gravity, aerodynamic forces - principally drag on the basket - and sensitive motors in the hoodoo ensured that the hose trailed correctly, leaving the basket to hang in the air almost motionless – in good weather at least.

Next, the instructors described tanking procedures.

Tanking sorties always started with a plan based on the distances each aircraft had to fly and the fuel required to do it in the forecast winds. It detailed how many refuelling operations were needed and the position of the blocks of airspace – refuelling brackets - within which they should start and finish. Most importantly, it had to guarantee that neither tanker nor receiver was ever in a position where they had nowhere to go if the refuelling process failed for some reason.

One complication was that tankers and their customers often came from different airfields, so a series of rendezvous procedures had been developed. These catered for tankers approaching from head on, behind, or from any conceivable angle in between. Most rendezvous were controlled using a combination, of radar, radio direction finding (DF) and air-to-air Tacan - equipment giving the range between two aircraft.

For instance, when a Victor tanker and a receiver were meeting head on, one of the tanker navigators would control the approach with radio bearings until, at a Tacan range taken from a graph catering for factors such as relative speed, the tanker would turn through 225° to end up two miles ahead of the receiver. This was a Bravo Rendezvous. Charlie and Delta Rendezvous were similar, but controlled by different forms of air-to-air radar.

I hoped our navigator understood it all because it sounded like wizardry to me. As it turned out, in the South Atlantic, we never had to manage the more complicated aerial ballets. Invariably, tanker and receive would both be departing Ascension, and although even two Hercs would take off at different times because differences in their weight would lead them to fly different heights and speeds, the rendezvous was usually pretty straightforward, the major complication being the weather.

There was one more complication though. To give receivers a margin of power as they guzzled fuel and became heavier, both tanker and receiver had to enter a shallow descent of 500 feet per minute, a manoeuvre known as tobogganing. In the case of a Herc receiver, if the tanker was a V-bomber, they'd toboggan at 230 knots (265 mph); if it was another Herc, they'd descend at 210 knots (240 mph).

So much for the theory.

We returned to Lyneham on Thursday to begin Herc-specific training with a group of instructors on the OCU.

The idea of turning the Herc into a tanker had been thought up and implemented in impressively little time. But it showed. Down the back, four large tanks, each holding 7,000lbs – 825 gallons – of fuel dominated the freight bay floor. They increased the fuel capacity to 91,000lbs, which often meant taking off from Ascension at the Military Operating Standard maximum weight of 165,000lbs, something most of us hadn't done since the height of the Falklands War.

The rest of the set-up was a truly Heath Robinson affair. Amid a jumble of electrical cables and fuel and cooling pipes, the hoodoo was fitted upside down on the rear ramp. Its hose fed through a four foot wide, two foot deep, port – hole - cut in the ramp. The port had a makeshift cover like a conservatory blind that could be closed manually when the hose had been reeled in. This was enough to maintain cabin pressure in normal flight, but when the hose was trailed to give away fuel, we had to depressurise and go onto oxygen.

Of course, to be a tanker crew, you also had to be able to receive fuel and this was the skill we had to learn first. No Herc tankers were available in the UK. We'd have to wait until we were in the South Atlantic to take fuel from one of them. The first of a potential eight receiver training trips was scheduled for the next day. It would be behind a Vulcan or Victor in a refuelling area to the south of the Cornish coast.

Once we were qualified, we'd be expected to receive fuel in any old weather. But for at least the first few training sorties, good conditions were essential. Disappointingly, the weather in the refuelling area on Friday was just too bad. It was the same story on Monday, but on Tuesday, the cloud cleared and we were off.

To my delight, our first receiver training sortie was to be behind a Vulcan.

I'm biased of course, but the mighty delta is one of those aircraft that just looks to be in its element when flying, a thing of functional beauty. I'd spent years crawling over, under and inside them on the ground, but I was looking forward to getting up close and personal in the air as well. So I was really excited when we established radio contact and the Vulcan closed up and overtook us on the left hand side.

And there it sat, about one hundred yards away, all graceful curves, despite its bulk. For the next 90 minutes, it flew backwards and forwards along what was known as a tow-line so that we could learn the rudiments of air-to-air refuelling. Initially, I'd given over my seat to an instructor, who would lead the captain and me through the process. The nav, eng and loadie had their own instructors on hand.

For the first thirty minutes or so, we forgot about refuelling while the boss re-familiarised himself with flying in close formation behind another aircraft, something he and most other Herc aircrew hadn't done since their flying training, in his case, nearly two decades earlier. Some navs, enges and loadies may never have witnessed tight formation flying.

Whatever our previous experience, I don't think any of us was fully prepared for the sight of a Vulcan hanging a few feet ahead of us, its foreshortened delta wings and high tailplane filling the flight deck windows. The air shimmered as the superheated exhaust gases roared out of the jet pipes of the Olympus engines and passed just above our heads.

We edged even closer, the boss aiming for a position where a series of marks and features on the Vulcan airframe lined up. It was the starting gate for the refuelling operation, but a bit difficult to visualise without a hose protruding from the tanker. That was the next step.

When the instructor deemed the boss ready, we moved out to sit about fifty yards to the right and slightly behind the Vulcan and watched it trail its refuelling hose from a port in the bottom skin a few yards from the back end. Above the port, what I had known as an electronic countermeasure bay now contained a hoodoo.

Once the tanker crew was satisfied the hose had trailed correctly, we were cleared to slide across. The boss took up the initial position he'd been taught, which put us about ten feet behind the basket. While he concentrated on the tanker, the instructor drew my eyes to the basket, teaching me to note the way it hung in the air and to check that its metal spokes and the thin canvas ring surrounding its two-foot circular opening were undamaged.

We'd discover all too soon that in turbulence associated with strong winds or bad weather, the basket would bounce randomly from side to side, up and down and diagonally, often by several feet. But on good days like this it tended to hang there, moving little, just the odd deviation of a few inches as zephyrs of air played on it.

To either side of the port from which the hose protruded, were three lights: red told us to stay back, amber that the hose was primed and ready to go, and green that we were plugged in and all the switches were made.

When the red lights turned to amber and the tanker gave us clearance, the captain nudged the throttles to establish an overtake - a fast walking pace was the advice – and flew us up and forward using features and marks on the tanker to guide him. If he kept these lined up, the shiny metal tip of the probe, like a small artillery shell with a rounded nose, would poke – prod - into the opening of the basket. Another couple of feet and the tip would plug into the end of the fuel hose, where spring-operated rollers would engage with a groove round the tip of the probe and *grip* it. The captain then had to push against slight resistance of the hoodoo motor to advance another seven feet to make all the connections, at which point, the green lights would illuminate and we could take on fuel.

The speed of advance was critical. Too slow and the tip of the probe could enter the hose with insufficient force to make a good contact, but enough to cause the hose to wind back in, leading to a delay while things were reset and it was trailed again. Approach too fast and we could pierce the spokes of the basket, or set up a whiplash in the hose that could damage the hoodoo and our probe. In the worst case, piercing the spokes of the basket could lock our two aircraft together, while even if we backed away safely, damaged to the spokes, hoodoo or probe would render the tanker unserviceable and us unable to refuel.

While the captain flew us toward contact, he had to resist the overwhelming temptation to glance at the probe and basket several feet to his right. If he did, especially in the early stages of training, he'd drag the controls that way and guarantee failure. He had to trust that using the features and marks on the tanker would prod the tip of the probe into the dead centre of the basket. In practice, he could actually afford to be up to a foot off in any direction, in which case the metal spokes of the basket would guide the tip into the hose.

Once he'd gained a green light, *all the captain had to do* was concentrate on keeping the marks on the tanker lined up so that we remained in the same position for up to twenty five minutes as we tobogganed down and fuel flowed along the hose, through our probe and the aircraft pipery into our tanks.

White bands every ten feet on the hose gave an indication of how much of it was protruding from the port. The ideal length for the hose to sit properly and for us to be a safe distance back from the tanker was for sixty feet. If an amber band on the hose fifty feet ahead of us approached the port, we were getting too close.

The principle was the same whether taking fuel from a Vulcan, a Victor or another Herc. But there were all sorts of complications. For a start, turbulence in the air streaming back from the tanker airframes, jet exhausts or prop wash tended to play over the receiving Herc and its high tailplane, causing it to swing like a weather vane atop a church steeple. The captain had to counter this to avoid pulling the hose too far in any direction and putting undue strain on the probe and its delicate tip. The leeway allowed was known as the cone of safety, a circle about twenty feet in diameter.

So how did I fit in?

My primary task was to assess the flight of the probe toward the basket and give the captain updates and hints, using phrases such as, *up a bit, left a bit, forward, back* or *steady*. But I was also meant to be a counsellor and medic, assessing his mood and spotting if he'd stopped breathing or begun hyper-ventilating, both of which I'd witness above the South Atlantic. So my armoury also included phrases like, *relax, take a stretch, don't look at the basket* and *breathe*! And finally, with the captain often fixated on his task to the exclusion of all else, I had to keep an eye on our safety, telling him to back off if we were getting too close to the tanker, or to pull out altogether if we were in danger of swinging outside the cone of safety and snapping off the tip of the probe.

Things became especially demanding when the basket was bouncing around in turbulence. On these occasions, with my help, the captain had to pick his moment to advance the throttles so that he nailed the basket as it swung through the central position. Each miss would risk damage to the probe and basket, and necessitate pulling back and trying again. Of course, some captains were better than others, some because they developed the knack of splitting their attention between the tanker, basket and probe to plug in almost every time.

Whether or not the boss was *cheating* in this way, he was one of those able to nail the basket in any conditions, which would be a godsend when we began tanking in anger.

Mine was a piffling role in comparison to his. About the only skill I required beyond a modicum of airmanship and empathy was an eye for parallax when assessing the progress of the probe toward the basket.

That first sortie lasted two hours, during which the boss practised closing up and making contact again and again, while I learned the things to look out for, what to say and when to say it, so that my input was a help rather than a hindrance. By the end, the boss was nailing the basket about every second attempt. He did well.

The next day, there were no serviceable tankers, but on Thursday morning, we practised behind a Vulcan again, although this time I flew the take-off and landing and stayed in my seat throughout. It was a beautiful day and the sight of a Vulcan hanging above us, filling the windshield, seemed so surreal that, at times, I found it hard to believe it was me sitting there. It was another experience I'd find hard to explain to anyone else, especially without appearing to brag. As a result, I've rarely mentioned it until now. The boss continued to improve, prodding the basket successfully on most attempts.

That afternoon we took off again, but this time to practise behind a Victor. If anything, the view from the flight deck was more impressive than when flying behind a Vulcan. The Victor hose extended from a port in the bomb bay skin about thirty five feet forward of the back end. So by the time you'd closed up to the basket and pushed it in several feet, the V-bombers' underbelly and huge crescent tail really were close, looming almost directly above us.

When Defence Secretary, Michael Heseltine, was being flown to the Falklands on the airbridge after the war, he expressed an interest in witnessing them taking fuel.

So, as they approached the refuelling bracket halfway to the Falklands, someone was sent down the back to invite him up. He was asleep in the VIP *caravan* they slid down the back end for such dignitaries, so by the time he climbed the steps onto the flight deck, they were already in contact and taking fuel. When he stepped forward and looked up to see the Victor tanker no more than a few feet away, his jaw dropped and his eyes opened wide like dinner plates. Unusually for a politician, he was speechless for several minutes.

Taking fuel from a Victor was also more demanding. Our proximity to its rear end meant the turbulence from its airframe and engines played over our tailfin, especially if we drifted high. This made the tendency to swing worse than when tanking behind a Vulcan. And although the boss was soon prodding into the Victor basket fairly consistently, staying in position for an extended period was proving more difficult. Not long after contact, we'd begin to sway from side to side, the motion building until we were making full use of the cone of safety. Tension was part of his problem, but there was another factor at play, a phenomenon called pilot induced oscillation, or PIO.

When the boss realised he was swinging left, he knew he had to counter with rudder and a bit of stick. But by the time the message from his brain had reached his feet, it was too late. The aircraft was already swinging right and his control inputs merely exacerbated the movement; which he tried to counter by moving the controls the other way, by which time we were already heading left…and so on and so on. As the swing worsened and we neared the edge of the cone of safety, either the boss had to recognise it and ease back to break contact or I had to tell him to do so.

The instructor assured him he wasn't the first pilot to struggle behind a Victor - something I was to find out for myself over the following months. A large part of overcoming the problem was the ability to relax. But of course, this was easier said than done, especially when the boss was so desperate to succeed. Failure would be a tremendous blow to his credibility.

No time to dwell on it, though, because this sortie extended into forty five minutes of night flying.

As the light faded, so did the giant aircraft ahead of us. Soon it was no more than a shadow blotting out the stars, a looming presence in the darkness. Strange as it seems, this could actually help some captains make contact and hold position. Gone were all the distractions daylight offered. At night, the floodlit guide marks and the basket were just about all that could be seen.

Friday saw us fly another one hour thirty five minutes behind a Victor. The boss became evermore consistent at plugging in and getting fuel to flow, but he still struggled to maintain contact for more than a few minutes before we had to back out. He always plugged straight back in, but in the South Atlantic, the hiatus risked us being unable to take the fuel we needed in the time, airspace and height available. The bottom line was, he had to stay in contact for longer. The pressure was mounting. Our next tanker training sortie would be on Ascension Island on Monday.

The remainder of the crew were to fly out by VC10 on Sunday, but I was up early Saturday morning to fly via Dakar in a Herc tanker captained by an instructor.

This was one of those occasions when things didn't go to

plan.

On the approach to Dakar on Saturday evening, we had a problem with a propeller and had to shut down an engine. After landing, an inspection revealed that we needed a new prop.

A couple of engine fitters and a replacement prop were flown out overnight and it seemed we might not be delayed too long. But unfortunately, either the new prop was faulty or it was damaged during fitment, because ground runs led to it too being rejected. In the end, we spent three days on the ground, leaving Dakar for an overnight flight and landing at Wideawake at 1.25 on Wednesday morning.

It was 13 months since the last of my dozen visits to Ascension. A warm south-easterly breeze was blowing in the smell of the ocean and I was looking forward to seeing the island again in daylight, where changes were afoot. But I could already see changes on the airfield.

Under arc lights, hundreds of contractors were busy laying a concrete dispersal area large enough to park a bigger fleet of aircraft than that that had overflowed the original pan during the War. The contractors were accommodated in a Portakabin village a few miles inland on Donkey Plain, where they were also in the final stages of building a permanent RAF station.

Until then, though, the resident Service personnel, mainly RAF with a smattering of Army engineers and Navy helicopter crews and tradesmen, were staying in what was grandly known as Concertina City. Just visible beyond the arc lights at the airfield, the City, more of a village really, was made up of tens of individual air-conditioned units on loan from the US military. These arrived flat-packed and opened out like, well, like concertinas. Most were about the size of caravans, but there were larger variations kitted out as kitchens, shower and toilet blocks; the Americans even had flat-pack churches.

I enjoyed my week in Concertina City. The atmosphere was not unlike that portrayed in the TV comedy, MASH, about a makeshift American military hospital in Korea. Like the TV series, there was plenty of black humour and banter between the different services and contractors, although, thankfully, there was much less blood and guts.

Anyway, the boss and the others had been able to catch a later VC10, so they hadn't had to spend three unproductive days on Ascension waiting for me. A little less than twelve hours after I arrived, we reunited in a tent on the airfield for another session of groundschool.

To get a Herc airbridge to the Falklands required two tankers, known as the short and the long tank. Increasingly,

Hercs were replacing the Victors, and when they did, both tankers departed Wideawake about five minutes apart, because of their different weights, with the airbridge following them about fifteen minutes later. Roughly three hours out of Ascension, the short tank would give fuel to the long tank and return to the Island.

About three hours after that, the long tank would rendezvous with the airbridge and give him enough fuel to attempt a couple of approaches to Port Stanley and divert to Uruguay if they couldn't land for some reason. The long tank would turn around and return to Ascension.

Our first training sortie was due the next day, but the tanker was unserviceable. It remained unserviceable all day. With few exceptions, like our recent delay in Dakar, I'd become used to Albert taking off on time and behaving himself, even on long and demanding routes. But the tanking equipment, and especially the hoodoo, was old and temperamental, prone to numerous faults that led to frequent delays, if not cancellations. It could be very frustrating, although there was a silver lining. It left more time for exploring Ascension

Our tanker and a receiver did get airborne the next day,

although only after another four hour delay. We flew for four hours ten minutes, during which we practised going onto oxygen, de-pressurising, streaming the hose and giving away a total of 10,000 pounds of fuel over several prods, to allow our nav to familiarise himself with the various switches and warning lights on his refuelling panel.

Giving away fuel could be as unnerving as taking it, but in a different way. When receiving, the hazards were all too plainly on view, a bloody great aircraft within a few feet of where you sat looking up at it. When you were the tanker, though, everything was happening behind you, out of sight. You knew nothing beyond the story told by the lights on the refuelling panel and the commentary of the loadmaster staring out of the port through which the hose was deployed. A rise in tension in the latter's voice was often the only indication that the receiving aircraft was edging too close or swinging too wildly, or both.

During training, any problems endangering our safety were generally the result of deliberate actions by the experienced crew taking our fuel, done to test whether we told them to back off, or put on the red light before things got out of hand. On actual airbridge operations, I was to discover that receiver captains struggling to stay within the cone of safety were usually, although not always, battling poor weather.

The Herc tanker was unserviceable again the next day and we went for a walk on and around Green Mountain. Over the next year, I never tired of being up there, walking among its lush greenery while looking out over a landscape of terracotta cones and lava stretching down to the blue Atlantic Ocean.

This walk also gave us our first glimpse of RAF Travellers Hill, the new camp nearing completion on Donkey Plain. On the way back to Concertina City, we drove in and had a brief tour.

About a mile to the west of the base of Green Mountain, the camp flowed for several hundred yards down a slight incline. Cascading from the top of the slope were three large buildings, the Officers', Sergeants' and Airmen's Messes respectively.

Clustered close to these were groups of large, air-conditioned, Portakabins, each nestling under its own pitched corrugated sunshade that extended over a small area of decking. We came to know these cabins as bashas, a term for a temporary shelter I'd heard on my CSRO course. Most accommodated about half a dozen servicemen or women. Finally, on level ground at the very bottom of the hill was a large, well-equipped, gym, a swimming pool and several sports pitches.

The whole site had been lovingly landscaped using local materials and plants. The light grey or duck egg blue accommodation units stood on large areas of red clinker threaded with black paths, while the Messes were surrounded with gardens of cacti, other succulents and saplings. As far as anything built on an otherwise pristine volcanic plain could be, it was tastefully done.

We managed two trips on Sunday, the first a tanker sortie, the second our first go at taking fuel from another Herc. In many ways, it was as impressive as sitting behind a Victor. The hose trailed from a port halfway up the ramp about twenty five feet from the back end, so by the time you'd made contact and pushed the basket in, Albert's wide posterior and high tail were startlingly close. You almost felt you could reach out and touch them.

The Herc tanker flew twenty knots slower than the V-bombers and its basket had to be a few inches wider to create enough drag for the hose to trail properly. So as we tobogganed down behind it, the basket was a bigger target and easier to plug into. Less welcome was the slipstream and propwash playing over our high tail. On occasion, it could create a swing as dramatic as that behind a Victor.

We only had one and a half hours with the Herc, and by the time we'd moved beyond practising formating on it, then prodding its basket, which the boss was soon doing consistently, there was too little time for him to practise overcoming the swing. His eccentric exploration of the cone of safety on the final attempt saw us have to pull out. It was a shame to end that way, because it would be three weeks before we had another opportunity to practise.

Before flying back to the UK on a VC10 on the evening of 31st January, we were lucky enough to see one of nature's greatest wonders.

Close to midnight, we were driven to Long Beach, the stretch of sand running north from Georgetown. Using our torches as little as possible, we made for the middle of the beach, where we sat, getting accustomed to the dark and the boom of ten-foot high rollers crashing onto the shoreline.

Over the next couple of hours, we watched a steady stream of Green Turtles emerge from the surf. I'd been told they'd be about a metre long and weigh two hundred and fifty kilograms, but that didn't really prepare me for the reality. They were huge. Watching them struggle out of the water and drag their great bulk up the beach was an amazing experience.

We followed one female about one hundred yards from the shoreline, where she stopped and, puffing, wheezing and sneezing, used her back flippers like shovels to dig a deep hole.

Into this, she laid up to one hundred rubbery-skinned eggs, which she then covered over with the excavated sand. All around us, we could see other turtles doing the same. Finally, we followed our female as she turned around and made her way back to the sea, passing others emerging from the water and making their way inland.

We knew the scene would be repeated all night every night for a couple of months on every stretch of sand around the Island, until several thousand females had laid their eggs. On later visits, I was lucky enough to see hatchlings a couple of inches in diameter dig their way into the night air and set off down the beach, tiny flippers going ten to the dozen. Most would reach the sea, but, thereafter, predation might mean that no more than one or two from each clutch would reach maturity.

As for the adults, each night, exhaustion would see some fail to make the sea or drown when they did. It wasn't until my visit with Geraldine in 2016 that I witnessed one of the casualties, a fresh carcass lying upside down on the tide line of Long Beach.

It was an incredibly moving sight.

When I returned to the squadron on 2nd February 1984, I was called into the boss's office. There were two surprises.

The first was a certificate and lapel badge marking that I'd flown 1,000 hours on the Hercules. Reaching such a milestone would normally take a whole three-year tour, probably longer, but I'd achieved it just twenty months after joining the squadron, a testament to the pace of operations, especially during my first nine months. I hadn't expected a certificate to mark the occasion.

The second surprise was also my second major challenge of the New Year. I was to be the next leader of the co-pilot section.

I'd known the man who'd held the post throughout my time on the squadron was leaving. With my Squadron Fund hat on, I was in the process of having a tankard engraved for him. But I'd had no inkling that I was to be his replacement. If I'd given the matter any thought at all, I'd have expected one of his existing deputies or some other, more experienced, co-pilot to take over.

So when the boss said, 'I want you to be my new co-leader,' I was flabbergasted.

Not that I could have turned the position down. As is the way in the military, the wing commander's words weren't the opening gambit in a negotiation, just his polite way of saying *you're it, like it or not.*

From my perspective, the outgoing man had done a good job. His longevity in the role backed this up. So taking over from him was a daunting prospect. The appointment was an indication that the squadron hierarchy had confidence in my ability to fill the position without it derailing the progress I seemed to have made in the air. I wasn't sure I shared their confidence, but I was flattered to be asked and resolved to give it my best shot, even though I knew it would lead to a much greater workload, and a change of lifestyle for both Geraldine and I.

From 8th February, weekdays I may well have spent at home when not flying would be spent in the office, allocating co-pilots to routes and other duties, while ensuring they were up to date in all manner of currency and training requirements. But I was also going to have less freedom to do things on evenings and weekends, when I'd invariably be the point of contact for the co-pilot section, ready to deal with any professional or personal problems that cropped up. As an example, I spent the next Sunday morning trying to discover the whereabouts and progress of an aircraft down route in order to soothe the concerns of an over-anxious wife whose husband had failed to contact her.

It was an early introduction to working when others were

relaxing, free of such responsibilities, and it set the pattern for the majority of my remaining time in the RAF.

Luckily, consoling wives took little of my time. Most was spent getting a bunch of independent-minded and, in some cases, downright ornery co-pilots to do things they might not want to do. There were meant to be twenty four of us, but we rarely numbered more than twenty, ranging in age from twenty one to early fifties, and in experience from a few hundred to several thousand flying hours. I had to be aware of the strengths and weaknesses of each so I could give each appropriate routes, training and support.

I quickly discovered those I could trust to keep on top of their own programmes and currency requirements, and those I had to chase to make sure they turned up for their next route or training event. An early lesson was that experience was not always a reliable guide to expertise. Some co-pilots straight out of training became proficient and trustworthy very quickly, while some with thousands of hours proved harder work. These individuals lacked self-awareness and humility, both failing to realise that their skills and application might be waning, and taking umbrage at any criticism or attempt at correction.

I'd meet a similar problem during other flying tours, most notably my last, when I was responsible for a unit of vastly experienced serving and retired pilots, a small number of whom caused me no end of problems, partly because they refused to acknowledge that their powers may have waned, and partly because they felt themselves to be above the rules. To complicate matters, they were usually several ranks above me, and keen to remind me of the fact.

Anyway, all that was to come. The co-leader post on 24 Squadron was my introduction to such things.

It wasn't until fourteen years later, when I became a supervisor responsible for a team managing the careers of 2,500 junior officers, that I realised how important being given such an early leadership role was to my subsequent career, especially as, after the six years as a ground tradesman, I was a late starter.

To be considered for promotion, officers need proven competence in their own specialization. But to be a contender, they need something to make them stand out from the crowd. Successful completion of a meaty secondary duty was one way of gaining extra recognition, but success in a demanding duty linked to their primary role could garner even more laurels. And, for a co-pilot, the meatiest role was leading their section. It gave an indication, in my case the first indication beyond the training environment, of my ability to manage and lead my contemporaries – or not.

In the end, if you'll excuse the immodesty, I think I did a pretty good job. I held the post for the rest of my time on the Herc.

One more thing before leaving this topic.

The RAF hierarchy, or at least, those representatives of it on 24 Squadron, had demonstrated through my selection that my humble origins and accent were no bars to advancement. There were many times throughout the rest of my career when I'd meet the odd individual who couldn't see beyond my lack of breeding and academic success, but *the system* was never anything other than fair. The RAF as an organisation was interested only in what I could do, not where I came from.

Of course, there were nuances. In one instance later in my career, my lack of formal academic qualifications led to doubts from the staff of a headquarters about my suitability to join the staff. But the system appointed me anyway. I went on to repay the faith put in me and perform well in the post. I was also barred from one overseas post I hankered after because I lacked a university degree. On paper, the same impediment debarred me from commanding a university air squadron. But, once again, the system appointed me anyway, not once, but twice.

So I think the RAF came about as close as any organisation

could to being a genuine meritocracy. It also provided genuine opportunities for social mobility.

LAS VEGAS

A week after taking over as co-leader, I set out on a trip taking in several North American airfields. I suspect my predecessor had put me down for the route as a parting gift. He knew that, from there on in, I'd be spending more time in the office than on the flight deck.

I had good reason to be grateful for his generosity, because Ascot 4973 proved to be another memorable trip. Flying XV178, we departed Lyneham on Monday 13th November for five consecutive nightstops: Gander and four USAF bases; Offutt, near Omaha, Nebraska; Nellis, near Las Vegas in Nevada; Kirtland, near Albuqurque, New Mexico; and Pease, in Portsmouth, New Hampshire. It was to be with a crew I knew well and liked, including a nav flight commander I'd completed the OCU alongside, and the loadie I'd last flown with on the Patrick/Andros trip of a lifetime.

It was a large crew, with two navs and two loadies, a ground engineer and, more surprisingly, four RAF policemen, joining us to guard the load we'd carry for part of the route. And then, as if there wasn't enough imprest paperwork already, three route checkers turned up in flight planning unannounced, one to assess me and the captain, one for the navs and one for the eng.

A route check was the last thing I'd expected, or wanted. I wasn't due one for another six months, at which point I might have been able to upgrade from a C to a B route Cat. Upgrading this early seemed unlikely, especially as time for planning had been limited. Most of the previous five days had been spent coming to grips with my new responsibilities as co-leader. Even collecting the imprest and route bags had been done in a rush.

And just to put the icing on the cake, the squadron leader examiner said he wanted me to be operating pilot for the first leg across the North Atlantic, something I hadn't done for ten months. To my relief, everything went well. Just five more legs to survive.

The nightstop in Gander was fairly quiet, that in Offut less so. It was St Patrick's Day and the beers we drank in several crowded bars in Omaha that night were all green. It was the first and last occasion I drank green beer, and with another assessed leg as operating pilot the next morning, I went to bed reasonably early. Not so the ground eng. He had no idea when he called it a night, but he made it only as far as the shelter of a bush in the hotel grounds. It was there that someone taking a stroll before breakfast discovered him, sound asleep.

Overnight temperatures in Nebraska in February could drop well below zero, so either it had been an unusually mild night, or the green beer had actually been anti-freeze. Either way, he survived to warm up and sleep it off on the flight to Nellis.

The routing to this USAF base five miles northeast of Las Vegas took us over the badlands of Colorado and the canyons, mesas and buttes of Arizona. The scenery, viewed from little more than 20,000 feet, was spectacular, topped only by the views of the Grand Canyon, its towering, multi-coloured cliffs winding between snow-covered heights.

There was another distraction on the skyline during the approach to Nellis. Las Vegas thrust from the desert a few miles to the southwest, a thin ribbon of high-rise buildings totally at odds with the surrounding landscape. There was little time to stare, though. I had to concentrate and fit in with tens of other aircraft fighting for one of the two main runways of a truly enormous airfield.

Nellis AFB, *the home of the fighter pilot*, housed more squadrons than any other USAF base. It also hosted more visitors than any other military airfield in the world. That morning, the dispersals, taxyways and air above were alive with aircraft of all shapes, sizes and nationalities. It was like Decimommanu on speed.

The comparison with Deci is valid. Nellis too sits amid a complex of exercise areas and weapons ranges, but they're much larger and more sophisticated than those in and around Sardinia. The visitors, most from NATO air forces, were there to hone their equipment, skills and tactics in conditions as close to war as could be imagined. Bombing missions were supported by fighter escorts, electronic countermeasure and intelligence gathering aircraft, tankers and forward air controllers. But they were also opposed by a vast array of ground defences and fighters, some part of a permanent aggressor force using similar aircraft and tactics to the Warsaw Pact.

We were carrying kit for an RAF detachment of Jaguars and Phantoms taking part in the largest and most complex annual exercise, Red Flag.

After a flight of just three and a half hours, we'd landed at ten in the morning on Wednesday. My second leg as operating pilot seemed to have gone okay, although predictably, the squadron leader route checker kept his cards close to his chest. Unusually, we had twenty four hours off, so we put the aircraft to bed and went to our hotel. Much to my surprise, this turned out to be what was then known as the Flamingo Hilton, about twenty floors of rooms atop a casino in the heart of the Las Vegas Strip.

Even on the drive into the city, I could tell Las Vegas was like nowhere else I'd ever been, so vastly different from Ludlow that it might have been on another planet. While my home town had an 11th Century castle and church, and many of its other buildings were at least five hundred years old, none of the concrete and glass complexes along the Strip seemed to have been around for more than a few decades, if that. The differences were even more apparent at night, when Ludlow would be lit by a few widely spaced and none-too-effective streetlights, while the Strip was almost as bright under the stars as it was under the desert sun.

The place held many other surprises for a Shropshire Lad.

I'd never been in a casino, so I had no point of comparison, but after check-in, the loadie walked me a few yards from the reception desk to look into the Flamingo Hilton's gaming floor. It was cavernous, a vast open plan room with a floor area bigger than several football pitches. I'd already decided to forego the wind down beers, keen to explore as soon as I'd showered and changed. It turned out that everyone else had reached the same conclusion, so we agreed to meet back in the lobby thirty minutes later.

My room on the seventh floor offered views of the desert to the east and the Strip to the north and south. It also had several brochures, some touting hotels and eateries, but others with tens, hundreds, of photos of glamorous young women. I was worldly enough to know that even Ludlow had its share of *escorts*, but if they ever advertised their services other than by word of mouth, it was on the back of public lavatory doors, not in brochures.

I've always been struck by the contrast between the apparent prudery of Americans and their use of sexualised images in advertising and entertainment. But this seemed to take such ambiguity to a whole different level. When I discovered the brochures were also lying around in reception and showed them to my fellow crew members, they delighted in confirming that the young women, and many more we'd see in the casinos and walking the streets over the next few hours, did indeed offer a full range of personal services. They never confirmed how they knew though.

The loadie said he was going off to play the tables, while the route checker explained that there was a whole different world in the suburbs beyond the Strip, and he was off to explore that. Had his tone not made it plain that it was a solo venture, I might have been tempted to join him, but, in truth, the lure of the Strip was too great. With a rough plan to meet up for dinner at a nearby eatery, the rest of us headed into the cavern.

Nearest the entrance in most casinos we visited were acres of one-armed bandits, people standing or sitting in front of them, most seemingly set for the long haul. I'd been warned that loitering and staring at the punters could lead to harsh words, even violence, but I found it hard not to linger and observe for at least a short while.

Most players held small plastic buckets or baskets. In a practised rhythm, they fed coins from these into the slot machines and pulled the handle. You could feel the air of anticipation as, one after another, the three tumblers wound to a stop. Usually, there was a flicker of disappointment before the next coin was on its way. Every so often, though, there'd be a smile, maybe even a fist pump, followed by the *ka-ching* of coins dropping into the metal slot below the tumblers. Most showers of change tended to be short-lived and go largely unacknowledged. But, on a couple of occasions, the clattering went on and on, drawing the attention of fellow gamblers. Some would exchange high fives, a gesture rarely if ever seen in the UK back then.

Beyond the slots, I was fascinated by the range of tables,

again covering acres of floor space. I recognised roulette, poker and blackjack, but there were other card games I'd never seen and never came to understand. The noisiest groups surrounded what I discovered were Craps tables, strips of green beige along which players rolled a pair of dice, loudly exhorting them to settle on a score meriting a payout, then whooping or groaning, depending on the result.

The process of taking everyone's money seemed incredibly manpower-intensive. Each gaming table had its croupiers or dealers, plus pit bosses to keep an eye on things. Standing a bit further back were dark-suited men, trying to look unobtrusive as they eyed several tables, ready to swoop at the first sign of trouble.

I wandered the floor of the Hilton for more than an hour, watching some of the more eccentric characters while trying to remain inconspicuous. It was impossible not to marvel at the amounts of money people were prepared to lose. Private rooms off to the sides housed games where I was told much larger sums were at stake. Around the fringes were areas akin to a conventional British betting shop, punters watching screens showing horse racing and other sports, like basketball and baseball.

For most punters, playing seemed more important than winning. Whether gambling for high stakes or low, most tried to control their features, but some were so obviously excited at every spin of a wheel or turn of a card that their nostrils flared like cavalry chargers hearing a bugle call. Any winnings invariably stayed on the table and I sensed that most would remain until their money had gone, or they were too exhausted to continue. It was a drug.

There were no clocks to reveal the passage of time, nor windows to differentiate night from day. And as long as someone was spending even relatively small amounts, like those on the one-armed bandits, the drinks were free, served by a small army of uniformed waitresses who wondered the floor taking orders and returning with trays of drinks. Later, we'd gravitate to Caesar's Palace, the one establishment even I'd heard of, and the one, I was told, with the youngest, prettiest and most alluring waitresses, dressed in white toga mini-dresses. When food was needed, there was no need to go far or spend much time away from the tables. Eateries ringed the gaming floor, their food fast and cheap, even free for some players.

Everything was designed to keep you spending freely for as long as possible. So what about me?

I think I can say with some confidence that my father failed to pass the gambling gene to me. I'd allowed myself $25 to play the tables, but I became bored after losing about ten and decided to keep the rest and spend it more fruitfully. Discounting charity raffle tickets, I've maintained the same philosophy to this day.

Whether you think my sobriety sensible or sad, it certainly stopped me spending more than I could afford, or losing my imprest, the supposed fate of one co-pilot carried away at the tables. And I don't mean his share of the imprest, but the whole shebang for the rest of the route, several thousand dollars. A very unhappy crew bailed him out and it's to be hoped he learnt his lesson, although I'm not sure addictions work like that.

Twenty years later, I was in a northern Italian city with a senior officer when we came upon a street hustler, hands a blur as, around the top of a foldaway table, he weaved three cups and a bean. After watching a few people lose small amounts trying to identify the cup with the bean beneath it when the movement stopped, my companion began to gamble, and lose. I looked on as he became increasingly agitated, betting again and again, locked in a battle of wills with the hustler. A small crowd had gathered by the time he'd emptied his wallet, at which point he turned to me, eyes blazing, and asked for more money. For the good of both of us, I refused and he became uncharacteristically abusive.

Watching a man I'd respected up to that point go from sane to un-hinged in the space of ten minutes brought home just how powerful and dangerous an addiction gambling could be.

Back in Las Vegas, we walked the Strip, visiting nearby casinos and show venues, like Circus Circus, the Oasis, Stardust, Dunes and, of course, Caesar's Palace. All had their own trademark decor and atmosphere, that is, until you entered their gaming floors, when the only real difference was the uniforms of the waitresses. The majority of us faced another day of route checking in the morrow, so, after a meal and a few beers, we returned to the Hilton earlier than we otherwise might have.

Two decades later, I spent two nights in Vegas when it bookended a family fly-drive holiday taking in the spectacular scenery of the south western national parks. We saw no brochures advertising escort services – they'd undoubtedly gone on-line - but the Strip was longer, higher, brighter and brasher, with many more themed hotels, some with rides and attractions to rival Disney. As a spectacle, we loved it almost as much as the parks.

I suppose I should be embarrassed at revelling in such tackiness and excess, but variety really is the spice of life.

ASCENSION AND THE FALKLANDS

The next morning, we left Las Vegas and, after a short flight over Arizona and into New Mexico, landed at an airfield shared by Albuquerque International Airport and Kirtland AFB.

I'd never heard of Kirtland, but as usual for US facilities it was enormous, occupying hundreds of square miles of real estate on the outskirts of Albuquerque city. It was home to a variety of flying and ground-based units, many linked to weapons research and development, including nuclear weapons.

We spent the night in Albuquerque in a cowboy, or, as the locals termed it, a shit-kicking bar, a slightly better varnished version of a saloon in a John Wayne movie, complete with live country and western music and line dancing. It was a fantastic night in the company of an engaging crew and friendly locals, men and women in check shirts, turned up blue jeans and cowboy hats and boots.

The destination for my third and final leg of the route as operating pilot was Pease AFB, near Portsmouth, on the Atlantic coast of New Hampshire. Once more, it shared its runway with the city's international airport.

That Friday, for the first time, the weather let us down and we rarely saw the ground during the five and a half hour flight. Pease lay beneath low cloud and poor visibility verging on fog. The resulting radar controlled approach to the runway gave the route checker the chance to assess my instrument flying. I'm glad to say it went well and in the subsequent debrief, he put me out of my misery and awarded me a B Route Category. It was a very pleasant surprise.

Of course, he could have taken it away again if I'd made a hash of the radio work on the next day's Atlantic crossing, but all was fine and we landed back at Lyneham at fifteen minutes to midnight on Saturday 18th February 1984.

Two evenings later, I was sitting next to the wing commander for our sixth receiver training sortie. After nearly three hours of day and night prods behind a Victor, during which the boss had consistently nailed the basket first time and rarely had to pull out, we landed and had our Cat Cards signed to say we were qualified to receive and dispense fuel by day and night. Our first detachment to Ascension as a tanker crew was three weeks away.

After a day trip to Oslo and Evenes in Norway, I had another pleasant surprise. The squadron awarded me a B Cat for Operational Efficiency. Things seemed to be going much better than my performance in flying training would have indicated. In fact, I was ahead of the curve, assessed as above average overall after just twenty two months on the Herc front line. There was no opportunity to bask in my success, though. The next Monday, I began two weeks of Periodic Refresher Training (PRT) on the OCU. The syllabus comprised five airborne and four simulator sorties, followed by a flying test and a series of questions about operating the Herc, known as a ground cat.

A respectable outcome from this, my second refresher training course, would be a C Operating Cat, which I could then upgrade to a B on my third PRT a year later. But having recently acquired two B Cats, I felt the pressure was on to get a third right then, early or not. Alas, it was not to be. In my diary, the comments after most flying and sim exercises are *not bad*, but there are also a couple of *could have been betters*. In the end, I came out with a *solid C Cat*. Unfortunately, I was posted off the Herc fleet before my third PRT, so I never had the opportunity to get that other B. Perhaps I'm being too picky, but it would have been nice to have had a full set to back up my overall above average rating.

Over the next nine months, I completed four detachments to Ascension, three of which included airbridge flights to the Falklands. Each detachment had its moments of drama and excitement, none more so than the first.

PRT finished on a Friday and I was due to fly to Ascension with the boss and the rest of the crew by VC10 the next Monday, 12th March. At the last minute, we were told to plan to fly a Herc down via Dakar the next day. Before cease work, though, things had changed again and we caught a VC10 the next morning.

Flexibility is the key to air power!

When we landed at Wideawake and descended the steps of the VC10 at seven in the evening, all seemed normal. The contractors were still working on the new dispersal area, but they'd finished the camp at Travellers Hill and the occupants of Concertina City had decamped to the accommodation there. We stepped straight onto a minibus to join them.

As the vehicle headed inland, the headlights picked out places where the metalled road had been partially or wholly washed away. The driver was forced to slow and pick his way around and through the damage, the result, he explained, of a storm the previous day. He offered no further explanation and we continued chatting amongst ourselves as the road climbed above Donkey Plain and we turned into the top of the Traveller's Hill site.

What we saw as we were driven downhill to our accommodation was a shock.

The headlights, streetlamps and pillar lights fringing the footpaths revealed wide scars in the red and black landscaping. Water running down the slope had gouged channels, some undercutting the Portakabin bashas, leaving a few tottering precariously above mini ravines.

It was a powerful example of the force of nature, but also, we'd find out later, an example of human folly.

It seemed the consultants and contractors had been aware of several small gullies a few feet deep meandering down the slight incline to Donkey Plain. They were watercourses, dry on all bar one day every ten or fifteen years, when enough rainwater was dumped on the Island for it to flow off the flanks of Green Mountain and the surrounding volcanic cones. Given the rarity of such an event, it seems the planners decided to discount them. The contractors had filled in the gullies, built over them and dug new drainage ditches to the side.

Unfortunately, the day before our arrival, and just a few weeks after the site had been occupied, a mega-storm hit, creating fast flowing streams. These largely ignored the new drainage ditches and followed their historical course, washing away the colourful landscaping as they raced around and beneath the bashas. It was several months before all was made good.

At least the damage was largely superficial, but when we gathered in the Officers' Mess bar after dropping off our bags, we learnt that there could have been a much more devastating human catastrophe.

In the early morning, an airbridge Herc had departed Port Stanley for Wideawake with a load of ninety passengers, mainly soldiers returning to the UK after long detachments on the Falklands. As usual for a remote destination with benign weather, the airbridge carried Island Holding Fuel, enough to loiter for an hour while any passing shower cleared away or an obstruction was pushed off the runway. And for added assurance, since the War, Ascension also had a tanker on standby to launch and top up any inbound Herc running short of fuel.

More than eight hours after leaving Stanley, the 30 Squadron crew had passed the point where they had insufficient fuel to land anywhere other than Wideawake. But all seemed to be going well.

Meanwhile, on Ascension, what should have been a passing storm had ground to a halt above Green Mountain. As the hours passed, the sky darkened, the cloudbase dipped below 1,000 feet and rain began falling over the whole island, steadily becoming heavier and heavier. If the cloudbase continued to lower, the airbridge wouldn't be able to land from an instrument approach. Worse, the visibility was becoming so poor they might not even be able to sneak in below cloud and find the runway threshold atop its two hundred and fifty eight foot cliff. Ascension Ops contacted the standby tanker crew at Travellers Hill, telling them to get down to the airfield ASAP and be prepared to meet the airbridge clear of the storm and pass enough fuel for both aircraft to divert to Dakar.

So far so good.

By this time, however, the rainwater running off the hills was sweeping through the camp, forming fast-flowing streams full of debris. This scoured the legs of the tanker crew, trying to reach their bashas and retrieve their flying kit. In the end, with time pressing, they resigned themselves to flying in civvies and headed for their minibus, only to find it listing at a precarious angle, nearside wheels in a newly formed ravine. They managed to find another vehicle and set out for the airfield, but had to pick their way along roads being washed away or covered in debris. Progress was painfully slow. As they soldiered on, they were sure they could hear a Herc.

They could.

Of course, only the airbridge crew really know how things unfolded on their flight deck, but the following narrative is woven from the story I heard in the Officers' Mess that night, and on many subsequent occasions.

Ascension Ops had told the airbridge crew about the storm on HF. Any doubts they may have had about its severity disappeared when the Island came within range of the weather radar just under two hundred miles out. Instead of the small dot they were used to seeing, there was an enormous dark blob. It was as if Ascension had been devoured. And when they established radio contact with air traffic control, things went from bad to worse. Every update included a lower cloudbase, down from 700 feet above sea level to 600, then 500, less than 250 feet above the runway.

The experienced, chain-smoking, captain was a figure of some renown on the Herc, being one of two pilots on the fleet with just one eye. In case of accidents with hot drinks, cigarettes or sharp pencils, he and his one-eyed colleague were banned from flying together, but otherwise, they faced no restrictions. His two-eyed co-pilot on the day of the storm was relatively young and inexperienced, as was one of the two loadies, who'd been on the same OCU course as me.

For the next hour or so, the captain called the shots, but did so while sitting back and smoking as the co-pilot flew the aircraft. The tentative plan was to descend early, stay clear of cloud, fly toward the Island until they sighted the MV Ascension, a large tanker moored a few thousand yards out on the extended runway centreline, fly over it on runway heading and hope to sight the runway lights and land.

Weather updates already indicated that this would be easier said than done. But when they found the large ship pitching and rolling in a boiling sea beneath leaden skies, it began to seem impossible. The cloud forced them down until they were just a few hundred feet above the towering waves, mere tens of feet above the runway threshold. Down the back, the loadies did their best to keep the passengers calm as the aircraft bucked and bounced in the turbulent air.

The co-pilot made a few tentative approaches, but, while they could sometimes pick out waves crashing into the coastline, they failed to see the runway lights before having to turn away for fear of smashing into the cliffs or the volcanic cones beyond them. Fuel was running low. If they couldn't find the runway, there were few options remaining, all involving ditching on the angry waters of the South Atlantic. None of the beaches were big enough to land on.

At that time, no Herc had ever been ditched successfully. On the few occasions it had been tried, the aircraft had broken up with the loss of all on board. Nonetheless, they had little choice but to consider one of three scenarios: ditch clear of the storm and wait for rescue; ditch next to the MV Ascension and hope to make it onto the ship; or ditch running in towards Long Beach, hoping to end up in shallow water or, ideally, the sand. The last option seemed to offer the best prospect of survival, so the chain-smoking captain told the co to aim for Long Beach if the next attempt on the runway failed. Down the back, the loadies briefed the passengers and prepared for the worst.

The tanker crew reached the airfield to find that the groundcrew had started the aircraft. They boarded and strapped in, a couple of them in shorts and flip flops. But there was no way they could attempt a take-off. Even if there'd been any hope of meeting up with the airbridge, the cones to either side of the runway were shrouded in mist and low cloud. It would have been suicide. Like everyone else on the airfield, all they could do was sit and peer into the mist beyond the threshold.

On the airbridge, the fuel state was becoming critical as the co set out on their final attempt to find the runway. Flying at three hundred feet, with the gear and flaps down, they were just forty two feet higher than the runway threshold as they crossed over the MV Ascension. Most of the co's attention was focused on the instruments, while the captain, nav and eng tried to pierce the mist with their five good eyes. Just when it seemed he'd have to turn away and set up for an approach toward Long Beach, the co heard a gravelly voice.

'I have control!'

He felt the controls wrenched from his grasp. So disoriented was he that when he looked to his front and saw lights, he thought the aircraft was upside down and falling into them. In fact, the captain, having seen the runway to his right, had seized control and banked hard toward it. The next manoeuvre, reversing the turn to level the wings for a landing only made the co's disorientation worse and he had no idea which way was up when the wheels touched the tarmac. The landing was remarkably smooth and, as the co's head cleared with the appearance of visual cues, he heard cheers from down the back.

The one-eyed captain was awarded the Air Force Cross for his hours of leadership and seconds of piloting brilliance, while the co and my loadie friend received Queen's Commendations for Valuable Service in the Air. The Herc force had narrowly missed the loss of an aircraft and everyone on board.

There was one other, slightly less serious, postscript to the storm. Ascension lost its place in the Guinness Book of Records for having the worst golf course in the world. In the weeks after the deluge, grass sprouted all over the Island, turning the clinker *browns* of the golf course into greens, just like almost every other golf course on the planet.

After a couple of days, we began to settle into the normal detachment routine, a long tank one day, the next day off, or on search and rescue cover. The working days started with a call at 3.15am for a take-off at 6.00. A couple of hours out of Ascension, we'd take 30,000+lbs of fuel from the short tank.

This was often the most testing part of the trip.

The boss still struggled to stay in contact for a complete refuelling bracket without nearing the edge of the cone of safety, so we usually had to pull out and plug back in again a few times. As a result, taking fuel would take us longer and involve more height loss in the toboggan than the norm, giving us a faster heart rate and a better view of the South Atlantic than most crews.

Then it was climb back up and fly on for another four hours or so until we were roughly midway between Ascension and the Falklands. There, we'd rendezvous with the airbridge, stream the hose and pass him 30 to 35,000lbs of fuel in a gentle toboggan. Afterwards, we'd bid him farewell as he climbed and carried on to Stanley, while we pulled in the hose and turned round to return to Wideawake. There, we'd land in the dark after a flight of twelve to thirteen hours and a crew duty day of fourteen to fifteen, if there were no delays. My longest crew duty day was eighteen hours twenty minutes following a delayed take-off.

Many would class the hours spent in the cruise between refuelling operations as boring. But, once again, I rarely if ever felt a lack of stimulation. If I wasn't on the HF radios collecting weather or passing or receiving messages, some in code, I enjoyed views of the clouds and the sea; and there was always the BBC or, on occasion, piped music, courtesy of someone rigging their Sony Walkman into the intercom and PA. Most crews can relate stories of listening to Simon and Garfunkel's *Bridge Over Troubled Water* as they flew either an airbridge or tanker above a stormy South Atlantic.

For much of each long tank, our diversion if anything was to go wrong was Rio de Janeiro and, whatever the time of year, I always assured the crew I had tickets for the Rio Carnival. Luckily, or sadly, depending on your point of view, we never had to divert.

There were other distractions.

On our first long tank on 19th March, our loadie spotted a mouse. An amusing interlude and not a great problem most people might think. But they'd probably be people who aren't flying thousands of miles from land above the South Atlantic, or anywhere else come to think of it.

Rodents can play havoc with electrical systems, gnawing through cables and disrupting power supplies. But, given time, they can also nibble their way through hydraulic pipes and control runs. The prospect of lights beginning to go out, or controls going slack when more than 1,000 miles from the nearest airfield was far from appealing.

Traps were baited and laid about the airframe, but to no avail. On the next flight, the mouse was spotted again. In truth, it was probably an infestation of mice rather than just the one rodent, but we continued to refer to it as *the mouse*.

What to do?

The problem had been passed up the line and one possible solution that came back was something we'd discussed among ourselves. Oxygen starvation.

The mouse had already been subject to de-pressurisation and low oxygen levels at 20,000 feet on the two occasions we'd given away fuel, but it seemed this was not enough. So on the way back to Ascension from the next long tank, we climbed to 30,000 feet, went onto oxygen and de-pressurised. Of course, there was always the chance we'd end up with a much more dangerous brain-damaged mouse. In the event, though, nothing more was seen of the poor little chap.

Another unheralded casualty of war.

The boss was keen to visit the latest 24 Squadron crew on a four-month detachment to the Falklands, and to see how they lived and operated. So, on March 28th, we flew the airbridge. For most of the journey, there was cloud at our operating heights, which made the refuelling bracket at the halfway point one of the most exciting I experienced. The episode is recounted in the Introduction to this volume. Luckily, conditions at our destination were much better and just over twelve hours after leaving Ascension we were able to see The Falklands nestling under blue skies.

Among our passengers was the new CO of a Phantom squadron. Much like our boss, he was visiting his crews at

Stanley, where they and a small number of Harriers provided air defence of the Islands. His presence led to a surprise, a welcoming committee of two Phantom air defence fighters. These performed a series of flypasts to either side of us before making a final high speed pass, twin afterburners aglow. An impressive sight.

Port Stanley airfield sits on a headland reaching out about four miles to Cape Pembroke, the easternmost point of the main islands.

The headland is no more than a mile across at its widest point and it would be an island were it not for a narrow causeway and a bridge, both carrying roads linking it to East Falkland. As we approached the Cape, we picked out the runway beyond it. A mile or so to the south west, the brightly coloured corrugated iron roofs of the adjacent town reflected the sunlight. No more than a large village in size, Stanley ran for a mile or so along the southern shore of a large natural harbour.

On this first viewing of the Falklands, with the blue waters and the hills stretching into the distance, it would be hard to contradict the oft-quoted comparison with the more remote areas of Scotland.

The damage caused to the 4,000 foot paved runway by the bombs of the Black Buck Vulcans had been repaired soon after the War by the Royal Engineers. They'd also used interlocking aluminium planking to extend the strip by another 2,100 feet. Six thousand one hundred feet was still pretty short for a Phantom, so arrestor cables were laid across the runway for the throwbacks to their aircraft carrier days, arrestor hooks, to snag when they landed. Our landing was much less dramatic and we slowed well before the runway extension.

On taxying in, I could see an immediate reminder of the War, a battle-scarred Argentinean Pucara fighter silhouetted against the skyline. We headed toward the dispersal area, where more aluminium planking had been used to make it large enough to take the resident Hercs, Harriers, Phantoms, a small fleet of helicopters and any visiting aircraft. We picked out a marshaller and followed his instructions to park close to the Portakabins allocated to HercDet, official title, 1312 Flight.

The Flight was manned by three crews drawn from 24 and 30 Squadrons. They worked a shift pattern of three weeks on and three days off to operate two tankers providing air-to-air refuelling for the Phantoms and Harriers, which generally flew only when a tanker was airborne. They also flew another, conventional, Herc, providing maritime reconnaissance of the waters round the islands, monthly mail and supply drops to the Royal Marine outpost on South Georgia, rescue cover for anything flying beyond helicopter range, including the airbridge, and a myriad of other, ad hoc, tasks. We spent the rest of the afternoon wandering the detachment, meeting people and getting a feel for the place before being driven to our accommodation.

Although the roads and most of the airfield had been cleared of Argentinean mines, much of the land beyond had not. It was the same around Stanley and many other parts of the islands. We were told to assume that anywhere beyond the roads and well-trodden footpaths around the accommodation were mined, whether there was anything to indicate it or not.

Something you were unlikely to encounter in Scotland, I thought.

Many of the military personnel around Stanley were accommodated in one of two coastels, large floating platforms moored adjacent to the shoreline between the airfield and Port Stanley. Atop each were four or five floors of shipping containers adapted to provide four-man accommodation units and most of the facilities needed to support their occupants, like laundries, kitchens and dining areas. Nearby was a floating NAAFI with a shop, bars and other recreation areas for diversions like table tennis and snooker.

It was all very functional and spartan, but as long as there was sufficient food and beer, and time for visits to Stanley and other parts of the islands during their few days off, people seemed to cope very well. In fact, while almost everyone hated the idea of being detached to the Falklands, once they were there, most tended to enjoy themselves, or at least make the best of it. After settling into our rooms on the coastel, we had a very enjoyable meal and a few beers with the Herc crews. We also witnessed the merciless but good-natured banter aimed, not only at the personnel of the other two services, but also the air and groundcrew of the other RAF fleets.

The next morning, the Boss and I accompanied the 24 Squadron crew on a routine maritime reconnaissance circuit of the Islands, cataloguing and photographing any vessels we came across. Most, we were told, would be trawlers from Eastern European and Far East fishing fleets, mainly Polish or Japanese. But there might also be a few ships with far more aerials than any fishing vessel could need. They'd generally be of Soviet origin, there to monitor British military communications and radar signatures. We aimed to find them so their movements could be tracked.

An immediate complication was the weather

Unlike the previous day, conditions around the islands were forecast to be dank, with low cloud and poor visibility. Not bad enough to cause a cancellation without having a look, though, so we set off, climbing into cloud shortly after take-off. Initially, as we headed out over the ocean and began our descent into the operating area, we were monitored by one of the air defence radar units. But a few thousand feet above the ocean, we dipped below their area of cover. From then on, still in cloud, we had to trust our altimeters to gauge our height above the waves. We also had to hope we didn't meet any other aircraft.

Sadly, just over a year later, in July 1985, a Herc flown by a 24 Squadron crew had a mid-air collision with an RAF Sea King helicopter. Both were in cloud below radar cover and neither was aware of the other until they hit. The Herc lost twelve feet of wing, but the captain managed to maintain control and return to Stanley. Sadly, however, the Sea King crashed into the sea with the loss of all four on board. I knew and had flown with the Herc captain. He emerged with nothing but sympathy and respect for his recovery of the situation. But, when I met him several years later, it was apparent that it had cast a permanent shadow over his life.

In such ways, The Falklands War continued to claim casualties long after it ended. You may remember that one of my flying training course at Linton, Byron Clew, had also been killed on the Islands when, in November 1983, his Harrier hit the ground close to Goose Green.

The Herc/Sea King collision demonstrates why descending in cloud without radar cover is best avoided. But here, around the Falklands, it had to be done, so the boss and I looked on with interest as the captain, a larger than life character I'd be on a course with a year later, flew ever lower within the grey shroud. Descending through 1,000 feet, we were still enveloped. It was the same at five hundred feet, and when an alarm on the radar altimeter sounded to indicate two hundred and fifty feet above the ocean. The captain levelled. At first, there was nothing but cloud below, but just as he was about to advance the throttles and climb, we caught sight of white-capped waves. Gingerly, he eased down another fifty feet and a sigh of relief rippled round the flight deck as we emerged below a fairly uniform cloudbase.

We found ourselves sandwiched between a grey sky and a blue-grey ocean, both stretching away to meld at an indistinct horizon a few thousand metres in every direction. The white horses flecking the swell provided some definition, but the lack of other visual cues made it classic conditions for disorientation, dangerous at the best of times, but especially so when manoeuvring at low level. It would be all too easy to enter a descending spiral from which there would be insufficient height to recover.

The captain was well aware of the dangers and briefed everyone to keep an eye on him when the fun started. And it didn't take long. For much of the next six hours, we manoeuvred among the various trawlers as we circumnavigated the Islands. Some were grouped into small national fishing fleets, others very much on their own. In the end, we found and photographed sixty three vessels, the vast majority genuine trawlers. But, as advertised, there were a couple of larger ships bristling with aerials and showing little interest in fishing.

We also visited one of the Falklands guard ships, the destroyer, HMS Nottingham. It was in the rougher seas further from the islands, plunging into wave after wave, great plumes of spray arcing back from its bows to cover much of the superstructure in white foam. The ship, all 5,000 tons of it, seemed to spend as much time beneath the waves as above them. As I watched it from a warm, dry and relatively stable flight deck, not only was my respect for mariners everywhere boundless, but I was also mighty glad I'd joined the RAF instead of the Navy.

Landing after six hours and fifteen minutes, most of which had been spent manoeuvring a couple of hundred feet above the sea, I felt drained. And I'd only been observing. A 24 Squadron pilot in the UK might fly only one short trip a year at low level during periodic refresher training, which made what the crews detached to the Falklands were doing all the more impressive and remarkable.

That night, we went to a CSE show.

During and after the Second World War, entertainers visited servicemen overseas to boost morale. The most famous would be singers like Vera Lynn. The Americans had a similar system with entertainers like Bob Hope performing for the troops. By the time of the Falklands War, a charity, Combined Services Entertainment, had taken on the role for the British forces, and CSE entertainers were regular visitors to the Falklands.

Our show followed what we were told was a fairly standard pattern, with a comedian cum compère telling risqué jokes and making fun of the officers in the audience. Over the course of a show pandering to the tastes of the target audience, he'd introduce a troupe of leggy female dancers and a singer or band, again, preferably pretty and female.

It was great fun, but I can't remember the names of any of the acts. I wouldn't have the same trouble the next time I met a CSE show.

The following day, we weren't due to depart until the evening, so we were taken into Port Stanley. The weather had picked up again and sunlight glinted off roofs in various shades of red, green and blue. It all seemed a million miles from the newsreels of a drab and damaged town we'd seen on our televisions in 1982. And yet, it was still evident there'd been a war.

For a start, the vast majority of vehicles on the roads were military, many of them Argentinean, liberated from their owners in June 1982. There were also far more military personnel in evidence than civilians. The latter tended to keep themselves to themselves, so much so, that I never spoke to an Islander during any of my visits. As a result, I was never able to confirm why they were known as Bennys, a reference to a none-too-bright character in a TV soap opera of the time, Crossroads.

When the military authorities banned the term Benny for fear of causing offence, the servicemen started calling them Stills, as in, Still Bennys. And when this nickname too was banned, they became Ands, that is, And Still Bennys.

Over the course of a morning, we walked much of the harbour frontage, stopping to pay our respects at an understated memorial to the war dead, and visiting the cathedral, passing a distinctive whale-bone arch guarding its approach.

On the way back to the airfield, we stopped to photograph a local landmark, the rusty hull and stunted masts of the Lady Elizabeth, a large iron-hulled sailing ship.

She was launched in Sunderland in 1879 and, in 1912, rounding Cape Horn with a cargo of wood, was damaged in a storm that toppled two of her three masts and swept four men overboard. While being towed to Port Stanley for repairs, she hit a rock and, although they managed to get her inshore before she sank, she never sailed again and was never broken up.

We also came across an Argentinean *jeep* swaying beneath the jib of a crane after being lifted out of a ditch. For a place with very few roads, it seemed there were a surprising number of road traffic accidents, this one apparently caused by the low sun dazzling the driver.

The return to Ascension was uneventful. Taking advantage

of the prevailing winds, it was completed in ten hours thirty minutes, exactly two hours less than the flight in the opposite direction. Most northbound flights were completed in a similar time and, as in our case, without the need for a tanker.

My next two tanking detachments, in July and September, were with a different crew. Its captain was another of those who had trouble maintaining contact when taking fuel. Added to that, he wasn't quite as good at plugging in as the boss. While taking fuel from the short tank about four hours out of Ascension, we always had to pull out and plug back in again several times, which made for some lengthy and, at times, stressful refuelling brackets.

The cancellation of a couple of airbridges meant we flew only four long tanking sorties during our twelve days on the Island in July. This left extra time for exploring and sport, but also made the detachment drag more than usual, so much so that I suffered an uncharacteristic bout of homesickness. Too much time to brood, I guess. Geraldine and I rarely communicated when I was down route, but during all my

Ascension detachments, we kept up a regular exchange of airmail letters – known as Blueys. Many of mine were written on the flight deck. I have one in front of me now. It starts, *Having a lovely time up here at 19,000 feet about 1400 miles south west of Ascension*. Riveting for her I'm sure!

During my next detachment, another CSE show was in the South Atlantic. The star turn was Jim Davidson, a well-known British comedian who enjoyed a somewhat seesaw career, rarely out of the tabloids for involvement in some controversy or scandal, whether real or fabricated. But throughout all his ups and downs, he remained a staunch supporter of armed forces charities, for which he was made an Officer of the Most Excellent Order of the British Empire – an OBE - in 2001. He also travelled widely to entertain the troops, which is what brought him to Ascension and the Falklands in September 1984.

The flying programme conspired to make us miss both his shows on Ascension, one the afternoon before he left for Stanley, one the day after his return. And in between, even though we were on the Falklands at the same time, he was performing at one of the more remote military sites, so we missed that show too. We were well recompensed, though, being part of a small group that spent several hours with him and some of his fellow performers in the Officers' Mess bar at Ascension on the night before he caught a VC10 back to the UK. It quickly became apparent that he was very familiar with the environment. More than that, he was in his element.

Over the course of the evening, he held court, a fund of jokes and stories, often about The Boys from Hereford – the SAS – for whom he seemed to hold a particular affection. A few months later, he repeated one of the stories I remember most clearly on prime time television, during one of his many appearances on the most popular British chat show of the time, The Parkinson Show.

Without his knowledge, his first performance on Ascension

had been opened up to the civilian workers on the Island, and their families. Whether he'd spotted them or not, he delivered his normal repertoire. So, the women and children in the audience were subjected to the full range of his ribald humour and ripe language.

That evening, the Island Administrator called him to his office in Georgetown and demanded an explanation for his *outrageous* behaviour. Jim duly explained that the show was for the troops and it wasn't his fault that others had been admitted, or that they'd been offended. The Administrator listened and, in his capacity as judge and jury on the Island, issued the entertainer an on-the-spot fine of twenty five pounds.

Jim leant over the man's desk, wrote a cheque and handed it him.

The Administrator looked at it and, raising a quizzical eyebrow, said, 'But you've made it out for fifty pounds,' to which Jim replied, 'yes. I'm doing another show when I get back from Stanley!'

My fifth and final tanking detachment was with the boss's crew. It was due to be over Christmas and New Year, but, for reasons I can't remember, the start date kept slipping, initially from the 19th to the 21st December, and then beyond Christmas. It was four in the morning of 28th December before we finally left Brize Norton on a VC10 for the journey south, arriving on Ascension that afternoon.

Over the course of the next 15 days, we flew an air test, an airbridge, four long tanks and, unusually, accompanied a Herc northbound to just beyond the Equator, where we dispensed enough fuel for him to make the UK in one hop. On days when we weren't providing search and rescue cover, the boss and I resumed our custom of walking to different parts of the Island. We also had an enjoyable, boozy, afternoon on the tanker, British Esk, moored a mile or so off Georgetown.

Our last hurrah, another airbridge, was memorable for several reasons. Among the passengers on the way down was a government defence minister, a member of the House of Lords. He spent much of the time after we reached top of climb on the flight deck. In fact, he occupied my seat for much of the flight, only relinquishing it for my final approach and landing at Stanley.

Although it was meant to be mid-summer down there, the weather was dank, and I spent the last fifteen minutes in cloud flying a radar approach. We popped below the cloudbase at about three hundred feet into a murky early evening and I plonked us down on the, mercifully, dry runway.

Many large military airfields with multiple runways and taxyways have what are known as Follow Me vehicles to guide visiting aircraft to their parking slots. Well, at Stanley, when we turned off the one and only runway onto the one and only taxyway for the short journey to the one and only dispersal, our path was blocked by two airmen on black service bicycles.

As we approached, they turned about and began to pedal away. A ripple of laughter went around the flight deck. On their backs, both had orange Day-Glo squares, one bearing the word, *Follow*, the other, the word, *Me*. We followed them the two hundred yards to our parking slot.

Without even getting off the aircraft, we knew that morale on 1312 Flight remained high.

A new airfield with accommodation for the garrison was being built thirty miles to the south west of Stanley at Mount Pleasant. It would open in May 85 and become fully operational a year later. But, until then, while the minister went to stay with the Governor, we headed for the coastel and another enjoyable night with the Herc crews.

The next day, the airbridge aircraft, XV300, returned to Ascension and we stayed at Stanley to spend the day with 1312 Flight. The weather was bad enough to curtail normal operations so there was plenty of time to chat. There was also time for another trip into Port Stanley, after which, we were driven to a sandy bay just to the north of the airfield.

You hardly expect to be in danger when viewing a bird that appears on Christmas cards. But, to reach the Magellan Penguins at Gypsy Cove, we had to follow a weaving path through a minefield. At its end, the birds looked as cute as you'd imagine, cute enough to hug, that is, if you were prepared to step over the barbed wire fence and walk past red signs bearing skull and cross bone symbols and the words, DANGER, MINES.

And yes, the penguins had been known to set off a mine, thankfully not when we were there.

The next morning, we discovered that, for some reason, the southbound airbridge had been cancelled, so we'd be spending an extra day on the Falklands. At the same time, out among the fishing fleet, a drama was unfolding.

A Polish trawlerman had fallen and sustained serious injuries that had somehow led to a tooth becoming lodged in his chest cavity. It hardly seemed credible, but apparently the tooth made it a life-threatening situation, requiring medical care beyond that available, either on his ship, or on the Falklands. As he was being recovered to Stanley on an RAF Sea King, a 1312 crew was planning to take him to Montevideo on board the flat-floor Herc, a journey of about three and a half hours. This would get him the treatment he needed as soon as possible, and keep the Herc and its crew out of theatre for the minimum time, probably less than ten hours.

But, and this is where my lifelong cynicism about the character and motives of politicians began, it seemed the minister wanted to return to the House of Lords to cast a vote vital to the survival of some government bill. And unbelievable as it might seem, this was deemed to trump the needs of the Polish seaman. More than that, the eventual solution, flying the casualty to Ascension in the flat-floor Herc for onward transfer to a hospital, probably in London, not only risked the man's life by greatly increasing the time it would take him to receive treatment, but also took the aircraft out of theatre for at least twenty four hours.

Now, I'm well aware that there may have been elements of the minister's predicament to which I may not have been privy. But my later dealings with politicians did little to change the low opinion I gained on this occasion. While I've met the odd one since who seemed decent, honest and truthful, I've met several others with inflated egos and a poor grasp of their briefs, if they even bothered to read them.

At least we were able to make ourselves useful. It was decided that we'd fly the minister and patient to Ascension, leaving all three 1312 Flight crews in theatre, if not all their aircraft. The flat-floor, XV206, was prepped, the patient loaded and we took off as soon as possible. I only fully understood the severity of the trawlerman's plight when I asked one of the medical team taking a quick break on the flight deck how his patient was.

The reply, 'I'll just go and see if he's still alive,' has stayed with me ever since.

At least the minister had the good grace to keep a low profile. We landed at Ascension after a flight of eleven hours and the patient was transferred to another aircraft. I'm sorry to say that I don't know what happened to him after that, but I've always chosen to believe that no news was good news. I can't believe there wouldn't have been some backlash against the minister if the man had died, although who knows.

We boarded a VC10 for our return to the UK ten hours after landing on Ascension.

My seventeen visits to Ascension and three to Port Stanley all had had their moments of excitement. I never returned to

The Falklands, and never really hankered to do so. But I fell in love with Ascension. It was, is, such an otherworldly place. My eighteenth visit with Geraldine in 2016 remains one of the high points of both our lives. I'd go back tomorrow.

BITS AND BOBS – OH, AND ETHIOPIA

As my predecessor as co-leader had predicted, most of my time between the five Ascension detachments during my final year on the Herc was spent in the office, fielding admin, keeping the programme up to date and making sure suitably qualified co-pilots were available to fill it.

Although there were moments when I wished I was free of the responsibility, especially when the programme changed at short notice, overall, my year in post was a rewarding and enjoyable experience. It meant I saw more of my fellow co-pilots than I otherwise would have and, as a result, I made several good friends. With one exception, my charges invariably did what was asked of them without too much fuss, while some, including my deputies, went above and beyond to be helpful. The exception needed chasing for absolutely everything. He was a liability and took up more of my time and energy than the other twenty combined, a phenomenon anyone managing people will recognise.

There were also periods of leave. Geraldine and I had a walking holiday along the Ridgeway, an ancient trail crossing much of south central England. There was also a short break in Paris and a couple of weekends in London, including visits to the theatre to see such plays as Noises Off and Private Lives, and the musicals, Singing in the Rain and West Side Story. A talk by Chris Bonington, a British mountaineer and adventurer, re-ignited an interest in the expeditions I'd read about as a teenager. His musings on his various encounters with Everest gestated for more than two decades, but I eventually made it as far as Everest Base Camp on a medical research expedition.

Although we continued to feel self-conscious and unsure about elements of etiquette, Geraldine and I still attended all the formal events on the station and squadron, and more informal dinners and parties around married quarters. Sometimes, we took friends and family to Summer Balls and Christmas Draws. Mostly, they seemed impressed, although Geraldine's parents were shocked at the behaviour of my fellow co-pilots when, at a 24 Squadron open day, they lifted OC 30 Squadron's staff car onto bricks. He'd only popped into his office for a few minutes and his face when he emerged was a picture. After enjoying his discomfiture for a few moments, the miscreants lifted the car down and, shaking his head, he drove away.

There were a handful of station exercises, practising a variety of more or less dire Cold War scenarios, and I gave a talk on conduct after capture and resistance to interrogation at a squadron training day. I usually flew a few times a month, mainly shorter tasks, such as Op Banner, shuttling between Germany and Northern Ireland. But I also completed a couple of Akrotiri runs, one involving a quick dash to Cairo, the other a night-stop on Crete to deliver groundcrew to a sick Lightning. The second Akrotiri trip, with a great crew, included a very enjoyable afternoon in a lock-up garage in Limassol, tasting wine, eating nuts and telling stories. I'm not sure we bought as much as we tasted, but the owner seemed happy.

The loadmaster was a real character, a fund of funny anecdotes featuring various experiences and escapades from his long and varied career. One of his more colourful pearls has stayed with me ever since. 'I've never been to bed with an ugly woman. Woken up with a few, though!' Not very PC, but political correctness was in short supply on the Herc force at the time; probably still is.

I also flew two trans-Atlantic routes, the first to Cold Lake, Edmonton and Calgary in western Canada, the second to Belize in Central America, via Gander, and Pope AFB, near Fayetteville, North Carolina. The visit to Pope was especially enjoyable, not least because it was with another crew that gelled and made the most of the night stops.

Pope sits on the northern edge of Fort Bragg, one of the largest military bases in the world, with an area of 250 square miles and a working population in excess of 50,000. It was the home of US airborne and special airborne forces, while Pope housed USAF Military Airlift Command and an enormous number of transport aircraft. After landing, we tailed a follow-me vehicle along tree-lined taxyways for miles before turning into a pan overflowing with what looked like tens of USAF C-130s, maybe hundreds. We wondered aloud whether RAF Lyneham would fit inside just that one area of concrete.

That night, we stayed in the Heart of Fayetteville Motor Inn and hit the town, including a visit to a bar with topless waitresses and pole dancing. Another eye-opener for a Shropshire lad.

Perhaps the most unusual and memorable single day during this period was June 6th 1984, when a small fleet of Alberts flew D-Day veterans, mostly sixty-plus years of age, to Caen in northern France to celebrate the anniversary of their landings in Normandy, forty years earlier to the day. We'd delivered them at eight in the morning, but when we returned in time to pick them up and get airborne again at eight in the evening, they were nowhere to be found.

After the official ceremonies, the veterans had decided it was time to party, and to do so at the cafés and bars they'd frequented in 1944, which were spread across the whole length and breadth of Normandy. By late evening, officials were desperately trying to round them up and get them to Caen Airport.

Much as we admired their spirit, it left us sitting on our

flight decks wondering if and when we were going to get away. One of the other co-pilots that evening was a newly-arrived Belgian exchange officer. About 20 minutes into our enforced stay, he climbed the steps of our aircraft with a handful of cold beers, secured from the terminal building.

I'd often heard that some of the Continental air forces had wine with their in-flight meals, but this was the first time I'd witnessed their preparedness to mix alcohol and flying. Our colleague was quite put out when we declined his offer.

It was 10.00pm before we had a full load of tired and emotional passengers and set off for Lyneham.

Monday 24th September, the day after my third Ascension tanking detachment, was another memorable day, although it had nothing to do with flying. It was the day Geraldine told me she was pregnant. We were both delighted. We also knew life was never going to be the same again.

Back in the professional realm, I've left one of the many high spots of my time on the Herc until last.

For ten years, the Soviet-backed regime of Colonel Mengistu in Ethiopia had been fighting a vicious civil war with rebels in the country's northern provinces and neighbouring Eritrea. Regular droughts and crop failures meant hunger was endemic in these regions, but Ethiopian government policies exacerbated the problem, turning starvation into a weapon of war, much like Stalin in the 1930s and Putin in the 2020s.

On 23 October 1984, BBC reporter, Michael Buerk, appeared on the evening television news holding an emaciated baby. He revealed to the world, *'a biblical famine in the 20th Century,'* and his powerful commentary and the accompanying images stirred widespread public outrage, forcing international agencies and governments to take note.

By mid November, Bob Geldof, lead singer of the punk rock band, The Boomtown Rats, was channelling his anger at the worsening situation into a monumental charity effort, whilst also harrying governments to do more. With the help of Midge Ure, lead singer of Ultravox, he produced a Christmas single, *Do They Know It's Christmas*, performed by Band Aid, an ensemble of music megastars. The funds raised generated shipments of grain and other necessities. The charity drive continued throughout the first half of 1985, climaxing in July of that year with simultaneous concerts in the US and UK, this time under the banner of Live Aid.

But long before this, just ten days after Michael Buerk's report, two RAF Hercs detached to Addis Ababa in the face of opposition from the Ethiopian and Soviet authorities. They said the situation didn't merit outside intervention, and anyway, there was no room at Addis Ababa airport for visiting aircraft. Neither of these things was true.

There were only a handful of Soviet Herc equivalents – Antonov An-12, Cubs – in theatre. Operated by the Russians, they flew once a day on flights that seemed to be more about population displacement than famine relief. Returning aircraft would disgorge hundreds of ragged refugees, who were shepherded out of the airport to an uncertain future in Addis Ababa.

On November 3rd, the two RAF Alberts began picking up food from the port of Assab and delivering it to airstrips in the famine areas. Unlike the Russians, they shuttled between the port and the strips three or four times a day, carrying more grain on each successive shuttle as they burnt fuel, then returning to Addis for the night.

Many of the strips were extremely rough, covered in shards of flinty rock that shortened the life of tyres and damaged the airframes. There were also security problems on the ground, with armed men of dubious allegiance among the thousands surrounding the aircraft, jostling for sacks of grain as they were being unloaded. After a few weeks, low level airdrops became the favoured method of delivery, difficult and sometimes dangerous, but safer for the aircraft and their crews.

The codename for the operation was Bushel. It lasted for a year, with strip landings and airdrops being performed by the crews of 47 and 70 Squadrons. My own contribution was piddling in comparison to theirs, but it was interesting nonetheless.

During the very early days of the operation, a Herc touched down on a rough landing strip next to a feeding station in the north of the country and its rear left tyre exploded. Flint and rubber shrapnel wrecked the undercarriage, dented one of the four propellers and punctured the aircraft skin. Some of the holes were as big as a fist.

Dusk was falling and the strip, barely visible by day, had no lighting, so it was too late for spares to be flown in before morning. Normally, they'd have sat on the ground and waited. But, after dark, the strip fell into the hands of Eritrean rebels. The Herc wouldn't survive the night, never mind the crew and their small team of movers.

Desperate times call for desperate measures.

The air eng had an aide memoire of battle damage repairs from the Vietnam War. Taking their cue from this, they strapped up the damaged wheel, started the engines, taxied to the end of the strip, and, trusting to three mainwheels instead of four, carried out a flawless take off. After a short flight with the gear and flaps down, during which several other problems became apparent, including a lack of pressurisation, they arrived overhead Addis Ababa airport. They were unsure how the undercarriage would react on touchdown, so the captain declared an emergency. This should have guaranteed a priority landing under the watchful eye of the fire and rescue services. Instead, an over-excited controller told them to hold off.

Only then did they spot the emergency vehicles clustered round an aircraft sitting in the rough ground beyond the end of the runway. How it had managed to overshoot 11,000 feet of tarmac was a mystery, but it turned out to be a twin-engined Russian An-10, Coke, with a number of passengers, including a VIP. He was due to be greeted by some of the Ethiopian colonels, who were adding to the chaos and confusion in the control tower. Unable to get sense out of anyone, the Herc captain took matters into his own hands and landed - without permission, but also without incident.

The Ethiopians were very unhappy, but when the dust had settled and he returned home, the captain received an Air Force Cross.

A few days later, I was the co-pilot on a crew flying in a replacement Herc, XV209. We were due to spend the night in Addis before flying the damaged aircraft, XV187, back to the UK, via Cyprus.

My captain was a bit of a legend on the Herc force, a hard-drinking, chain-smoking specialist aircrew flight lieutenant, thoroughly professional, but determinedly un-military. This was my first route with him and an eng I'd known as a fellow airman at Scampton. In one of the saddest tales of my whole time at Lyneham, he'd lost his wife to an ectopic pregnancy while he was on detachment in the Falklands. I'd flown several times with the other crew members, an experienced nav and loadmaster, the latter a particular favourite, ever ready to lighten up an otherwise dull day.

While collecting the cups from our first round of tea or coffee on a flight stretching ahead for several hours, he'd ask if anyone wanted anything else before he shut the galley. Those who didn't know him would look around, wondering if he was serious. In a similar vein, at the start of a route lasting several days, he'd distribute teabags with our names on and explain that they were ours for the rest of the route. To prolong the joke, after first use, he'd hang them up to dry on a line of cord strung across the rear of the flight deck. Silly, but fun.

Before he could pull one of these stunts, though, the route had already been full of incident. A series of problems had kept us on the ground at Lyneham for six hours. This would normally mean scrubbing until the next day because Akrotiri closed to visitors just after lunchtime. But such was the priority of our flight that they were told to stay open to receive us. It was late morning before we took off with me as operating pilot.

The snags before departure had already made it feel like a simulator trip. And then, crossing the Mediterranean with the sun dipping toward the horizon, a warning light appeared. Most, if not all other captains would have jumped in and taken control at that point. They'd also have retained control for the rest of the flight. But our captain sat back and left me and the eng to work through a diagnostic process that led to a precautionary engine shutdown. He also let me make the asymmetric landing at Akrotiri, my first in anger, and at night from an instrument approach. It felt like another rite of passage, and gave a further welcome boost to my confidence.

The engine snag was fixed overnight and we took off for Addis Ababa the next afternoon. The transit over Egypt and Sudan proved uneventful until we tried to contact Ethiopian air traffic control. Either they didn't want to speak or we were too low for them to pick up our transmissions. In the end, it was a Russian captain who piped up in a sixty a day growl to relay our messages and our clearance to enter Ethiopian airspace. It was dark by then, so we saw nothing beyond the lights of scattered communities as we flew on toward Addis Ababa.

The city's airport and its 11,000 foot runway were tucked in to the southeast of the southern suburbs. It was 7,625 feet above sea level, 1,500 feet higher than Erzerum, the highest airfield I'd flown into before this. Our groundspeed on landing would be fifteen knots faster than that appearing on the Air Speed Indicators in the cockpit. So, although he had plenty of runway to play with, the captain still had to make sure he didn't exceed the nosewheel limiting speed or burn out the brakes.

We couldn't see it in the dark, but the Soviet aircraft that had run off the end of the runway a few days earlier still sat there.

Its Russian pilot had landed long and then burnt out his brakes in an effort to stop in the little runway remaining. It had come to a halt when the undercarriage collapsed. And believe it or not, there was another Soviet aircraft hidden in the brush at the other end of the runway.

Anyway, our landing was uneventful and the crew door opened just before 10.00pm, admitting the heat and distinctive aroma of Equatorial Africa, and a squadron leader. After a few words of welcome, he informed us that although they still hoped we might get away the next day, fixing the damage to XV187 was taking longer than anticipated. He also told us there was a curfew between eleven at night and six in the morning, so we shouldn't delay getting ourselves and our luggage onto the waiting bus. This drove us five miles due north to the British Embassy, along streets that were already eerily quiet for a major city.

Having turned off a residential road and parked to the side of what, in the gloom, could have been a large country house in Wiltshire, we grabbed our bags and followed a guide round the back. Although we weren't carrying much or walking far, I sensed an uncharacteristic shortness of breath, the effect of jumping without acclimatisation from sea level in Cyprus to above 2,000 metres in Addis in just a few hours.

Later, the detachment would be in hotels, but, for the

moment, they were living under canvas. We stopped outside a large olive drab tent nestling among several others. Armed guards patrolled the grounds, there to protect us from potential intruders, including hyenas. We'd seen one during the drive, rummaging among rubbish like a nightmarish urban fox. That night, the possibility of encountering such a creature, or being mistaken for one, during the short journey to and from the ablutions tent overcame my usual urge to get up and pee.

We were acutely aware of other people trying to sleep nearby, so we sank a couple of wind-down beers in near silence, before undressing and slipping into sleeping bags on camp beds that seemed to tip at the slightest excuse. There were a few muttered expletives in the dark before all was quiet; that is, until the captain fell asleep.

The volume of his snoring would have rivalled a Vulcan scrambling for take-off. The rest of us lay there, sliding, as the minutes passed, from conspiratorial sniggers, to world-weary sighs, and then groans. It was impossible to shut out the booming death rattles and whistles that accompanied each breath. And then there were the pauses, just long enough for you to imagine, even pray, that he'd stopped breathing altogether, before the next gurgling inhalation. After my Everest expedition years later, I'd have confidently diagnosed chronic sleep apnoea exacerbated by altitude. But whatever the cause, if anyone within a fifty yard radius was sleeping, I'd have been amazed. The strange surroundings on their own would have made sleep a challenge, but our captain's snoring made it impossible.

Confronted as we boarded the transport for the airport next morning, he laughed the whole thing off. We shook our heads, wiped bleary eyes and consoled ourselves that, unlike his wife, we wouldn't have to put up with it again.

In the morning light, the Embassy looked even more like a Wiltshire manor house, albeit with idiosyncratic thatched annexes and outhouses and more exotic flowers and shrubs. We drove out of the wrought iron gates and discovered there would be a short diversion for breakfast.

A few miles to the south-east of the Embassy, our driver turned off the dusty streets onto a long tarmac drive. It was lined by lush green pasture divided into rectangular enclosures by bright white fences. Each held a small herd of cattle, anything from African Longhorns to Herefords. At the top of the drive was a low-rise complex of buildings.

We were in the International Livestock Centre for Africa – ILCA, a non-governmental organisation aiming to improve the provision of livestock to alleviate hunger and poverty in Africa.

As we walked into ILCA's pristine refectory, I for one was wrestling with the contrast between the images of Ethiopia and its famine on our television screens, the embassy and our current surroundings, which included a large selection of breakfast fare. More than anything since walking the streets beyond the international hotel in Sri Lanka, this breakfast brought home my good fortune. It also made me feel guilty for the same reason, although not guilty enough to want to swop places with those outside the wire.

When we reached the airport, we discovered that we were to have more time to experience the contrasts of life in Addis than expected. XV187 wasn't yet fit for the flight to Cyprus. They kept discovering more damage, and getting replacement parts and fitting them took time and effort the detachment could little spare.

While the rest of us toured the RAF tented village adjacent to the pan, the loadie went on to the flight deck and came back with packets of earplugs. They'd be nowhere near enough to neutralise the sound of the captain's snoring, but they might muffle it a bit.

That morning, as well as spotting the BBC reporter, Kate Adie, whose presence indicated the depth of the crisis in Ethiopia, I witnessed one of the Russian population displacement flights.

A few days earlier, one of the biggest aircraft ever built had arrived. The Soviet Air Force Antonov An-22, Cock, had been parked on a pan several hundred yards away. A monster in all respects, the tips of its twin tailfins were forty one feet above the ground and it had a wingspan of two hundred and eleven feet, each wing bearing two turbo-prop engines with enormous, contra-rotating, propellers. Its one hundred and ninety foot fuselage could carry four large armoured vehicles or up to two hundred and fifty troops, although only the twenty eight at the front would be lucky enough to fly in a fully pressurised compartment.

I was chatting to one of the RAF groundcrew who'd watched it start up - a long-winded process taking about thirty minutes - and fly out that morning. As we talked, it reappeared, coming in to land and turning off the runway to return to its dispersal. The engines wound down and the propellers came to a stop, at which point the rear cargo ramp and door opened. I gasped as hundreds of ragged refugees poured out, some in obvious distress, leaning on others.

'They don't look too good,' I said, before noticing something else and asking, 'are they all men?'

'Usually,' the airman said, 'as far as we can tell from this distance. And they always look to be in poor shape, which we put down to a combination of age, sickness and a long flight in a compartment with no pressurisation and little if any heating.'

As figures continued to pour out and disappear behind the giant airframe, I was called away to be taken for a leisurely lunch at ILCA. When I asked more about what I'd witnessed, I was told that sometimes up to four hundred people were disgorged and herded away from the dispersal. Soon after, the cargo bay would be hosed down, another indication of how appalling conditions must have been during the flight from the north.

It was hard to believe the Russians were moving these men for humanitarian reasons. It was more likely that potential rebel fighters were being displaced to an uncertain fate. No-one seemed to know what happened to them once they left the airport.

After lunch, we were driven around to get a flavour of the city. The centre was decked with bunting and banners in celebration of the tenth anniversary of the colonels coming to power. Among other extravagances, they were said to have spent hundreds of thousands of dollars on alcohol, for both their anniversary and events surrounding a meeting of the Organisation of African States, taking place over the following few days.

Otherwise, Addis Ababa seemed little different to Dakar or Nairobi, the other major African cities I'd visited. Beyond the more affluent suburbs, the roads were lined with areas of dusty scrubland, where there were signs of poverty, but not starvation.

The market areas had small flocks of goats and sheep wandering about, while food, household goods or ironmongery were laid out under parasols on trestle tables or the ground.

One scene, however, has stayed with me ever since, haunted

me even.

We stopped at a set of traffic lights. To the side of the road an old woman hobbled, bowed almost double under a bundle of brushwood. To her side, several healthy young men walked alongside donkeys, each carrying much less than the old woman. I leaned forward and asked the driver why the division of labour was so skewed in favour of the pack animals.

'Donkeys are very expensive,' he replied, no hint of irony in his voice.

Of course, it may be that putting the woman's load on a donkey would have taken away her livelihood. But what I took away from the exchange was that the welfare of the donkeys was more important than the welfare of an old woman

The next day, Saturday, the aircraft was still being fixed. It was hoped we'd get away some time on Sunday. The captain had volunteered us to spend the day flying one of the shuttle aircraft, but he was turned down. We lacked the necessary clearances for strip landings and air dropping freight.

Rather than lounge around at the airfield or in the embassy grounds, the loadie and I decided to catch a taxi to one of the places mentioned the previous day, the largest outdoor market in Africa. Mal enjoyed shopping and haggling, and I had a motive beyond sightseeing.

When we were in Turkey, the nav had bought a baby's crib of woven reed from a local market. At the time, it had seemed presumptuous in the extreme. His wife wasn't even pregnant. Geraldine would have been very unimpressed if I'd done the same before we were sure she was pregnant. But now she was, I thought I'd try and buy a similar item. The market seemed the best bet.

Our taxi was an ancient, rusting, Renault, its driver a weather-beaten old man or, more likely, a middle-aged man who'd had a hard life. We spoke none of the local tongue, Oromo, but in a way that never ceased to amaze me, he had at least enough English for us to confirm the destination and agree the fare before we set off. Only then did we notice the floor beneath the clutch, brake and accelerator pedals. It was largely missing, giving us an unwelcome view of the dusty road speeding by. And it certainly sped by. In another similarity to Sri Lanka, our driver leaned over the steering wheel with a manic grin as he weaved in and out of the traffic, making regular use of the horn and expansive hand gestures.

At least the brakes worked, as we discovered when the cars to our front suddenly swerved onto the rough ground to the side of the road, throwing up clouds of dust. Seconds later, a phalanx of police motorbike outriders appeared. Lights flashing and sirens blaring, they forced us off the road with the others, making way for a convoy of black limousines. These sped past, bonnet flags fluttering.

Now I know politicians and royalty in most countries have outriders that clear or close off roads to ease their progress, but the way we'd been brushed aside seemed unnecessarily dramatic, violent even. Luckily, our vehicle wasn't quite in the ditch, but others were, and they were definitely going to need help to regain the tarmac.

The taxi continued to climb out of the city until it stopped next to a large market hall atop a hill. We paid the driver, who promised to return to the same spot in two hours. We nodded our agreement, although I for one felt it would be nice to find a more roadworthy vehicle.

'Aston Villa!'

We'd barely waved farewell to the taxi, when an Ethiopian in his early 20s appeared in front of us.

'Aston Villa,' he repeated, pointing to the yellow heraldic lion on his claret and blue football shirt.

I don't remember how the rest of the conversation went, but about a minute later, it seemed we had a guide, whether we wanted one or not. In truth, we did. We were two lone Brits a long way from the embassy with little real idea of where we were and how we'd get back once we headed in the direction our taxi driver had indicated, downhill, away from the market hall.

I suppose there were very real risks in putting ourselves in the young man's hands, but Mal and I shrugged at one another and followed him into what turned out to be a dark warren of busy, twisting, alleyways between stalls. These were generally larger and more substantial than those we'd seen on the side of the road the day before. They also carried a wider range of goods, which tended to be grouped, household produce here, ironmongery and tools there. The first hundred yards or so was mainly food, including a vast array of fruit, vegetables and spices. To our eyes, the meat stalls looked pretty disgusting, cuts of unidentifiable fatty flesh and offal hanging from hooks and lying on slabs, dripping or oozing blood. Luckily, it was the spices that filled the twisting passageways with their pungent aromas.

At first, the faces confronting us were stern. Our guide spoke earnestly with some of the stallholders and shoppers, and at the word British, the hostility melted into smiles. It seemed that although our guide had had no difficulty identifying us as British, many of those we passed had suspected a different nationality.

'They thought you were Russian,' he said, bowing his lips.

'Pah! We hate the Russians.'

Whether they understood all his words or not, the Ethiopians around us echoed the sentiment, pulling faces that made their dislike of their government's international sponsors all too plain. And from then on, as if the news had preceded us, we passed only smiling faces and kind words.

'Welcome to Ethiopia,' or, 'thank you for coming to help us.'

It was very moving, and humbling, especially as Mal and I didn't merit the adulation. That belonged to those manning the Addis Ababa detachment and delivering the grain. It was impossible to explain such subtleties, though, so we took the plaudits on their behalf. Chatting with our guide as we walked, we discovered that much of the English we heard, including his, was learned watching British football, which was immensely popular, with many showing fanatical allegiance to their chosen teams, in his case, Aston Villa.

On occasions when the stalls gave way to open spaces, we could see the market stretching out in every direction, seemingly without end. I explained that I was looking for a crib and we were led through another network of alleys to a clearing ringed with stalls selling all manner of woven reed and wicker items, including bags and baskets. Each stall was a cottage industry, one man front of house, encouraging passers-by to look at his wares, men, women and children in the darkness at the back weaving the goods.

We hunted among the stalls as our guide told the holders what we wanted. Soon, we were surrounded by eager men and boys holding up evermore baskets. But, although these came in a range of styles and sizes, with the best will in the world, none were meant to be, or would even double as, cribs. In the end, our minder intervened, shooing away the disappointed traders and creating enough of a lull for us to head off.

For our remaining time, we soaked up the atmosphere as we wandered. The loadie haggled for both of us as he bought a few knick-knacks and I bought some fruit. We guessed we were nearing the market hall when there were shouts from behind and a young man ran up. He was holding a crib. Breathing heavily, he held it out for inspection. It was about the right shape, but made from wicker rather than reed, and rough old wicker at that. Chopped ends stuck out, and some of the weaves had splintered into wicked spikes. Any baby laid in it would risk life-threatening scratches and stab wounds, no matter how well swaddled.

I realised straight away that the choice of material and the poor finish were a result of the haste in which the crib had been woven. It had probably been done in about fifteen minutes, given that the young man then had to find us. Who knew, there could have been another ten men and boys from other stalls chasing us down as we stood there? The crib was useless, but I didn't have the heart to turn the trader away. After the briefest of haggles, and much to the loadie's disgust, I paid close to the asking price – next to nothing to me – and the young man walked away, wreathed in smiles.

Even now, remembering the effort that had gone into producing the crib and getting it to me makes me feel quite emotional. But it really was a dangerous bit of kit. Even before I reached the market hall, it had scratched, pinched and stabbed me.

Our guide was as good as his word, and so was the taxi driver. He gestured, smiling and opening the rear door as we walked toward him. We didn't have the heart to look around for an alternative, so putting our lives in his hands again, we signalled our intention to honour our agreement, then turned to say farewell to Aston Villa.

At no time had we felt at all threatened in his company, and although we were now to pay him for his hospitality, it was well worth it. I often wonder what has happened to him in the intervening years. I think he would be just the type of enterprising young man to make the perilous journey to Europe when his situation in his home country became unbearable. And who could blame him?

The taxi journey to the embassy was as much of a white-knuckle ride as the outbound leg, although we weren't actually forced off the road this time. And the driver seemed a little bemused, if ultimately happy, to receive a wicker crib in addition to his tip.

The next day, the engineers spent the morning doing final checks on the undercarriage and air conditioning. When we arrived in the early afternoon, there were still concerns about both systems, but such was the pressure on pan space and manpower that we had to get the airframe away, at least as far as Cyprus, where more groundcrew and equipment would be available.

Although the departure date and time had kept slipping, our diplomatic clearance to overfly and, if necessary, land in Saudi Arabia was still valid. So I submitted a flight plan nominating Cyprus as our destination and Jeddah, halfway up the west coast of the Arabian Peninsula, as our diversion. I declared the number of persons on board as thirteen, five crew and eight passengers, including one we'd picked up at the last minute: the defence correspondent of a British tabloid newspaper.

Most of us were surprised the paper had a defence correspondent, but here he was, a short, thin, middle-aged man, twitching with nervous energy. As he boarded the aircraft, he looked decidedly uncomfortable, like a rodent pushed into a bird of prey enclosure. Given the somewhat uncertain state of our airframe, we wondered why he wasn't waiting for a later flight. Had he upset someone in the Ethiopian hierarchy?

All he'd say was that he was eager to get home and file a report on the RAF famine relief effort. He hoped it would make the front page.

During take-off from Addis, the loadmaster watched the left undercarriage through a small, grease-streaked, glass panel in the freight bay wall. It didn't provide a very clear view, but he reported that, as far as he could see, all seemed well as the wheels retracted and the door closed around them. We climbed to the north towards Djibouti and the Gulf of Aden.

The terrain was spectacular, tall peaks and plateaus reaching up to and beyond 10,000 feet to either side of the deep, dark, scar of the Great Rift Valley, the line of which we were following.

Passing about 15,000 feet, the eng piped up, 'Air conditioning's failed, Captain.'

Not a complete surprise, but without pressurisation we couldn't fly much above 10,000 feet without going onto emergency oxygen, not a pleasant prospect on a long flight, especially for the passengers. Ideally, we'd have turned back to Addis, but that was the last thing the detachment needed. The captain decided to press on, well aware that we had insufficient fuel to reach Cyprus at this height.

'Good job we've got that diplomatic clearance,' he said cheerily. 'Looks like a quiet night in Jeddah.'

A quiet night anywhere sounded bliss after three listening to him snore, so there was no dissent. The Saudi Arabian city was still two hours away, though, and as we knew from our inbound journey, it wouldn't be long before we lost contact with Ethiopian air traffic control and the few navigation beacons in the area. So the captain and I hit the radios to tell everyone what was happening and what we intended, while the nav dug out his maps and moved forward to stand behind me.

Initially, we could see well enough to weave round those peaks that reached up to and above our height. But then we began to notice large thunderstorms ahead and to either side. The bases of their dark clouds sat on the higher plateaus, while the mountains became shrouded in cloud or behind curtains of torrential rain, turned silver and gold by frequent flashes of lightning.

We needed to steer well clear of the storms or risk lightning strikes, icing and severe turbulence, not to mention, high ground. The weather radar was useless among such terrain, so, as the light faded, the loadie joined us to add another pair of eyes to those already looking out for hazards.

The captain seemed to be enjoying himself.

Smiling, he said, 'Just like going into Teheran in a Hastings back in the day.'

After what the rest of us had found a pretty tense thirty minutes, dodging storms and wasting precious fuel, we cleared the worst of the weather, and the high ground. We were still too low to raise Saudi air traffic control, though, so an American Airlines captain 25,000 feet above offered to relay our messages. We heard his transmission but not the Saudi response, which he relayed a few seconds later in an apologetic tone.

'They say you're denied entry to their airspace.'

While we digested the unexpected rebuff and the American sought clarification, the captain began to outline our options if the Saudi's stuck to their guns.

'Well, much as I'd like to, we can't just blunder into Saudi airspace. At best, we'll be arrested. At worst, they might shoot us down.'

It sounded melodramatic, but who knew?

'And it's very nearly dark,' he continued, 'so we can't get back to Addis at this level. We'd never see the storms or the mountains. So, we'd have to climb and get everyone on oxygen. Even then, we'd have to dodge the bigger storms, and I'm not sure we can spare the fuel. So where else...?'

The American interrupted to relay a further message.

'They say you've declared thirteen persons on board, when your diplomatic clearance is for twelve.'

The defence correspondent! He'd been included on the flight plan, but not the diplomatic clearance. Luckily, he wasn't on headset, so he missed the captain discounting the option of throwing him overboard - for the time being!

The American Airlines jet wished us well before he flew out of range and the Red Sea was fast approaching when I finally managed to contact Saudi air traffic control. A controller with an east coast American accent said the Saudi's had denied us entry. Sensing a potential ally, I explained, apologetically, that the extra passenger, a reporter, had been added at the last minute, and that we'd suffered a pressurisation failure that made a return to Addis Ababa impractical. As a result, we were requesting diversion to Jeddah in line with our flight plan.

The controller said he'd do his best and left us on tenterhooks. After what seemed an age listening to nothing but radio static, we were preparing for the worst, when he came back with clearance to Jeddah. You could almost hear the collective sigh above the beat of the engines. I offered him our heartfelt thanks and we trundled on. No-one voiced the thought that the reporter, maybe even the rest of us, might still be arrested on landing.

At 2,500 feet on the approach to Jeddah airport with scattered lights appearing, the loadie returned to the inspection panel in the freight bay wall and we commenced the landing checks. On the call for landing gear, I lowered the handle and listened to the familiar rumble of the undercarriage moving.

'Fuck me!' the loadie shouted.

'What is it?' the captain asked.

'It's difficult to see with the torch,' the loadie replied, 'but

I think something dropped out as the wheels went down, Captain.'

'A wheel?' the captain voiced all our thoughts.

'No. They're still attached. But something.'

The tension mounted as we closed on the runway. Were we missing some vital piece of the landing gear? Having seen the refugees disgorged from the Russian aircraft, I couldn't help thinking there was another, unpleasant, possibility, but I kept my counsel until there was an opportunity to discuss it in private. In the event, the landing was fine, and a quick inspection revealed nothing wrong with the gear, which added to the mystery.

After a delay in the airport while our paperwork was checked and double-checked, we were all allowed into Saudi Arabia, reporter included. The eng and a couple of groundcrew stayed to work on the aircraft while we were driven to our hotel. Once there and in a party room without beer, we openly wondered whether the loadie had witnessed some poor stowaway falling from the undercarriage bay. And had the poor man already been dead from hypothermia or, more horrifically, had he lost his grip as the gear went down, only to fall, fully conscious into the outskirts of Jeddah?

The loadie tried to quash the speculation. He didn't think the object had been that big. At the time, we took his words at face value, and no stories emerged to cast doubt on his view. Nonetheless, I've never been able totally to shrug off the possibility that we left a body lying somewhere in the suburbs of the city, maybe in some poor family's home, having crashed through their ceiling.

The next morning we discovered that the engineers had been unable to fix the air conditioning. Given this, we should really have declared XV187 unserviceable. But this would have meant spending several days in Jeddah waiting for spares and manpower to fix it. This was an unattractive prospect for many reasons, some practical and diplomatic, others personal, not least the wish to avoid staying in a country where alcohol seemed totally unobtainable. The topic was closed when the captain made it plain that he refused to stay a minute longer than necessary in a country that didn't serve beer.

I think that, like many Herc aircrew at the time, I was, to all intents and purposes, a functioning alcoholic. Where the next beer was coming from was never far from my thoughts. I remained like this for the rest of my career and, although I now drink a lot less than in those days, the title still fits. So the thought of several days on the ground without beer filled me with almost as much horror as the captain. He just saved me the effort of saying it.

The problem was that one of the conditions of our entry into Saudi Arabia was that we should fly direct to the UK on departure. And there was no way we could do that at 10,000 feet. Nonetheless, I filed a flight plan with Lyneham as our destination and Brize Norton as our diversion. I have a copy of the document in front of me now. Once airborne and passing 10,000 feet, we advised Saudi air traffic control that the pressurisation had failed again and requested a diversion to RAF Akrotiri in Cyprus.

We landed at Akrotiri after a flight of three hours fifteen minutes offering stunning views of the Arabian and Egyptian coasts of the Red Sea, the Gulf of Suez and the Sinai Peninsula. XV187 was immediately grounded.

Before we said goodbye to the defence correspondent, who was due to board another RAF aircraft for the last leg home, he trotted off to a phone to file his story, looking happier than at any time in the last thirty six hours. When he returned, though, the cares of the world had descended on him again. His editor had just received word that a famous footballer, George Best, had been in an altercation in a nightclub. Knowing the editor as he did, the downbeat reporter moaned that, not only would he lose his front page, but he'd be lucky to get a paragraph anywhere in the paper.

A few days later, we discovered he'd been right. The

George Best story had monopolised the first five pages, and his Ethiopia story had been relegated to a few well-hidden paragraphs.

After an enjoyable three days in Cyprus, I arrived back at Lyneham on 15th November.

I'd only been away eight days, nearly six of them on the ground waiting for XV187 to be fixed and then re-fixed. But, from the engine shut down on the first day, to the days on the ground in Addis and the storm-tossed flight into Jeddah, it had felt like a real adventure. And it may seem to be over-egging it, especially as I flew none of the dangerous famine relief missions, but I am as proud of my small contribution to Op Bushel as anything else in my career. In humanitarian terms, it was probably the most important thing I did, the epitome of a later public relations strap-line that positioned the RAF as *a force for good*.

My strongest memories of the time are still triggered by music. Firstly, when the Band Aid single, *Do They Know It's Christmas*, leaks from shop doorways in the run up to Christmas, but more powerfully still when I hear the record, *Drive*, by the Cars.

During Live Aid on Saturday 13th July 1985, it was the backing track for a film of the famine shown on big screens in Wembley, and on our television. Beneath the images of emaciated children lay our three-month old son, healthy, well fed and, at that moment, gurgling happily. The contrast had Geraldine and me in tears, and the song still makes me emotional to this day.

A couple of years later, one of my flying training students explained why *Drive* had a similar effect on him. He'd been at Live Aid, and as he and the thousands around him listened to the song and watched the accompanying images, above them, a cloud the shape of Africa moved across the sun.

FAREWELL TO ALBERT

My tour as a co-pilot on 24 Squadron was due to end in April 1985. I already knew I wanted nothing more than to stay at Lyneham as a captain, flying the world with a group of people who, in the vast majority of cases, I liked and admired. I hadn't really contemplated any other eventuality. But my aspirations weren't the only consideration. Before I'd left for my final Ascension detachment in late December 1984, the co-pilots of my generation went before what was known as a Captains' Board.

As the name implies, the Board's members had to decide whether we had proved ourselves suitable to be captains on the Herc fleet. On this element at least, I went before them with some confidence. I'd arrived at Lyneham having barely survived flying training, and was coming to the end of my tour assessed on my last annual report as above average in both flying and leadership. I also had a strong recommendation for captaincy.

Whatever the Captains' Board thought of us, though, it could only make recommendations. The final decision on our next posting lay in the hands of the RAF personnel staffs, then based at RAF Barnwood in Gloucester. They would balance the recommendations of the Board with our personal aspirations and the requirement to fill vacancies across the RAF, anything from Herc captains to flying instructors and a multiplicity of other jobs, both in the air and, God forbid at this stage of our careers, on the ground.

Naively, I thought they'd see the sense of me remaining at Lyneham. For a start, weren't my three years as a co-pilot a second apprenticeship, like the one at Halton, only this time to be a captain rather than an airframe/propulsion fitter? And the six years I'd spent as an airman meant I was several years older than my peers. They could leave Lyneham for an instructor tour and still return to become a Herc captain by the age of thirty. I was already nudging that age, so surely it made sense for me to become a captain first.

However, things were conspiring against me. During and after the Falklands War, the flying training system had been starved of pilots from the Herc fleet. Worse, instructors with a recent Herc background had been recalled to Lyneham from the flying training units. Now, it was time to repay the debt. Six Lyneham co-pilots were needed on the next instructors' course. And unfortunately, although my squadron and the Board had strongly recommended me for captaincy, they'd also said I had the attributes to be a flying instructor.

Two days after arriving back from Ascension in mid January, I received a posting notice informing me that I was to begin training as a Qualified Flying Instructor at the RAF Central Flying School in February. I was devastated. All my personal aspirations had been dashed. I suddenly envied those deemed unsuitable for instructor duties, most of whom would be staying at Lyneham as captains. And to make matters worse, I was destined to train as an instructor on the Jet Provost, the aircraft I'd struggled to fly with any proficiency during my own flying training just a few years earlier.

The primacy of *the needs of the Service* meant there was no use railing against my posting to instructor duties. But with the benefit of hindsight, I should have requested a change of aircraft from the Jet Provost to the Bulldog, the piston-engined trainer the other five co-pilots had been earmarked to fly. At the time, though, I reasoned that if the Service had selected me to train as an instructor on the Jet Provost, that was what I should do, whether I wanted to or not.

Geraldine had her own reasons to be disappointed with the impending move. With five weeks notice, she had to leave a job she enjoyed and was very good at, clean and pack up another house, unpack and clean another one that we knew we'd live in for no more than six months, and all when she was five months pregnant. To her eternal credit, she just got on and did it, as she did throughout the rest of my career, enduring another ten, similarly disruptive, moves. We didn't know it at the time, but we'd spent longer at 86 Eider Avenue than we would at any other house over the rest of my career.

Frequent moves are one of the reasons Service spouses who follow the flag struggle to get jobs, or just accept that they'll never do anything other than temporary work. It's also why they struggle to get consistent health and dental care, not to mention continuity of education for their children. They had many crosses to bear, which is why so many decided not to follow their partners, but to put down roots and see their other half only at weekends.

Of course, one of the ironies of all this is that just over a decade later I was on the staff of the Personnel Manning Agency, by then at RAF Innsworth, also in Gloucester. For two years, I was the one making personnel decisions that had the potential to dash the aspirations of a proportion of the 2,500 junior officers my six desk officers managed. And when viewing *the needs of the Service* from the other end of the telescope, on occasion, I had to be hard-nosed. Knowing the disappointment my decisions were likely to cause didn't make them any easier.

I spent most of my last month on 24 Squadron manning the office as co leader and contact man, completing just one route, two days shuttling between RAF Laarbruch in Germany and Decimomannu in Sardinia. It was a low key ending to three and a half years that had seen me travel the world in the company of an amazing cast of characters.

I'd go on to do other jobs I enjoyed, some very much, but my time on the Herc was the most enjoyable, and the period providing the most abiding memories.

To me, Lyneham will always be a little island in the Caribbean, where the sun always shines and the bar is always open. Ludicrous of course. Even at the time, there were dark days when nothing seemed to go right. But I don't remember those. What I remember are the friendships, the laughter and the incredible places I visited.

And, of course, Fat Albert.

They say that complex machinery is never happier than when being worked hard. That was certainly true of Albert. Robust and dependable, it worked its socks off during my time at Lyneham, hardly ever letting me, or anyone else, down. Subsequently, it and its crews went on to work even harder, taking part in both Gulf Wars, Afghanistan and the Balkans, to mention but a few of its many operations. My time on the flight deck was all too brief, but I pay tribute to those that came before and those that followed. Sadly, Albert is due to leave RAF service in 2023. We owe it an enormous debt.

Somehow, as I drove away from Lyneham on 20 February 1985, I knew that no matter how hard I tried, I'd never go back. It really was farewell, Albert.

AUTHOR'S NOTE

Once again, I reluctantly decided not to name individuals. The potential to cause upset and offence is just too great, even when you think you're bathing someone in a favourable light. Where, despite trying to be discreet, I've still caused upset, I apologise.

Also, having discovered that my readership invariably comprises aviation buffs, I decided to focus this volume almost exclusively on the professional aspects of my time at Lyneham. The personal aspects were no less important to me, but I now know they are of less interest to most of you.

As I'd feared, my re-introduction to the Jet Provost proved painful. For the only time in my career, I went beyond struggling to failure. But a change of aircraft cleared the mental block and I became a successful instructor on the Bulldog. So the next volume will chronicle one tour as a flying instructor, one as an instructor of instructors and two as a unit boss at different ranks. Each included another cast of amazing characters - students and staff - excitement, tragedy, humour and royal connections.

You can find out more about me and my other books – Wings Over Summer; Wings Over Malta; The Battle of Britain, Hitler's First Bloody Nose; and Volumes 1 and 2 of this memoir - Preparation For Flight and On The Buffet - from my website: http://www.ronpowell.co.uk.

ACKNOWLEDGEMENTS

Special thanks go to Martin Butler for the cover design; to Wing Commander Steve Phelps RAF (Retired), for his invaluable comments and corrections; and to my writing group, The Tiny Writers of Penarth, all published themselves under the names, KJ Rabane, Jan Marsh, Robert Darke, Pam Cockerill and Iona Jenkins. Thanks also to anyone I've missed.

Most of the source documents were my own, but I acknowledge the help of Wikipedia, The Concise History of Ascension Island by JE Packer and thehistorypress.co.uk.

Similarly, most of the illustrations are my own, taken with an old Kodak Ektralite folding camera kept in the bottom leg pocket of my flying suit, or on a digital camera during my 2016 visit to Ascension. The satellite photo of the Island is attributed to NASA and I'm grateful Graham Macaulay, a member of my basic flying training course, for the photo of the approach to Port Stanley airfield.

ABOUT THE AUTHOR

After 32 years in the Royal Air Force, from which he retired as a Group Captain (full Colonel) running the first stage of flying training for the British Army, Royal Navy and Royal Air Force, Ron moved to south Wales to pursue his long held ambition of becoming a writer.

Since then, in addition to this title, he has written a Battle of Britain novel, Wings Over Summer; a sequel, Wings Over Malta; a concise illustrated history, The Battle of Britain, Hitler's First Bloody Nose; and two earlier volumes of this memoir, the first, Preparation For Flight, about growing up in rural England and his first few years in the Royal Air Force, the second, On The Buffet, about his flying training. All are available as e-books and paperbacks on Amazon, while both

Wings books are also available as audio books on all major platforms.

More detail on Ron's RAF career, talks and samples of his writing can be found on his website, http://www.ronpowell.co.uk.

RON'S OTHER BOOKS

Wings Over Summer

Over 14 days at the heart of the Battle of Britain, Spitfire pilots Jack and Alex struggle to survive the savage battles raging in the air over southern England.

Several times a day, they fly against overwhelming odds, witnessing the death and disfigurement of friends and enemies, and wrestling with the knowledge that the same could happen to them at any moment.

Brief periods on the ground offer little respite, with Biggin Hill subjected to frequent air raids, during which many more friends are killed.

Both Jack and Alex find love, but the Battle takes its toll.

The flying scenes in Wings Over Summer are especially vivid, perhaps because Ron Powell spent much of his 32 years in the RAF as a flying instructor, teaching young men and women to turn upside down, jink and spin in light aircraft. He also met several Battle of Britain veterans and, more than anything, hopes Wings Over Summer will stand as a tribute to their courage.

A masterpiece of historical fiction.
I can't remember the last time a book moved me so much.
The best description of aerial combat I have ever read.

Wings Over Malta

In March 1942, Battle of Britain Spitfire ace, Jack Williams, is one of 15 pilots flying the first Spitfires to reach the most heavily bombed place on Earth: the tiny Mediterranean island of Malta. Their task is simple, regain control of the air.

But when not sheltering from incessant bombing by Luftwaffe forces based only minutes to the north on Sicily, Jack and his fellow pilots are hunted from take off to landing by tens of Messerschmitt 109Fs.

Can they, and the Island, survive?

Puts you in the seat of a Spitfire in troubled times.
A gripping fictional account of the defence of Malta.
An excellent story brilliantly interwoven about real events and people.

The Battle of Britain, Hitler's First Bloody Nose

A concise and incisive narrative supported by illustrations that not only brings to life the battle fought in the skies above southern England in the summer of 1940, but also describes who the pilots on both side were and how they were trained, their equipment and tactics, and some of the controversies that raged at the time. A cross-section of pilots are highlighted, some well known, others unheralded. They include the inspiration for much of Ron's life and writing, Pilot Officer Laurie Whitbread, shot down and killed in September 1940; and two survivors he was privileged to meet, Squadron Leaders Geoffrey Wellum and Tony Iveson.

Finally, he highlights the historical importance of the Battle and provides a fitting tribute to all those that sacrificed their lives to give Hitler his first bloody nose.

If I could keep only one book on the Battle, it would have to be this.
The most balanced history of the Battle I have read.
Devoured your book. I loved it.

Shropshire Blue Volume One – Preparation For Flight

A flight with the Red Arrows sparks in Ron Powell a desire to tell the story of his early life and 32-years in the Royal Air Force, from engineering apprentice to group captain (full

Colonel) pilot. The result is Shropshire Blue: A Shropshire Lad in the RAF.

The first volume, Preparation For Flight, opens with him growing up in Ludlow, a historic town on the English/Welsh border, where his interest in the RAF is sparked by a headstone in a local cemetery.

He joins the Service as a Halton apprentice, suffering under a harsh regime preparing him to parade before HM The Queen just five weeks later. It's a duty he performs another ten times during his three year apprenticeship.

On graduation, Ron works on Vulcan nuclear bombers that are poised to fly into the heart of the Soviet Union. He conveys the power and menace of these amazing aircraft, while painting a vivid portrait of life on a Cold War airbase.

After selection as a potential pilot, he begins officer training. Once again, the regime is harsh, but he knuckles down, relating many, often humorous, episodes on the way to gaining his commission.

Oh what a great book of memories.
It kept me amused, entertained and interested right to the end.
I loved this book and can't wait for the next instalment.

Shropshire Blue Volume Two – On The Buffet

If you've ever wondered what it would be like to train as an RAF pilot, this is the book for you. But don't expect a tale of seamless progress and glamour. Ron Powell had a difficult journey.

Following on from Preparation For Flight, this second volume of memoir follows Ron's progress during the run up to first solo and on to the thrills of spinning and aerobatics, the advanced skills of navigation and formation flying, and his personal demon, flying on instruments.

Much of the time it seemed that no matter how hard he worked on the ground, he just couldn't produce the results in the air. And yet, after three demanding courses, he gained his wings and could look forward to flying on the front line.

Makes the reader feel as if he's right there with him in the cockpit. Excellent read and great insight into flying training.
He has captured perfectly the rollercoaster of emotions and physical stress.

GLOSSARY AND ABBREVIATIONS

AEF: Air Experience Flight – small units utilising volunteer pilots to give air experience flying to members of the RAF-affiliated cadet forces, notably the Air Training Corps and the RAF sections of the Combined Cadet Force.

AFB: US Air Force Base.

Banner: The codename given to operations in Northern Ireland.

Bushel: The codename given to the Ethiopian famine relief operation.

CFS: The Central Flying School, the oldest flying school in the world, responsible for the training of the RAF's instructors and the examination of flying units to ensure they maintain the highest standards.

CO: Commanding Officer.

CPT: Co-pilot Training.

Corporate: The codename given to operations in the South Atlantic.

Echelon: A formation position in which each successive wingman sits alongside the tailplane of the aircraft in front, so the formation flows back diagonally from the leader.

Flaps: Surfaces on the inboard rear of each wing, lowered on final approach to increase lift, allowing a lower nose attitude and stalling speed.

FRCs: Flight Reference Cards – cards bearing list of checks, such as the Starting, Take Off or Landing checks; and others to help with emergencies, such as Engine Fires or Forced Landings.

FSO: Flight Safety Officer.

GMT: Greenwich Mean Time.

HDU: Hose Drum Unit, known as a Hoodoo.

Imprest: The money and paperwork carried by the co-pilot to pay for meals and other incidental expenses down route.

ITCZ: Inter-tropical convergence zone – a band around equatorial regions where the northern and southern trade winds meet, causing rising air and thunderstorms.

Line Astern: A formation in which aircraft fly one behind the other, generally no more than a few yards apart.

MOD: Ministry of Defence – The overarching headquarters of Britain's armed forces.

NATO: North Atlantic Treaty Organisation – Alliance of countries that guarantee to come to the aid of any that is attacked.

NOTAM: Notice to Airmen – a system for notifying airmen of anything that might affect the progress or safety of their flight, such as other aircraft operating in their area.

OASC: Officers and Aircrew Selection Centre.

OC: Officer Commanding.

OCU: Operational Conversion Unit – the units that train aircrew to fly and operate the aircraft they are to fly on the front line.

OIC: Officer in Charge.

PIO: Pilot Induced Oscillation – a problem caused by a pilot's actions being out of synch with his thoughts to produce ever-larger deviations from the required flight path, typically on landing or when flying in formation with another aircraft.

PRT: Periodic Refresher Training, undertaken on the Herc OCU, ideally, 6 months after joining a squadron and annually thereafter.

QRA: Quick Reaction Alert

SOPs: Standard Operating Procedures.

UKMAMS: UK Mobile Air Movements Section – the people responsible for loading aircraft of the UK air transport force, universally known as movers.

USAF: United States Air Force.

Z: Greenwich Mean Time

Printed in Great Britain
by Amazon